OPERATIONS MANAGEMENT

OPERATIONS MANAGEMENT

Peter Jones and **Peter Robinson**

OXFORD
UNIVERSITY PRESS

Great Clarendon Street, Oxford, OX2 6DP,
United Kingdom

Oxford University Press is a department of the University of Oxford.
It furthers the University's objective of excellence in research, scholarship,
and education by publishing worldwide. Oxford is a registered trade mark of
Oxford University Press in the UK and in certain other countries

© Peter Jones and Peter Robinson 2012

The moral rights of the authors have been asserted

First Edition copyright 2012

Impression: 1

British Library Cataloguing in Publication Data

Data available

Library of Congress Cataloguing in Publication Data

Data available

ISBN 978–0–19–959358–3

Printed in Italy on acid-free paper
by L.E.G.O. S.p.A. – Lavis TN

This book is dedicated to:

Roy and William Faull
and
Rosemary and Philip Robinson

Acknowledgements

This text has come into existence through the hard work and dedication of a large number of people. We would therefore like to acknowledge and thank the following for their contribution to this handbook.

First, our thanks to all those colleagues in industry that agreed to be interviewed and to take us on 'factory tours'. Almost without exception, when we asked them for their assistance, they said 'yes' without any hesitation. They are truly the most amazing group of colleagues—incredibly knowledgeable, fantastically professional, and so committed, to both operations management and its implementation within their organizations. It has been a joy to work with them. We thank them for their trust in us to produce something worthy of their efforts.

Second, a special thanks to colleagues from those firms that agreed to have videos made about their operations—Brompton Bicycle, Center Parcs UK, Domino's Pizza, and Pipex. Filming a 30-minute video takes a lot more time than you would think, so we greatly appreciated their patience during this process. Also thanks to our videographer and his team for making the filming process both highly professional and enjoyable.

Third, we would like to thank our academic colleagues. Our colleagues at Surrey provided inspiration, ideas, and support for some of the chapters, based on their specific expertise in some aspects of operations management. Colleagues elsewhere reviewed a draft of each chapter and became 'critical friends'—highlighting areas for improvement and making suggestions as to how to do this.

Fourth we must pay credit to our families whose support has been invaluable. In particular, Alexandra and Elizabeth Robinson who were willing to read numerous case insights to see whether the wording and content were suitable for university students.

Finally, our thanks to all those at Oxford University Press who assisted during all stages of the process in getting this book to print.

Prof. Peter Jones and Peter Robinson
October 2011

The authors and publishers would like to thank the following people for their comments and reviews throughout the process of developing the text and the Online Resource Centre:

Dr Tolga Bektas, University of Southampton
Briony Boydell, University of Portsmouth
Dr P.J. Byrne, Dublin City University
Dr Hing Kai Chan, University of East Anglia
Dr Karen J. Fryer, Glasgow Caledonian University
Dr William Green, University of Leicester
Dr Canan Kocabasoglu-Hillmer, Cass Business School

Dr Maneesh Kumar, Cardiff University
James Rowell, University of Buckingham
Jamie Rundle, Sheffield Hallam University
Simon Snowden, University of Liverpool
Prof. Marcel van Assen, Tilburg University
Dr Ying Yang, Newcastle University Business School

Thanks also to those reviewers who chose to remain anonymous.

The publishers would be pleased to clear permission with any copyright holders that we have inadvertently failed to or been unable to contact.

Preface

About this book (for students)

Why operations management is important

If you think about a normal day, you are surrounded by products and receive services all the time. From the alarm clock that wakes you up, the radio station you listen to, the bus that takes you to work or university, the coffee you drink during the day, right up until you get into your bed at night. Every man-made thing you see, touch, use, or experience has had to be conceived, designed, and delivered to you in one way or another. This has only been possible through the application of operations management principles and practices.

Not only does this discipline impact on our everyday lives, but in most organizations it is the most significant activity. Most people in an organization work in the operations function, most of the cost is spent on operational activities, and probably most of the value created derives from operations. This applies to offices, shops, factories, hospitals, banks, schools, and airports. In fact, nearly every building that you see, not being used for domestic housing, exists because operations are going on within it.

How the book is organized

Given the huge scope of operations management, explaining how it all happens is quite a challenging task. In this book, we start where most firms and organizations start—with the customer. Firms get and keep customers by developing capabilities which are termed 'order winners' (OWs)—these are the things that make a customer choose one firm, organization, or product over another. There are five core OWs—quality, cost, flexibility, speed, and dependability—but within each there are more specific OWs on which firms compete. For instance, quality order winners include aesthetics, reliability, and serviceability. All in all we identify 32 basic ways of competing—either by bundling these together into a multitude of different strategies, or by simply outperforming the competition. Think about how you chose your university—it was either because it had features that others did not have, or because it appeared to be better at some things than other universities, or a combination of both.

We then go on to review the way that firms organize themselves to deliver their OWs—through their operational design, facilities, supply chain, inventory, capacity, customer handling, and quality standards. We follow this by considering how processes are created, new products and services are developed, how work is designed and employees managed, and how projects are planned and directed. Finally, we consider how many organizations integrate these different aspects of operations into a strategy which is designed to give them competitive advantage within their industry sector.

How the book works

We think that organizing the book in this way is the best way to explain operations management. It is how we have been teaching operations management to students for many years. But we also know that academic colleagues in universities around the world may see it differently. So a feature of this text is its flexibility (this is one of our 'order winners'). This book of 17 chapters is organized into four parts:

- Part A is concerned with introducing and understanding the discipline.
- Part B focuses on managing operations.
- Part C is about designing and developing operations.
- Part D is about operations strategies.

So if the teacher—or the curriculum—requires it, these Parts can be read in any order (although we recommend that you start with Part A).

To illustrate the principles and practices outlined in the book, we use lots of industry examples, many of which are household names—such as Thorntons, easyJet, and Rolls-Royce. But we also use examples of firms that do not sell directly to consumers, but provide products and services to other firms—such as Pipex, Ashford Colour Press, Lindum Group, and AgustaWestland. These case studies are designed to illustrate how theory is put into practice. They range over nearly every industry sector you can think of—from ice cream to aerospace, hotels to pharmaceuticals, and from vacuum cleaners to smoothies.

In every chapter there are 'Research insights'. These summarize a major research study or paper that underpins the specific content of the chapter. These demonstrate that much of the 'theory' (or the principles and practices) outlined in the book derives from research studies of real operations. Each chapter also ends with recommendations and suggestions as to where further information can be obtained, if you wish to research that chapter's topic in more depth.

Some of this you might be familiar with, if you have been employed in some way, as most young people get work in operational areas, such as shops, hotels, restaurants, and other sectors. But even if you have no previous experience, the book is designed to explain not just what happens in operations, but why it happens the way that it does. To help with this, there is a range of learning tools in an integrated media package. This includes animated diagrams, podcasts, links to web-based videos, and QR codes in the text so you can use your mobile to go directly to additional online material.

'Walking the talk'

Finally, as operations management people themselves, the authors are keen to engage with their customers and to continuously improve their product. To this end, you can follow, and contact, the authors through their personal social networking media—Twitter, Facebook, and the Jones & Robinson blog.

About this book (for lecturers and tutors)

As explained earlier—in the section 'How the book works'—this text is very flexible and is designed to fit with a range of different syllabi and schemes of work. Each chapter is accompanied by a PowerPoint presentation covering key aspects, and includes animated slides that bring the concepts to life.

As well as written cases and research insights, the book is also accompanied by bespoke video interviews, which explain in more detail exactly how operations are managed in four different companies—Domino's Pizza, IKEA, Brompton Bicycle, Pipex, and Center Parcs UK. In these videos, a range of managers responsible for different aspects of operations management are interviewed to explain how they help to deliver their organization's order winners. Live action footage of the operations in action is also included, to enable students to see real people working in, and talking about, operations.

Contents

Detailed contents

PART A Understanding operations management

PART B Managing operations

PART D Operations strategies

List of case material

Author profiles

Professor Peter Jones heads up the Hospitality and Food Management Group at the University of Surrey, where for ten years he was the ITCA Chair of Production and Operations Management. He is the author, co-author, or editor of 12 textbooks, many of which are in the field of operations management. He also serves as associate editor on a number of editorial boards, where he is responsible for publishing journal articles with an operations focus. His own published research articles have been on a wide range of operations management topics—such as mass customization, statistical process control, revenue management, and productivity. He also writes a regular column for an industry magazine—*Onboard Hospitality*—as well as blogging and tweeting on operations management issues. As a consultant he has advised major European companies, and has devised and run service management development workshops for them. He has an MBA from London Business School and a PhD from the University of Surrey.

Peter Robinson is a tutor in operations management at the University of Surrey Business School. Since 2006 he has taught operations management and project management at undergraduate level and MSc levels as well as operations strategies at MBA level. Prior to that he worked for ten years as a board member for an international automotive supply company and has additional experience in implementing new technology into both manufacturing and administrative sections of a number of businesses. He has a BSc (Hons.) degree in Chemistry from Liverpool University and is a Professional Member of the Institute of Materials, Minerals and Mining (MIMMM).

Take advantage of our:

 Bespoke video case material—free online for all registered adopting lecturers

Video case material consisting of interviews and processes tied to each chapter are broken down into five minute clips, and can either be shown in relation to a chapter topic, or as a whole film demonstrating how one company utilizes many aspects of operations management.

This has been specifically designed to support lecturers as they deliver their module, and to challenge students to think about real business issues and what they might encounter in their future careers.

 Annotated library of links to 'Operations in Action'

For each chapter there are annotated links to video content demonstrating various operations in action in the real world.

Resource title: SSP UK - BIA - The Movie
Brand and/or topic: SSP Travel Caterers
Resource description: Video of a typical day for the caterers at Belfast International Airport.
Channel: Vimeo
URL: http://vimeo.com/24953344

Resource title: A look inside the Cessna factory
Brand and/or topic: Cessna aircraft
Resource description: This video explains how Cessna changed their approach to operations and how this enabled them to consolidate production in one factory.
Channel: YouTube
URL: http://www.youtube.com/watch?v=0DcDko3E-V8

Within each chapter read the:

 Case insights

Each chapter opens with a case study focused around a well-known company, which sets the scene for the topics to be covered in that chapter. Questions accompany each case to encourage students to start thinking critically about the subject.

CASE INSIGHT
White Stuff—a culture designed for design

This company was founded in 1985 and in 2011 had 78 UK stores and a home shopping channel. It has been described as a 'charming lifestyle boutique selling lovely clothes for lovely people'. The staff are described as a 'chilled out bunch' who had one the lowest levels of reported stress of any company entering the Times 'Best Companies to Work For' competition in 2009. This very much stems from the philosophy of the firm's two founders—Sean Thomas and George Treves—who started the company by entitlement, staff based in the London Head Office could have two 'duvet days' or 'afternoon naps' every year. The staff were also treated to free massages and subsidised yoga sessions. Reiki and beauty treatments were also available in the therapy rooms. The company organized lots of events for their employees, such as two day surfing trips to Cornwall, trips to theme parks, their own fancy-dress Olympics, and even karaoke nights. As a result employees were reported to spend a lot of time together outside

 Operations insights

Each chapter is packed with short, topical real-life mini-cases which help students apply the theory to a well-known company. These are accompanied by questions to guide student analysis of each example.

OPERATIONS INSIGHT 7.2
Club 18–30—planning the summer season

This tour operator specializes in providing low-cost holidays in resorts that appeal to a specific age group. In 2011, it offered air travel from six different UK airports to ten summer holiday destinations, with a choice of up to 80 different hotels to stay in. In order to do this, the company has to forecast demand one year ahead for the following season and then negotiate contracts with airlines for airline seats, coach companies for transportation to and from the resort, and hotels in which its customers will stay. The forecasts have to be very detailed. Demand will vary over the course of a summer season, with July and August being the peak demand, and other months being periods of lower demand. The company also has to estimate the strength of demand in different regions of the UK, as most holidaymakers prefer to fly out from the airport nearest to them. Finally, it has to estimate the relative popularity of

End of chapter cases

Every chapter ends with a long case study which pulls together the central themes of that chapter, and enables students to see the application of the topics in a real-life situation. Case studies are accompanied by questions to ensure they get the most out of these examples.

END OF CHAPTER CASE
Center Parcs—busy 24/7 and 365 days of the year

Center Parcs' development in the UK began in 1987 with the opening of a village in Sherwood Forest, near Nottingham. In 1989, a second UK village, at Elveden near Thetford in Norfolk was opened. The third UK village was opened in 1994 at Longleat near Bath. Finally in 2004 it acquired a fourth village—located in the Lake District in northwest England, therefore serving all parts of the country.

The selection of these sites was highly strategic. They have to be located within two to three hours'

or three nights Friday through to Monday. This means there are around 3000 bed spaces to fill on 102 occasions throughout a year. There is not a total of 52 three-day breaks and 52 four-day breaks because guests must book a seven-day break over Christmas and the New Year. Despite this high capacity, each village achieves an annual occupancy in excess of 95%.

Running Center Parcs presents many kinds of capacity challenges. The first is how to fill over 3000

Attempt the:

 ## Web-based activities

These interactive online activities encourage students to undertake web-based research in order to enhance their understanding of operations in practice.

Overview
This activity will introduce you to two leading operations management associations serving people interested in the field of operations management.

Activity Description
Visit the websites for The Association for Operations Management and the Production and Operations Management Society and compare and contrast them.
Consider the following:

1. Their establishment, history and development over the years.

2. Their mission and/or vision.

3. Who are their target audiences and where do they reside?

 ## Tutorial activities—free online for all registered adopting lecturers

A range of hands-on activities to help enliven lectures and seminars and facilitate development of students' practical skills.

Activity Description

This activity draws on material in Chapter 1.

All public companies registered in the UK must publish an annual repor financial statements, these reports usually include a statement on the o activities by the Chairman, the CEO or both. Students should be asked different annual reports – one on a manufacturing company and the oth firm – and review these statements to see what is said about operation:

In particular students should be asked to identify any specific examples aspects of OM identified in Table 1.

Features on the Online Resource Centre (ORC) can be found here

www.oxfordtextbooks.co.uk/orc/jones_robinson/

Don't forget that all online resources can be uploaded to an institution's Virtual Learning Environment to allow students to access them directly!

How to use this package . . .

. . . to test understanding of operations management

Get to grips with the main concepts through the:

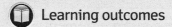 **Learning outcomes**

A bulleted outline of the main concepts and ideas indicates what you can expect to learn from each chapter.

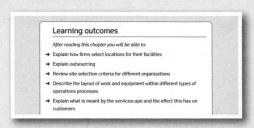

Learning outcomes

After reading this chapter you will be able to:

→ Explain how firms select locations for their facilities
→ Explain outsourcing
→ Review site selection criteria for different organizations
→ Describe the layout of work and equipment within different types of operations processes
→ Explain what is meant by the servicescape and the effect this has on customers

Chapter summary

Linked to the learning objectives, each chapter concludes with a summary of the most important concepts students need to take away.

Chapter summary

To consolidate your learning, the key points from this chapter are summarized as follows:

- Explain the concept of the 'service encounter' and how it should be managed

  A service encounter is that period of time during which the customer and the service organization interact face-to-face, over the telephone, or through other media. Many customer processing operations involve a series of such encounters. Blueprinting or flow charting the process and specifically identifying the employee/customer interfaces enables the process to be designed efficiently and employees trained appropriately.

- Explain the principles of queuing theory and the psychology of waiting lines

  A queue is a situation in which the customer is passively engaged with the process, waiting

Key terms and downloadable flashcard glossary

Key terms are highlighted where they first appear in the textbook and definitions placed in the margin. These are also collated with their definitions in the glossary at the back of the book.

 The glossary terms are available online in an interactive flashcard format, and can be downloaded to an MP3 player or smartphone allowing students to check their understanding of important key concepts on the go.

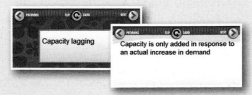

Complete the variety of questions available:

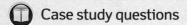 **Case study questions**

Each chapter opens with a case study focused around a well-known company, which sets the scene for the topics to be covered in that chapter. Questions accompany each case to encourage students to start thinking critically about the subject.

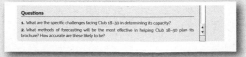

Questions

1. What are the specific challenges facing Club 18–30 in determining its capacity?
2. What methods of forecasting will be the most effective in helping Club 18–30 plan its brochure? How accurate are these likely to be?

Review questions

These short end of chapter questions test students' understanding of the chapter's central themes.

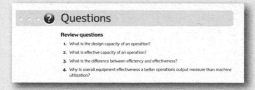

Discussion questions and suggested answers

These carefully devised end of chapter questions encourage students to reflect more widely on the topic covered and enhance their critical thinking skills.

Pointers and suggested guidelines on how to answer these questions are available to all registered adopting lecturers to help save them time when marking.

Multiple choice questions

A bank of self-marking multiple choice questions is provided for each chapter giving instant feedback and page references to help students focus on areas that need further study.

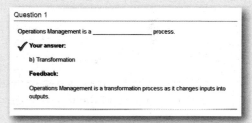

Test bank—free online for all registered adopting lecturers

This ready-made electronic testing resource, which is fully customizable and contains feedback for students, will help lecturers to save time creating assessments.

Features on the Online Resource Centre (ORC) can be found here

www.oxfordtextbooks.co.uk/orc/jones_robinson/

Don't forget that all online resources can be uploaded to an institution's Virtual Learning Environment to allow students to access them directly!

How to use this package . . .

. . . to take learning further

Understand the concepts behind the figures:

QR code images link to animated diagrams with audio

QR code images are placed throughout the book and link through to an animation of that figure online.

These animations are accompanied by an author commentary to expand and develop student understanding.

QR Code images are used throughout this book. QR Code is a registered trademark of DENSO WAVE INCORPORATED. You can scan the code with your mobile device to launch the relevant animated model from the Online Resource Centre. If your mobile device does not have a QR Code reader visit this website: www.mobile-barcodes.com/qr-code-software.

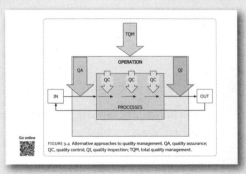

FIGURE 9.4 Alternative approaches to quality management. QA, quality assurance; QC, quality control; QI, quality inspection; TQM, total quality management.

Undertake further research with guidance from the:

Research insights and links to seminal papers

The summaries of seminal papers provided throughout each chapter support and strengthen the theory discussed and encourage students to carry out further research into these topics.

The weblinks to these academic papers are then provided online. These are available on the types of electronic databases subscribed to by most universities worldwide.

RESEARCH INSIGHT 10.2
Biazzo, S. (2002) Process mapping techniques and organizational analysis: lessons from sociotechnical system theory, *Business Process Management Journal*, 8(1), 42–52

Having discussed technology in some detail, it is worth reminding ourselves of the importance of human beings in most systems. In this article, Biazzo compares and contrasts three different approaches to process mapping commonly adopted in the 1990s. He then goes on

Source
Mingers, J, and Taylor S. (1992) The Use of Soft Systems Methodology in Practic *Journal of the Operational Research Society*, 43, 4, 321-332.

Jones and Robinson Commentary
There is no better way to understand a technique than to hear from the people th
This article reports on a survey of managers and others that actively and enthus

Further learning guide

At the end of each chapter the authors provide a short guide to related further reading and relevant websites to encourage students to actively explore the themes of the chapter further.

→ Further learning guide

A good place to start is the Kaizen Institute (**www.uk.kaizen.com**). Although a consulting company, their website has a great deal of information and case studies on CI tools and their implementation. One of the values of the Association for Manufacturing Excellence is continuous improvement (**www.ame.org**). It is based in the USA, but publishes online a great newsletter, with articles not just on CI but a range of other operations topics. You should also look at the crowdsourcing websites and compare the business models of Innocentive, NineSigma, and Yet2, each of which is slightly different. Finally the Brompton Bicycle company has a great website that explains how its folding bikes are design and manufactured (**http://www.brompton.**

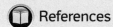 References

Consider reading the original articles and books in the wider references lists provided at the end of each chapter to discover more about the issues raised within this topic.

Interact with the authors:

 The Jones & Robinson Blog

Follow and contact the authors through their personal social networking media— Twitter and Facebook, as well as the Jones & Robinson Blog, to receive up-to-date thoughts and opinions on recent industry news—all accessible via the Online Resource Centre.

In addition to the lecturer support materials already mentioned, we also provide:

 PowerPoint slides—free online for all registered adopting lecturers

Accompanying each chapter is a suite of customizable slides to be used in lecture presentations.

 Tutor guide—free online for all registered adopting lecturers

A comprehensive guide containing teaching notes to help prepare for lectures and seminars. This also includes suggested answers to the Review questions and Operations insights questions found in each chapter, as well as a guide to how the video content can be integrated into teaching.

Features on the Online Resource Centre (ORC) can be found here

www.oxfordtextbooks.co.uk/orc/jones_robinson/

Don't forget that all online resources can be uploaded to an institution's Virtual Learning Environment to allow students to access them directly!

Part A

Understanding operations management

Chapter One

Introduction to operations management

AgustaWestland—getting into operations

Stuart is 23 years old and has three years of operations management experience. Whilst studying for a business management degree, he undertook a professional training placement for a year. It was spent working for AgustaWestland (AW), the aerospace engineering company that manufactures helicopters in Somerset. On graduating, Stuart returned to work in operations for them—as a graduate management trainee.

As their graduate employment brochure explains, AW takes on a number of graduates each year. As well as the two-year graduate programme, there are a number of other training and development opportunities, including the AW personal development programme 'Leading Edge', and the Finmeccanica Learning Induction Programme (FLIP) which encourages interaction with graduates across the Finmeccanica Group (AW's parent company). With over 230 trainees, from apprentices to graduates, the company also creates a social network through regular organized events to integrate newcomers.

AgustaWestland, the aerospace engineering company, takes on a number of graduates each year. Copyright AgustaWestland NV.

Here Stuart talks about his operations management experience:

I've always been interested in working in operations because I have always found anything a bit of a puzzle interesting. I found a placement with AgustaWestland through the Placement Office. I was attracted to the opportunity to work in aviation as I had been an air cadet. The firm organizes placements by having trainees line managed by the Training Department and then seconded to production departments for a period of time. During my year out, I had six months in two very different areas. The first of these was in the production of aircraft and the second was in a process improvement team in customer support. The first role involved long-term production planning and scheduling of different sections of the aircraft. During the second six months I looked at a variety of support processes and was involved in facilitating process improvement events.

The graduate scheme I am now on is made up of working in four or five specific areas over a two-year period. This is designed to deliberately develop expertise and skills within a host directorate. In my case this is Customer Support. In this directorate there are three main areas—technical services (which coordinates responses and resolutions to aircraft failures or breakdowns, as well as issuing technical communications), materials services (which deals with materials and logistics of spares, repairs, and overhauls), and aircraft services (which maintains aircraft for those clients that have outsourced this back to us). During my two years on the scheme I worked in materials services. Hence I have had four different roles relating to process development and improvement, standardization across aircraft platforms, capacity planning, and developing reporting structures in relation to supplier performance, and analysing these.

Every working day is interesting and challenging. This is partly because graduate trainees are given different projects to do and partly because of the dynamic nature of this business. The environment is ever changing because technology is changing all the time. So it is a very innovative sector. It is also very international as support has to be provided to clients across the globe.

Source: authors' primary research

Questions

1. What appears to be the key roles an operations manager might play in an organization?

2. What might be the major operations-based issues that face AgustaWestland?

Introduction

What is **operations management** (OM)? You may not have thought about it before but actually you are surrounded by the outcomes of this activity. Everything you see that is not in nature has been designed and produced by someone. Everything—buildings, aeroplanes, clothes, furniture, cosmetics, jewellery, and even the food we eat—is produced by people engaged in operations. So operations management actually underpins most of human activity and shapes the society in which we live. A simple definition of operations management is the planning and organizing of the production of manufactured goods and delivery of services. It is one of the core functions within an organization—the others typically being marketing, human resources, and finance and accounting.

As a discipline, operations management has evolved over the years. Originally it was referred to as production management. This reflected the focus on how best to manage manufacturing in factories, which in the 1900s was the predominant form of large-scale economic activity. This was the era when goods such as motor cars, aeroplanes, refrigerators, and radios were being mass-produced for the first time. Production management tended to focus on the internal activities of the firm and was preoccupied with how best to organize equipment, employees, and work within the factory setting. But over time, it became clear that an organization's performance did not simply depend on what happened within the factory, but also on how its suppliers performed and how well it distributed its products to customers. This widened the focus to include the supply chain—'upstream' from the manufacturer—and onwards distribution—'downstream' from the factory. This coincided with the growth of large-scale service firms, such as hotel chains, banks, and retailers, who did not have factories anyway. As a result this led to the adoption of the term operations management. So OM can be defined as the management of processes that convert inputs (such as materials, labour, and energy) into outputs (in the form of goods and services). Or to put it another way, it's all about how things get built or made and how services get delivered.

In many respects operations management is a 'sleeping giant'. That is to say many people have not recognized the importance of this function, nor indeed have even realized that they may work within this function. In some organizations, some management job titles clearly identify managers with an operations role—such as operations director, production manager, and customer services manager. But there are many roles where this is less obvious—such as bank manager, reservations manager, and quality manager.

In recent years, the value and importance of operations have begun to be recognized. For instance, the original success of Japanese companies in sectors such as car manufacturing and electronic goods was seen to be based on their ability to manage their operations more efficiently and reliably than European or American competitors. Likewise, reform of the National Health Service in the UK is also partly based around reviewing and revising clinical practices and procedures. This is not surprising because operations in most organizations are by far the most significant part of what the organization does. Generally most of the employees are engaged in operations, most of the revenue generated and costs incurred derive from operations, and most of the organization's assets, such as its buildings, plant, and machinery, are used for operational purposes. In other words, the success, or failure, of most organizations depends upon the management of their operations. So let us begin by looking at how firms are organized and the role that operations play within the organization.

> **Operations management** the management of processes that convert inputs (such as materials, labour, and energy) into outputs (in the form of goods and services)

What is the nature of operations in an organization?

In this section we start by considering what an organization is like before going on to look at different types of organization. We then look at how operations management fits into such organizations and how the operations function itself is organized.

What is an organization?

Even one person working on their own needs to be organized to ensure that the activity is done well. So when two or more people come together in order to perform an activity there has to be some form of organization. This is especially the case when an organization is made up of many thousands of managers and employees. There are four basic issues that need to be addressed in relation to organizational design:

- The nature of the hierarchy
- The degree of centralization
- The extent of formalization
- The level of complexity.

The hierarchy of the organization determines the basic shape of an organization—how many layers there are between the chief executive officer (CEO) that leads the organization, and those working on 'the shop floor'. A so-called 'tall' organization has many layers, whereas a 'flat' organization is one where there are few layers of management between the CEO and the workforce. Tall organizations also tend to have narrow 'spans of control', that is to say a small number of employees reporting to the manager above them. This tended to be the shape of early industrial organizations because they were modelled on the only form of organization that existed at that time—the military. Over time, the trend has been for commercial organizations to reduce the number of levels and widen the spans of control of managers in order to 'flatten' the organization.

The degree of centralization in an organization is all about how power is distributed within an organization. In highly centralized organizations, power is held at the centre, with all decisions about policy and procedure made by the CEO or senior managers at 'head office'. In decentralized organizations, relatively low-level managers have delegated authority to make decisions and take action.

The third issue in organizational design is formalization. This refers to how work is organized and how explicit and rigid this is. Formal organizations have a large number of policies, procedures, and rules that are typically written down in standards of performance manuals or some other form of documentation.

Finally, complexity refers to the number of subunits within the organization and the degree of difference between them. Some organizations have a high degree of standardization because they make a single product or deliver a simple service, hence they are not complex. Other organizations may make a wide range of products and deliver services to many different customers in many different locations.

As a result of these four issues, organizations can take a number of different forms. This is discussed in the next section.

Organizational forms

There are five basic organizational forms—simple, functional, divisional (or product), conglomerate, and hybrid (or matrix).

The simple form of organization is typically how most small and medium-sized enterprises (SMEs) are organized. In such organizations the original founder or entrepreneur is typically in charge of all aspects of the business.

Functional organizations are divided into different areas of management activity, typically Operations, Sales and Marketing, Human Resources, and Accounting and Finance. When organizations become larger, the owner or CEO cannot do everything, so employs specialists in these functional areas to manage those aspects of the business.

Divisional organizations are either organized around product categories, customer markets, or regions of the world. Then each division will have its own resources and functional organization. For instance, GSK (previously GlaxoSmithKline) is a UK-based pharmaceutical company employing 99,000 people in 100 countries. In 2010, it was organized into four major regional divisions for North America, Europe, Asia Pacific/ Japan, and Emerging Markets.

Conglomerate organizations are made up of a variety of different businesses, which may or may not have similarities between them. A typical conglomerate is General Electric, which is, according to Interbrand (2010), the world's fifth best brand. Originally a manufacturer of electrical appliances it moved into financial services and the media business in the 1980s. In 2008, GE's divisions included GE Capital (including GE Commercial Finance, GE Money, and GE Consumer Finance), GE Technology Infrastructure (including GE Aviation, the former Smiths Aerospace, and GE Healthcare), GE Energy Infrastructure, and NBC Universal, the television and film company.

Hybrid organizations, sometimes referred to as matrix structures, are organizations that deliberately mix the four organizational forms just described. In the 1990s some of the major petrol companies such as BP adopted this form. Hence there may be both regional divisions and functional departments.

The relationship between the issues of organization and organizational form is illustrated in Figure 1.1. This shows that as organizations become more complex the degree of centralization decreases. With regard to formalization it tends to be the divisionally organized firm that has the highest level, reflecting the fact that it typically has narrow

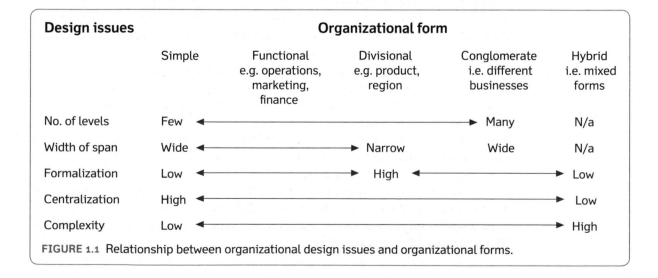

FIGURE 1.1 Relationship between organizational design issues and organizational forms.

spans of control. Conglomerates tend to have more levels than other firms, but this is mostly due to these being the larger organizations. The importance of this from an operations perspective is that managers of individual operations, whether they be a factory, shop, or medical practice, may have very different responsibilities and freedom to act, depending on the degree of organizational centralization and formalization.

It should be noted that organizational form and structures are not fixed—they change over time. Operations insight 1.1 illustrates how Starbucks in the USA decided to change its structure and identifies some of the operations issues that arise from such reorganization.

OPERATIONS INSIGHT 1.1
Starbucks—mega corp. or local store?

In 2008, Starbucks in the USA conducted an organizational review that had implications for how its operations were managed and for its 170,000 employees. Clearly the decision to reorganize was a difficult one, as the Starbucks CEO stated that he was 'struggling' with the issue and was aware that it could be 'painful' for some employees. This was because the reorganization removed 600 positions and hence staff were made redundant.

The purpose of this was clearly to cut costs and make the organization more efficient. It was hoped that it would strengthen Starbucks' focus on the customer in its outlets, by consolidating many of the support functions at head office and in regional offices. Hence it was decided to have four operations divisions—Western/Pacific, Northwest/Mountain, Southeast/Plains, and Northeast/Atlantic—instead of just two. The idea behind this was to enable regional managers and support teams to work more closely with the managers and employees in each Starbucks outlet. It was also hoped that the approach adopted by the new regional leaders would be more customer-centric, that is to say, listen more carefully to consumer feedback and respond appropriately. Each of these new divisions was to be led by a senior vice president, who would report directly to the US president of Starbucks. Within each division, managers responsible for Store Development, Marketing, Partner (i.e. Human) Resources, and Finance report directly to their respective executive managers at head office, while being responsible for results at the divisional level.

Starbucks' organizational review aimed to strengthen its customer focus. © istock/john shepherd.

Starbucks also reorganized support functions which up to this point had consisted of:

- US Store Development
- US Licensed Stores
- US Finance
- Partner Resources
- Marketing

- In-Store Experience
- Global Supply Chain
- Global Communications
- Partner & Asset Protection.

Most of these were merged to create fewer departments and improve coordination across the organization. As a result, Starbucks shifted some of the operational responsibility down from head office to the regional offices and reduced the number of levels between the CEO and the outlet managers.

Source: based on a press release issued by Starbucks CEO Howard Schulze in Seattle on 21 February 2008

Questions

1. What form of organization structure has Starbucks adopted?
2. How centralized and formalized will Starbucks be after the reorganization?

As well as the long-standing forms of organization already described, newer so-called post-bureaucratic forms have emerged, such as team organizations, networks, and even virtual firms. Team structures tend to be based around projects within organizations that cut across conventional functional boundaries within organizations. Well-known organizations that have partially adopted this approach include Xerox, Motorola, and Chrysler. Such manufacturers have done so in order to achieve better coordination between sections of their manufacturing process that might previously not have communicated with each other. Network organizations are ones that have significantly reduced their workforce and outsourced or contracted out the work to other organizations, who may be able to do this better or more cheaply than could be done within the organization. This is the case with some firms that used to manufacture their own goods, but now have completely outsourced the making of products to other companies, as seen in the clothing industry in the UK. Finally there are some 'organizations' that are virtual, being based almost entirely on the Internet. An example of this might be Linux, which is a community of software developers from around the world that have developed the Linux operating system and related software applications. Another example is Salon Consulting, which is made up of many independent consultants who collaborate together on projects as and when necessary, depending on the size and complexity of the work and the expertise required for its successful completion.

How is the operations function organized?

Having identified in the introduction that most organizations have operations, and that operations managers are often responsible for most of the assets, people, and money, we now turn to how the operations function itself is organized. The same issues identified earlier—hierarchy, centralization, formalization, complexity—which affect the whole organization also affect operations. We can see how these factors influence the organization of operations if we look at a single industry, such as the motor manufacturing sector. Firms in this sector vary from global companies such as VW and Toyota with a wide range of cars, to relatively small firms producing specialized vehicles, such as

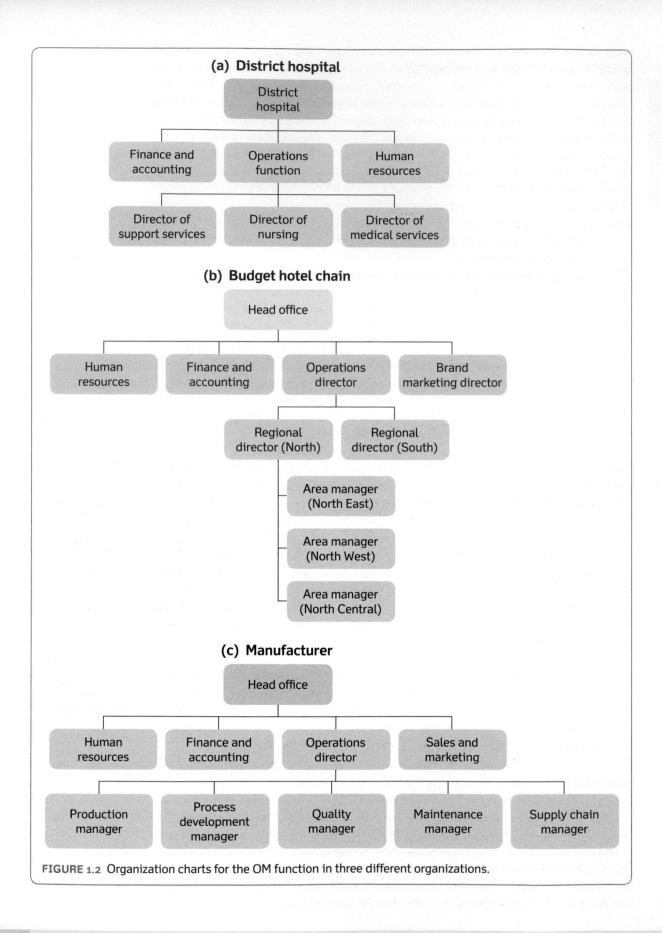

(a) District hospital

- District hospital
  - Finance and accounting
  - Operations function
    - Director of support services
    - Director of nursing
    - Director of medical services
  - Human resources

(b) Budget hotel chain

- Head office
  - Human resources
  - Finance and accounting
  - Operations director
    - Regional director (North)
      - Area manager (North East)
      - Area manager (North West)
      - Area manager (North Central)
    - Regional director (South)
  - Brand marketing director

(c) Manufacturer

- Head office
  - Human resources
  - Finance and accounting
  - Operations director
    - Production manager
    - Process development manager
    - Quality manager
    - Maintenance manager
    - Supply chain manager
  - Sales and marketing

FIGURE 1.2 Organization charts for the OM function in three different organizations.

Lotus. Toyota manufactures over 22,000 cars a day; Lotus has made 29,300 Lotus Elise cars in 16 years, roughly five per day. Toyota has a product range of 40 cars; Lotus has four models of sports car. Toyota has hundreds of suppliers of parts for its cars; Lotus manufactures some of its own components and buys the rest from a small number of suppliers (such as complete engines from Toyota). Toyota has 53 manufacturing facilities outside Japan; Lotus has a facility in Norfolk. Toyota employs over 300,000 workers; Lotus employs nearly 1300. As a result, Toyota has a divisional approach to its operations function, with operations managers responsible for different factories in different countries, other managers in charge of aspects of operations (procurement, research and development, quality management), and other managers responsible for certain product categories (saloon cars, sports cars, SUVs). Lotus, on the other hand, has a relatively simple and flat structure. But both Toyota and Lotus are at the leading edge of automotive engineering.

Differences between how the operations management function is organized are even more marked when we compare organizations in different sectors. This is illustrated in Figure 1.2. In all three organizations, operations are clearly separate from the other functional areas of marketing, finance, and human resources. But the operations function itself is subdivided on different criteria. In the hospital it is broken down into three different groups of employees with different sets of expertise—doctors, nurses, and support staff. In the budget hotel chain, operations is organized geographically. This is because each hotel is very similar but they are located throughout the UK. Finally the manufacturer has organized operations into five areas each of which is related to different aspects of the manufacturing process—supply chain, production, maintenance, quality, and development.

Figure 1.2 seems to suggest that the distinction between what is operations and what is some other function is very clear. In reality this is not always the case. This can be explained by understanding systems behaviour (Wilson, 1990). A **system** can be defined as a clearly identifiable, regularly interacting or interrelating groups of activities, as discussed in more detail later in this chapter. A feature of systems theory is the concept of a 'boundary' around the system. The boundary determines what is in the system and what is not. The reason that it is sometimes difficult to be clear about boundaries is that often outputs of one system are the inputs of another. This leads to another systems concept—namely '**simultaneous multiple containment**' (SMC). Many systems are interrelated and are made up of subsystems and are themselves subsystems of a larger system. Moreover many systems exist as subsystems of more than just one system. If SMC sounds confusing—it can be.

In Figure 1.2a we look at a simple example of how the operations management function might be organized in a hospital. In medicine, hospital doctors tend to specialize in one specific area. There are two main areas of expertise—surgical and medical. Surgeons engage in operative treatment and may become specialists in specific types of operation such as heart or brain surgery. Medical doctors treat patients non-surgically, usually with drugs. They, too, can specialize—in either different parts of the body (for instance, cardiologists are heart specialists and dermatologists are skin specialists) or different types of patient (paediatricians treat children and geriatricians treat the elderly). So hospitals are organized in this way in terms of teams of doctors and wards in which to care for patients. But patients do not necessarily fit easily into this system. For example, an elderly person with heart problems may be taking drugs for their condition and need surgery. Which ward do they go to and which doctor cares for them? It is clear in this case that the boundaries created by the hospital, based on its subsystems of staff and wards, need to be flexible enough to cope with the patients it cares for.

System clearly identifiable, regularly interacting or interrelating groups of activities

Simultaneous multiple containment describes how a process may have subprocesses and how these subprocesses may also be part of a different process

This idea that boundaries may be blurred, or flexible, is of major concern when it comes to understanding the relationship between operations and the other management functions. The line between operations and marketing is particularly blurred. As we shall shortly see, in service operations there are many implications of having the customer in the operation itself. But one specific issue is that as well as serving the customer there is direct marketing going on as well. The customer might be reading promotional material, whilst the server may be making recommendations or giving advice. This overlap is even more pronounced if you consider one of the key foundations of marketing, namely the marketing mix or so-called 4Ps of product, price, place, and promotion. Quite clearly the operations function has a key role with respect to the first three of these. It is operations that actually make the product, its ability to do so hugely influences the price that has to be charged, and operations ensures that the product is distributed ('place') effectively and efficiently. Likewise, if most of the employees in an organization work in operations, then this function has a huge responsibility for human resources. So despite organization charts showing these functions as separate entities, a key aspect of any organization is its ability to ensure collaboration across the different functional areas, as illustrated by the earlier hospital example.

TABLE 1.1 Responsibilities of operations managers

System features	Key responsibilities	Chapter
Developing and maintaining the system's infrastructure	Selection of a location for the operation Organizing the physical plant Maintaining and assuring the security of the plant equipment and other assets	4
Managing the system inputs and distribution of outputs	Deciding on whether to make in-house or buy from suppliers Selecting suppliers Managing the supply chain Distributing goods and services to customers	5
Controlling material inputs within the system	Determining stock levels Organizing materials flow	6
Managing customer inputs within the system (i.e. as 'co-workers')	Organizing customer flow (queuing etc.) Managing self-service technologies Responding to breakdowns in service	7
Managing the rate of flow through the system	Forecasting demand Scheduling work and employee time Adapting demand	8
Assuring the quality of system outputs	Setting standards Manage quality processes Monitor output quality	9
Developing and enhancing the system's processes	Monitoring productivity of employees and efficiency of technology Adapting work systems to improve performance	10
Designing and developing human work systems	Implementing principles of work design Managing employees, teams, and organizational culture	11
Developing new outputs (i.e. products and services)	Developing new concepts Assessing feasibility of new concepts Turning concepts into reality	12

What does an operations manager do?

Having identified the operations function within organizations, we now consider what the managers in this function are responsible for. There are key issues in relation to the 'system' that they plan, organize, and control, as illustrated in Table 1.1. The table also shows in which chapter each of these issues is discussed and explained.

Managing the short term and long term

Another key aspect of operations management is time. Operations managers are responsible for the very short term—operational activity within the factory, shop, or whatever on a minute-by-minute basis—but also the very long term—the development and investment in processes that will lead to the organization's future success. Table 1.2

TABLE 1.2 Managing operations in the short term and long term

	Short-term examples	Long-term examples
Developing and maintaining the system's infrastructure	Adding, replacing, or reorganizing equipment Setting up maintenance schedules	Selecting a site for a new operation and constructing the facility Major investment decisions on new technology
Managing the system inputs and distribution of outputs	Ordering stock Managing warehousing and logistics	Tendering contracts for new suppliers Outsourcing decisions
Controlling material inputs within the system	Setting stock levels Scheduling speed of production	Adopting new approaches to materials flow such as manufacturing resource planning (MRP II) or just-in-time
Managing customer inputs within the system (i.e. as 'co-workers')	Monitoring queues Overseeing self-service technologies (SSTs) Dealing with service failures and recovery	Redesigning the servicescape Selecting and siting new SSTs Improving service performance
Managing the rate of flow through the system	Forecasting for days or weeks ahead Devising work rotas Taking orders for goods or reservations for services	Forecasting for months or years ahead Planning manpower needs Planning scale of production and width of product range
Assuring the quality of system outputs	Checking output against standards Monitoring quality performance	Benchmarking standards against competitors Adapting and improving processes
Developing and enhancing the system's processes	Monitoring system performance—productivity of employees and efficiency of technology	Planning new systems to improve productivity and efficiency
Designing and developing human work systems	Monitoring hourly or daily workforce performance Reviewing ergonomics of equipment or work stations	Redesigning tasks, jobs, and teams Evaluating and adopting new human/technology interfaces
Developing new outputs (i.e. products and services)	Modifying and extending existing products and services	Adding new and original products and services to the range

RESEARCH INSIGHT 1.1

Hayes, R.H. and Wheelwright, S.C. (1984) *Restoring Our Competitive Edge*,
John Wiley: New York, pp. 24–45

Hayes and Wheelwright are two of the founding fathers of operations management. Their ideas and concepts have significantly influenced thinking in this field. In this ground-breaking book, they discuss the emergence of manufacturing strategy. In Chapter 2 of their book, they suggest a four-stage model of how operations could increasingly improve operational capability and hence simultaneously increase its strategic impact. These four stages are:

1. Internal neutrality—simply corrects the worst problem areas

2. External neutrality—identifies and adopts best practices

3. Internally supportive—links operations with strategy

4. Externally supportive—delivers competitive advantage through operations.

This model also demonstrates a shift from a focus on the short term, towards a long-term view of operations. Although the article was written in the mid-1980s, much of what they have to say is relevant today. Most especially it identifies that firms can succeed, i.e. achieve competitive advantage over their competitors, by organizing their operations in the right way. In the final four chapters of this book we look at this concept of 'operations strategy' and three specific examples of such strategies—lean manufacturing, continuous improvement, and globalization.

takes the nine systems features of Table 1.1 and gives some examples of what an operations manager may be concerned with in the short term and the long term.

Processes—the heart of operations management

We have briefly described operations as a system, with inputs, processes, and outputs. So central to what an operations manager does is the management of process. One way or the other, all the activities identified in Table 1.2 are about this. Just as a mechanic can look under the bonnet of a car and tell if the engine is working smoothly, an operations manager has to be able to look at any process, big or small, and identify if it is running well or not.

One way for a manager to be able to undertake such a diagnosis is to understand an operation's four Vs—**volume**, **variety**, **variation**, and **variability**.

Volume the size or scale of the output, i.e. how many items are manufactured or customers served in a specified time period

Variety the size of product range or number of services offered

- Volume relates to size or scale of the output, for instance, how many items are manufactured or customers served in a specified time period.

- Variety relates to the size of product range or number of services offered. For instance, Virgin Atlantic only flies long haul to selected destinations, whereas British Airways has both short-haul and long-haul flights to over 100 destinations.

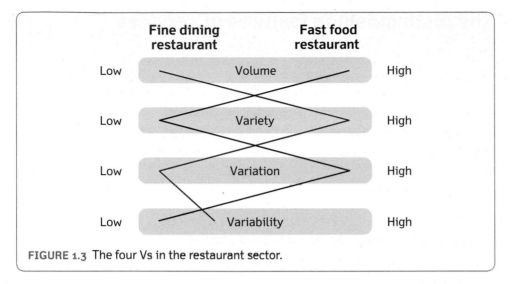

FIGURE 1.3 The four Vs in the restaurant sector.

Go online

- Variation describes how the level of demand changes over time and thereby affects the volume of outputs. This may be short term (hourly or daily)—such as lunchtime in a restaurant, as well as seasonal—such as the demand for umbrellas or tickets for outdoor events.
- Variability refers to the extent to which each product or service may be customized or not. For instance, in a restaurant the French fries will be standardized, but the steak might be grilled rare, medium, or well done.

The impact these have on an operation is illustrated in Figure 1.3 which compares two different kinds of operation in the restaurant sector. A typical fast food restaurant in a busy high street location may serve up to 30,000 customers a week (high volume), whereas a fine dining restaurant such as those operated by Gordon Ramsey may serve around 700 customers a week. The fast food menu has relatively few choices, many based around the same concept such as hamburgers, chicken, or fish (limited variety), whereas Ramsey's restaurant will have a menu with a wide choice of different dishes and this menu may be different from one day to the next. In the fast food sector demand for meals varies on a daily basis, with peaks in demand at lunch and dinner times and is influenced by factors such as the weather—more shoppers using the restaurant if it is raining (high variation). The fine dining restaurant may only be open at certain times and only take diners who reserve a table, so that it is always full. Finally, the fast food restaurant uses standard ingredients and standard recipes to try to ensure that every item sold is consistent (no variability), whereas diners in the fine dining experience may be asked how they like their food and it is then cooked to their specification.

Variability the extent to which each product or service may be customized or not

Variation how the level of demand changes over time and thereby affects the volume of outputs. This may be short term (hourly or daily), as well as seasonal

Services versus manufacturing

For the last 30 years there has been a debate as to whether service industries are fundamentally different from manufacturing. This is important because if they are different, then operations managers have to manage service operations differently from the way in which manufacturing operations are managed.

The distinguishing features of services

In 1978 a group of Harvard professors published their ground-breaking book *The Management of Service Operations*. Sasser et al. (1978) argued that there were four features of services that made then fundamentally different from manufacturing goods—namely **intangibility**, **heterogeneity**, **perishability**, and **simultaneity** (sometimes referred to as inseparability). Each of these will now be briefly discussed and debated.

Intangibility

Intangibility the lack of tangible characteristics of a service operation

This refers to the concept that services do not physically exist but are directly experienced by consumers. Moreover once a service has been purchased and experienced there is no physical evidence of it ever being consumed. The classic example of this is an overnight stay in a hotel. The guest arrives, stays in the hotel, pays, and leaves and has no evidence of having purchased anything—except for their bill. The operations management implication of intangibility is that it is extremely difficult to ensure services are delivered in the correct way, because it is extremely difficult to measure these intangibilities. For instance, the hotel guest buys a 'good night's sleep'.

But are services really intangible? Or perhaps, to put it another way, are products really tangible? It is difficult to think of anything that is more tangible than a motor car. A car is a large, significant artefact for which a huge amount of tangible data can be collected—such as how much it weighs, how fast it goes, and how much fuel it consumes. But there is evidence to show that many cars are purchased not on the tangible evidence of their performance but on their intangible aspects—their aesthetics. People buy cars because they like the colour, or the shape, or the comfort of the seat—using their subjective opinion rather than objective 'facts'. So clearly products have many intangible features. It can then be argued that services have tangible features, just like products. These often relate to the environment in which the service is delivered and how functional it is—such as how queues are designed, and how the technology works. Service companies routinely put a great deal of effort into how they design their operations to make the customer experience effective and efficient (this is discussed in more detail in Chapters 4, 7, and 10).

Heterogeneity

Heterogeneity the variety of responses consumers may have to a service experience

This refers to the idea that consumers have unique experiences of services that are not shared with, or are the same as, other consumers. This follows on from intangibility. If there is no tangible product, then it is easy for each customer to interpret their experience in different ways. Using the hotel example, the same hotel room may be used by hundreds of guests but each of them could have different experiences and different levels of satisfaction with that experience. For operations managers, heterogeneity means that managing the customer experience is very challenging. Even if services are delivered to a precise standard, different consumers will react to these in different ways. Indeed, the same customer using the same service on different occasions may have different reactions each time. Hence measuring consumer satisfaction is a challenge.

The case against heterogeneity distinguishing services from products is very simple—consumers' opinions about products are just as heterogeneous as they are for services. If cars are purchased not for their features but because they 'look nice', then there can be a huge variation in consumers' opinions as to what 'nice' is.

Perishability

It is argued that services cannot be inventoried or put into stock. An airline seat available today, if not sold, is therefore a sale that is lost forever—it cannot be sold twice the following day. The operations imperative that follows from perishability is that it is essential to ensure services are used to their maximum. The capacity of the operation has to be effectively managed—as discussed in Chapter 8. This is why hotels are happy to sell rooms at a discount on or near the date requested, as it is better to have some revenue to cover costs than have a half-empty hotel.

Products, on the other hand, tend to be non-perishable—although some products such as foodstuffs (meat, vegetables, dairy products) have relatively short shelf lives. But very few products have an indefinite shelf life. Consumers generally want to buy the latest model. So even if a mobile telephone manufactured a year ago works perfectly, customers may be reluctant to purchase it as it does not have the latest features (functional or aesthetic). In terms of services, they also have a 'shelf life'—it is all the time that leads up to the specific occasion when the service needs to be sold (such as in a hotel or on an aeroplane). For instance, airlines and hotels started taking bookings for the London Olympics in 2012 from 6 July 2005 onwards—the day it was announced that London was the venue. That's a 'shelf life' of seven years, which is considerably longer than most manufactured goods.

Perishability the inability of service providers to inventory their services

Simultaneity (or inseparability)

Services are produced at the same time (or place) as they are consumed, unlike a product which can be purchased and used whenever (and often wherever) it is needed. Therefore a service depends on direct interaction between the consumer and the service provider. Although simultaneity and inseparability tend to be used interchangeably to describe this concept, they in fact refer to two different things. Simultaneity refers to the idea that service is provided at the same time as it is requested; whereas inseparability refers to providing service in the same place as the consumer. In high street retailing, the customer only experiences the shop's services if in the outlet itself. The operations management issue that results from simultaneity is that service provision has to be matched closely to consumer demand—but it may be difficult to predict this demand. So a shop may know that it is busy on Saturdays and have extra staff on duty to deal with this. But the shop does not know if shoppers will arrive in a steady stream over an extended period, in which case they can be served without delay, or whether 30 or 40 will arrive within ten minutes of each other, so that queues build up and some customers have to queue to be served. Clearly, not matching supply to demand means that often the quality of the service suffers, leading to low levels of customer satisfaction.

Simultaneity the co-production and delivery of a service in the consumer's presence

Given these proposed differences between services and manufacturing, are service firms and their operations managed differently? As Research insight 1.2 shows, some would argue strongly that they are.

RESEARCH INSIGHT 1.2

Heskett, J.L., Jones, T.O., Loveman, G.W., Sasser, W.E., and Schlesinger, L.A. (1994) Putting the service-profit chain to work, *Harvard Business Review*, Mar/Apr, 72(2), 164–70

A number of Harvard professors have been researching and writing about services for many years. In this article they collaborate to discuss what they call the 'service-profit chain'. This model argues that the most successful service companies, so-called 'breakthrough firms', focus on their employees and customers. They suggest that in this new service paradigm, successful service managers heed the factors that drive profitability—investment in people, technology that supports front-of-house workers, redesigned recruiting and training practices, and pay linked to performance. As a result the service-profit chain suggests relationships between profitability and customer loyalty, as well as employee satisfaction, loyalty, and productivity.

Whilst Heskett et al. (1994) make a convincing case for the service-profit chain, this does not mean that service is different from manufacturing. Investing in people, adopting the right technology, recruiting and training employees, and performance-related pay are probably also important and essential in manufacturing. So, in this book we argue that the single key difference between these two main types of operation is simultaneity/inseparability. In services, having the customer 'in the factory' means that service employees cannot make mistakes and have to respond in quite sophisticated ways to the emotions, feelings, and behaviours of the customers.

Processing materials, customers, and information

So far we have identified that operations management is all about processes and that there may be some difference between services and manufacturing, notably that customers are involved in the creation and production of services. Given that the concept of a process is that of a flow through a system, it is now time to consider what flows through. The answer is that it can only be three things—materials, customers, or information (or a combination of these).

Therefore Johnston and Morris (1994) suggest there are basically three types of operation:

- Materials processing operation (MPO)—more commonly referred to as manufacturing
- Customer processing operation (CPO)—typically described as a service
- Information processing operation (IPO)—mostly considered as services.

But in many cases, an operation is not uniquely an MPO, CPO, or IPO—it is a combination of all three. For instance, during the customer experience in a restaurant materials are processed (food and drink prepared for consumption, transported to the customers), information is processed (customer selects from menu, order taken, bill prepared), and customer processing occurs (customers' requests are responded to, social interaction takes place). This is further illustrated in Operations insight 1.2 on motor repair services.

The reason why these three basic types of operations are important is that materials, customers, and information each behave in very different ways. Materials are physical and come in all kinds of shapes and sizes. When not being handled they remain inert, interacting with their environment very little—although food may deteriorate and iron may rust if left for too long. However, when being handled, each kind of material has specific properties. Some materials are liquid, such as petrol and wine. Many materials are solids, such as wood and metal, although these two materials behave in very different ways when shaped and heated. Other materials may be both liquid and solid—glass for instance is 'liquid' when being heated to shape into objects, but a solid, albeit a fragile one, when cooled. Because of these physical and chemical properties the behaviour of each material can be precisely understood and managed in any given state. Hence processing materials should be entirely predictable.

It might be thought that managing customers is also relatively straightforward. Although customers come in all shapes and sizes, they are all fundamentally 'made of the same material'—flesh and blood. This homogeneity should therefore mean that all customers will react and behave in the same way in any given situation. But as we all know this is not the case! People have minds of their own. Moreover, unlike passive materials, they can physically transport themselves from one place to another. This can be an advantage if they choose to move in the way the operation expects them to (for instance, by joining the end of a queue) but a disadvantage in that some customers may not choose to cooperate. Disney Paris discovered this when they first opened their theme park. Although highly experienced operators, they were used to visitors following instructions and following certain queuing rules. They found that their French visitors were unaware of, or chose to ignore, such conventions. In order to avoid delays and queues these early visitors would access rides using exits, push into queues, and take other inappropriate action.

Finally there is information. This is clearly neither material nor human. At its simplest, information is a collection of facts or data. This of itself is not much use, so in terms of operations when we talk about information processing operations we are actually talking about the movement or communication of information from one place to another. Just as materials processing has been transformed over the centuries through various 'revolutions'—the agricultural revolution, the industrial revolution, and the Internet revolution—so information has developed—from the spoken word, to writing and then printing, and the digital revolution. This now means that information systems can do what previously was difficult for humans to do, such as handle large amounts of information, perform complex calculations, and control many processes at the same time. Processing information is now so important that many organizations have not only a CEO and chief financial officer (CFO), but also a chief information officer (CIO). And there are some sectors of commerce and the public sector which predominantly deal with information, such as financial services, education, and mental health care.

SMC Renault Minute—servicing cars and serving people

SMC Renault Minute in Woking, Surrey is a subsidiary of a main Renault car dealership, SMC Renault, which was established in 1986. Working as a wholly owned subsidiary, SMC Renault Minute was set up a short distance from the main dealership in 2005. It occupies premises of some 10,000 square feet and has four service bays. It specializes in fast-fit services, from exhausts, batteries, and tyres to brake pads and shock absorbers, but also carries out full repair services and MOT testing. There is a small car parking area where cars are held awaiting service, a small reception area, and a viewing area for customers to see their car during MOT testing. Primarily set up to handle Renault vehicles it now services most makes of car. There are ten members of staff including four full-time motor technicians. There are two additional motor technicians who work at SMC branches locally who can be called upon to cover for sickness, holidays, or a large influx of work.

There are two modes of operation. Firstly the most usual option is through appointments. Each job has a standard time associated with it and the experienced service administration staff estimate the amount of time that the job will take and can advise the customer of the likely cost. This helps to maximize the use of the company's valuable resources and it also allows time for any spare parts required to be ordered and made available before the car enters the service bay.

The second mode of operation is a 'While-U-Wait' option in which customers can arrive without an appointment and then wait until a service bay becomes available. Demand for this service is obviously unpredictable but it offers an opportunity for SMC to make use of otherwise unused service bay capacity.

In common with many small and medium-sized enterprises it uses a mixture of manual and computerized systems to help plan and organize its operations. The process is illustrated in Figure 1.4 which shows the flow of the customer, information, and materials through the operation of a typical service repair. Bookings are made via a manual diary system but when the vehicle arrives it is given a computerized job number. Information about the make and model of car are included in a job sheet together with the work to be carried out, which then builds up a job history. This allows the company to keep in contact with their customers by providing a reminder service for upcoming service or MOT testing. If an unforeseen problem comes to light that will require additional expenditure then the service administration staff will contact the customer to seek approval for the work to be carried out. After the job is finished the motor technician completes the job sheet and signs it to say that the work has been carried out in accordance with the required specification. A computerized invoice is then provided for the customer, who pays for the service, receives the keys, and retrieves the car from the parking area.

In this operation the flow of the customer, information, and materials can clearly be identified. Figure 1.4 illustrates the role that information has in managing an operation, namely it links the flow of the customer and the flow of materials through the system.

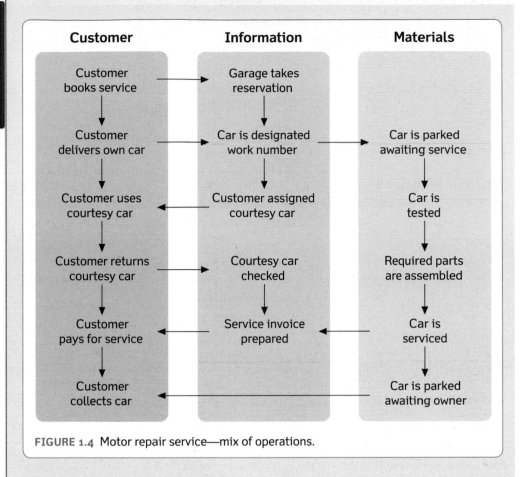

FIGURE 1.4 Motor repair service—mix of operations.

Go online

Questions

1. What are the advantages to the company of having an appointments system?

2. Can you think of any other ways of organizing this operation to make best use of their resources?

Operations as systems

So far we have identified that operations take inputs and process these to produce outputs, and we mentioned that this can be thought of as a 'system'. This is often shown as illustrated in Figure 1.5a. However, this diagram simplifies operations too much, because there is another kind of 'input' that we have not yet discussed, namely the resources that a firm needs in order to conduct its business. These resource inputs are called 'transformational inputs', whereas the inputs that flow through the operation, such as materials, customers of information, are 'transformed inputs'. The transformational inputs are of two kinds—the physical assets of the firm, such as its buildings, machinery, and equipment, and the human assets, its employees. Moreover these transformational inputs can be back of house, that is to say unseen or unused by customers, or front of house, so that customers enter the operation and use the services provided. Figure 1.5b illustrates

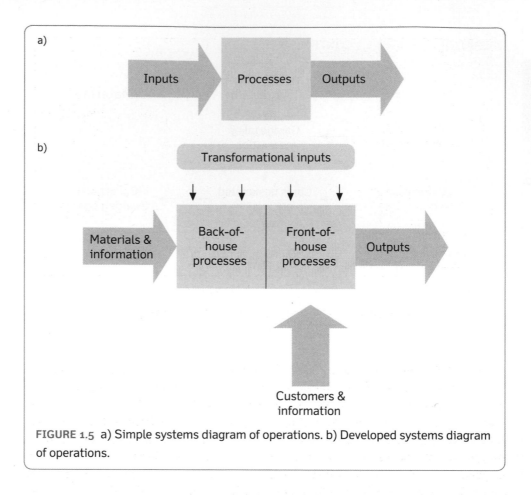

FIGURE 1.5 a) Simple systems diagram of operations. b) Developed systems diagram of operations.

this. Most manufacturing operations have no front of house, because they do not process customers. All service businesses have a front of house, and probably have a back of house too (as we have seen in Operations insight 1.2 about Renault).

The servuction system

Another way of thinking about the relationship between customers, information and transformational inputs is the so-called **servuction system**, originally conceived by Langeard et al. (1981). This is illustrated in Figure 1.6. The concept of 'servuction' is a blend of the words service and production. It recognizes that operations which process customers can do so in two ways—through their physical infrastructure, such as buildings, plant, and equipment, and/or through their staff. Of course in most cases they use both. This system model adds another dimension to understanding operations, namely that the customer experience is not simply affected by what the operation provides but also by other customers using that operation, i.e. the so-called co-consumers. In other words the experience of customer A is affected by the service they get from the infrastructure and staff and by their interaction with customer B. For instance, your enjoyment of an evening out at a restaurant, club, or cinema can be spoilt by other customers behaving in ways that you find annoying or offensive.

The model is also extremely helpful in demonstrating and explaining some of the ways in which customer processing operations have been changing over the years. First,

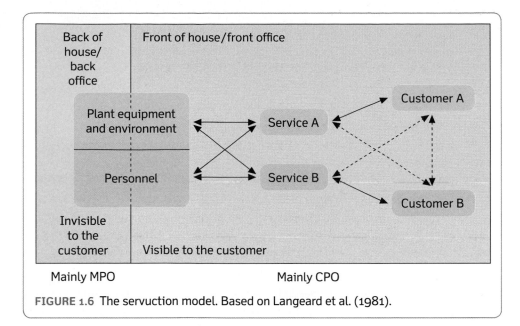

Go online

FIGURE 1.6 The servuction model. Based on Langeard et al. (1981).

the extent to which service is provided by infrastructure or by staff has changed. The customer has increasingly taken responsibility for their own service and in effect become a co-worker through using self-service technologies. This has led to the idea that service encounters can be either 'high-tech' or 'high-touch'. High-tech services have little or no staff input, customers usually interact just with technology, such as when they use a cash machine outside a bank. High-touch on the other hand has high levels of personal service, as you would expect from a hairdresser or doctor. Second, the barrier between back office and front office has been shifted or taken down altogether. The fast food sector was one of the first to do this. In the traditional restaurant setting, the kitchen was back of house and the dining area was front of house, and customers could neither see nor enter the kitchen. In fast food there is no wall between the service area and the production area, the back of house is open for all to see. This was done for two reasons. First it helped fast food employees to see front of house to gauge how busy the restaurant is, thereby enabling them to speed up or reduce the scale of production. Second it reassured the customer that low-cost food was safe to eat because they could see for themselves how clean and well operated the kitchen was. Operations insight 1.3 looks at how the servuction system has changed in the banking industry.

OPERATIONS INSIGHT 1.3
Financial services—from counters to couches

Over the last 30 years, the financial service sector has been transformed, fundamentally changing the nature of the relationships between the bank and its customers. There have been two major driving forces of this change—deregulation and technology. Deregulation was of three kinds—a reduction of restrictions on competition, an enabling of banking, insurance, and securities services to be combined, and the harmonization of regulations across

Europe. In simple terms, banks (who largely focused on offering current and deposit accounts) were able to merge with building societies (who focused on mortgage lending). As a result, organizations merged in order to provide the full range of financial services, as well as to take advantage of economies of scale.

At the same time, information technology and then the Internet enabled nearly all of the paperwork associated with financial services to be digitized. As well as speeding up transactions, this also enabled customers to directly interface with the technology and serve themselves, either through automatic teller machines (ATMs) or, more recently, Internet banking.

Both of these trends have led to the design and layout of banks changing. In the old-style bank, where the majority of transactions related to withdrawing or depositing cash, a bank comprised a long counter and glass screen, behind which tellers sat to serve customers. The paramount concern was security, so access from the front office area to the back office was kept very secure. If a customer needed to speak with their bank manager, they normally had to make an appointment, and then met with the manager in a private office. But in modern banks, the type of financial services on offer varies more widely, so transaction times vary. Moreover, bank employees are now expected not just to deal with customers but to sell financial products to them. So banks have become more like open-plan offices. There still is a teller's counter for security reasons, but there will also be open desks, comfortable seating, and display areas. At the same time, the exterior or lobby area has been redesigned to incorporate ATMs.

A contemporary bank interior—very different from how banks used to look. © istock/gerenme.

Financial service companies have therefore adopted both 'high-tech' and 'high-touch' approaches to service. This concept—'high-tech/high-touch'—was first used by John Naisbitt in 1982 in his book *Megatrends*. He argued that as business, and society in general, introduced more and more technology, it needed to be balanced by 'human ballast', i.e. social contact. Technology is particularly good at doing some things (complex data manipulation and transfer) but very poor at doing others (responding to human emotions). So bank customers who wish to engage in fast simple transactions have high-tech facilities to enable this, whilst other bank customers, who need questions answered and alternatives discussed, are provided with comfortable and relaxing surroundings in which to do this on a face-to-face basis with a bank employee.

Questions

1. How has the back office/front office interface changed in retail banks over the last 20 years? (Use the servuction model in Figure 1.6 to illustrate this.)

2. How has the role of technology and the role of employees changed over the same time? (Use the servuction model in Figure 1.6 to illustrate this.)

Conclusions

This introductory chapter has been designed to set the scene. It began by highlighting the importance of operations management, before going on to discuss different ways in which organizations can be structured. The same issues that emerge from organizational design—hierarchy, centralization, formalization, and complexity—also affect the way in which the operations management function is organized. The role of the operations manager was then discussed, both in terms of their short-term responsibilities and their longer-term, strategic responsibilities. The rest of the chapter was then devoted to ways in which operations may or may not be different from each other. In this book we propose that there is less difference between manufacturing and services than might be supposed. The key issue is that in some operations the customer is present and this has implications for how the operation is designed and operated. We also saw how operations may have very different combinations of volume, variety, variation, and variability. Finally, the role of technology and employees, either back of house or front of house, was discussed.

This chapter demonstrates that the scope of operations management is huge. It ranges from very big issues such as the long-term success of major corporations, right through very specific issues such as to the nature of a single service encounter and a customer's satisfaction with that experience. It also ranges across every single activity that humankind engages in. In the first few minutes of every day, the average person will have interacted with the outputs of hundreds of different manufacturers or service providers—when they clean their teeth, listen to the radio, get dressed, make breakfast, catch the bus, and continue on through their daily routine. How are operations managers able to make so many different things? And provide so many different services to make our lives as comfortable as they are? That is what the rest of this book is devoted to explaining.

END OF CHAPTER CASE
Domino's Pizza UK—using operations to drive success

On 15 February 2011, Domino's Pizza UK & IRL plc released its latest results for the trading year 2010. System sales had increased by 19.3% up to £485.3 million. Operating margins were 20.2%, up from 19.4% the year before. Profit before tax was increased by 27.3% to £38.0 million. And like-for-like sales were up by 11.9%. Not surprisingly, earnings per share for shareholders were also up by 25.7% and total dividend increased by 31.6%. These were outstanding results by any standards, but especially good in the context of the UK's flat economy and in a sector where margins are traditionally tight. However, 2010 was not an exceptional year for the company. Domino's had had double-digit growth every year for the last five years and had plans to continue this through for the next five years, so that by 2015 its turnover would be in the region of £1 billion.

In 2005, the CEO had identified a number of initiatives that would drive the business forward over the following five years. These were agreed by the board and called Vision 2010. Each of these had contributed to driving sales, or reducing costs, or both. These initiatives included improving customer service, especially in relation to delivery time; product quality; new product development; supply chain efficiency; and the development of online ordering systems.

Pizza topping was one of the processes reviewed. Copyright Domino's Pizza Group Limited. All rights reserved.

Heatwave bags keep the pizzas hot during transit. Copyright Domino's Pizza Group Limited. All rights reserved.

A key feature that attracts customers in the home delivery market is delivery time—the time it takes for the food to arrive at the customer's door after the order has been placed. The industry standard for this, and what most customers expect, is 30 minutes. In 50 years of trading, Domino's had always been very aware of this and had striven to design systems that would enable this performance standard to be met. Delivery time has two main components—'out-the-door' time (OTD), i.e. the time it takes to process the order in store; and transportation time, the time it takes to get from the store to the customer. In terms of transportation time, Domino's have limited control over this. It is a function of how far away the customer is from the store and the prevailing traffic conditions. Stores are located so that their delivery area is nominally no more than eight minutes away, which is roughly two miles. But the majority of orders are placed by customers less than a mile away.

So if delivery time is to be systematically improved, the focus has to be on OTD, as reducing this will affect the speed of delivery for all customers. In 2006, OTD was identified as being 17 minutes on average. Hence the decision was made to try to reduce this by at least 3 minutes. This would have the effect of improving performance to the point where 98% of customers would get their pizza within 30 minutes of ordering it. However, reducing OTD was hugely challenging. So a detailed review was begun of all the processes that made up this time. These were order taking, pizza dough preparation, pizza topping, oven cooking, boxing, and dispatch. To drive this review an in-store display panel was installed that showed managers and workers what that store's OTD performance was in real time. Data was updated every 30 seconds. Moreover, this panel also displayed the average OTD times of other stores in the region, as well as for the whole system, so that each store could benchmark its OTD performance as it happened. This led to stores competing against each other to get better times, by making lots of small incremental changes that helped speed up OTD, such as layout of workbenches, number of staff on duty, ensuring production lines were stocked, and so forth.

Domino's regards itself as fanatical about product quality. It had not compromised on this, even though there was pressure on commodity prices and maintaining margins was a challenge. Unlike some of its competitors, it did not use frozen dough balls, but chilled dough, which has to be constantly held at 1–3 degrees throughout its movement along the supply chain. It also used 100% mozzarella cheese and fresh tomato paste (not concentrate). And to maintain product quality from store to customer, Domino's introduced the first heated delivery bags, called Heatwave, to keep the pizzas hot during transit. Quality is also managed through unannounced operations audits, which take place three times a year. These audits measure in detail every aspect of the store operations, but especially OTD and hygiene. In 2010, stores averaged a score of 4.4 out of 5, demonstrating a high level of quality performance. Regular high scores on the audits results in the franchisee being rated as 'approved to expand', that is to say they will be offered any new store openings in their region, and they are able to buy franchises from other franchisees who are exiting the business. If a store scores below 2, another audit is scheduled within 30 days. If that is failed, another audit is conducted within 7 days. Three failed audits result in a franchisee being given 60 days to sell their franchise (usually to another franchisee) at the going market rate.

There is a dedicated new product development (NPD) team at Domino's head office. All products are systematically tested and trialled before being rolled out across the chain. This team developed a spicy pizza called 'Meltdown – the Revenge' creating a challenge amongst its customers to try this spicy pizza, and in 2010 introduced a new pizza base called the 'Basil Burst Base'. Occasionally franchisees, sometimes influenced by customers, come up with product ideas. This was how the 'Reggae Reggae' pizza was developed. But all product ideas go through the same NPD process.

The company has also trialled other formats and service times. In 2009, Domino's launched its first mobile unit in the UK. It also started to target the lunchtime crowds and launched a specific lunchtime menu in July 2010. Later in 2010, the first 24-hour store opened in Manchester, offering breakfast, as well as lunch menus. Despite the development of specific products for these day parts, experience suggests that customers continue to order a pizza and a soft drink at any time of the day and night. This is especially the case where sections of the local population may be employed in shift work.

Domino's Pizza has chosen to have tight control over its supply chain, hence it has three commissaries or distribution centres, two in the UK and one in Ireland, from which goods are supplied to stores, and its own fleet of trucks to deliver these. Stores typically receive stock three times a week to ensure that it is fresh. So that delivery does not interfere with store operations, deliveries are made at night. Each driver has keys and access codes that enable entry onto store premises. This means that not only are the goods delivered, but they are properly placed on the correct shelving in each store. This ensures tight inventory control, but also contributes to maintaining proper in-store hygiene and food safety standards.

In order to stand out, Domino's has an innovative approach to e-commerce. It was the first pizza delivery company that offered online and interactive TV ordering. The company also offers a pizza tracker which was designed for the customer to follow their order. In September 2009 the company launched its iPhone app which achieved sales over £1 million by December. The company plans to also be the first to develop an app for android smartphones and for the iPad. In 2010, e-commerce sales in the UK and Ireland totalled £128 million compared to £78.5 million in 2009. The success of Domino's e-commerce initiatives can also be illustrated by its website usage, as it consistently drove higher rates of visitation than its three major competitors. Another recent development is a Domino's Pizza Facebook page, which in March 2011 had over 160,000 fans. This allows Domino's to publicize its products and promotions and network with its customer base. In many cases, customers use the page as an opportunity to complain, either about the service or the product. Domino's has a team of eight people constantly monitoring this and other sites, and replying to every single issue of concern as quickly as possible after it has been posted. The policy is not to remove complaints, but show that the company is listening and trying to put things right. In some cases, postings are removed because they are offensive. Facebook has also been used to run competitions, such as one called 'Superfans'.

With a very small head office, geographically dispersed stores, and a workforce employed by many different franchisees, Domino's Pizza UK's CEO believes that Domino's strong culture is the 'glue' that holds the organization together. This culture originated in the USA with the company's founder Tom Monaghan. It is based around being informal, proud of being 'whacky', goal-oriented, and fearless. Organizational commitment is reinforced in stores throughout the world by the company chant. This goes:

- Leader: 'Who are we?'
- Employees: 'Domino's Pizza!'
- Leader: 'What are we?'

- Employees: 'Number 1!'
- Leader: 'What do we do?'
- Employees: 'Sell more pizza, have more fun! Sell more pizza, have more fun!'

In 2010, nearly every Vision 2010 target had been exceeded. In particular, financial performance was better than planned—average weekly unit sales of mature stores were £400 more than target, and for new stores more than £1000 higher. Total annual sales were £10 million higher than forecast and the firm's market capitalization was almost double the target set in 2005.

Questions

1. Describe how Domino's processes materials, information, and customers.

2. Identify what Domino's servuction system looks like.

3. What short-term actions (refer to Table 1.2) are Domino's operations managers taking?

4. What long-term actions (refer to Table 1.2) are Domino's operations managers taking?

 # Chapter summary

To consolidate your learning, the key points from this chapter are summarized as follows:

- **Define what is meant by operations management**

  OM can be defined as the management of processes that convert inputs (such as materials, labour, and energy) into outputs (in the form of goods and services).

- **Understand the nature of operations within an organization**

  Operations management is one of the core functions within an organization—the others typically being marketing, human resources, and finance and accounting.

- **Explain what an operations manager does and the role he/she plays in an organization**

  An operations manager has responsibility for developing and maintaining the system's infrastructure, managing the system inputs, controlling material inputs within the system, managing customer inputs within the system (i.e. as 'co-workers'), managing the rate of flow through the system, assuring the quality of system outputs, developing and enhancing the system's processes, designing and developing human work systems, and developing new outputs (i.e. products and services).

- **Discuss the similarities and differences between the manufacturing and service sectors of the economy**

  Services have four features which are supposed to differentiate them from manufacturing—intangibility, heterogeneity, perishability, and simultaneity (sometimes referred to as inseparability). Intangibility proposes that services do not physically exist but are directly experienced by consumers. Heterogeneity refers to the idea that consumers have unique experiences of services that are not shared with, or are the same as, other consumers. Perishability argues that services cannot be inventoried or put into stock. Simultaneity and inseparability identify that services are produced at the same time, and in the same place, as they are consumed. It is argued that it is mainly simultaneity/inseparability that differentiate services from manufacturing.

- **Explain the similarities and differences between customer processing operations, materials processing operations, and information processing operations**

  Materials are inert until they are handled, whereupon they behave in specific ways derived from their physical and chemical structure. Customers are people and as such are able to transport themselves from one place to another and to interact with their environment. Information is the communication of facts or data, often in very large quantities and in ways not visible to the human eye.

- **Discuss the relationship between the two 'Research insights' in this chapter.**

  Research insight 1.1 by Hayes, R.H. and Wheelwright, S.C. (1984) introduced the idea that firms, predominantly in the manufacturing sector, could achieve competitive advantage through their operations. Research insight by 1.2 Heskett et al. (1994) discusses how 'service breakthrough firms', those achieving competitive advantage in their service business sectors, seem to be doing this—through the so-called 'service-profit chain'.

Questions

Review questions

1. What is the difference between 'production management' and 'operations management'?

2. Why is operations management important in most organizations?

3. What are the four key features that explain an organization?

4. What key issues emerge from organizational design and what types of organization are there?

5. What are the four Vs?

6. How are services and manufacturing supposed to be different?

7. Consider a professional football club. What operational decisions have to be made in the short term? What are the long-term operational issues?

8. What is the servuction system? How has it changed over the years?

9. What ethical issues might an operations manager have responsibility for?

10. In what way might operations management have implications for sustainability?

Discussion questions

1. If most of the employees in an organization work in operations, what aspects of human resource management should be the responsibility of the OM function and what aspects should be the responsibility of the human resource function?

2. How unique (or heterogeneous) are customers' perceptions and behaviours? Later in this book (in Chapter 7) we identify that customers tend to behave in very similar ways, which is why they queue for services. In everyday life, in what ways do people behave differently from each other, and how do they behave similarly?

3. If a service provider does not take reservations, does this make their service more or less perishable? Or neither? Why?

4. Can you think of any operation that only processes materials, or only information, or only customers?

5. Visit a local service operation. Draw its servuction system identifying the kinds of technology that are being used, the number and types of staff, whether this is back of house or front of house, and the nature of interaction between customers. How might the servuction system be changed in order to make it more high-touch?

 # Further learning guide

There are very large numbers of textbooks, journals, and associations in the field of operations management. The two key research journals are the *Journal of Operations Management* (JOM) and the *International Journal of Productions and Operations Management* (IJOPM). In addition there are more specialist journals focusing on specific aspects of operations, such as the *Journal of Purchasing and Supply Management*. With regard to operations management associations, some focus on industry professionals—such as the Institute of Operations Management (**www.iomnet.org.uk**) and Institute of Logistics and Transport (**www.ciltuk.org.uk**) —whereas others tend to be mainly academic associations—such as the European Operations Management Association (**www.euroma-online.org**). All of these can give you insight into the field of operations management.

 # References

Interbrand (2010) *Best Global Brands 2010*, Interbrand Report

Langeard, E., Bateson, J., Lovelock, C., and Eiglier, P. (1981) *Marketing of Services: New Insights from Consumers and Managers*, Report No. 81–104, Marketing Sciences Institute, Cambridge

Naisbitt, J. (1987) *Megatrends: Ten New Directions Transforming Our Lives*, Warner Books: New York

Sasser, W.E., Wyckoff, D.D., and Olsen, M. (1978) *The Management of Service Operations*, Free Press: Boston, MA

Wilson, B. (1990) *Systems: concepts, methodologies, and applications* (2nd ed.), John Wiley: New York

Chapter Two

Winning customers and competing effectively

Learning outcomes

After reading this chapter you will be able to:

→ Explain the concept of order qualifiers (OQs) and order winners (OWs)

→ Explain how firms compete on the basis of OQs and OWs

→ Understand how operations are affected by market structure and identify alternative structures

→ Identify alternative approaches to industrial market segmentation and customer market segmentation and explain the implications of this for operations management

The British Broadcasting Corporation originally developed television (TV) in the UK in the 1930s and has remained a publicly funded service, paid for by TV licence payers. However, in the new age of satellite broadcasting and digital television, the market structure of broadcasting has changed significantly. This has brought into question how the BBC should be funded and how different market segments view the Corporation.

For some time the licence fee has been regarded as the least worst way of financing the BBC and supporting its role as a public service broadcaster. However, research in 2009 conducted by Ipsos Mori for MediaGuardian showed that a significant proportion of the public might no longer agree with this. Whilst 61% of respondents identified BBC1 as their favourite channel, 41% agreed with the licence fee being an 'appropriate' way to fund the BBC, with 37% disagreeing with the concept of the TV licence. Most respondents did not think the licence fee was good value.

However, different age groups and people from different parts of the UK do not share the same views. In particular, only 31% of 15–24-year-olds thought the licence fee was not the best way to support the BBC, whereas this rose to 45% of the 35–44 age group. This compares with the BBC's own research and perspective which is that it has least support from amongst young people, as they watch fewer of the BBC's television channels and listen less to its radio stations than their parents.

In reporting on this research, the *Guardian* suggests that this could be seen as 'encouraging for the BBC', as it suggests that support for the licence fee is not necessarily based on how television is watched or radio listened to. A BBC executive is quoted as saying 'Young people perhaps appreciate the quality of the BBC's output more. They have travelled more and are used to consuming television in different ways.'

All in all, the BBC is left with a dilemma. Different studies show different levels of support from amongst different groups of people. With four television channels and six radio stations, along with the BBC iPlayer and other Internet services, the Corporation is clearly trying to serve everyone in the UK, partly because everyone who owns a television has paid for a licence (or should have). But other stakeholders, such as satellite broadcasters, politicians, and the media, argue that the BBC is simply duplicating programming that commercial broadcasters put out, and that the BBC should only focus on its public service mission. Moreover if it did this, the licence fee could be significantly reduced, as some of what the BBC now does, it would no longer do, Radio One being the example most cited.

Sources: 'MediaGuardian poll on BBC licence fee', Owen Gibson, the Guardian, *18 August 2008; www.bbc.co.uk*

Questions

1. Who are the 'customers' of the BBC and what do they expect the BBC to provide them with?

2. How should the BBC respond to increased competition from satellite broadcasters?

Introduction

In the first chapter we have identified that a basic model of operations management is 'inputs—process—outputs'. And we described processes as being at the heart of operations, along with the notion that three things flow through operations, namely materials, customers, and information. But to further understand operations, we now switch our attention to outputs—what is it that the operation is trying to produce? This because a firm can be very well organized and have highly efficient processes, but if no one wants its goods or services then it will not stay in business.

In the Preface to this book we explained that we believe that to understand and explain operations management it is necessary to adopt a customer perspective. This chapter is central to this approach because it examines in some detail what consumers expect products and services to provide. This is illustrated in the opening Case insight about the BBC. It is an independent corporation but funded by a licence fee imposed by government. As the case illustrates, how much money it should have and what services it should provide are constantly under review. The case also illustrates how different groups of consumers have very different views about this issue. So even not-for-profit organizations, such as charities and government agencies, need to be clear about providing for consumer needs and understand how they access the resources to do so. Charities compete for donations from the public against other charities; and government agencies compete with each other for their slice of tax revenues.

Hence, we begin by considering the concept of **order qualifiers** (OQs) and **order winners** (OWs)—the competitive criteria by which firms use operations to meet the needs of their customers. We then go on to explore different forms of market structure and the influence this may have on OQs and OWs, as well as the nature of supply chains and distribution channels an operation may have. We then consider different ways in which firms position themselves relative to these markets, especially through segmentation. Surprisingly, market structure and market segmentation do not get discussed very much in the operations management field, perhaps as a hangover from when the focus was on production management rather than operations management (see page 5). It might also be because two of the topics of this chapter are generally seen as within other disciplines—market structures in economics and market segmentation in marketing. We think this is a mistake. In fact we would argue that it has only been possible for firms to develop operations strategies, such as those discussed in Part D of this text, because they have fully understood markets and customers. Markets are only a different way of describing a key aspect of operations management—namely supply chains, since a market describes the structure in which buyers and sellers interact with each other.

> **Order qualifiers** characteristics of a product or service that are required for it to be considered by a customer

> **Order winners** characteristics of a product or service which directly contribute to winning business from customers

Order qualifiers and order winners

The ability of firms to identify customer needs and to develop an appropriate range of products or services to meet these needs is essential for successful operations. This in turn increases a firm's profitability. Hill (1993) identified certain competitive factors which firms could use to both tender for and then win business. He called these terms order qualifying and order winning factors respectively.

Order qualifying factors are characteristics of a product or service that are required for it even to be considered by a customer, such as holding a recognized quality standard (e.g. ISO 9000) or being able to deliver directly to a customer. Having more of these factors will not normally give firms opportunities to do more business.

Order winning factors, however, are those characteristics which directly contribute to winning business from customers, such as speed of delivery or the flexibility to increase or decrease production output to meet demand. They are the key reasons for customers to purchase goods or services and improving the performance of these factors may result in increased business.

These factors are unlikely to remain the same over time in any particular industry sector as customers' requirements change, competition increases, and technologies improve. What were once seen as order winners can quickly change to order qualifiers and a new 'bundle' of order winners is required to maintain or improve market share. The automotive industry is a good example of this. Ten years ago air conditioning and power steering were both offered as added extras (at additional cost), and could be order winners. Nowadays these come as standard on almost all family saloon cars, so these features are order qualifiers. The manufacturers have had to respond to customers' needs by increasing the amount of technology in new cars, from satellite navigation systems to fully automated engine management systems.

Order qualifying and order winning factors can be translated into the following five internal performance objectives:

- Cost

- Quality

- Flexibility

- Dependability

- Speed.

Subsequently Neely (2008) has analysed each of these in more detail. Based on this framework, we can now discuss each of these in turn and see how they may be used to provide a competitive advantage.

Cost

The ability to provide products or services at a price the customer is willing to pay whilst still retaining a profit for the organization is the essence of good cost control. Within the category of costs Neely (2008) suggests there are five main cost factors, as illustrated in Figure 2.1 and described in detail later in this section. Providing low-cost products or services does not necessarily mean lower quality. Many companies have adopted lean operations (as explained in Chapter 15) whereby waste of all kinds is eliminated and quality has improved.

There are five main categories of cost, which may serve as OQs or OWs (as shown in Figure 2.1). These are discussed as follows:

- Manufacturing costs—this refers to the actual cost of making the product or delivering a service. It is all the direct costs associated with the operations activity. Particularly in business-to-business (B2B) markets, customers often have a very clear view of

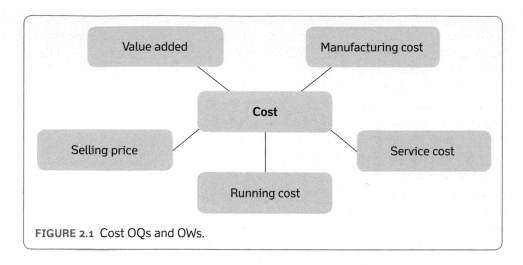

FIGURE 2.1 Cost OQs and OWs.

Go online

what the cost structure of their supplier is likely to be as they can benchmark one supplier against another. Alternatively they may have previously been backwardly integrated into this market and therefore have some direct experience themselves of the manufacturing costs. For instance, a number of major airlines have owned and operated their own flight kitchens, so although they no longer do so and outsource their in-flight meals, they have a good idea of what the cost should be of such production.

- Value added—this refers to the activities carried out by an organization that increase the worth of a product or service and for which the customer is willing to pay. These are created by a set of operations which together are often referred to as the value chain. Managing the value chain and therefore reducing non-value-adding operations (i.e. waste) is referred to in more detail in Chapter 15 when we discuss lean operations.

- Selling price—the price at which a product or service is priced will very much depend on the sensitivity to price of the particular market. Some markets are so keenly priced that they sell products to the nearest penny or even fraction of a penny. For instance, petrol was being sold in 2011 for around 135.9 pence per litre and many products are priced at one penny less than a rounded amount, such as £9.99.

- Running cost—the running cost of a product refers to how much it will cost the buyer to use and operate whatever they have purchased. For instance, this is a major concern of many buyers in the transportation industry. Bus companies and haulage contractors want to know how much it will cost them to run the vehicles that they operate.

- Service cost—some products, such as motor cars, may need regular maintenance and servicing, which have to be paid for.

Adopting a cost leadership operations strategy has been widely used by supermarkets, such as Lidl and Aldi, and low-cost airlines, such as easyJet and Ryanair. In both of these industry sectors this move has forced mainstream operators to follow suit. Most supermarkets now offer a range of own-label, lower-priced goods and many leading airlines have, or tried to have, a budget airline subbrand.

easyJet is a low-cost airline started in 1995. It ran an advertising campaign that showed exactly how they had cut costs.This shows many of the key features of the low-cost airline business model. Such airlines tend to operate fleets of aircraft that are almost identical, in easyJet's case the Airbus 319 and 320. This makes scheduling aircraft to routes, maintaining aircraft, and training and staffing aircraft very much easier and cheaper. Low-cost carriers (LCCs) fly only short haul from airport to airport on a network basis, unlike scheduled airlines that have short-haul routes that feed a 'hub airport' out of which long-haul flights take off. LCCs' network approach means that they avoid the expensive 'hub' airports such as London Heathrow and Frankfurt, by flying from secondary and regional airports, such as London Gatwick and Manchester. This results in lower ground handling charges, as well as lower air traffic control and landing fees.

LCCs also have one class of passenger, economy, so that the number of seats in the aircraft is maximized. Moreover they do not provide complimentary meals to passengers. Their approach is to have 'retail sales on board', that is to say sell snacks and beverages to those passengers that want them. This helps them to reduce turn-round time, as trolleys do not have to be loaded and offloaded every time the aircraft lands. In addition, easyJet is very efficient at disembarking and loading passengers. This is helped by not allocating seats to passengers, so they hasten to get on the aircraft in order to secure their preferred kind of seat, such as near a window or in the aisle. This also helps to keep ticketing costs down, which have fallen even further with the increased purchase of tickets via the Internet.

The use of secondary airports and fast turn-round times means that easyJet and other LCCs tend to utilize their fleet of aircraft more efficiently than scheduled airlines. It also helps to ensure that service standards are high, in terms of taking off and arriving on time.

Questions

1. What operational activities does easyJet do at lower cost than other airlines?
2. What key decisions have resulted in easyJet being able to operate at lower cost?

Quality

Quality (as an order winner) the ability to provide products and services that meet customers' expectations

The quality of a product or service is almost certainly one of the most important criteria for customers to evaluate, both before and after purchase. However, this is not always as simple as it seems. What may be a perfectly acceptable product in terms of functionality to one customer may not suit another's needs. The intangible nature of service encounters also influences how customers perceive the quality of the service they receive, which affects future transactions. Organizations need to determine what customers like or dislike about their product or service as this will help drive continuous improvement programmes. Quality management is therefore as much a philosophy as it is a science and the ability to satisfy or exceed customers' expectations is at the heart of most quality management programmes. We will cover this in more depth in Chapter 9.

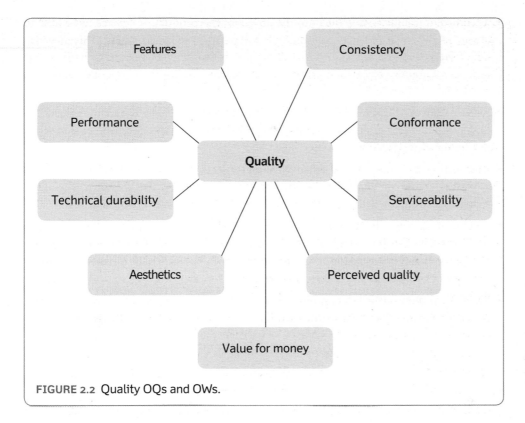

FIGURE 2.2 Quality OQs and OWs.

Go online

Quality standards exist for most industry sectors and these are seen as important order qualifiers. But quality can also be a major order winner, as in the luxury goods sector. Rolex, for example, the Swiss watch manufacturer, produces around 2000 watches a day. From rough materials to packaging it takes about one year to produce each Rolex watch. Rolex produces its own machines, tools, and supplies for the manufacture of the watch movements and other components. This includes automated and computer-controlled processes. This exceptional commitment to quality and excellent brand marketing has made Rolex an iconic watch manufacturer whose products are worn by high-profile public figures. A Rolex watch is also a prized long-service award for employees at the Hard Rock Café.

Neely's (2008) categorization of quality criteria is shown Figure 2.2 and discussed here:

- Performance—this refers to how well the product or service does what is it is meant to do, i.e. how well it meets its product or service specification. This is the primary requirement for the product or service. For instance, many lipsticks are advertised as being long lasting or long wearing. If they do not last for eight hours or more, then their performance quality is low.

- Features—these are the added product or service refinements which support the primary requirement. We have already identified that motor cars now have many different features.

- Consistency (referred to by Neely as 'reliability')—this refers to the ability of the product or service to consistently perform to its specification over time. This can be measured by the average time between occurrences of faults.

- Conformance—this refers to the product or service meeting its technical specification.

- Technical durability—this refers to the ability of the product or service to be able to absorb slight variations in conditions and still perform to specification. This may also be referred to as robustness and work to measure. This was pioneered by the Japanese engineer Taguchi, whose methods still bear his name today. Products, such as toys in particular, need to be durable.

- Serviceability—this refers to the ability of a product (or to a lesser extent a service) to be maintained and continue to work acceptably over an extended time period without undue deterioration.

- Aesthetics—this refers to the sensory characteristics of the product or service, i.e. its look, feel, sound, or smell. This will also include the appearance and suitability of the service location, for which the term servicescape has become widely used.

- Perceived quality—this is the notion of customer satisfaction and whether there is a gap between customers' expectations and perception. Many service encounters are not immediately measurable in quantitative terms but organizations use comment cards or questionnaires to collect this data.

- Value for money—this is a combination of cost and price. Customers may be willing to accept a lower specification for a product or service offered at a lower price.

Flexibility

Flexibility (as an order winner) the ability to change a product or service offering to suit customers' needs

The ability to change a product or service offering to suit customers' needs has become ever more important to modern companies. Whether it is changing the quantity or the range of a product or service a growing number of companies have learnt to use agile operations and mass customization to best serve their customers' changing needs in a timely fashion.

Traditionally flexibility was considered to be in one of four areas, namely product or service flexibility, mix flexibility, volume flexibility, or delivery flexibility. Neely (2008) has expanded these as shown in Figure 2.3 and discusses them as follows:

Go online

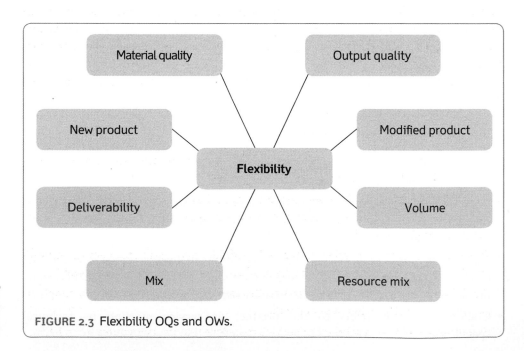

FIGURE 2.3 Flexibility OQs and OWs.

- Material quality—this refers to the ability of the organization to adapt its operations to be able to absorb small differences in raw material quality without unduly affecting the final product. For instance, a furniture manufacturer will have to use wood from many different trees, each of which will be slightly different.

- Output quality—this refers to the organization's ability to offer different standards of output. An airline is flexible in that it offers different output quality on the same plane, by having first class, business class, and economy class cabins.

- New product—this refers to the ability of the organization to introduce new products or services into the market. Research has shown that first movers in this area get the majority of the profits. Apple's success with the iPhone and the iPad derived partly from being first to market with this kind of product.

- Modified product—this refers to the ability of the organization to modify its existing products or services.

- Deliverability—this refers to the organization's ability to react to changes in delivery times requested by customers.

- Volume—this refers to the ability of the organization to increase or decrease output to meet demand.

- Mix—this refers to the organization's ability to provide a wide range of products or services.

- Resource mix—this refers to the ability of the organization to offer product or service flexibility by virtue of having a mix of resources available (machinery, manpower, and time), either internally or through buying in, to satisfy demand. Printers are very good at this, being able to print a variety of materials (such as brochures, flyers, and magazines) in a wide range of volumes (or 'print runs').

Dependability

This is the ability of an organization to consistently meet its promises to the customer. Whether this is delivering component parts on time to an automotive assembly line on a just-in-time basis (as explained in Chapter 5) or ensuring that supermarket shelves do not run out of essential supplies, dependability has become a very important performance measure in the supply chain. A key element of managing supply chain relationships is the building of trust between buyers and sellers, and dependability is a major feature of this.

Dependability (as an order winner) the ability of an organization to consistently meet its promises to the customer

Neely's types of dependability are shown in Figure 2.4 to which we have added a fifth—safety. These are discussed here:

- Schedule adherence—this refers to the ability of the organization to meet customers' scheduled requirements. These may be long or short term.

- Delivery performance—this refers to the ability of the organization to meet a required standard for delivering the product or service. This is usually based on on-time delivery and complete quantity.

- Price performance—this refers to the ability of the organization to meet its commitment to the customer for delivering its product or service at the agreed price.

- Ability to keep promises—this refers to the ability of the organization to supply its products or services when it says it will.

- Safety—the ability of a product or service to ensure that its user comes to no harm.

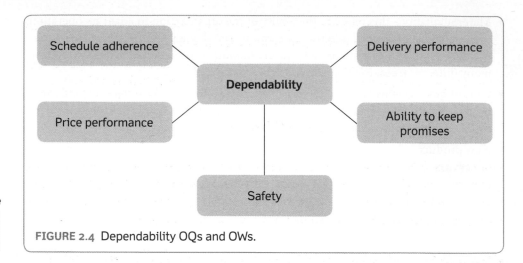

Go online

FIGURE 2.4 Dependability OQs and OWs.

Speed

Speed (as an order winner) the ability to provide products or services with as short a time delay as possible between customer order and delivery

The ability to provide products or services with as short a time delay as possible between customer order and delivery is essential in many industries. The growth of the fast food industry depended on this ability. McDonald's has over 30,000 restaurants worldwide and serves over 39 million customers every day. By a combination of efficient lean management systems and innovative use of the latest technology it is able to prepare a freshly cooked hamburger to a customer in less than 30 seconds from the order being placed.

According to Neely (2008) there are five forms of speed (shown in Figure 2.5):

- Quote generation—this refers to the time the organization needs to prepare a quotation to the customer once the final concept and specification have been agreed. This generally applies to either long-term contracts between two organizations or to high-value goods.

- Delivery speed—this refers to the time taken for the organization to deliver the product or service to the customer once an order has been received.

- Delivery frequency—this refers to the number of deliveries per day, week, month, etc. that the organization makes to its customers.

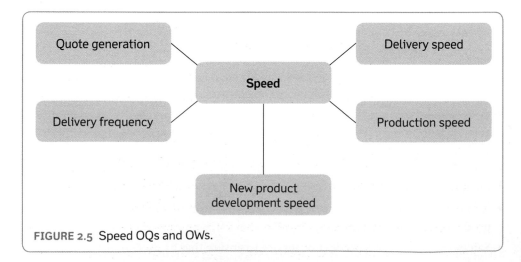

Go online

FIGURE 2.5 Speed OQs and OWs.

- Production speed—this refers to the overall time taken internally by the organization to produce its product or service and be ready for delivery.

- New product development speed—this refers to the time taken for the organization to introduce new products to the market from initial concept to final prototype.

Putting the OQs and OWs into practice

The concept of OQs enables firms to be clear about what they absolutely must achieve in order to meet the most basic expectations of their customers, and then OWs enable firms to develop their products and services in such a way as to give them a competitive edge against other similar firms competing for the same customers.

RESEARCH INSIGHT 2.1

Berry, W.L., Hill, T., and Klompmaker, J.E. (1999) Aligning marketing and manufacturing strategies with the market, *International Journal of Production Research*, 37(16), 3599–618

Terry Hill developed the concept of order qualifiers and order winners in his textbook published in 1993. In this article, he and colleagues explain this concept further and demonstrate how it can be applied to a specific firm—a clothing company in Thailand.

However, it cannot be assumed that sellers and buyers necessarily agree on what the OQs and OWs are. Research by Horte and Ylinenpaa (1997) found across a number of markets that manufacturers believed their customers were purchasing their goods on the basis of certain OWs, whereas the buyers were purchasing on different criteria. For instance, a manufacturer of shop refrigerators thought their OWs were price, delivery speed, delivery reliability, and after-sales support, whereas their customers identified that they purchased from that manufacturer on the basis of price and conformance quality.

Turning OWs into operations strategies

What has emerged is that some firms, and some sectors, have bundled together potential OWs in specific ways, so that competition in these sectors is based on similar operations activity. When this is done, we can clearly identify these as operations strategies, that is, long-term approaches to creating competitive advantage. Often the firms that are the originators of the strategy emerge as market leaders and become closely associated with that strategy. Examples of this are:

- Lean production and Toyota—based around cost and quality OWs

- Low-cost airlines and easyJet—based on dependability and cost OWs

- Agile manufacturing and Benetton—based on flexibility and speed OWs

- Mass customization and Dell—based on flexibility and cost OWs

- E-commerce and Amazon.com—based on flexibility and speed OWs.

The final four chapters of this text explore some of these strategies in detail.

OPERATIONS INSIGHT 2.2
The fast food industry—from quick 'n' easy to good for you

The fast food industry provides an excellent overview of the key issues in applying the concepts of OQs and OWs. First, a number of chains explicitly identified, and trained their employees to deliver, key operational targets. In the case of McDonald's, for many years it operated by focusing on QSCV—quality, service, clean, and value. Likewise in the case of Taco Bell, in 1989 its research identified that customers wanted 'FACT', i.e. fast, accuracy, cleanliness, and at the appropriate temperature. Whether it is QSCV or FACT, it is apparent that these are OQs or OWs—clean is almost certainly an OQ whereas service or fast is an OW.

Healthy fast food has become an order winner for many restaurants. © istock/Burwell and Burwell Photography.

However, these explicit performance criteria have not persisted as markets and consumer tastes have changed. Whereas originally speed may have been an order winner, it became an order qualifier—something that customers expected automatically. Fast food restaurants were then increasingly expected to compete on flexibility. They have responded to this in a number of ways. They have introduced the concept of making the product to order, in McDonald's case through their 'made for you' programme. This required them to slightly modify their product. For instance, the bun was modified so that it could be toasted more quickly. They also widened their product range, i.e. increased their 'mix'. Now a major customer concern is diet and healthy eating. So the major fast food chains are engaged in new product development in order to meet these needs.

Questions

1. What were McDonald's OQs and OWs when it first started out in the fast food industry?
2. What are McDonald's OQs and OWs now?

In some markets it is not easy to create unique bundles of OWs, so in these cases firms compete on the same criteria but seek to outperform their competitors in one or more of them. For instance, in the overnight parcel delivery business it is difficult to distinguish between the different service providers—after all, the parcel either arrives the following day or it does not. These companies therefore focus on aspects such as aesthetics (how smart and clean their trucks and employees are) or value for money (offering special deals to loyal customers).

But we cannot simply assume that firms are free to pick and choose their order winners. The market structure that a firm operates in can have a great influence on how firms behave, as we discuss in the following section. It can limit what they are able to do, if they have little relative power either as sellers or buyers, and it can also influence how they have to compete against other firms. For instance, in the UK there is controversy as to the level of market power enjoyed by major supermarket chains, and the extent to which this has driven down food prices so much that farmers can no longer operate profitably. Whatever the context, the way in which organizations then seek to exploit their OWs is to select specific segments of their market at which to direct their outputs. Whilst notionally sellers seek to meet the specific needs of their identified segments, in reality organizations are always constrained by their resources and their capabilities in terms of what they are actually able to do.

Market structures

Markets are basically 'structures' which enable the exchange of goods and service for money (usually money, though sometimes it may be for other goods and services). Since operations management is largely about processes this means they are made up of 'transactions' and 'relationships'. And markets are one major way in which transactions and relationships are organized. Market 'structures' can be physical—such as a street market, or a contractual relationship between firms in a supply chain, or virtual markets, such as the derivatives market traded on the stock exchange.

Fresh organic food at the world-famous street market at Portobello Road, London. © istock/fazon1.

Markets typically have certain characteristics, such as:

- Level and types of competition
- Relative strength of buyers and sellers
- Level of industry concentration, i.e. the level to which the market is dominated by a few large firms
- Degree of collusion amongst sellers and/or buyers
- Extent of product differentiation
- Ease of entry into and exit from the market.

These different characteristics can vary, leading to seven basic types of market structure. These are:

- Perfect competition—many buyers and sellers, none being able to influence prices.
- Imperfect competition—many buyers and sellers, but due to buyers' imperfect knowledge of prices there are some opportunities for sellers to control prices.
- Oligopoly—several large sellers who have some control over market mechanisms.
- Duopoly—two dominant sellers with considerable control over supply and prices.
- Monopoly—single seller with considerable control over supply and prices.
- Oligopsony—several large buyers with some control over demand and prices.
- Monopsony—single buyer with considerable control over demand and prices.

Here we are not interested in the economic principles by which these different markets operate. But we do need to understand the implications that these different structures have for how operations are managed.

Perfect versus imperfect markets

There are very few markets that trade under conditions of perfect competition. The one example that is usually given of a perfect market is the stock market, where stocks and shares are traded. Supposedly all buyers and sellers have access to the same information and there are very large numbers of both. Trading on the basis of 'insider information'—being aware of something that the market does not know and using this to buy or sell shares—is expressly forbidden. Apart from the stock market, most other markets are imperfect. This is because it is almost impossible for all buyers to know all prices. This means that cost is not necessarily the dominant OW, and firms can compete on speed, flexibility, quality, and dependability. One of the interesting aspects of the Internet revolution is that price comparison sites are now enabling consumers to know a lot more about prices than they have ever known in the past. In some markets this is leading to the so-called 'commodification' of products and services, i.e. firms find it difficult to differentiate their output so that it has become a commodity traded on price alone. In this context, cost tends to be the major order winner.

Power of sellers

In some markets, sellers may have power and hence be able to control market conditions and prices. The most extreme case of this is a monopoly, where there is a single seller. In most cases, governments tend to intervene in such markets and break up monopolies. In the UK there is a Competition Commission (formerly the Monopolies and Mergers Commission) that adopts this role, as illustrated in Operations insight 2.3. However, it is not unknown for markets to be dominated by two (duopoly) or a few (oligopoly) sellers. This is usually the case when:

- There is industry concentration, i.e. few sellers each with a significant market share. This is the case in pharmaceuticals, where a relatively small number of drug companies dominate the market. In the aircraft industry there is almost a global duopoly with Boeing and Airbus making more than 95% of the world's passenger aeroplanes. In both these cases, firms tend to compete on non-price criteria such as product features, serviceability, conformance, technical durability, and delivery speed.

- There are significant switching costs, i.e. it is costly and complex to switch from one supplier to another. For instance, in the PC market Microsoft is a dominant supplier of operating systems. It can be argued that a key role of operations management, and especially of product research and development, is to create and design products for which there will be strong demand but that other firms will find difficult to replicate. This is often achieved by seeking patent protection on new products.

- Suppliers might forwardly integrate, i.e. suppliers have both the potential and capability of taking over the customer's business. Historically many sectors have seen such integration. For instance, in the UK many brewing companies purchased licensed premises, i.e. pubs, through which to distribute their products. This was seen by the UK government as anti-competitive, so in the 1990s these integrated companies were broken up and forced to choose between being brewers or pub operators. Some stayed as brewers, such as Courage, whereas others disposed of their brewing capability and became hospitality chain operators, such as Whitbread.

Typically suppliers are weak under the opposite conditions:

- There are many suppliers. Food producers are generally weak because this market is made up of many, many relatively small farms producing products that are very similar to each other. From an operations perspective, this creates the need to try to differentiate the product or service from other suppliers in order to be able to charge a premium price for it—hence the growth in organic farming.

- The product is highly standardized or a commodity. For example, tyre manufacturers make a product which is relatively homogeneous, so that auto manufacturers can easily switch suppliers if they wish to. If products cannot be differentiated, the function of operations is to ensure that the product is produced to the required standard at the lowest possible cost.

- There is a threat of backward integration. Firms that rely on specific materials for their operation are often tempted to secure their supply of such materials by taking over their suppliers. There have been examples in the paper industry of manufacturers purchasing timber companies for this reason. The concept of producing in-house versus outsourcing is a key issue in operations (see Chapter 4) and one that is fundamental to supply chain management (see Chapter 5).

It is not always possible to identify markets in which suppliers are strong, as they may often appear in the market as different brands. In the fast-moving consumer goods market, there are several very large firms, but despite selling many goods to consumers, they remain relatively unknown. For instance, Unilever operates all over the world and has many well-known brands such as Flora, Marmite, Knorr, Walls, Ben & Jerry's, Persil, Cif, and Dove.

RESEARCH INSIGHT 2.2

Porter, M.E. (1979) How competitive forces shape strategy, *Harvard Business Review*, March/April, 137–45

Michael Porter has been one of the major influences on understanding business strategy and his 'five forces model' has been applied in many industries and formed the basis for much research. This article, published over 30 years ago, was the first to introduce this framework. In it, Porter discusses the importance of supplier power and buyer power, which is a key issue affecting how operations are managed. In this article he stresses the implications of selling to powerful buyers, namely that firms will only make good profits if they are the lowest-cost provider or if they have some unique product or service features. As we have discussed earlier, this has implications for operations management in terms of the OWs a firm must develop in order to be competitive.

Power of buyers

Buyers are strong or weak for similar reasons to sellers. Buyers are strong when:

- There are few buyers. With a single buyer, a market is termed a monopsony, and with a small number, an oligopsony. This tends to be true in the defence industry. Military equipment is generally only purchased by governments.
- Buyers purchase a significant proportion of total demand. In the UK there has been concern about how major supermarket chains now dominate the market and are therefore able to hold prices down to the detriment of food producers.
- There is a threat of backward integration, i.e. buyers threaten to take over their suppliers.

Buyers are weak when:

- Buyers are fragmented. This is the case with most consumer products.
- Switching costs are high. Airlines are reluctant to operate a fleet of aircraft from different manufacturers as this increases their maintenance costs and parts inventory.
- Buyers rely on one supplier or a few suppliers. PC manufacturers have found themselves in a relatively weak position due to their reliance on Intel to supply them with computer chips.
- There is a threat of forward integration, i.e. suppliers threaten to take them over.

Profit versus not-for-profit

Not all organizations seek to make a profit. Such organizations are mainly of two types—they are in the public sector, run by central or local government, or they are charities. But even in this not-for-profit sector, effective operations management is important because stakeholders in these organizations expect them to be run efficiently. Taxpayers or donors to charities do not expect their money to be wasted nor the services provided to be substandard.

B2B versus B2C

A key feature of markets is whether or not a business is selling to other businesses (B2B) or directly to consumers (B2C). In most cases, B2C firms will be in a situation where buyers are weak and they are strong. For B2B firms, the situation is less clear cut. As we have seen from examples discussed earlier, in some sectors sellers will be powerful, whereas in others it may be the buyers, depending on the different market structures. When placed in the context of supply chains this may mean that there are different market structures at each stage of the chain. This is illustrated in Figure 2.6. This shows many small producers of raw materials, a few manufacturers of roughly equal size, two large distributors, and a number of retailers varying in size. Within this supply chain, it is likely that the distributors have significant power as there are only two of them. One specializes in distribution to large retailers, the other to small retailers.

The influence this has on the operations function on firms within this sector can be summarized as follows:

- Small producer—has little market power, therefore operations have to ensure costs are kept under control.

- Manufacturers—great rivalry between firms of roughly equal size. Raw material costs are roughly the same for all, so operations have to seek ways in which to process materials at lower cost than competitors, or produce goods of higher quality, or be more dependable, or react speedily to the needs of the market, or be very flexible and responsive in their operations. Or a combination of these things.

- Distributors—have significant market power, and so can dictate prices to both manufacturers and retailers. Moreover they have reduced competition between themselves by each focusing on different market segments. The firm that distributes to large retailers will achieve scale economies by delivering in large lot sizes; the other firm will have to focus on efficient scheduling of its transport fleet to distribute relatively small lot sizes.

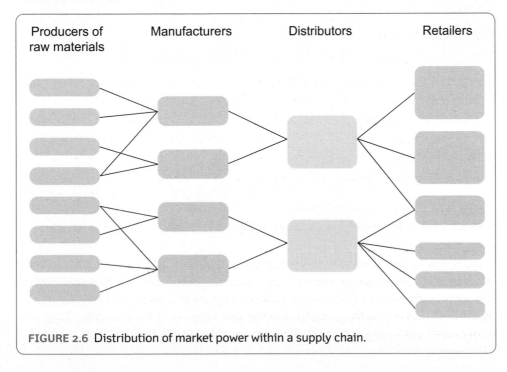

Producers of raw materials   Manufacturers   Distributors   Retailers

Go online

FIGURE 2.6 Distribution of market power within a supply chain.

- Retailers—some have more power than others due to their size. Large retailers are likely to compete on price; small retailers are likely to specialize and to sell unique product lines from specific manufacturers.

A real-life example of this might be the paper industry. Timber producers may be weak (because there are many of them), paper manufacturers may be weak (because paper is largely a commodity product), and some users—such as print media firms and publishers —may have market power (due to their high usage of paper), whereas others—such as small printers—may not (due to their small size).

Category management

One specific example of how operations is affected by market structure is the growth of so-called '**category management**'. Very large retailers and supermarkets with multiple product lines break down their products into categories. Fast-moving consumer goods (FMCG), or grocery, categories might be soups, shampoo, or soap powder. Each category is then managed strategically, in that sales and profit targets are set and specific promotions planned. This has inevitably led the retailers to work closely with suppliers in order to collaborate over new product introductions, national advertising campaigns by the supplier, and in-store merchandising. In many cases, retailers designate a 'category captain', that is, the leading supplier of that product category. The aim behind this collaboration is to increase sales across the category, but it can also be perceived as anti-competitive. Category management is hugely important from an operations perspective as it enables manufacturers of FMCG to be able to predict much more precisely their production volumes and logistic needs. This is explained further in the End of chapter case.

> **Category management**
> the strategic management of product groups through trade partnerships which aim to maximize sales and profit by satisfying consumer and shopper needs (Institute of Grocery Distribution)

OPERATIONS INSIGHT 2.3
Live Nation Entertainment—becoming too big?

The proposed merger of Live Nation, the world's biggest concert promoter, with Ticketmaster, one of the world's largest ticketing companies, was challenged in 2009, in view of concerns about the potential risk to competition. The UK Competition Commission launched an inquiry, after the Office for Fair Trading (OFT) expressed concern that the deal could give the merged company too much market power. In 2009 Live Nation was the largest live events company in the world with a turnover of more than £2 billion. Unusually for a concert promoter, it had also begun signing artists, such as Madonna and rapper Jay-Z. Likewise, Ticketmaster had become a very large event ticket seller following its recent acquisition of the secondary ticketing company getmein.com. The combined company would be renamed Live Nation Entertainment.

The £550 million deal was announced in February 2009. At the time it was claimed that it would result in better prices for customers. But Ticketmaster at that time sold between 40% and 50% of all the tickets to live music events, whilst Live Nation staged up to 20% of live music events. Bruce Springsteen was one of the high-profile entertainers who expressed concern. He posted on his website a message that said 'The one thing that would make the current ticket situation even worse for the fan than it is now would be Ticketmaster and Live Nation coming up with a single system, thereby returning us to a near-monopoly situation in music ticketing'.

The OFT said it was particularly concerned about the potential for CTS, another of Europe's largest ticketing agents, being disadvantaged in the UK market should the merger go ahead. However, in December 2009 the OFT announced that at least as far as the UK was concerned the deal could go ahead,

There were concerns the merger would cause a monopoly situation in live music ticketing. © istock/ Shawn Gearhart.

so long as the merged business did not prevent other ticket agencies from selling tickets to its concerts, or refused to sell tickets for rival events. Similar concerns had been raised in the USA, and the US Department of Justice required Live Nation to sell off one of its ticketing subsidiaries, Paciolan, before the merger could take place. It also had to license the Ticketmaster ticketing system to AEG for at least five years, as well as agree to terms also designed to maintain competitive conditions.

Sources: Rosie Swash, the Guardian, *11 June 2009, Robert Lindsay,* Times Online, *22 December 2009, and Live Nation Entertainment* 2010 Annual Report

Questions

1. What kind of market structure exists in the event ticketing industry in the UK?
2. The OFT ruled in favour this merger. Why do you think it did this?

Customers and market segments

As the previous discussion highlights, most markets are not homogeneous. They are made up of many different buyers of different sizes. The underlying principle of segmenting markets is to identify these differences so that for each specific cluster of consumers their OQs and OWs become apparent. In order to do this, segments need to meet five criteria. A segment must be:

- Identifiable and measurable
- Differentiable from others, i.e. have unique needs
- Accessible and actionable so that it can be sold to
- Substantial enough to justify selling to it
- Durable over time.

We shall now look at the operations management implications of operating in a B2B environment compared with a B2C market.

Industrial market segmentation

Although consumers are familiar with organizations that serve them, there are actually many more firms who operate on a B2B basis than B2C. Hence we begin by considering how B2B firms segment their markets, i.e. industrial market segmentation. One of the most common approaches applied in industrial markets today was developed by Wind and Cardozo (1974), who suggested industrial market segmentation should be based on a combination of macro-segmentation and micro-segmentation.

Macro-segmentation focuses on the characteristics of buyers, in the form of companies or institutions. This means that markets may be segmented by:

- Size of buyers—this has the advantage of being one of the most practical and easily identifiable characteristics. Size may be measured by the buyer's revenues or volume of business.

- Geographic location—this, too, is relatively easy to establish. This may be important in terms of physical distance between the seller and buyer thereby creating additional transportation costs. But it also influences the seller–buyer relationship in terms of communication and culture. Communicating with buyers in different countries adds complexity, as does understanding the cultural norms of foreign buyers.

- Product segmentation—different groups of customers buy the same products for different reasons, and may value specific product features. For example, bed manufacturers produce beds for several sectors—hotels, hospitals, and homes. Each of these places emphasis on different features of the bed. For instance, home owners may want a bed to provide storage space in drawers under the bed, a feature not required by hotels.

- Performance segmentation—different organizations may prioritize certain aspects of the product or service over other performance criteria. Advertising agencies may buy office furniture based on its aesthetic appeal, whereas a university might do so based on durability.

- Procurement segmentation—different organizations purchase in different ways. Some organizations have a centralized purchasing division, others delegate this function to their separate units. Some require a wide range of deliveries at intermittent periods, whereas others need a continuous supply of standard items. Increasingly, large manufacturers require just-in-time deliveries (see Chapter 5).

Having narrowed down the potential buyers by using one or more of the macro criteria, the market can be further divided by **micro-segmentation**. This requires a higher degree of knowledge of factors that will affect the business relationship between sellers and buyers. Such factors include:

- Buying decision criteria—this relates to the concept of order qualifiers and order winners previously discussed.

- Purchasing policies—in some industries and some organizations it is common to tender for business with a sealed bid in response to an invitation to do so. In others, buyers may purchase as a result of a simple sales contact.

- Perceived importance of the product to the customer's business—some industries are unable to operate without access to raw materials or key components.

- Nature of the decision-maker—in some industries products are purchased by procurement specialists with no specific product knowledge; in others a high degree of expertise may be required. For instance, the purchase of complex industrial machinery may mean that an engineer makes the purchasing decision, whereas no great expertise is required in purchasing stationery.

Figure 2.7 shows the market segments of the engineering company BUFAB, who specialize in engineering and manufacturing fasteners and small parts. It clearly has products aimed at specific segments—telecoms, engineering, furniture, automotive, process, construction, aerospace, and offshore.

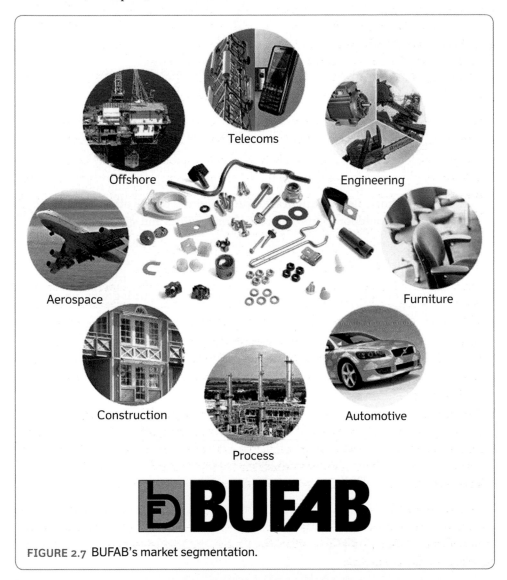

FIGURE 2.7 BUFAB's market segmentation.

RESEARCH INSIGHT 2.3

Harrison, M., Hague, P., and Hague, N. *Why is Business-to-Business Marketing Special?* B2BInternational, www.b2binternational.com/library/whitepapers/pdf/b2b_marketing.pdf

This is not a conventional journal article or book chapter, but a 'white paper' written by three of the founders of a market research company that specializes in B2B marketing. It is included here because it clearly identifies the ten main ways in which B2B marketing is different from B2C marketing, and what the implications of these differences are for the firm. They suggest that these factors make B2B operations significantly more challenging.

Consumer market segmentation

For marketers segmentation is important because it enables a specific marketing mix (i.e. the 4Ps of product, price, place, and promotion) to be put together aimed at each specific segment. This is why segmentation is also important for operations managers, since it determines the specific 'bundle' of order qualifiers and order winners that each different segment requires.

There is a wide range of ways in which consumer markets may be segmented. These can be divided into four main categories—geographic, demographic, psychographic, and behavioural.

- Geographic variables include such criteria as region of the world, country, or region of a country; population density; climate type; or degree of urbanization (city, town, rural). For instance, hotel chains develop different brands for urban and rural or resort settings. Urban hotels typically have conference and meeting rooms, large car parks, and function catering facilities. Resort properties on the other hand may have larger bedrooms, outdoor sports, and recreation facilities and spas.

- Demographic variables include gender, age, family size and type, income, occupation, education level, religion, and ethnicity. Often these are combined into specific clusters that combine several variables, such as 'Yuppie' (young, urban, professional), Dinks (double income, no kids), and empty nesters (couple with grown-up children that have left home).

- Psychographic (or lifestyle) variables are based on consumers' activities, interests, attitudes, opinions, and values. These are typically established through consumer surveys which lead to the creation of segments or clusters based around specific lifestyles.

- Behavioural variables are based on how consumers act towards certain products and services. These relate to factors such as usage rate (light, medium, heavy users), loyalty, readiness to buy (potential buyer, first-time buyer, repeat purchaser), and the occasions when a purchase is made (such as routine business purchase or special occasion social purchase).

Conclusions

Operations management is all about transactions and relationships which are driven by markets and the customers in them. Managers in a service setting know this because they deal with customers all the time. In manufacturing, it is not quite so obvious that this is the case. For some organizations, the customer is a member of the public, but often the customer can be another firm. The buyers may be small or very large, and the quantities of goods and services they purchase can vary from just one item up to many hundreds of thousands. Hence it is not possible to know what products to make or services to prepare without understanding customer needs and wants. It is also not possible to know how many to make or prepare for, nor when, without market insight. Because most markets are complex, firms and organizations simplify this by engaging in segmentation. B2B companies engage in industrial market segmentation; B2C adopt customer market segmentation. This enables them to identify the specific order qualifiers and order winners that each segment wants. However, a number of factors—new technology, competition from other providers, and changing market tastes—mean that these OQs and OWs need to be constantly reviewed. Throughout this textbook we shall constantly be considering and reviewing how the principles and practices of operations management enable firms to deliver their OQs and OWs.

END OF CHAPTER CASE
Hozelock—how operations management helps drive market share

Hozelock is a UK-based manufacturer of gardening equipment, especially related to the watering of lawns and gardens, as well as pond pumps and equipment. It is the market leader in this field, with nearly 70% of the UK market and a growing market share in a number of other countries.

In 2007, the firm decided to consolidate its manufacturing capability from five separate factories onto a single site in the West Midlands. This new facility is on a 33,400 square metre site and incorporates every operation from design through to distribution, including an Engineering Centre of Excellence. A further £1 million was invested in modern product test facilities and new production equipment. By operating from a single site the company was able to make cost savings on transport and energy, improve communication within the organization, and better support agile production. In addition, overall capacity was increased to allow for future growth (as discussed in Chapter 7).

From an operation perspective, this new plant has facilitated Hozelock moving to a so-called 'pull system', that is to say, setting production targets based on customer orders. The effect of this was to reduce work in progress by 25% and considerably reduce lead times, i.e. the time it takes between starting to make the product and selling it to the customer. Its supply chain also changed to reflect this, as suppliers began operating to just-in-time delivery schedules. For example, one of Hozelock's key suppliers is a packaging company based in Holland, but it now holds strategic stock (as discussed in Chapter 5) at a UK warehouse only a short distance from Hozelock's West Midlands facility.

As well as modifying its supply chain, Hozelock has also changed how it distributes its products, adopting a category management approach with its customers, who are predominantly large-scale garden centres. This has enabled it to eliminate warehousing, and it now delivers direct to customers. There are around 1000 major stores that are delivered to on a weekly basis. But Hozelock's system monitors daily the level of its key customers' stock through electronic point-of-sale (EPOS) devices, i.e. tills, and distributes stock to them accordingly. This has taken stock out of the supply chain, so that less space is taken up with inventory and less money is tied up in stock. This also means that Hozelock products are on the shelf, available for sale, 99% of the time. This means that when a customer is shopping they will find what they are looking for. This is of major concern to retailers because if customers are disappointed they will probably go elsewhere. As well as maintaining shelf stock, Hozelock's distribution system also minimizes excess purchasing. This combination of very short delivery lead times and personalized delivery is a level of service superior to Hozelock's competitors, especially foreign competitors who have to import stock from overseas.

Because gardening products are used outdoors, customers have seasonal buying habits. Hozelock's business is significantly affected by the weather, so it began subscribing to both short- and long-term weather forecasts. It used these to help schedule production, order materials, and establish staffing levels. Through analysis, it has found a correlation between the weather and its EPOS data on purchasing habits. For instance, spray guns and sprinklers are likely to be in high demand during periods of hot summer weather. On the other hand, during cold winters garden equipment is often damaged by frost and ice so that spring will bring high demand for replacement hoses and reels. As well as these long-term weather effects, Hozelock uses weekly short-term forecasts to adjust its temporary staff volumes to cope with expected increases in demand.

Due to this seasonality, Hozelock's turnover is around £10m in the winter and increases to around £150m of business during the periods of peak demand. Hence, over a year, there are substantial differences in production levels and requirements. For this reason, the company has adopted fully flexible assembly lines, which can be operated by between 4 and 20 employees, depending on the production level scheduled. Such flexibility also contributes to managing stock levels, production output, and efficiency.

Hozelock believes that innovation is required not only in terms of its processes, but also in terms of the products it supplies. New product development has explicitly been incorporated into its strategic plan. Such innovation helps the company to respond to the changing environment and occasional crises. For instance, in 2006 13 million people in southeast England had a hosepipe ban, whilst only one year later there was severe flooding across the country. Such events created real challenges with regard to predicting consumer demand and operating production efficiently. To counter the threat of hosepipe bans, Hozelock developed and launched 14 new products designed to save water and use it sparingly, which they called 'water-wise' products. These included their AquaPod drip watering system, a Water Butt Pump, and Water-Storing Gel and Feed. These new products more than doubled sales of irrigation systems, as well as winning Hozelock recognition in a variety of ways. For instance, the AquaPod and Gel won the UK water industry's new Waterwise Marque in recognition of the contribution they made to reducing water wastage. The company also introduced a new range of hose accessories, including different types of hose guns and their Aqua Control Pro Electronic Water Timer. This timer allowed gardens to be watered overnight so that less water was lost to evaporation, and it could also be fitted with a rain sensor, so that watering was only done when needed. As well as its existing range of pumps, Hozelock also launched a Flood Pump to help property owners whose homes had been flooded. Such new product development was also assisted by the consolidation on one site, as it was easier to attend meetings and conduct production trials. The single site also encouraged cross-functional team working on new product ideas and development.

As well as developing its home market, Hozelock developed its export markets. In 2009 this accounted for 45% of sales. The advantage of international sales is that they smooth out demand fluctuations in the UK market. Each of Hozelock's markets—in Australia, Russia, Poland, Greece, and Spain—has different periods of peak and trough demand due to their specific weather pattern.

Sources: www.hozelock.com, 'Hozelock in Bloom', The Manufacturer *March 2010, 'Hozelock, Fit for all Seasons',* The Manufacturer *April 2008*

Questions

1. What are Hozelock's order winners (OWs)?

2. How has it designed its operations to deliver these OWs?

3. What is the nature of Hozelock's market structure?

Chapter summary

To consolidate your learning, the key points from this chapter are summarized as follows:

- **Explain the concept of order qualifiers (OQs) and order winners (OWs)**

  OQ factors are characteristics of a product or service that are required for them even to be considered by a customer, such as holding a recognized quality standard (e.g. ISO 9000) or being able to fly directly to a customer's destination airport. OW factors, however, are those characteristics which directly contribute to winning business from customers, such as speed of delivery or the flexibility to increase or decrease production output to meet demand. They are the key reasons for customers to purchase goods or services and improving the performance of these factors may result in increased business.

  There are five main performance objectives:

  - Cost
  - Quality
  - Flexibility
  - Dependability
  - Speed.

  Each of these can be subdivided into more specific objectives. For instance, cost is made up of factors such as value added, manufacturing costs, and selling price.

- **Explain how firms compete on the basis of OQs and OWs**

  Firms compete in two main ways. First they can seek to combine the many alternative OWs in unique ways in order to differentiate themselves from their competitors. Second, they can adopt the same OWs as competitors but simply do them better than anyone else.

- **Define market structure and identify alternative structures**

  Markets are basically 'structures' which enable the exchange of goods and service for money (usually money, though sometimes it may be for other goods and services). There are basically seven types, which are:

  - Perfect competition—many buyers and sellers, none being able to influence prices.
  - Imperfect competition—many buyers and sellers, but due to buyers' imperfect knowledge of prices some opportunities for sellers to control prices.
  - Oligopoly—several large sellers who have some control over market mechanisms.
  - Duopoly—two dominant sellers with considerable control over supply and prices.
  - Monopoly—single seller with considerable control over supply and prices.
  - Oligopsony—several large buyers with some control over demand and prices.
  - Monopsony—single buyer with considerable control over demand and prices.

- **Identify and explain alternative approaches to industrial market segmentation.**

  Industrial markets can be segmented by:

  - Demographics: industry, company size, customer location.
  - Operating variables: company technology, product/brand use status, customer capabilities.

- Purchasing approaches: purchasing function, power structure, buyer–seller relationships, purchasing policies, purchasing criteria.
- Situational factors: size of order, urgency of order, product application.
- Buyers' personal characteristics: personality, style.

• **Identify and explain alternative approaches to customer market segmentation**

There are four main approaches to customer segmentation—geographic, demographic, psychographic, and behavioural. Geographic relates to the specific physical location or setting of the customer. Demographic relates to social and economic aspects of consumers. Psychographic is concerned with people's attitudes and values. Finally, behavioural segmentation is based on how the product or service is used by the consumer.

• **What are the similarities and differences between how Berry et al. (1999) in Research insight 2.1 and strategist Michael Porter (in Research insight 2.2) discuss competition between firms?**

Berry et al. (1999) discuss how a firm competes in terms of the action its takes relative to its competitors. Porter (1979), on the other hand, focuses on the external factors that influence the behaviour of firms, and indeed whole industry sectors.

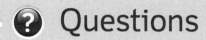 **Questions**

Review questions

1. What is the difference between an OQ and an OW?

2. What are the five main OQs or OWs?

3. How many forms of market structure are there?

4. How are market structures different from each other?

5. How does market structure affect operations management?

6. What is category management?

7. How can firms segment industrial markets (B2B)?

8. How can organizations segment consumer markets (B2C)?

9. What ethical issues might arise out of different forms of market structure?

10. In what way might each of the OWs have implications for sustainability?

Discussion questions

1. If you were a UK-based plastics fabricator, which industrial markets would you consider trading in and why?

2. If you are the owner of a toy shop, which suppliers would you choose to buy from and why?

3. What are the specific OQs and OWs for a budget airline or for a motorcycle manufacturer?

4. Consider the OQs and OWs for a traditional fast food operator. In what way has Pret A Manger developed and competed on new OWs?

Further learning guide

Order qualifiers and order winners are discussed in any standard textbook on operations management. For a slightly different view of these concepts, textbooks on performance management may also discuss these. To get a sense of the issues associated with market structure, the OFT website (**www.oft.gov.uk**) is a good place to go. The OFT's mission is to make markets work well for consumers and its website explains how it does this. It also provides a series of reports into specific markets that it has investigated. For more information about category management there is the Category Management Association (**www.cpgcatnet. org**). For a marketing perspective on B2C segmentation, you might want to read Chapter 6 in Baines et al.'s (2010) *Marketing*. Likewise for an insight into B2B marketing read Chapter 14 of Baines et al.

References

Baines, P., Fill, C., and Page, K. (2010) *Marketing*, Oxford University Press: Oxford

Hill, T. (1993) *The Essence of Operations Management*, Financial Times Press: London

Horte, S.A. and Ylinenpaa, H. (1997) The firm's and its customers' views on order winning criteria, *International Journal of Operations & Production Management*, 17(10), 1006–19

Neely, A. (2008) *Business Performance Measurement: Unifying Theory and Integrating Practice* (2nd ed.), Cambridge University Press: Cambridge

Wind, T. and Cardozo, R. (1974) *Industrial Marketing Management*, Elsevier Scientific Publishing Company: New York

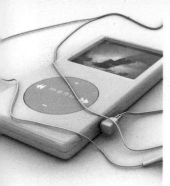

Chapter Three

Operations processes and life cycles

Learning outcomes

After reading this chapter you will be able to:

→ Explain how process types have evolved

→ Define and explain process choice

→ Explain the role of operations management during the stages of the product life cycle

→ Explain the role of operations management during the stages of the service firm life cycle

Vision Express is one of three major UK optician retailers that control 70% of the British market for spectacles and contact lenses, the others being Specsavers and Boots Opticians (which includes Dolland & Aitchison). Part of the French-owned Grand Vision group since 1997 it was incorporated in 1987 and has a head office in Nottingham. It has 320 UK retail outlets and together with its major rival, Specsavers, has revolutionized the provision of prescription spectacles. It has done this by providing a service to customers whereby they can be seen by an optician, have their eyes tested, and receive a new pair of glasses in just one hour.

Prior to this most spectacles were made by hand by opticians using precision tools making them to fit individual clients. Faces vary in terms of the width of the bridge of the nose and the size of the eyes. Hence frames had to be made to order. Likewise different lenses had to be made to ensure a client's eyesight was adjusted correctly for each eye. The process was time consuming and costly, often requiring many fittings and readjustments.

Vision Express simplified the whole process, by stocking in their stores semi-finished lens blanks or stock prescription lenses, together with mass-produced spectacle frames. As well as speeding up the process, this has also brought the cost down, so that glasses are now seen as commodity products and many customers have more than one pair. In fact eyewear, as it has become known, is now a common feature in many fashion magazines.

Each Vision Express retail store has five dispensing machines and materials are tracked using sophisticated computer software which has improved customer service delivery from 87% to 96% in the last year. To ensure stores always have the correct stock of frames and lenses, Vision Express has a central distribution centre from which orders are filled within 24 hours. By using inventory control and warehousing software, the company can ensure 99.5% accuracy with regard to restocking stores. The same software also helps to keep inventory levels (and hence costs) low in the distribution centre.

Sources: www.visionexpress.com; www.boots.com/en/Opticians; www.danda.co.uk

Questions

1. What would make a customer buy their 'eyewear' from Vision Express, i.e. what are its order winners (OWs)?

2. How does Vision Express operate so that it delivers the product/service that customers want?

Vision Express has 320 retail outlets. © Vision Express 1988–2011

Introduction

We have established in the opening chapters that there are different forms of organization, markets, and ways for organizations to compete in these markets. We have also identified the role of operations management (OM) and emphasized that at the heart of OM is the idea of managing processes. In this chapter we explore in more detail the different kinds of process an operations manager may be responsible for. We also look at the issue of time, or rather how the role of the operations manager may change during the growth of a service firm or lifetime of a product. This was illustrated in the Vision Express Case insight at the start of this chapter, which shows how this company transformed the optician market by redesigning the traditional processes associated with making spectacles, so that the customer's experience is significantly improved.

There is a very important reason for understanding processes—namely that what an operations manager does in one kind of process is not the same as what they do in other kinds. For instance, we saw in Chapter 1 how Lotus custom builds cars in what is called a job shop (explained in a later section), whereas Toyota does so on an assembly line. This means that the workforces in these two types of operation have very different skills, the equipment that they use is different and is organized differently, and the speed of operation is different. As we shall see, these different process types are linked to the 4Vs—in particular, volume and variety. We saw that the 4Vs for a fast food restaurant are very different from those for fine dining (discussed on page 15); this means they have different process types, and this also means that a manager that works in one kind of food service context would not find it easy to manage in the other.

It is not only process type that influences management behaviour; so-called 'life cycles' also affect how managers behave. For materials processing operations there is the product life cycle, and for customer processing operations the so-called 'service firm life cycle'. How operations are managed in the early stages of these life cycles is very different from how they are managed in the later stages. So in this chapter, we begin by looking at how process types have emerged over time, before going on to explore the concept of 'process choice'. We then consider the different kinds of life cycle that may affect operations management and how this affects the operations manager.

Evolution of process types

In order to further understand operations management, it is useful to understand how different types of operation developed over the years. According to Brown et al. (2000) there are three main eras of operations management:

- The craft era—this was the time before the industrial revolution when artisans made individual goods, usually working in their own small business.

- Mass production era—this was the period of large-scale production and the growth of large operations which fabricated relatively standard outputs. More strictly speaking, **mass production** refers to assembly of products on a production line.

- Strategic operations era—this period covers the last 30 years, in which features of the craft era, such as individualized products, have been incorporated into features of mass production, most notably low-cost output.

Mass production the manufacture of standardized products in large quantities, based on standardized components and assembly-line processes

These eras are shown in Figure 3.1. This also shows that operational activities may lead to goods or services that are a single unique output, or multiple replicable outputs. Within the second kind of activity, output may then be produced on a discrete (item by item) basis, or on a flow process basis (as discussed later in this section). Although we talk in terms of 'eras', it is important to note that process types developed many years ago still continue to this day. So over time new process types have been developed, but the old process types have continued. For instance, skilled craftspeople still work in their own small businesses making exclusive individual items.

The 'craft era'

Before the industrial revolution, all goods and service were provided by artisans, often organized into guilds of skilled craftsmen. Some of these skilled trades no longer exist, such as bowyers (longbow markers), scriveners (writers of letters), and loriners (stirrup makers), but many of the guilds still exist although members are not required to be skilled workers, rather members of a profession linked to that industry. However, many of these skilled trades still exist, so goods and products continue to be made in this way. The types of operation that can be identified with this craft era are as follows:

- Simple **project**—craftspeople, groups of artisans, or skilled professionals work together to produce a unique output that depends on their variety of skills. A typical example of this is housebuilding, which requires bricklayers, carpenters, plumbers, and other trades.

- **Job shop**—this can be defined as 'the production of small batches of large numbers of different products, most of which require a different set or sequence of processing

Project a planned set of interrelated processes executed over a predetermined time

Job shop the production of very small batches of different products, most of which require a different set or sequence of processing steps

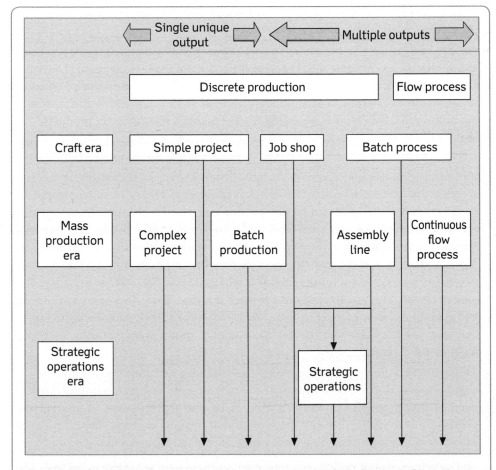

FIGURE 3.1 Evolution of operations. This figure is derived from *Strategic Operations Management*, Brown, S., Lamming, R., Bessant, J., and Jones, P. (2000) Elsevier.

Go online

steps' (Chase and Aquilano 1995). Typical examples of job shops are the blacksmith's forge, auto repair shops, and print shops.

Batch process production of small batches using flow processes

- **Batch process**—this type of operation combines raw materials, typically mined, quarried, or grown (such as wood, iron ore, foodstuffs, or barley), by processing them through a variety of stages into finished products. Examples of batch process operations are in the areas of micro-brewing, viticulture (wine making), and rubber.

The 'mass production era'

The industrial revolution transformed operations in two main ways. Firstly the scale of production increased significantly, and secondly processes were rationalized to enable costs to be kept down. This resulted in more standardized products, simplified and less skilled work, large factories and mills, along with the emergence of four new types of process:

- Complex projects—this involved outputs on a much larger scale and of more complexity than could be achieved as a simple project. Such projects were a result of three main influences—the availability of entirely new materials such as composite metals and plastics; the mechanization or automation of some elements of the activity; and the development of specialist expertise, such as architects. Examples of complex projects are the development of transport infrastructure (railways and motorways), skyscraper construction, and nuclear energy plants.

Batch production a production system in which an operation is broken down into distinct processes that are completed on a small number or 'batch' of products at a time

- **Batch production**—by mechanizing some elements of a typical job shop process, along with the use of some interchangeable parts (components that could be used in the production of more than one product) the batch production process type emerged. It is sometimes referred to as a 'standardized job shop'. An example of this type of operation could be a small engineering works making a wide range of products.

- Assembly line—this also evolved due to mechanization, the simplification of work tasks, and interchangeable parts, linked to the development of the moving assembly line, or in services replacement of the production worker by the customer (i.e. self-service). The phrase 'assembly line' is often credited to Henry Ford, who applied it to car production in 1913, but he got the idea and possibly the term from vegetable canners, meat wholesalers, and others who were using 'flow production' methods for many years before then (Bryson 1994). It had taken 14 man hours to produce the Model T Ford motor car in 1910, but assembly-line methods cut this down to just two hours by 1913. As a result, Ford was selling this car for $850 when it was first manufactured, but by 1916 had cut the price down to $345. This approach to work and operations has subsequently been described as Fordism. Examples of this type of operation are television and refrigerator assembly, motor manufacturing, and computer manufacturing.

Flow process production a series of processes through which a product moves or flows continuously

- **Flow process**—flow process operations are the almost continuous production of commodity products. The discovery and exploitation of new materials, the development of new products that derived from these, and the discovery of new ways of processing such materials drove the evolution of this process type. The most typical examples of this type of operation are paper, oil, and steel production.

In this switch from craft skills to mass production there were some key individuals who had a significant impact on operations management. Eli Whitney in the USA introduced the concept of interchangeable parts when he won a contract with the American government to manufacture muskets. In the UK, Brunel and Maudsley introduced assembly-line principles to manufacture blocks for the Royal Navy in Portsmouth. Frederick W. Taylor developed the idea of 'scientific management' wherein processes were analysed in detail so that they could be organized and scheduled in the most efficient manner. Henry Ford is then credited with recognizing that standardized parts could be used to manufacture cars on an assembly-line basis, although such lines were already being used in the mail order business at that time and Ransom Olds had patented the concept a few years earlier. One of the things that made assembly lines possible in the early 1900s was the availability of a reliable and consistent power source—electricity—something we all take for granted today.

Firms also found benefits from producing in high volumes, known as **economies of scale**. Increasing the volume of production usually drives the average price of each product down for a number of reasons. These factors include:

- Purchasing—large-scale production requires a high volume of parts, so manufacturers are able to negotiate long-term deals with their suppliers by buying in bulk.

- Marketing—the cost of advertising, promotion, and other marketing costs is spread over more outputs.

- Technical—some kinds of equipment and plant such as vats, tanks, and other 'containers' have increasing returns to scale. That is to say, as they increase in size their capacity increases at a greater rate than the materials needed to make them. For example, if you double the size of the metal sheets used to make a cubic container, its capacity is trebled.

- Financial—large firms producing on a large scale can generally negotiate better deals with their banks than smaller firms.

- Managerial—large firms can develop managers and specialists that smaller firms cannot.

The four basic types of process developed in the mass production era each responded to different characteristics of customer demand, in terms of the four Vs (volume, variety, variation, and variability). This is illustrated in Table 3.1. In addition, mass production

TABLE 3.1 Process type, four Vs, and order winners

Criteria	Project	Job shop/ batch production	Mass production/ mass service	Continuous process
Volume of output	Low	Low	High	Very high
Variety of product or service	High	Medium	Low	Usually one product only
Variation in demand	High	Medium	Low	Low
Variability (degree of customization)	High	Medium	Little	None
Typical OQs	Price Quality conformance	Price Quality conformance	Quality conformance	Dependability
Typical OWs	Design Quick response times	Flexibility	Price	Price

had shown that by organizing work onto assembly lines, manufactured goods could be produced at very low cost, but products were highly standardized. On the other hand, job shops produce highly customized goods, albeit at a high price. So each of these types predominantly delivered just one of the five main order qualifiers/winners—cost, speed, flexibility, reliability, and quality.

The 'strategic operations era'

All seven of these operational types, discussed earlier, exist today. But the last 20 years have seen the emergence of a new, 'strategic' approach to operations. This has led to a number of alternative ways of configuring manufacturing and service delivery that have features of both a job shop operation (notably variety) and assembly line (in particular, low-cost, high-volume throughput).

Strategic operations refers to the way in which firms have recognized that operations can lead to competitive advantage in much more complex ways. In this era, firms found ways to deliver on more than just one order winner. A number of alternative operations strategies exist, and some of these are discussed in much more detail in Part D of this text. Here they are briefly explained.

- Lean production—this strategy was originally developed by Toyota in Japan and has spread to become the industry norm in automobile manufacture and other sectors of industry. Essentially 'lean' refers to the stripping out of all kinds of waste from any process to make it as efficient as possible. (See Chapter 15.)

- Agile manufacturing—The National Science Foundation defines agility as 'the ability to alter any aspect of the manufacturing enterprise in response to changing market demands'. Such agility and flexibility have been strongly influenced by the introduction of information technology (IT) into design and production processes, and it often involves 'postponement'—delaying the assembly of the product until the last possible moment. For instance, Benetton adopted agile manufacture when they began making garments from undyed wool and then dying the garments in one of their 'United Colours of Benetton' once they could see which colours were selling well that season (also discussed in Chapter 15).

- Mass customization (MC)—there is some overlap between 'lean', 'agile', and MC. This is because MC seeks to produce low-cost goods customized for individual customers. Hence a key feature of MC is 'modularity'—the creation of modular components and processes that can be combined in a wide variety of different ways. Also MC usually involves making the product to order. Dell makes computers in this way, and BMW manufactures Minis adopting this strategy.

- Servitization—refers to manufacturing firms becoming service providers with added-value services for customers who buy their products. For instance, IBM was originally the world's largest manufacturer of mainframe computers. But by 2008 over half its revenue was generated from services such as maintenance agreements, project management, and consulting.

- Ubiquitization—is a strategy adopted by service firms in order to physically distribute their products and services 'everywhere'. Examples of this are banks who have installed ATMs in a wide variety of locations, soft drink manufacturers who distribute their products through vending machines, and hotel and food service chains that seek to maximize their geographic coverage in order to create a critical mass of locations to support customer loyalty.

- E-business—the advent of the Internet and its adoption by a high proportion of the population has led to new business models being created that exploit this marketing channel. The archetype of this approach is Amazon.com, who revolutionized the sale of books and subsequently other products through their online shopping strategy.

- Innovation and continuous improvement (CI)—the main difference between innovation and CI is the scale and speed of change. Rapid and significant change is innovation, whereas CI is incremental change. All firms and their operations have to change over time as consumer tastes change, new competitors emerge, and new technologies become available. Some firms use innovation to be first into the market with new products or services, and/or use CI to seek to stay ahead of the competition in their market. In the UK, firms like Virgin Atlantic and Dyson have a reputation for being innovative. (See Chapter 16.)

- Low-cost competition—new business models have also emerged whereby firms are able to compete on costs that are significantly lower than the established players in the market. The airline industry has been revolutionized by so-called low-cost carriers, first in the USA with Southwest Airlines, and then in the UK with easyJet and Ryanair.

- Globalization—it can be argued that globalization is not simply an operations strategy, but a corporate strategy. However, making products or delivering services on a global basis has very significant implications for how operations are managed. (See Chapter 17.)

RESEARCH INSIGHT 3.1

Lowson, R. (2003) The nature of an operations strategy: combining strategic decisions from the resource-based and market-driven viewpoints, *Management Decision*, 41(6), 538–49

Robert Lowson was one of the most original thinkers with regard to strategy in operations management. This article is selected because it provides an explanation of the concept of operations strategy, explains how it evolved, and reviews two alternative ways of thinking about it—the resource-based view and the market-driven view. These two viewpoints (or 'paradigms') occur throughout the operations management literature and influence different researchers' interpretations of nearly every aspect of operations. Once again, this article makes reference to the five main order winners—quality, speed, dependability, flexibility, and cost—demonstrating how important these are. It also introduces issues that we shall go on to explore in more detail later in this text—the supply chain, technology, and human resources.

An important point emerges from this analysis—there are some industries which have operated or continue to operate only in the context of one era, whereas others span two or all three eras. For instance, hairdressing and sculpture remain craft-oriented operations; likewise petroleum refining is solely a flow process operation. However, building construction can be either craft or mass production, as discussed in Operations insight 3.1, whilst car making may be craft, mass production, or mass customization.

The traditional way of building a house is essentially craft-based. A number of specialist craftsmen or women—bricklayers, carpenters, electricians, plumbers—each contribute their skills to the project. The house is assembled from basic raw materials such as bricks, cement, beams and planks of wood, copper piping, electric wiring, and other materials (as illustrated in Figure 3.2a). This means that each house can be unique, constructed on the basis of an individual set of plans and designs, often drawn up by an architect. However, this approach means that conventional housebuilding is relatively slow as all the materials have to be delivered to the site and be custom-built for that location. It also requires a great deal of coordination and collaboration between the various trades on site.

A more recent and modern approach to housebuilding is to use prefabricated parts, which are then assembled on site (as illustrated in Figure 3.2b). In this instance, walls (including their doors and windows) are manufactured under factory conditions, transported to site, and fitted together on the foundations. Manufacturing off-site has the potential to reduce the cost, as large-scale production generally leads to economies of scale (see page 63), as well as reducing the time needed to construct the house on the site itself. However, this approach means that a large number of identical houses are built.

Questions

1. What kind of process type is traditional housebuilding?

2. What issues might arise from building houses on production-line principles using prefabricated parts?

a)

b)

FIGURE 3.2 a) Traditional housebuilding. © iStock/clubfoot. b) Prefabricated housebuilding. © iStock/mabe123.

Process choice

The question of whether or not organizations have a real choice in material processing operations is an interesting one. Research insight 3.2 by Hayes and Wheelwright (1979) would have us believe that there are five fixed process types which operations would neatly fall into by virtue of their volume of output and variety of product. However, as we have illustrated earlier through the evolution of process types, the strategic operations era brought with it many different ways to satisfy an increasingly demanding customer base, leading to agile and flexible processes such as mass customization. This is illustrated in Figure 3.3 which shows the five original categories along the diagonal of

RESEARCH INSIGHT 3.2

Hayes, R.H. and Wheelwright, S.C. (1979) Link manufacturing process and product life cycles, *Harvard Business Review*, January/February, 133–40

This article first established the concept of process choice and how volume and variety lead to basic process types. In fact it did so by linking process type to time, specifically the product life cycle, suggesting that as a product developed it needed to be produced in different ways. The article was significant for a number of reasons. Not only did it link the volume of output to process type, but it also identified how the task of management was different in each of these operational settings. We have built on these ideas and expanded them. In the previous section we have discussed how OM differs from one type of operation to another. In the next section we discuss how OM varies from one stage of a life cycle to another.

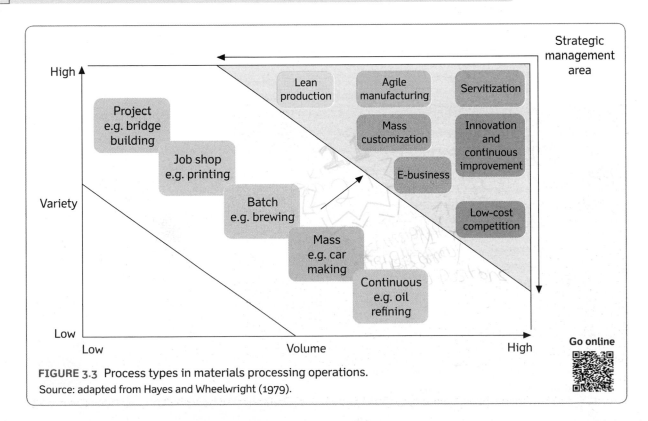

FIGURE 3.3 Process types in materials processing operations.
Source: adapted from Hayes and Wheelwright (1979).

Go online

the figure plus the move towards the top right of the diagram delivering higher variety with a higher volume under the influence of the strategic era. It is interesting to note that in 1979 when Hayes and Wheelwright wrote their article the notion of high volume coupled with high variety was seen as unnatural, stating that 'a company that allows itself to drift from the diagonal without understanding the likely implications of such a shift is asking for trouble'. However, the area in the lower left of the diagram is still today left unutilized as the combination of low volume with low variety leads to high unit costs.

This was followed by other researchers who looked specifically at customer processing operations, most notably Silvestro et al. in 1992. They proposed a similar diagonal matrix based on volume and variety in which they identified three operations types, namely **professional services**, **service shop**, and **mass service**.

- Professional services—these are generally services that are provided uniquely to each customer or client. Examples would include medical advice and treatment from a doctor, legal services from a lawyer, and building designs from an architect.

- Service shop—an operation in which relatively small numbers of customers have a variety of service features that they can experience. Examples would include table service restaurants, hospital accident and emergency departments, and hairdressing salons.

- Mass service—an operation which provides identical or very similar services to a large number of customers at the same time. Examples of this type would be supermarkets, fast food stores, and cinemas.

The Silverstro et al. matrix is recreated in Figure 3.4 and again is adapted by the authors to show the development towards some of the same concepts within the customer processing operations, such as mass customization, innovation, and continuous improvement.

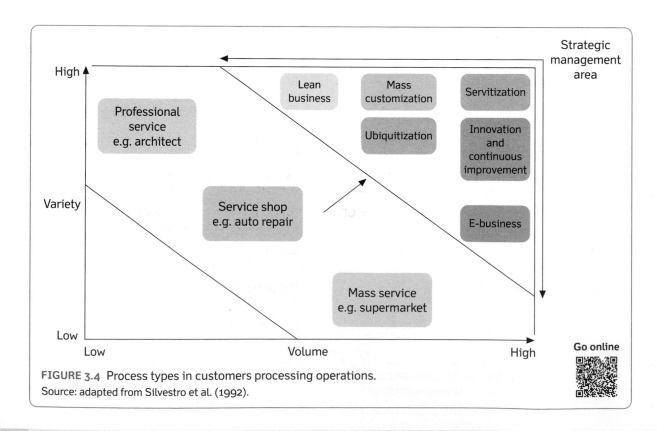

FIGURE 3.4 Process types in customers processing operations.
Source: adapted from Silvestro et al. (1992).

It should be noted that such classificatory schemes or matrices are not without controversy. Collier and Meyer (2000) compare three different approaches to classifying service operations (including Silvestro et al.'s) and conclude that defining precisely the criteria on each axis can be a challenge, and that statistically the two axes might be correlated to each other. In other words, increasing volume leads to less variety or vice versa. They concluded that further work needs to be done in order to understand what exactly differentiates between different process types.

Whether organizations have materials processing or customer processing operations, there are a number of key factors which are common and some which define the particular process type. These are shown in Table 3.2. Generally speaking, projects are highly flexible, whilst continuous process is the least flexible. This applies to how the process is designed, the layout of plant and equipment, the level of output (capacity), the nature of work that employees do, and whether costs are fixed or variable. The relative flexibility of each process type then has implications for other characteristics such as the speed of work flow—the more flexible the process, the slower it becomes. Likewise, flexible processes require a skilled workforce, whereas workers in the less flexible operations, such as mass production and continuous flow, follow set routines. Process type even influences the way in which quality is managed. All of the criteria listed in Table 3.2 are discussed in more detail in the chapters indicated in the table.

TABLE 3.2 Characteristics of process type

Criteria	Project or professional service	Job or service shop	Mass production or mass service	Continuous process	Relevant chapter
Process flexibility	Highly flexible to suit customers' needs	Some flexibility	Little flexibility	No flexibility	10
Layout choice	Fixed layout	Process or cell layout	Product layout	Product layout	10
Supply chain	Not fixed Variable demand	Not fixed Variable demand	Fixed Some variation	Fixed and predictable	5
Level of inventory	Low	High	Low	Low	6
Typical work flow	Slow throughput times	Medium throughput times	Fast throughput times	Fast throughput times	10
Capacity management	Variable Chase demand	Capacity lagging Chase demand	Capacity leading Level capacity	Capacity leading Level capacity	7
Quality management	Control (QC) and assurance (QA)	Inspection (QI) and control (QC)	Total quality management (TQM)	Statistical process control (SPC)	9
In-process design changes	Many	Some	Very few	None	10
Employees	Skilled staff	Some empowerment	Mainly follow set routines	Mainly follow set routines	11
Job content	Flexible. Highly skilled workers	Flexible. Typically do more than one job	Predictable. Lower skilled employees	Set processes. No change	11
Cost control	Low fixed & high variable costs	Medium fixed & medium variable costs	High fixed & low variable costs	High fixed & low variable costs	3

The product life cycle

A number of life cycle models have been proposed concerning aspects of business. These are typically in the form of a S-shaped curve, which illustrates a slow build-up in the beginning, a period of rapid growth, and then a slowing down in activity, as illustrated in Figure 3.5. In this section we look at two life cycle models—the **product life cycle** which has implications for managing materials processing operations, and the service firm life cycle which has implications for customer processing operations.

Levitt (1965) was one of the first to suggest that products follow the kind of sales growth depicted in Figure 3.5 and that this should be exploited. As this figure illustrates, the initial sales for a new product show a very small increase during the introduction stage following a period of innovation and new product development. This could be a completely new invention or one that is new to the company, but equally could be a radical change to existing products. Market awareness will be low and the operations manager needs to find ways to manufacture the product to allow the company to bring it to the market's attention. Slack et al. (2010) suggest that the dominant performance objectives at this stage are to deliver flexibility and quality. This may require developing new processes, adopting new technology, and investing in new equipment. This has implications for training staff who may have to adopt new ways of working. Planning will be challenging as there is no data on which to forecast. Therefore the volume of output remains largely unknown and a variety of production runs will need to be planned for.

During the growth stage, customer acceptance increases and sales increase. The quantities required increase rapidly. The operations manager will be focused on building up capacity at no loss in quality and in redesigning manufacturing processes to take advantage of economies of scale. Often this entails adding additional production lines identical to the first one. It may also involve adding additional shifts so that the plant is used more intensively. The performance objectives at this stage may become speed, dependability, and quality.

During the maturity stage it is likely that competitors will have entered the market. Sales growth will slow and the operations manager will need to further reduce cost,

Product life cycle the sequence of stages which products or brands follow after being developed, namely introduction, growth, maturity, and sales decline

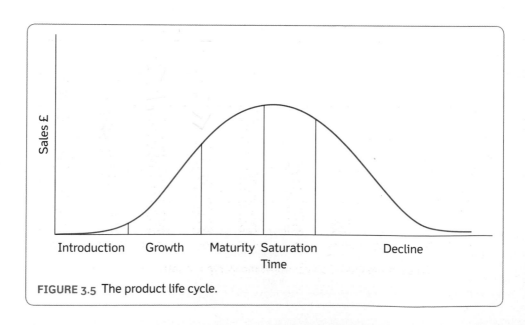

FIGURE 3.5 The product life cycle.

improve customer delivery speed, and be prepared for minor modifications to the product to help retain a competitive advantage. Hence cost and dependability are the performance objectives.

During the saturation stage sales growth will slow further as most potential customers will have already purchased the product and the company will be relying on replacement sales. It may be that to maintain market share firms can only compete on cost. At this stage (or ideally just before), the organization should engage in more innovation to redesign and redevelop the product. This time the innovation process will most likely be a facelift of or an extension to the existing product range.

In the decline stage sales will fall off quickly and the operations manager will be engaged in bringing the revised product on line as quickly as possible.

OPERATIONS INSIGHT 3.2
Apple iPod—an archetypal product life cycle

Apple was originally a computer company set up by Steve Jobs, an entrepreneurial American business colleague of Bill Gates, the Microsoft entrepreneur. Throughout its history Apple has been seen as synonymous with innovation and design. In 2001, the company launched the iPod. This was a new type of portable media player using digital technology to store the music. Since then the company has developed new versions of the product such as the hard drive-based iPod Classic, the touchscreen iPod Touch, the video-capable iPod Nano, and the compact iPod Shuffle. In order to bring the early concepts of the iPod to the market they used Internet advertising extensively and relied on the network of loyal users of their already successful Mac version of the personal computer to spread the word.

Total sales of iPod players have now exceeded 200 million worldwide, as illustrated in Figure 3.6. What Apple did best was to pre-empt demand by keeping in close contact with customers through the Internet and focus groups to frequently bring out enhanced versions

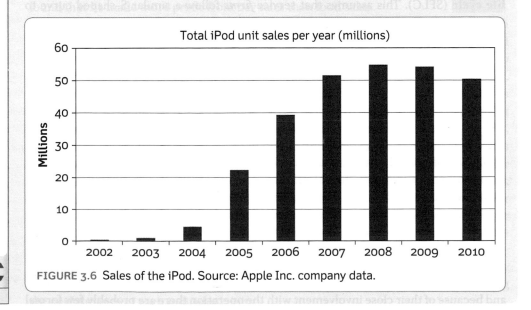

FIGURE 3.6 Sales of the iPod. Source: Apple Inc. company data.

TABLE 3.4 A model of the plural form

Challenge	Company	Plural processes	Franchise
Unit growth	Centralized	*Additive Socialization*	Decentralized
Uniformity	Budgets Information systems	*Modelling Ratcheting*	Incentives, contracts
Local response	Centralized	*Local learning*	Decentralized
System-wide adaptation	Central expertise	*Market pressure Mutual learning*	Local experience

Source: Bradach (1997)

However, despite this somewhat trial and error approach to chain growth, Bradach (1997) argues that the outcome, i.e. the plural form, 'may enable organizations to escape their natural tendency to ossify over time by creating a built-in constructive tension between parts that keeps the organization receptive to new influences, yet in control'. Bradach goes on to identify 'plural processes' that enable such firms to meet the challenges of chain operation. These are illustrated in Table 3.4.

The additive process refers to chains seeding new markets with company units, followed by franchisees. Companies therefore become good at seeking general locations, whilst franchisees find specific sites. This also overcomes the limits of company capital. The socialization process relates to the fact that it is common for company people to become franchisees. This overcomes the shortage of suitable people to fuel more rapid growth, but supports more strongly the need for brand standards and uniformity. The modelling process describes how franchisees model the franchisor by growing their number of units to form 'mini-chains'. Such growth is aided by organizational learning from the franchisor. The ratcheting process explains how system-wide benchmarks lead to healthy competition between company and franchisee units. Likewise, company managers and franchisees tend to focus on different views of the market, with the former more concerned with national trends and volumes, whereas the franchisee focuses on very local market issues. Finally, learning processes refers to how the company learns from franchisees (local responsiveness) and franchisees learn from the company (system-wide adaptation).

Conclusions

In this chapter we have considered the link between processes and life cycles. This was first discussed by Hayes and Wheelwright in 1979 and continues to be of huge importance today. The key point that emerges from this discussion is that operations managers in one kind of process type do not face the same challenges as in other types, and hence do not manage in the same way as managers in other types of process. Likewise how you manage a materials processing operation at one stage of the product life cycle, or a customer processing operation at a stage in the service firm life cycle, is not the same as at other stages. This introduces the concept of 'fit', i.e. that what a manager does and how it is done have to fit with the context of the operation.

Unilever is one of the world's largest fast-moving consumer goods (FMCG) companies, making and marketing many of the brands commonly found in households in the UK and throughout the world. It is an Anglo-Dutch company that was formed in 1930 by the merger of a soap-making company, Lever Brothers, with a Dutch margarine producer. The rationale for this merger was that the manufacture of both soap and margarine is based around the processing of palm oil. Today the company has operating companies and factories on every continent. It also has research laboratories in England, the Netherlands, the USA, India, and China.

In the late 1990s, Unilever undertook a review of all its different businesses with the aim of focusing on the strongest core areas, which were ice cream, margarines, tea-based beverages, detergents, personal soaps, skin care products, and prestige fragrances. As well as these, several other areas were identified as having potential: frozen foods, culinary products (sauces and side dishes), hair care products, oral care products, deodorants, household care products, and industrial cleaning products. All the other businesses not in these areas that Unilever operated at this time were sold off. This process continued in 1999, when Unilever launched its 'Path to Growth Strategy' which rather than rationalize businesses, rationalized brands. It ceased to make around 1200 of its brands to focus on making 400 or so regional or global brands, that between them accounted for almost 90% of the company's revenue in 1998. This significant reduction in the product portfolio was designed to increase annual growth rates from 4% to 6–8%, as well as save the company £1 billion a year. Unilever now focuses on what it calls 'billion-dollar brands'. It has 13 such brands, each of which achieves annual sales of more than €1 billion. Seventy per cent of sales come from Unilever's top 25 brands, which fall almost entirely into two categories: food and beverages, and home and personal care. By 2010 Unilever operated 257 manufacturing sites in 68 countries.

A typical Unilever billion dollar brand is the Sunsilk range of shampoos. The product in the UK was launched as Sunsilk Liquid shampoo in 1954, and within five years it was marketed in 18 different countries. Sunsilk was a different kind of shampoo as it only needed one application, resulting in the retention of more natural oils in the hair. In 1956 a product designed for dry hair was launched—Sunsilk Cream shampoo—and in 1960 Sunsilk Tonic shampoo was launched, aimed at caring for the scalp. By the 1960s all shampoos were liquid, so the original brand was relaunched under the name Sunsilk Beauty shampoo and by 1962, there was a full range of Sunsilk shampoos for different hair types. Four years later, with the introduction of olive oil into the formula, new variants were launched.

As well as the formula of the product the packaging also changed. Originally sold in large bottles, in 1958 a transparent polythene tube was introduced. Then in 1969, all Sunsilk shampoo was repackaged in PVC bottles, enabling a larger bottle size at no increase in cost. Five years later an economy-size shampoo bottle was introduced. Product development continued throughout the 1970s and 1980s. The Sunsilk conditioner range was launched in 1971 for different types of hair. In 1980, the whole Sunsilk range was relaunched, with improved formulations and packaging design to bring the brand into the 1980s. Further relaunch and repackaging were undertaken in 2003.

In 2010, Unilever spent €928m on research and development across all its brands, employing over 6000 people in this area. The company typically makes around 300 new patent applications a year. A successful shampoo brand has to meet certain criteria. These include creating a soapy foam that can be easily rinsed from the hair, have a thick or creamy feel and pleasant fragrance, be suitably coloured, cause little or no eye or skin irritation, and cause no damage to the hair. In addition, features that users may be unaware of are that it must have low toxicity (i.e. not be poisonous if ingested) and be biodegradable. Manufacturers like Unilever continuously engage in research and

Chapter Four

Locating, designing, and managing facilities

Learning outcomes

After reading this chapter you will be able to:

→ Explain how firms select locations for their facilities

→ Explain outsourcing

→ Review site selection criteria for different organizations

→ Describe the layout of work and equipment within different types of operations processes

→ Explain what is meant by the servicescape and the effect this has on customers

→ Explore trends in operations design

Monty's Bakehouse—who does what where?

Monty's Bakehouse was set up in 2004 just south of London. It specializes in producing a hot, hand-held, premium snack product that can be reheated from frozen very easily and be served to consumers quickly and simply. By 2010 it was distributing 6 million products a year to sports stadia, cinemas, and travel companies, such as airlines, train, and ferries.

From the outset, the founder—Matt Crane—was faced with the 'make or buy' decision. Should they manufacture their own products or outsource this? Since Matt's background was in marketing for a major UK supermarket chain, his expertise was in branding, packaging, and food marketing—not food manufacturing. Moreover to set up a plant in which the products could be made would require an initial minimum investment of over £1 million. He therefore decided to outsource production to an existing manufacturer. But finding such a partner was not easy. Bakery product manufacturers in the UK are of two basic types. The first is relatively small, vertically integrated companies that make, distribute, and retail their products, often locally or regionally. Matt found that these firms had great expertise and passion, but neither the capacity nor drive to manufacture for someone other than themselves. The second type of manufacturer operates on a much larger, industrial scale producing bakery goods in large volumes for sale nationally through major supermarket and retail chains. Matt was concerned that firms such as these would not be able to produce the kind of premium product he wanted to make, nor be willing to make the relatively small production batches he would order.

To find the first manufacturer (of savoury pastries), Matt created a short list of possible partners by attending trade shows, consulting the British Retail Consortium's list of grade A facilities, and identifying firms that used a specific type of packaging machinery that he had identified as being the best for his type of product. He then visited a number of plants before selecting a manufacturer in South West England. This manufacturer had relatively modern equipment and facilities, an excellent food safety system in place, a good environmental health record, and very low product recall rates—all of which reassured Matt that product quality would be good. The company also had spare capacity and was keen to expand, as it specialized in producing pasties for sale through local outlets, which was highly seasonal. Last but not least, Matt found that the attitude and approach of the senior managers in this firm was very similar to his own. As he says, 'We were a good match for each other.' Since then Monty's Bakehouse has expanded. It outsources pizza products to a specialist firm in Scotland, Scoffins™ are made in the South East, and both the wraps are produced and the packaging manufactured in the North West.

As a result, Monty's Bakehouse only has 14 employees, focusing on developing new products, quality assurance, marketing, and distribution. A key part of what Matt and his senior team do is manage the outsource relationship, creating a 'partnership', rather than simply a supplier–customer link. However, this does not mean giving suppliers an easy time. A sample of every batch a manufacturer produces has to be sent to the Monty's Bakehouse office for quality assurance purposes. For a supplier to agree to such stringent tests, the relationship between the two parties has to be close. So staff from Monty's Bakehouse visit each of the plants on a weekly basis, and Matt himself meets with the suppliers routinely once a month. In addition, Matt has provided investment in new equipment for some suppliers, as well as initiated an employee recognition scheme within his supply chain's workforce. As a result suppliers engage in supporting new product development. For instance, the packaging company makes its computer-aided design system available when new packets need to be developed. From the suppliers' point of view, Matt's exacting standards have 'raised their game', so that what they have learned from producing the Monty's Bakehouse range of products, they have applied to the other products they make. In this case, outsourcing has been truly a win–win situation.

Source: author's primary research

Questions

1. How important is the location of the Monty's Bakehouse head office?

2. Why did Monty's Bakehouse outsource production?

Introduction

In this chapter we consider why operations are located where they are and why they are the size they are. As well as selection of the right site, over the years an increasing emphasis has been placed on facilities management—how an organization's buildings are equipped and serviced. In customer processing operations, there has always been an emphasis front of house on ensuring interiors and equipment meet customer expectations, as we saw when we considered the servuction model (see page 23). This customer environment has been termed the 'servicescape', that is to say the physical and psychological setting in which a service experience is organized and delivered by service providers and experienced by consumers. But there is growing evidence to show that creating the right environment for materials processing is equally important. This does not just mean setting out the equipment in the most efficient way, but also creating a pleasant work environment for employees. We refer to this as the 'manuscape'.

In this chapter we go from the macro issue of location, where in the world to place your operations, through to how to find specifically the right site on which to have your facilities, and then down to the micro issue of how to organize the equipment and layout of those facilities. In considering an operation we look at both the servicescape and the manuscape, before going on to examine how operations managers ensure that their facilities are kept secure and well maintained.

> **Servicescape** the physical and psychological setting in which a service experience is organized and delivered

> **Manuscape** the physical and psychological setting in which manufacturing is organized and delivered

Selecting locations for operations

The objective of finding the right location is to ensure that an operation is in the best possible place relative to its customers, suppliers, and other related facilities. As such, each organization is seeking to derive competitive advantage from the location of its operations. If it makes the wrong choice, this is often difficult to rectify due to the investment and sunk costs in the facility. So an organization can end up operating in the wrong place for many years.

There are a number of factors that influence the choice of a location. These are usually broken down into two main types—physical and socioeconomic factors. Physical factors are related to geographic/environmental issues. They include:

- Access to raw materials. Some operations are based around raw materials. Obviously extraction industries such as mining and quarrying can only be sited where these materials are found. Other industries process these raw materials and hence they can be sited close to their source or further away. Most iron and steel works are located close to coal mines or mineral deposits or both, whereas in the oil industry, processing is usually conducted in oil refineries that are not adjacent to oil wells—sometimes for obvious reasons, such as wells in the North Sea.

- Availability of energy supply. Some operations, such as glassmaking, need significant amounts of energy in order to process their materials or goods.

- Provision of other utilities such as water supply, drainage, etc. A surprising number of industries require a constant and large supply of fresh water. In some cases the water itself is processed, as in whisky distilleries or breweries; sometimes it is used for cooling purposes, as in power plants; and sometimes it is used for washing or cleaning purposes, as in flight catering kitchens. It is for this reason that some operations are typically located next to rivers or other sources of water.

- Nature of transportation networks. Whether to enable the supply of raw materials or components into the facility or to distribute finished products and services, an operation needs to have suitable transport links. Some outputs may be bulky and heavy, requiring transportation by rail or heavy goods vehicles. Other outputs may be light and fragile, and may be delivered individually direct to customers through the postal service. Some outputs are perishable, requiring specialized transportation, such as tankers or chilled lorries. And customer processing operations need to be close to customers, whether driving by in their cars or walking along the street.

- Nature of communication links. Some operations require a highly sophisticated communications infrastructure to operate effectively. Call centres and information technology (IT) support centres need access to high-bandwidth fibre optic networks, for instance.

- Availability of land or property. New infrastructure requires land on which to be built. In the UK there is an increasing shortage of land that has never been built on before, so-called 'greenfield sites', so more and more industrial and commercial property is being built on 'brownfield' sites, i.e. land that has previously had buildings on it. Certain types of operation may have very specific needs. Notably large assembly plants are most efficient when operating on one level, so require flat land on which to be built. However, many operations are located in existing buildings—most retail shops, offices, and small job shop operations are leased from property developers that have built shopping malls, office blocks, or industrial estates.

Socioeconomic, or human, factors include:

- Local labour markets. The skills and expertise of a workforce can vary widely from one locale to another, often due to the dominant industry in that area. For instance, Center Parcs operates holiday resort villages located in very different labour markets. Elveden holiday village in Suffolk has a workforce the majority of whom have previously worked in agriculture or rural industries, whereas the Nottingham village has access to a workforce who previously worked in manufacturing or extraction industries. And in the case of the Whinfell Forest village, Center Parcs became the largest single employer in the Carlisle area and found it difficult to recruit sufficient numbers of staff.

- Access to markets or customers. Most service industries locate their operations where it is easy and convenient for their customers to access and use the facilities. In many cases this means selecting sites with either high pedestrian traffic outside or high vehicle traffic.

- Proximity to or distance from competitors. In principle, the best way to create a local monopoly (and hence make more profit) is to be the only supplier of those goods or services in that location.

- Business climate. Locations are selected where the general business climate will support the firm's activities. This is especially the case when firms seek to expand internationally (see Chapter 17 on globalization).

- Government policies. Finally, governments at all levels may offer incentives for firms to locate in certain areas. In the UK such incentives may be provided by central government, development agencies, or local authorities.

RESEARCH INSIGHT 4.1

Hayter, R. (1997) *The Dynamics of Industrial Location: The Factory, the Firm and the Production System*, Chapter 4, 79–110, Wiley: Chichester

In this chapter from his book, Hayter examines in depth the factors that influence where factories are located. He goes on to explain the processes that firms go through in order to select locations and suitable sites. He also identifies that firms do not simply have factory facilities, but may also have head offices, research laboratories, and support facilities, and he goes on to discuss how these may be sited.

Despite there being clear criteria why an operation might be located where it is, there are no absolute rules. Some organizations and industry sectors appear to routinely select locations that appear to run counter to the factors identified previously, i.e. that 'break the rules'. Examples of this kind of behaviour are:

- Competitive clustering. This refers to operations that co-locate next to each other, i.e. deliberately site their operation next to one or more competitors. The reason for this behaviour is synergy, that is to say operators that co-locate attract more customers in total than if they did not. This has always been the case with regard to retail markets and shops. Imagine a street with market stalls on one side, many of which are selling almost identical goods, such as fruit and vegetables, flowers, and haberdashery. On either side of the street there are then shops that also sell similar products, such as clothes, shoes, or mobile telephones. Creating shopping areas like this attracts very large numbers of customers because they know that whatever they are looking for can be found there. It also enables customers to easily compare quality and price—something that most consumers like to do before they purchase. As well as retailing, other sectors now follow this approach. For instance, IT companies now cluster together, not for access to customer markets but for access to skilled labour markets. So for instance the Thames valley around Reading is known as the UK's 'Silicon Valley'.

- Saturation marketing. This refers to a single company co-locating lots of its operations together so that it creates market dominance. In the last chapter, we talked about Lettuce Entertain You, a restaurant chain that has 38 different restaurants—all in Chicago.

- Marketing intermediaries. Some firms choose to be physically close to suppliers who assist in their downstream or marketing activities. For instance, tour operating companies may have offices near airports.

- Personal preferences. Sometimes a location is selected for no other reason than the founder or owner wants to locate there. To a large extent, this was the case with the Monty's Bakehouse head office.

Trends in location

Make or buy decision

Make or buy
the decision whether manufacturing fabrication should be in-house or done by a supplier

One of the most fundamental decisions an organization has to make is what it actually does. What activities are going to be undertaken by the firm, and which are going to be provided by other organizations? In materials processing this is called the '**make or buy** decision'—should the products being manufactured be made entirely within the firm or not? Like Monty's Bakehouse, some very large companies that would appear to be manufacturers may actually do very little materials processing themselves. Unilever, for instance, sees itself as a marketing-led company whose expertise is in brand management. This means that it prefers to use its available capital to invest in developing new products, and in marketing and advertising. For example, some key products are manufactured by third parties, and the warehousing and distribution operations are operated by third parties.

Clearly if a firm decides not to undertake some activities it needs to find suppliers who will do so for it. This leads to the development of the supply chain—which we discuss in the next chapter. If a firm has previously performed some activities itself and then decides not to, this is referred to as **outsourcing**, especially if it transfers resources to the outsourcer to enable it to supply the firm.

Outsourcing
the shift of production from in-house to a supplier

Outsourcing

Organizations can outsource some of their business activity at a variety of levels. They can outsource entire functions of the organization such as human resources, information technology, facilities, real estate management, and accounting. They can also outsource elements of each function. So the marketing department might outsource its telemarketing, web development, and market research. In the operations area, outsourcing has been applied to computer-aided design (CAD), drafting, manufacturing, engineering, customer support, and call centre functions. Firms may also decide to move an activity to another country, usually with a low-cost economy. This is known as '**offshoring**'. In many cases, offshoring is linked to outsourcing, but it need not be.

Offshoring
moving an operational activity to another country

There are many reasons to outsource, which include:

- Reduced operating costs. Suppliers may be able to produce goods or supply services at a lower cost because they have economies of scale or are simply better at doing so.

- Restructuring costs. By transferring activities to suppliers the firm may be able to reduce its fixed assets (i.e. buildings and plant), amount of capital employed, amount of inventory it holds, and number of employees. All of these things change the ratio of fixed costs to variable costs, thereby affecting its financial liquidity, increasing flexibility, and ultimately enhancing shareholder value.

- Focus on core business. Shareholders increasingly take the view that firms that are focused on their core business outperform those that are not. This is partly because it is easier to value a business that is focused. For instance, in the hotel industry 'bricks', i.e. the hotel properties, have been separated from 'brains', i.e. the hotel operating companies. This is because the hotel business operates to a very different economic cycle than the property business. It also requires very different expertise.

- Access world-class capability. Clearly if other firms focus on their core business, then suppliers should also be better at what they do. They invest in their technology, processes, and people so that they produce high-quality products or services at low cost. Moreover such suppliers are more likely to be innovative thereby ensuring the customer is always at the leading edge of any new developments in their field. This is discussed in Operations insight 4.1.

In a survey of outsourcing undertaken by the Outsourcing Institute there were also reasons for outsourcing which may not be best practice. These included:

- Cash infusion. Outsourcing may involve the transfer of assets such as equipment, facilities, vehicles, and licences from the customer to the supplier. Depending on the value of these, there may also be a cash payment to the customer. Furthermore they may be sold at book value which is typically higher than the market value. In effect this represents a 'loan' from the new supplier to the customer. Such a 'loan' is repaid over the lifetime of the contract through the prices charged by the supplier. This is a one-off benefit that cannot be repeated.

- Function out of control. In some cases, firms have outsourced parts of their business that have been difficult to manage or are underperforming. Simply outsourcing may not solve the problem, however, since if the firm cannot manage these things itself, they will find it difficult to specify in the outsourcing contract how they should be managed and to communicate this to a supplier.

- Catalyst for change. An organization seeking to change the way it does things may use outsourcing as a means of achieving or influencing this.

- Accelerate time to market. Firms that are anxious to get their new products to customers may not have enough capacity themselves to do so rapidly. Hence they outsource their production to suppliers. However, the danger is that in doing so they risk the quality of that product.

Although outsourcing is a major trend, it is not without its disadvantages, as the Boeing Dreamliner Operations insight 4.1 illustrates. These disadvantages may be:

- Financial costs. Outsourcing may incur higher costs due to the cost and difficulty of managing suppliers. All supplier contracts incur costs, called transaction costs by economists, which derive from conducting negotiations, managing the tendering process, and oversight of supplier performance.

- Loss of control. Clearly, handing over activities to another party means that these are no longer under the direct control of the organization. This may lead to a loss of continuity of supply or quality control should the supplier not perform as expected. For instance, the supplier may have industrial relations problems that lead to a short-term loss of supply. In a worst-case scenario the supplier may even declare bankruptcy and cease to exist.

- Increase in risk. By transferring activities out of the organization there may be a loss of in-house expertise which might never be possible to regain. Moreover losing experts may make it difficult to manage the contract effectively. Working with suppliers may also involve commercial secrecy or confidentiality as they inevitably become aware of their customers' operations and performance.

- Size of the trading area. This refers to how far customers are expected to travel to get to the operation. Center Parcs considers two hours' drive to be about the average travel time to one of its villages, whereas a supermarket chain might expect most customers to live no more than 15 minutes from the store. Likewise some operations rely on passing trade, whereas others are destinations in their own right. This is why retail stores, who often depend on passing traffic, cluster together in shopping centres in order to create a 'destination' that shoppers will travel to. The trading area is often described in terms of travel time rather than distance because road layout, bottlenecks such as bridges, and barriers such as rivers can affect the ease or difficulty with which customers can reach a site. Sometimes these barriers are psychological rather than physical, so customers will not travel through areas that they might perceive to be unsafe.

- Market structure. Most customer processing operations appeal to leisure customers who typically spend their own money (so-called 'discretionary spending') or business customers who are buying services on expenses. Hence the restaurant market in London is very different in the City where a large proportion of customers are on business, compared with the West End where they are mostly shoppers or tourists.

- Demographics. The market will also be made up of individuals with potentially marked demographic differences. If the operation is designed to appeal to a younger market segment it must be sited in a property that appeals to that segment.

- Travel patterns. A large number of people engage in routine travel—such as commuters on their way to work and students on their way to college. They very rarely alter or change these patterns of behaviour, so understanding these patterns is vital to ensure sufficient customers pass by an operation that depends on this. The growth in the number of food outlets at railway stations is an indication of this.

- Access. Customers need to be able to get into and out of the operation easily. If they use motor transport there has to be adequate signing so that customers can find the site and then sufficient parking.

- Visibility. Most operations, especially those that rely on passing traffic, need to be seen.

In order for these different criteria to be applied to different sites a variety of evaluation methods are used. One of the most straightforward is the weighted factor technique. An operator selects the most important criteria in relation to a site and then weights them according to their relative importance. For instance, a specified demographic might be weighted 30% but visibility may only be 10%. Then sites are scored against each criterion before the weighted score is calculated. Only sites that meet a certain score are then developed. A more sophisticated approach based on statistics is to undertake regression modelling of each site. This identifies which combination of variables produces the best site. On the other hand it is not unknown for some operators to adopt expert estimation, which is largely based on previous experience and intuition.

A feature of modern business is the emergence of so-called location intelligence. This combines geographic data, such as aerial maps, demographics, and business information, to facilitate site selection, the optimization of branch operations, and expansion planning across a wide range of industry sectors. Indeed it is argued that this kind of approach can enable a wide range of other activities such as risk management and supply chain collaboration—as illustrated in Figure 4.1. This shows the extent to which an integrated approach to selecting locations or specific sites is desirable, as where operations are situated has implications for so many aspects of the business.

A location-intelligent company

Risk management
Location-aware security
Contingency planning
Product and market trends

Customer service
Sales info inquiry
Help desk
Transaction status

Supply chain collaboration
Available to promise (ATP)
Advanced planning engines
Product information management

Distribution and logistics
Logistics planning
Soft goods delivery
Inventory management

Operations
Order processing
Asset utilization
Resource allocation

Customer acquisition
Site selection
Defining sales territories
Sales collateral distribution
Online promotion and targeting

FIGURE 4.1 Outline of a 'location-intelligent company'. Yankee Group, 2011.

Determining facility capacity

This will be dealt with in Chapter 7 in more detail when we will be discussing the issues involved in meeting short- and medium-term demands from customers. However, determining the capacity of a facility in the long term is essential before you can make decisions about its location and layout. Decisions on facility size will depend on the likely size and variety of orders and also the geographic location of the facility relative to its customer base. If the customer base is widespread then it is more likely that a number of small or medium-sized facilities will be chosen, each located near to a major customer market. If most of the demand is local then a single large unit may be the best option. This is due to the impact of logistical supply chain decisions (which we will discuss in Chapter 5) and will also depend on the flexible nature of the business.

We will see in Chapter 7 that operating capacity is in fact a variable. Although processes will have a design capacity, i.e. the maximum output that can be delivered in a set time, there will be a number of factors which will influence the actual capacity a facility can offer. For example, employee, machinery, storage, or transportation limitations can all play a part in determining the actual capacity available.

Layout in different process types (the 'manuscape')

Determining the most appropriate layout for a particular process is a key decision for an operations manager. This will influence throughput of customers or materials and ultimately the cost of the process. There are four basic layout types and each is associated with one or more process type.

planned in advance or be reactive, for instance, conducted in response to a breakdown or failure of some kind. In both cases, it is necessary to consistently record what service has been delivered, as well as measure its quality, to ensure the contract is being fulfilled across all sites. To achieve this, each of the suppliers uses a networked management information system which enables work to be recorded in real time, as it happens. This information is used for measuring the key performance indicators and for managing operations effectively in terms of scheduling work, cost control, asset management, productivity analysis, and capacity planning.

In 2011, Roll Royce extended MITIE's contract to include its facilities in five other European countries, as well as the UK. In conjunction with this, MITIE has created a new brand name— 1 team—for its Rolls-Royce contract and increased the 1 team workforce to over 1000 employees.

Sources: www.pfmonthenet.net/featuresarchive/article.aspx?ArticleID=11157 and www.mitie.com

Questions

1. Does the outsourcing of its facilities management have any implications for Rolls-Royce Aerospace's ability to deliver its order qualifiers and order winners?

2. What type of operations (job shop, batch, etc.) and layout (fixed, process, etc.) are involved in facilities management?

Ethics and sustainability

It can be argued that the location and siting of operations are one of the most contentious areas of operations management. One only needs to think about the controversies reported in the media, such as stories about the construction of new nuclear power plants or waste incinerators, the closure of local factories, the building of hotels and resorts in areas of outstanding natural beauty, or the demolition of old buildings to make way for new shopping centres, to appreciate this.

So sustainability is having an increasing impact on operations locations. Brownfield sites (i.e. sites on which there has already been development) rather than greenfield sites are being preferred, and the carbon impact from vehicle emissions of the transport required to service the operation are being considered. And governments, at both national and local level, are influencing this through the tightening of planning regulations and granting planning consent. Unilever, for example, has a three Cs strategy, where any developments must balance the requirements of providing high levels of customer service while minimizing cost and carbon emissions.

The effective layout of equipment and organization of work also has ethical considerations in terms of the pace at which employees can work. In discussing flight catering operations earlier, we reported that there was higher employee satisfaction when working at work stations than on assembly lines. In office environments a major cause of

TABLE 4.1 Worker fatalities by main industry in the UK 2008/09

Industry sector	Fatalities	Deaths per 1000 workers
Agriculture	26	5.7
Construction	53	2.4
Manufacturing	32	1.1
Services	63	0.3
Total	174	0.6

Source: www.hse.gov.uk/statistics/fatals.htm

concern has been damage to workers' eyesight when staring at computer screens for long periods, repetitive strain injury from using keyboards, and back pain from poorly designed office chairs. This has led to the development of ergonomic design wherein workplaces and equipment are specifically designed to reduce physical stress on employees.

Layout and design are linked to the idea of health and safety at work. In the UK, employers have a statutory duty to comply with legislation in this area, but may also be open to civil litigation in cases of negligence. The Health and Safety Executive publishes annual statistics on deaths of employees whilst at work, as well as work-related injuries and illnesses. In 2008–2009, agriculture, followed by construction, were the most dangerous operations to be engaged in, and services the safest, as shown in Table 4.1. The adoption of total productive maintenance (TPM) as discussed later in Chapter 14 is one way that operations may be made safer.

Conclusions

In many industries, locating operations on the right site is fundamental to success. The cost of setting up an operation is so high that organizations spend a great deal of time and money finding and selecting the right place. Once established it is extremely challenging and costly to move to a new site. This is why many established companies such as Pilkington Glass and Vauxhall are still making their products on sites that were established over 100 years ago. Exactly how to choose a site will vary from one type of business to another. Extraction industries are sited where their materials are found, distribution centres on major transportation links, and retail stores cluster together to create critical mass. A newly emergent field is so-called 'location intelligence' which enables firms to enhance their capabilities through better site selection, distribution, and logistics.

Organizations also have to decide how much of their operation they will undertake themselves and how much they can outsource to suppliers. Outsourcing has been a major business trend in the last 20 years, as more and more companies focus on their 'core' business. But as we saw in Operations insight 4.1 about Boeing Dreamliner, this is not without risk. Linked to this decision is the issue of how large any facility should be and how processes should be laid out within it. There are four basic types of layout—fixed, process, cell, and product, plus a hybrid mix of all or some of these. In customer processing operations, it is not just the work flow that needs to be considered, but the effect the environment has on customer behaviour. This is referred to as the servicescape, in which colours, lighting, music, noise, and even smells all play their part in the consumer's experience.

Finally, facilities need to be managed. The field of facilities management has also developed in the last 20 years so that there are now firms that specialize in this activity. This was illustrated in Operations insight 4.3 about Rolls-Royce. This enables firms to outsource their facilities to such specialist firms, who will look after the property, maintenance, security, utilities, waste management, and reception services.

END OF CHAPTER CASE
IKEA—UK locations and store design

IKEA is an international retail chain that specializes in furniture and home furnishings. The company entered the UK market in 1987, by which time it had stores in many European countries, southeast Asia, and North America. By 2011, the company had 18 stores across the UK. Four were located in outer London (Croydon, Edmonton, Wembley, and Lakeside), sited on so-called 'out-of-town' retail parks. The 14 other stores are located in major cities such as Belfast, Cardiff, Glasgow, Birmingham, and Leeds. The majority of these are also sited out of town, but two—in Coventry and Southampton—are on city centre sites. In order to manage their facilities, IKEA has a property team of ten people based in their UK head office. This team includes a property manager, two acquisitions managers, and three members of the construction team. They are responsible for site acquisition, construction, and facilities management. Each of the team members is professionally qualified and has 10 years or more of experience in the retail property discipline.

In looking for a site, the property team will take into account a number of factors. With regard to physical features a key factor is access to road and public transport infrastructure, good visibility, and proximity to other existing retail locations. Because IKEA customers may be shopping for large and relatively expensive items, the company believes that they will take time to do so. This means they may want to browse and visit more than one retailer to compare products and prices, and maybe even visit IKEA more than once before they make a decision. Hence being co-located with other retail outlets means that a visit to IKEA becomes part of the total shopping experience. The company has no preferred stores that it would like to be located near. As well as these physical factors, a store would be located within one hour's drive time of a population of one million people who have the right socioeconomic demographics. In order to identify and select sites the property team use a modelling software system that takes into account travel distance, income levels, Acorn categorization, along with a checklist of requirements for the store. This checklist details the factors identified earlier—accessibility, public transport, and visibility. Often IKEA has been the first to take a site on newly developed retail parks, but more recently it has located on existing retail parks or shopping areas. Most of its facilities are freehold, owned by IKEA, but there are a few stores on a very long leasehold. Both freehold and leasehold stores are operated in exactly the same manner.

In order to supply its chain of stores, IKEA also has a UK distribution centre located near Peterborough. However, it handles slightly less than 50% of deliveries as, where possible, suppliers deliver their products directly to each store. Restocking is an automated process based on data derived from the store's electronic point-of-sale (EPOS) system. This sends orders to both suppliers and the distribution centre each day. Suppliers can take between one week and two months, depending on the product, to meet these orders. However, the distribution centre will meet its orders within two days. Store deliveries are made every day of the week and every week of the year and are made between 3.00 am and 9.00 am. Most stock is taken directly from the delivery lorry to the shopfloor, where it is displayed ready for sale. Stores have very limited amounts of BoH storage space and racking, which is used mainly for safety stock so that shelves can be replenished over the course of a busy day

A typical store needs a very large area of around 13 acres (the size of more than seven football pitches). As the cost of land, either to buy or lease, is very high, it is rare for each site itself to be 13 acres in size, as parking is created by having it under the store or as a multistorey car park adjacent to it. This is because the stores would like to have parking for up to 1000 cars in the immediate vicinity. One of the principles behind the shopping experience at IKEA is that customers purchase their goods and take them home with them. Since these products can be large and bulky, having vehicular access is fundamental to the operation. The stores themselves are typically between 33,000 and 45,000 square metres (the size of 14 average houses).

Public perception of the typical store is that it is a very large, low-rise warehouse-type building, with few windows, painted in IKEA's distinctive blue colour. And this may be true of some of IKEA's older stores. But newer IKEA outlets have moved away from this very functional approach. Many stores now incorporate skylights and windows to allow more natural light into the stores. This means that energy costs are lower and natural light shows off the products more effectively. It may also have a positive effect on employees. It is also the case that some stores are no longer laid out over one or two floors.

For instance, the IKEA store in Coventry has seven floors and it illustrates how the operation is laid out. On the ground floor there is a street café, access to parking and some parking spaces. On floors 1 and 2 there is further parking for up to 806 vehicles. On floor 3 there are the checkouts, 22 of them, as well as 'Smaland', which is the free play area for children. Floor 4 is used for customer services and employee areas, such as changing rooms, cafeteria, and training rooms. Floor 5 is IKEA's 'market hall', where smaller items are stocked, Finally, floor 6 is their showroom where goods are laid out in room settings, up to 45 different ones in this instance. The top floor also has a 450-seat restaurant. In a typical store, 80% of space is given over to FoH operations, and 20% is used for BoH operations, mostly made up of employee areas, storage, and plant (utilities) room.

IKEA's basic concept is to provide well-designed but functional furniture and furnishings at a low price. What was different about IKEA, and remains a distinctive feature of its stores, was that it displayed its products in room settings, that is to say laid out as a series of different rooms in a house—kitchens, living rooms, dining rooms, bedrooms. This is because its products are designed in ranges that are coordinated, for example, a bed, wardrobe, drawers, bedside table, and accessories would all be styled the same. Hence many of IKEA's customers are not simply buying a single replacement item; they are seeking to refurbish entire rooms in their home. In order to do this, the customer goes from one room setting to another and makes a note of what items they wish to purchase. They might then go to the market hall with a shopping trolley in order to purchase smaller items, like curtains, lamps, or cushions. Then they go to the self-serve warehouse to find the larger items they made a note of. These are often in flat-pack form, which reduces storage space and keeps costs down, as the customer has to assemble the product when they get it home. Finally they go through the checkout. For larger, bulkier items the customer may pay at checkout and then collect them from a storage area located adjacent to a loading area.

As the stores are very large, partly due to setting out room layouts, customers can spend quite a long time in each store. Indeed the IKEA website refers to the idea that customers should plan it as 'a family day out'. This is why each store has facilities for customers to eat in, as well as for children. Children's facilities include Smaland (or small land) which is a supervised play area where kids can be dropped off whilst their parents shop. Parents are given a pager so that if they are needed they can return to their child. Stores also have unsupervised play areas at other locations, as well as organizing play activities for children. Another feature of the operation is the long opening hours, with stores staying open in the evening until 9.00 pm or 10.00 pm. Supporting the in-store shopping experience are IKEA's catalogue and website. Many customers browse through these before going to a store in order to identify what they might be interested in. But they still like to go and see it for themselves 'for real'.

Sources: authors' primary research and www.ikea.com/gb/en

Questions

1. How important is store location to IKEA's success as a business?

2. How does the site of an IKEA store contribute to delivering IKEA's order winners?

3. How does the design of an IKEA store deliver order winners?

Chapter summary

To consolidate your learning, the key points from this chapter are summarized as follows:

- **Explain how manufacturing firms select locations for their facilities**

  Materials processing operations usually depend on the supply of raw materials or components. They may also need access to energy, water, or some other natural resource, labour markets, customer markets, transportation, and communication links. In addition, the business climate and government policies will have an influence. Draw on Hayter's Research insight 4.1 to discuss this in more detail.

- **Explain how customer processing organizations select locations for their facilities**

  Customer processing operations need to be located close to customer markets and have good communication links. Initially it will depend on the structure of the market and the relative size of the firm within it. Selection criteria would then be size of trading area, demographics, travel patterns, access, and visibility. Increasingly sophisticated modelling techniques such as the weighted factor technique, regression modelling, and location intelligence are used.

- **Explain outsourcing**

  If a firm has previously performed some activities itself and then decides to have a supplier do these instead, this is referred to as outsourcing, especially if it transfers resources to the outsourcer to enable it to supply the firm.

- **Describe the layout of work and equipment within a job shop**

  A job shop layout is arranged such that the product to be made is transported between the required pieces of process equipment. Typically this is used for low-volume products to meet customers' special requirements.

- **Describe the layout of work and equipment within an assembly line operation**

  An assembly line or mass production operation is arranged as a sequential process from one operation to the next, often in a line. It is typically used for large-volume products where there is very little flexibility and high repeatability.

- **Explain what is meant by the servicescape and the effect this has on customers**

  The servicescape is the physical environment of an operation encompassing several different elements such as the overall layout, design, signage, and décor of those parts of the facility used by customers. Draw on Bitner's (1972) article (Research insight 4.2) to discuss this in more detail.

- **Explore trends in operations design**

  There are four major trends in operations design—production-lining, decoupling, self-service, and co-branding. Production-lining refers to the introduction of technologies into service operations in order to automate production. Decoupling refers to the separation in terms of location and production time activities that take place back of house from those that take place front of house. Self-service is the involvement of the customer in the production of their own product or service. And co-branding is the use of the same facilities or technologies to deliver more than one brand or service.

Questions

Review questions

1. What criteria might influence the choice of location for engineering firms?

2. What criteria might influence the choice of location for clubs and discos?

3. What are the advantages and disadvantages of an organization outsourcing its call centre to India?

4. What criteria would be used to select a site for a new hospital?

5. What factors influence the size and scale of an operational facility?

6. How is equipment laid out in the different types of process (job shop, batch production, assembly line)?

7. How is the servicescape of a bank different from that of a home furnishing store like IKEA?

8. What are the main trends in operational design in terms of the servicescape?

9. What are the key features of facilities management?

10. How do health and safety at work vary from one industry sector to another? Why might this be?

Discussion questions

1. Pilkington makes glass at a plant in St Helens in Lancashire. Why St Helens?

2. Compare and contrast the locations of Holiday Inn Hotels with Holiday Inn Express in the UK (look on Holiday Inn's website). In what ways are the locations similar and different? Why?

3. When Disney built its theme park near Paris, what factors influenced its size?

4. How is a garage that undertakes general car repairs organized and laid out? How is this different from the layout in a tyre and exhaust replacement operation, such as Kwik Fit?

5. What is the archetypal servicescape of a dentist's or doctor's waiting room like? How could it be improved and why?

 # Further learning guide

To get a hint of how factories are designed try **www.autodesk.co.uk**. This company produces computer-aided design software that helps design buildings, plants, and factories. Moreover their design suites can turn these plans into three-dimensional images, as well as simulate materials flow through the factory. For everything you might want to know about outsourcing go to the Outsourcing Institute website (**www.outsourcing.com**). If you are interested in the servicescape search out websites devoted to design and interior design in relation to different services, such as retail, banking, hotels, and restaurants. Finally, many of the topics that have been covered in this chapter can be explored in more detail in specialist textbooks. One industry sector that has a wide range of such texts is the hospitality industry. For instance, the Educational Institute of the American Hotel & Lodging Association publishes books on international hotel development, facilities management and design, hospitality engineering systems, security and loss prevention, and even quality sanitation management.

 # References

Bitner, M.J. (1992). Servicescapes: The impact of physical surroundings on customers and employees, *The Journal of Marketing*, 56(2), 57–71

Tombs, A. and McColl-Kennedy, J.R. (2003). Social-servicescape conceptual model, *Marketing Theory*, 3(4), 447–75

Chapter Five

Managing supply chain relationships

Learning outcomes

After reading this chapter you will be able to:

→ Define supply chain management and explain its structure

→ Describe and explain an organization's procurement function

→ Understand supplier relationship management

→ Explain how logistics operates and alternative modes of delivery and storage

→ Identify and explain trends in supply chain management

Thorntons chocolates—300 ingredients from every continent

In 1911 Joseph Thornton opened a small chocolate shop in Sheffield. In the late 1980s, Thorntons developed an operational base in Alfreton, Derbyshire, where the company now has its headquarters and produces, packages, stores, and distributes its products. By 2009, Thorntons owned 377 stores like the one pictured in Banbury, Oxfordshire. It has franchised 200 more stores, distributed through supermarkets, and sold directly to consumers through its website. Within all these distribution channels, Thorntons is vertically integrated, a supply chain strategy which we will discuss in more detail later in this chapter. This means that it operates its own fleet of vehicles and employs its own drivers. This is because it considers agility as a key order winner and it can maintain ultimate control over deliveries through ownership rather than partnership or outsourcing. In 2009 Thorntons had a net turnover of £215 million, and a market share of around 50%. In 2010, following the sale of rival Cadbury to Kraft of the USA, it became the largest independent chocolate and confectionery company in the UK.

A Thorntons chocolate shop in Banbury, UK.

The product range has huge variety in terms of milk, plain, and white chocolates, different mouldings and decorations, and of fillings, such as praline, mousse, nougat, or fudge. There are between 17 and 22 chocolate block ranges available at any one time, as well as standard chocolate boxes and four limited-edition boxes each year. Packaging may be in boxes, tins, trays, pouches, and packets. In addition there are speciality products such as Advent calendars, hampers, and gift boxes.

Thorntons has adopted corporate social responsibility and applies this to its operations. The company applies ethical, social, and environmental standards to its supply chain. It visits and audits over 95% of its suppliers on a regular basis. The main aim of these audits is food safety but they also consider health and safety, employee pay, employment conditions, use of child labour and environmental policies and practices.

Thorntons uses over 300 different raw materials, sourced from all over the world. Cocoa trees only grow 10° either side of the equator, so most cocoa is supplied from the Ivory Coast and Ghana but Thorntons also has supplies from Madagascar, Venezuela, Ecuador, and Papua New Guinea. All of its cocoa is bought from suppliers who actively support the International Cocoa Initiative (ICI) and World Cocoa Foundation (WCF) programmes. These schemes are designed to improve the well-being of cocoa farmers and their families as well as promote responsible labour practices. By ethically sourcing cocoa it is hoped to minimize the likelihood of purchasing cocoa from sources which illegally exploit child labour. Thorntons is a member of the WCF and has registered as a member of GreenPalm, which promotes certified sustainable palm oil production and seeks to maintain rainforests.

Traditionally, chocolate boxes were filled by hand. In 2004, the company introduced a robotic packing line and another in 2009. Such lines can pack around 900 chocolates a minute, automatically sensing the product, measuring it to make sure it is the right size, picking it up, and placing it in the box at the correct orientation. The company also invested in a £2 million moulding line which allows it to make moulded chocolates and hollow spun products like Easter eggs and models. Automation such as this has improved production speeds and helped to ensure a higher level of quality control. This also means that it has developed a close relationship with the international specialist packaging supplier who provides equipment and packaging materials. The automation of the packaging process is critical to Thorntons achieving its delivery and quality targets. The equipment supplier with its technological expertise is a key partner in supporting the company's drive for higher volume production.

Sources: 'Thorntons, Thorntons Packaging', The Manufacturer December 2010; 'Thorntons, A Thorntons Moment', The Manufacturer November 2010; www.thorntons.co.uk

Questions

1. In what ways does Thorntons' supply chain match its order winning criteria?

2. What are the implications of having a sustainable supply chain?

Introduction

Almost no organization exists without suppliers. It could be argued that extractive industries which take raw materials out of the ground have few suppliers. But even they purchase plant and equipment from suppliers, probably have it maintained by those suppliers, and might even feed their workforce using external suppliers. For large-scale manufacturers, as we can see in the Case insight on Thorntons, the number of suppliers can be very high and because many of them come from different geographical regions the relationship with them can be hugely complex. Moreover, given that often suppliers and their customers are not located near to one another, the movement of goods from one to the other is also hugely complex. To get some idea of this, simply stand on a bridge over any motorway or major road and count the number of lorries that pass by in five minutes. Every single lorry is one tiny link in some organization's **supply chain**.

In this chapter we consider four main topics. First we look at the nature of supply chains, and in particular how they are structured. We will use an example of the automotive supply chain as most people are aware of this and it helps to illustrate a number of changes that have been made in **supply chain management** over the years since the gradual domination of Japanese motor manufacturers. We then go on to examine the procurement function—how organizations go about selecting suppliers and ordering goods from them. This leads on to a discussion about logistics, which is concerned with the movement of goods between suppliers and customers. Finally, we look at significant trends in supply chain management.

> **Supply chain** a sequence of business and information processes that link suppliers of products or services to operations and that link operations through distribution channels to end users

> **Supply chain management** the planning, design, organization, and control of the flow of information and materials along the supply chain in order to meet customer requirements in an efficient manner

Supply chains or networks and tiers of supply

A supply chain can be defined as a sequence of business and information processes that link suppliers of products or services to operations, and which then link those operations

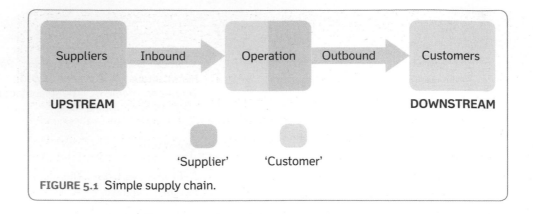

FIGURE 5.1 Simple supply chain.

through distribution channels to end users. These processes in a supply chain plan, design, organize, and control the flow of information and materials in order to meet customer requirements in an efficient manner. A simple supply chain is illustrated in Figure 5.1.

As information and materials are designed to flow between suppliers and customers this idea extends to the terminology used in supply chain management. Suppliers who are operating before the subsequent operation are deemed to be upstream and those who operate nearer the ultimate customer are deemed to be downstream. So you can think of the whole supply stream as a river. This is a good analogy as the objective of all of the organizations involved is to keep material and information flowing smoothly. As we shall see later in the chapter when we discuss logistics, those supplies that are brought in to the operation are termed inbound and the materials and information that are passed further downstream are termed outbound.

Figure 5.1 suggests that an operation (or the organization that owns or controls it) is one link in a chain of single suppliers taking in various materials and information and then processing them before passing them on to customers. But most operations will have more than one supplier, and those suppliers in turn may well have multiple suppliers. Indeed many operations are acting as both customer and supplier in these supply relationships as illustrated by the colour coding in Figure 5.1. In addition many operations require multiple sources of their key materials to ensure continuity of supply. This is illustrated in Operations insight 5.1 which shows the complex network of relationships between automotive suppliers and their customers.

Tiers of supply and demand

Tiers of supply and demand the levels in the chain or network, determined by how near they are to the operation

First-tier supplier those suppliers directly serving the operation

Intermediary organizations in supply chains are termed '**tiers**' of supply, the nearest to the finished process being a **first-tier supplier**, the next nearest a second-tier supplier, and so on. It then follows that competition is not just between firms but between alternative combinations of suppliers and their tiers, as the ability of an organization to deliver its order winners will be dependent on the efficiency and effectiveness of the specific network of suppliers that supports that organization. Consequently, supplier coordination and cooperation have become a key driver in the success of many businesses in different market sectors such as retail clothing, consumer white goods, computer software, and even financial services where the speed of access to new product information is vital.

The automotive supply chain is an excellent example of materials processing organizations collaborating at both local and global levels. There are many thousands of parts that go into a modern motor vehicle and they all have to be sourced and brought in to the assembly plant in time to be fitted into the final vehicle. Coordination of this is a hugely complex task as any excess material in stock would cause unnecessary cost to the company, whereas too little inventory would result in not enough cars being assembled. Figures 5.2 and 5.3 illustrate this to show the tiers of supply and tiers of distribution of a typical automotive manufacturer.

Figure 5.2 shows three tiers of supply and is a good example of a business-to-business (B2B) supply relationship that was discussed in Chapter 1 on types of business. A first-tier automotive supplier could be the engine manufacturer; a second-tier supplier could be the metal machining company that supplies engine components and a third-tier supplier could be the steel supplier. As the colour coding shows, the intermediate tiers of supply act as both customers and suppliers, which increases the complexity of the relationships involved.

On the distribution side there are again intermediaries, or tiers. Figure 5.3 illustrates this. Here we see an example of a business-to-consumer (B2C) relationship. It is not appropriate for automotive companies to sell their products at the factory gate and so they use retail showrooms. These help to increase customer service and loyalty by showcasing the latest models available and providing an efficient ordering system via computer link to the factory

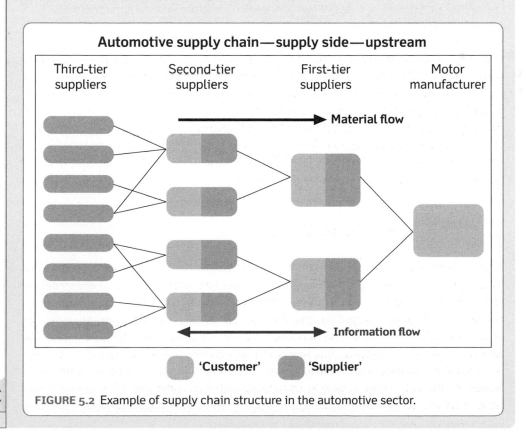

FIGURE 5.2 Example of supply chain structure in the automotive sector.

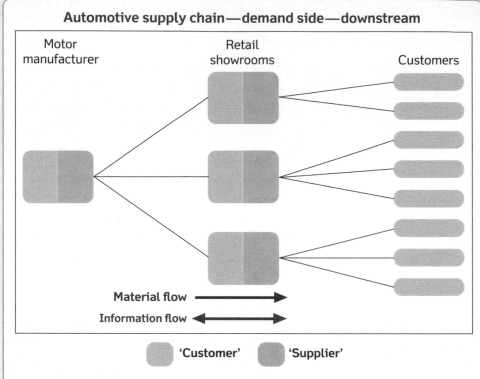

FIGURE 5.3 Example of supply chain distribution structure in the automotive sector.

to inform customers when the vehicle will be available for delivery. The showrooms are often associated with service and repair garages to encourage the customer to return regularly and therefore view the latest models available. There is normally some inducement to make this happen, usually achieved by having a warranty period of up to seven years in some instances during which time certain defective parts will be replaced free of charge so long as the vehicle has been regularly serviced by a registered dealer. Again some tiers in the distribution supply chain act as both customers and suppliers.

Questions

1. What features of the automotive supply chain make it easy to manage? What features make it more challenging?

2. How does geographic location affect the configuration of the supply chain?

Although the term supply chain has been used for many years, in the increasingly complex world of business it is being recognized that in many instances the relationship between supplier and customer is more sophisticated than a simple chain. Today it is more realistic to think in terms of supply networks. This means that in the automotive supply chain example, there may be any number of other relationships within the network, such as tier-three suppliers also supplying tier one, tier-one suppliers supplying each other, or suppliers supplying direct to customers.

RESEARCH INSIGHT 5.1

Lamming, R., Johnsen, T., Zheng, J., and Harland, C. (2000) An initial classification of supply networks, *International Journal of Production and Operations Management*, 20(6), 675–91

This was one of the first articles to question the concept of the supply chain, and examine the nature of supply networks. The authors identify that three aspects of the product being supplied impact on the way supply networks should be managed, namely the degree of product innovation, product uniqueness, and product complexity. They use case studies of 16 different types of firm to support this argument.

Procurement: buying from and working with suppliers

A **procurement** system is concerned with ensuring the right suppliers are used and that the purchasing process is itself controlled. In order to ensure the 'right' suppliers there has to be a system for selecting them, establishing a supply relationship (including the nature of the contractual link), and of supplier evaluation. These are largely strategic issues. The purchasing function is then concerned with the types of item being purchased and the purchase process itself, i.e. largely operational issues. It is clear from this overview of the purpose of the system that successful procurement performance can be measured not simply by cost but also by continuity of supply, value of stock held, and the quality of the relationship with suppliers.

> **Procurement** the process involved with selecting suppliers, negotiating contracts, purchasing items, and evaluating suppliers

Types and numbers of supplier

In view of the number of different types of process, and the concept of a supply network, it is clear that the number of suppliers can vary quite widely. In some cases, there might simply be one supplier, which is referred to as **single sourcing**. The advantages of this are:

> **Single sourcing** obtaining all of one type of product or service from one supplier

- Higher level of product quality with less variability
- Ability to establish a partnership relationship
- Makes engaging in new product and service development easier
- Able to vary delivery schedules more easily as only one supplier to deal with
- Opportunities to achieve cost savings by ordering in larger quantities
- Lower administration costs
- Essential if volume and value of products are too small to divide between competitors.

Multiple sourcing is deciding to purchase the same items but from more than one supplier. The advantages of this approach are:

> **Multiple sourcing** obtaining the same type of product or service from more than one supplier to ensure continuity of supply

- Reduces the risk of supply disruption if one supplier is unable to deliver
- Increases flexibility if demand increases are significant
- Creates competition between suppliers, so forces down prices
- Essential if the volume or value required is too great for one supplier.

The advantages of single sourcing can also be seen as disadvantages for multiple sourcing and vice versa.

Single sourcing can create major problems for companies. A recent example of this concerns British Airways who, like many airlines, outsource their flight catering to specialist companies. In 2005 they were single sourcing their in-flight catering at London Heathrow airport to Gate Gourmet, a well-established firm who also had supply contracts with American Airlines and Qantas. However, the company was not profitable and proposed to reduce costs by making a number of changes to its working practices. In August 2005 an industrial dispute broke out at London Heathrow in response to this reorganization. Gate Gourmet workers at their main flight kitchen went on strike, which meant that British Airways were without meals on most of its flights for several weeks. As a temporary measure passengers had to be issued with vouchers that enabled them to buy food and drink at the airport before their departure. Furthermore, ground staff at the airport took wildcat action for two days in sympathy with the Gate Gourmet workers. This grounded all British Airways flights from the airport, leaving more than 100,000 passengers stranded, and costing the airline an estimated £40m.

Two years after this event, BA put their contract at Heathrow out to tender, and decided to multiple source. It awarded its long-haul contract to Gate Gourmet, but its short-haul contract to a new entrant into the market—a consortium of Northern Foods and DHL. This decision drives price competition but it also reduces British Airways' exposure to future disruption as supplies can now be obtained from either company in case of any shortage.

In highly technical or regulated environments such as Formula 1 motor racing it is not so straightforward. The need to have a continued supply of parts for each race is obvious but quality is hugely important too, as any minor difference in the technical characteristics of a component part could result in slower lap times. When races may be won or lost by tenths or even hundredths of a second then this is critical, therefore single suppliers tend to be favoured in these circumstances.

Selecting suppliers

There are two basic ways in which suppliers can be selected. The first and most straightforward approach is to rely on secondary sources, such as company websites, promotional material from suppliers, trade association data sheets, and word of mouth from industry contacts.

The second and more professional approach is to gather primary data from potential suppliers and systematically compare alternative suppliers on clearly established criteria. Investigating suppliers in this way can take a variety of forms:

- Request for information (RFI). In this instance suppliers are asked for general information about their capabilities and performance. Such information may be about their range of products, delivery speed and reliability, prices, or specific issues such as environmental policy and sourcing policy. In some industry sectors buyers might only source from suppliers who have met certain accreditation criteria, such as

ISO 14000 (the international standard on environmental action) or ISO 9000 (the international standard on quality and customer service, which is discussed in Chapter 9).

- Request for proposal (RFP). Rather than ask for general information, the buying organization may present potential suppliers with a brief and ask them for a business solution, i.e. describe the way in which they would go about meeting the specific needs of their customer.

- Invitation to tender. Similar to a RFP, a tender also requires the suppliers to provide a full cost breakdown for their proposal.

- Request for quotation (RFQ). This is more specific than a tender and largely involves the suppliers in quoting a price for supplying a product or service that is tightly defined by the buying organization. This might also include meeting certain technical or quality specifications.

Supplier relationship management

Supplier relationships can be thought of strategically (i.e. in the long term), but also operationally in terms of the type of contractual arrangement between the two parties.

There are three basic types of strategic relationship—conventional, associated, and partnership. The conventional relationship is the one that most people think of—an arm's-length agreement between two organizations in which one is the supplier and the other is the buyer. This can be a one-off, i.e. the buyer only uses that supplier once; or routine, albeit that the buyer is not proactive in either selecting the supplier or evaluating them. The strength of the relationship is relatively weak and based solely on the commercial exchange of goods and services. The associated relationship is usually based on a long-term link between the two parties that involves more sophistication in managing the interaction. Often suppliers will guarantee quality of delivery, thereby reducing the buyer's need to check all deliveries, both in terms of the quality of what is provided and the time at which it is delivered. A partnership between buyer and seller is the strongest form of relationship. As well as guaranteeing delivery quality, partners typically work together on new product development, jointly invest in new technology, and create a seamless logistics system between the two parties.

These relationships are then supported by contracts. Jonsson (2008) suggests there are four broad types of contractual relationship:

- Direct competition—this refers to a buyer deciding who to buy from on each occasion an order is placed. Suppliers compete to win an order on whatever criteria the buyer has stipulated—typically cost but not exclusively so. The number of suppliers is relatively high under these conditions, but the total purchase value of each order is relatively low. For example, an organization might purchase its office consumables on this basis.

- Contracts in direct competition—this is similar to direct competition, but instead of competing for single orders, suppliers compete against each for a contract to supply over a specified time period. This may require the buyer to stipulate a minimum order quantity for that period. In the restaurant industry it is common for there to be these nominated suppliers from whom each restaurant orders its goods.

- Operative contracts—these tend to be based on supplier performance rather than on comparing one supplier against another, as in the former two cases. Contracts are entered into for the medium term, say three to five years, and tend to be renewed so

TABLE 5.1 Examples of contract terms and conditions

Type	Example	Terms
Financial	Fixed-price contract	A price is agreed on and applies to the full term of the contract
	Cost-related contract	The cost of supply varies according to an agreed rate in relation to the volume supplied
	Price protection clause	This enables buyers in long-term contracts to compare prices with other suppliers and switch to them if their supplier does not match it
	Escalation clause	This incorporates some kind of formula that allows the cost of products to fluctuate according to the market conditions for materials needed to produce those products
	Buy-back clause	Suppliers agree to buy back at a guaranteed price any stock not sold by the customer
	Revenue sharing clause	The supplier is partly paid a fixed price and additionally shares in the revenue of any products sold by the customer.
Legal	Termination	A clause that explains under what circumstances either party can terminate the contract before its term
	Business continuity	A clause that explains how either party will meet its obligations should it cease to exist (through merger or acquisition, for instance)
	Force majeure	How the contract deals with events outside the control of either party
Performance	Quantity flexibility clause	This enables the buyer to order varying quantities, often within specified limits
	Delivery speed clause	This specifies the time between when an order is placed and it actually being delivered to the buyer

long as the supplier has performed well against the pre-agreed criteria. Airlines tend to have these types of contracts with flight caterers.

- Strategic contracts—there are likely to be relatively few suppliers in these arrangements, but the value of their contracts is likely to be high. These tend to be long term and there may not even be a termination clause in the contract. Such contracts tend to be used in the context of 'partnership' as described previously and examples would be in the transport infrastructure and construction environments where public private partnerships (PPPs) are common.

Within these broad types of contract there is then a wide range of contract types or contractual clauses, reflecting different aspects and terms of the agreement. These are outside the scope of this textbook, but some of those which are financial, legal, or performance related are illustrated in Table 5.1.

Supplier evaluation

As well as the legal contract referred to previously, suppliers and their customers may also have a service level agreement. A service level agreement is used to supplement the contract and in effect to 'operationalize' it. It aims to explain in practice how the terms of the contract will be met. The agreement will be linked to the various order winners the supplier has and on which it seeks to win customers. This was discussed first in Chapter 2 (see page 33). So the way in which suppliers are evaluated will reflect the wide range of criteria for selecting suppliers in the first place, as well as their performance in delivering these.

In supply chain management, suppliers often compete on cost. More specifically this may be on criteria such as:

- Selling price—the price at which a product or service is supplied will vary according to the sensitivity of the buyer towards price and the nature of the procurement item.
- Value added—this refers to the activities carried out by an organization that increases the worth of a product or service and for which the customer is willing to pay. As we shall see later in this chapter, suppliers can do far more than simply deliver goods and services. For instance, they may manage inventory on behalf of their customers.

Often suppliers are also evaluated on their dependability, which includes features such as:

- Schedule adherence—this refers to the ability of the supplier to meet customers' scheduled requirements.
- Delivery performance—this refers to the ability of the supplier to meet a required standard for delivering the product or service. This is usually based on on-time delivery and complete quantity.
- Ability to keep promises—this refers to the ability of the supplier to supply its products or services when it says it will.

Buyers may also require their suppliers to be flexible. In these cases they may evaluate suppliers on the basis of:

- Deliverability—this refers to the supplier's ability to react to changes in delivery times requested by customers.
- Volume—this refers to the ability of the supplier to increase or decrease output to meet demand.
- Mix—this refers to the ability of the supplier to provide a wide range of products or services.
- Product or service modification—this refers to the ability of the supplier to be adaptable and modify its existing products or services.
- New product development—this refers to the ability of the supplier to introduce new products or services into the market, either on their own or in collaboration with their buyer.

Suppliers will inevitably have to also meet some quality characteristics so they may be evaluated on:

- Performance—this refers to the ability of the supplier to provide products which meet an agreed specification during use and which continue to do so over an appropriate time.
- Aesthetics—this refers to the look, feel, touch, or aroma of the product.
- Perceived quality—this refers to the notion of 'value' put on the product by the buyer.

Finally, suppliers may meet buyers' needs through their speed. This includes:

- Response speed—this refers to the time the supplier needs to respond to a RFI, RFP, invitation to tender, or RFQ (discussed earlier in this chapter).
- Delivery speed—this refers to the time taken for the supplier to deliver the product or service to the customer once an order has been received.

- Delivery frequency—this refers to the number of deliveries per day, week, month, etc. that the supplier is willing and able to make.

- Production speed—this refers to the overall time taken internally by the supplier to produce its product or service and be ready for delivery.

- New product development speed—this refers to the time taken for the supplier to introduce new products to the market from initial concept to final prototype.

Purchasing policy and procedures

One of the factors that influence the choice of supplier and the nature of the relationship is the type of items that are being purchased. It also has a significant impact on how purchases are made and delivered.

Purchase items

There are basically six kinds of item purchased:

- Raw materials are normally purchased in large volumes and include items such as timber, metals, and unrefined materials. They invariably require storing before being further processed by the buying organization.

- Components come in two types—standard and special. Standard components are also called commodities. Purchasing is relatively simple, and contracts are often long term. The purchase itself can be directly linked to the manufacturer's own control systems, such as enterprise resource planning (ERP) systems (see Chapter 6) or to a retailer's point-of-sale data. Special components have to be sourced more carefully since specifications need to be drawn up and the customer needs to be assured that the supplier can meet these.

- Consumables refer to items that are needed for the organization to operate but are not central to its production capability. Examples of such items are cleaning materials or office supplies. Another category of consumables is spare parts. These, too, are only used when needed, but their significance to the organization is much greater as without them production may be delayed.

- Plant and equipment are items that are relatively infrequently ordered. Unlike the first three types of item, plant and equipment are used to undertake the production process, rather than flow through it. As such, plant and equipment may vary widely in terms of cost and sophistication, depending largely on the type of technology being utilized by the organization. For instance, transportation and delivery businesses need a fleet of vehicles; oil refining requires heavy drilling equipment; farmers need tractors and an assortment of interchangeable special purpose attachments; and food manufacturers require large-scale food processing equipment. In some cases such equipment may be specially built to order, or it may be ordered from suppliers' stock.

- Services. Traditionally supply chain management has tended to be applied solely to materials processing operations and specifically to the materials procurement activities. However, an increasing number of organizations are outsourcing other activities and functions to suppliers. Indeed it is even possible to outsource many of the stages in the supply chain process. It therefore follows that many of the concepts of supply chain management—the relative strategic importance of items, building supplier relationships, selecting and evaluating suppliers, and the purchasing function—apply just as much to customer processing operations as they do to materials processing ones.

- Labour is not normally thought of as a 'purchase item' because most thinking about supply chain management has been applied to materials processing operations. But labour is a key element for operating customer processing operations, and even organizations that process materials are dependent on their workforce. In fact, there are many ways in which organizations 'procure' workers which resemble supply chain practices. Most notable is the way in which recruitment companies enter into long-term contractual arrangements to provide agency staff to organizations. Likewise some organizations recruit trainees from specific sources, such as colleges and universities, so they in turn are given 'preferred supplier' status. Similarly the contracts that employees have can include many of the types of clause outlined in Table 5.1—such as incentives, minimum hours worked, and revenue sharing.

However, there are two arguments that might be put forward to dispute this suggestion—that employees are a procurement item. Firstly, treating employees like goods that can be bought and sold dehumanizes the workforce. This might be so, although as the second point illustrates, it is for precisely the opposite reason that it is proposed. Secondly, it is inappropriate to discuss selecting and hiring employees in an operations management textbook, because this is a human resource issue. But in a way that is precisely the point. If operations managers spent as much time and care 'procuring' employees as they do procuring goods and services, then the whole organization might benefit. Leaving it solely to the human resource function in an organization to do only increases the possibility that amongst the large percentage of employees who work in operations, many might not really be suitable in their role. This is discussed more fully in Chapter 11.

For all of the described types of purchased items, the significance of the item to the customer and its relative availability on the marketplace tend to influence the nature of the relationship with the supplier. This is shown in Figure 5.4.

- Raw materials are typically leverage items—that is to say they have great importance to the buyer but are relatively easily acquired through the marketplace. Their purchase and supply will need to be coordinated using an order model based on the quantity ordered and time to deliver. We will discuss different types of ordering pattern in Chapter 6 when we talk more specifically about materials and inventory management.

- Special components are also of high importance, but they have to be specially procured from suppliers, so they are strategic items. Hence there needs to be a longer-term arrangement between buyer and supplier to ensure these are available.

- Standard components have relatively low significance for the buyer, but are not readily available in the market, so they are bottleneck items that require secure delivery.

- Finally, consumables are non-critical items which require efficient purchasing routines as they are readily available from many different suppliers but are not of great significance to the buyer. The exception to this is spare parts. Although these are often thought of as consumables, they are bottleneck items and delivery needs to be secured, as without them production may be halted.

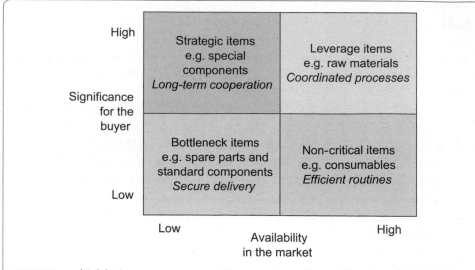

FIGURE 5.4 Link between procurement items and supplier relationship. Adapted from Kraljic (1983).

The purchase process

There are a number of potential stages in the purchase process. Depending on the nature of the product being supplied, not all of these may be necessary. Non-critical items can simply be ordered and received, without any intervening steps, whereas strategic items probably need to include all of the following seven stages:

- Purchase order—the documentation that specifies the items required and their volume.

- Order confirmation—an acknowledgement of the order from the suppliers confirming the items are available and will be delivered on time (if specified).

- Delivery monitoring—the buyer may choose to monitor or track where in the supply chain the items have got to. This can be done these days using radio frequency identification (RFID) technology.

- Delivery notification—confirmation from the supplier as to when the goods will be delivered.

- Delivery reception—the process that buyers go through upon receipt of the goods. Depending on the nature of the items, these may be meticulously inspected (also called goods-in inspection) to ensure they conform to specification, or simply signed off.

- Returns—these are items not accepted by the buyer and returned immediately upon delivery.

- Payment—systems will be put in place depending on the nature of the supplier–buyer relationship on the terms of payment, e.g. number of days' credit, penalties for late payment, etc.

The documentation that supports purchasing will also vary according to the mode of delivery used (see later in this chapter).

Supply chain integration

In addition to the supply chain relationships described previously (conventional, associated, and partnership) some supply chains become vertically integrated. When organizations decide to own a greater part of the supply network, it is known as **vertical integration**. We mentioned this earlier in this chapter in the Case insight about Thorntons where distribution has been vertically integrated. There are clear advantages to taking a greater financial control over suppliers and/or distributors, because by doing so a firm will have much greater management control of the entire supply network. This will help to ensure products are delivered on time and that quality controls are consistent and appropriate throughout the network. However, due to factors such as the relative size of the participating companies, location, or market segmentation it may not always be a wise decision to vertically integrate either upstream, i.e. towards the supply end of the network, or downstream towards the customer end of the supply network.

There are a number of alternatives:

- Acquisition or merger. This refers to the complete takeover of either suppliers or distributors. An example where this has happened is in the UK brewing industry. Brewing companies acquired upstream suppliers, such as the farms which grew hops, and downstream distributors, namely the pubs that sold their beer.

- Joint venture. In many cases firms are constrained from merging and hence set up a joint venture, especially in new and emerging markets such as China. A joint venture is a collaborative agreement between two (or more) organizations to manage a business activity.

- Strategic alliances. A strategic partnership or strategic alliance could be entered into to try and cement a relationship over the medium to long term. In this way firms can obtain the expertise of the partner in a joint ownership deal which has benefits for both parties, delivering a more efficient process for the original firm and additional business for the partner. An example of this type of arrangement is given later in this chapter in Operations insight 5.3 which discusses Halfords and Unipart Logistics working together. A potential disadvantage of these arrangements can be the fact that each company must be able to work openly and therefore a level of trust is required, which some firms may find difficult, particularly when it involves sharing confidential financial or market data.

- Virtual integration. The increasing use of the Internet and e-business in general has led to collaborations online in a process which has become known as virtual integration. Barriers between suppliers and distributors are less rigid and this has become a very popular way of working when suppliers, distributors, and customers are located far away from each other. Extensive use is made of telecommunications and data transfer technology, such as electronic data interchange (EDI). It is possible for these companies to collaborate at a lower cost than would be possible with a physical partnership or an alliance.

> **Vertical integration** the extent to which a company owns the upstream supply side organizations, the downstream distribution organizations, or both, in its supply network

The supply chain operations reference (SCOR®) model

One way that helps to integrate the processes used by collaborating companies within a supply network is to adopt a framework of agreed practice. One such framework

Supply chain operations reference (SCOR®) model a framework that sets clear guidelines on the management of the key processes in the supply chain (plan, source, make, deliver, and return)

developed and introduced by the Supply Chain Council is the **supply chain operations reference model**, known as the SCOR® Model (www.supply-chain.org). This focuses on five key processes which are repeated throughout the network by all participating companies:

1. Plan. This concerns the development of a supply chain strategy which aligns requirements with the resources available. This involves ensuring that the plan is communicated to all parties in the network and is supported by a business plan and a financial plan.

2. Source. This concerns meeting demand with effective procurement of goods and services by selecting suppliers, scheduling deliveries, and managing inventories.

3. Make. This concerns producing what is required by effective production scheduling, manufacturing, testing, and packaging.

4. Deliver. This concerns managing and fulfilling orders and transporting goods to the customer and providing an invoice.

5. Return. This concerns managing customer returns and the related processes required to support them, including transportation, verification, repairs, disposal, or replacement, and crediting the customer when necessary.

Each separate company adopting these practices ensures that each link in the network is equally strong.

Logistics

The physical activities involved in the procurement, movement, storage, and accounting for raw materials, partially processed goods, and finished goods have developed into an industry in their own right. Finished goods need to be distributed either directly to customers or via wholesalers or retail outlets. In addition, goods which are returned by unhappy customers need to be handled in a similar way, but in reverse.

Logistics the physical activities involved in the procurement, movement, storage, and accounting for raw materials and partially processed and finished goods

The term **logistics** has been used since the early 1900s in military operations. The correct supply of men, machinery, and ordnance is seen as key to successful military campaigns. The term was introduced in a business context in the 1950s and is today universally acknowledged as a key business operations process. Efficient logistics operations have become a very important part of the business supply chain due to customers demanding more flexibility in the availability and delivery of goods and services.

The Council for Logistics Management (CLM, 2003) states that 'Logistics management is that part of supply chain management that plans, implements and controls the efficient, effective forward and reverse flow and storage of goods, services, and related information between the point of origin and the point of consumption in order to meet customer requirements.'

Logistics involves a number of key material flows which must be controlled by the operations manager in addition to a corresponding number of information flows necessary to keep customers' deliveries being completed on time and for the necessary payment systems to account for all of the activities. These are shown in Figure 5.5. It is clear that there are material and information flows both upstream, towards the supply end of the chain, and downstream, towards the customer end of the chain. As we saw earlier in the automotive supply network example, here the operation is acting as both supplier and customer in the supply relationship.

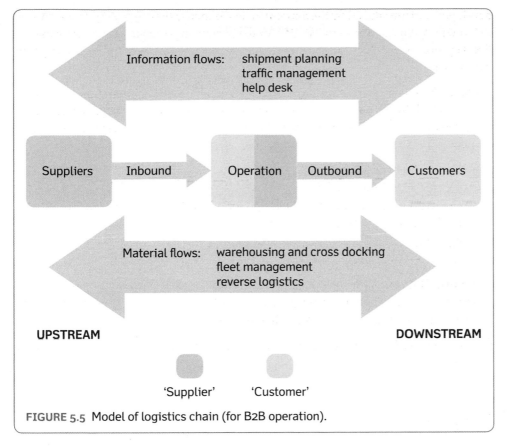

FIGURE 5.5 Model of logistics chain (for B2B operation).

Go online

The key issues in the material flow to consider are:

- How and where goods are stored—stock rooms, warehousing, and logistics centres
- What mode of transport is used—fleet management
- How goods are physically moved from large to small shipments closer to the delivery point—cross docking.

The key issues in the information flow to consider are:

- Shipment planning
- Traffic management
- Payment systems.

Each of these will be discussed separately.

Stock rooms, warehousing, and logistics centres

Most supply networks will have storage facilities on the premises of all parties in the network. These may be separate buildings with rows of racking to house the materials on, or areas within the manufacturing space, either racked or pallet stacked. Modern warehouse facilities now have very high bay racking with narrow aisles that are operated by automated pick and place robots. These then transfer products to unmanned automated guided vehicles (AGVs), which run on tracks throughout the premises to deliver the materials to the next process operation. When an item is needed it is removed

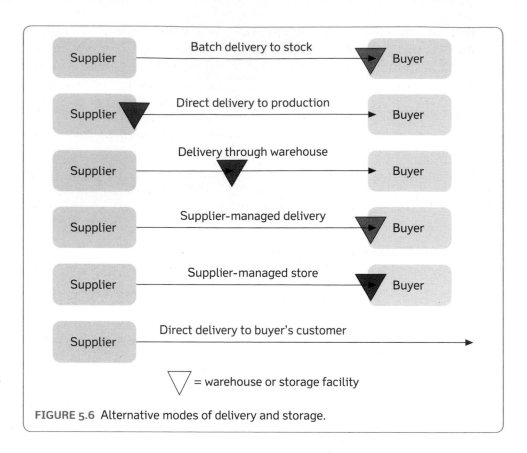

Go online

FIGURE 5.6 Alternative modes of delivery and storage.

from its storage location, tagged with an identifier, and leaves the warehouse for its destination.

However, the precise location of a large-scale warehouse facility, and who manages it, will vary according to the process type of the buyer (i.e. whether it is a job shop, batch process, or mass production). The alternative approaches to storing and delivering materials are illustrated in Figure 5.6. This reinforces the notion that the supply 'chain' is really a network, as an operation may have more than one approach to how items are delivered and stored, although one approach is likely to predominate. The alternatives are as follows:

- Batch delivery to stock. This is the simplest form of delivery pattern. The supplier fulfils an order from the buyer for a specified range and level of stock. The goods are delivered to the buyer's stores or warehouse. Examples of this may be any retail operation such as high street clothing or books.

- Direct delivery to production. This is a key element of so-called just-in-time (JIT) operations (discussed in more detail in Chapter 6). Goods are delivered directly to the production point where they are needed without ever going into storage. The buyer has to develop ways to check these goods in to the premises, often carry out an inward inspection process (either visual or some kind of testing), then arrange for them to be racked or stored and their location recorded. Any future usage or movement of these raw materials then needs to be monitored and recorded so that replenishment orders can be generated to ensure that there is no shortage of supply. This needs to be carefully coordinated with forward sales projections to take account of fluctuations in demand. This is used extensively in automotive assembly operations.

- Delivery through warehouse or logistics centre. In this mode of delivery, a logistics centre is placed between the supplier and the buyer. This may be due to the fact that the supplied goods may come from a number of different sources or locations and hence need to be consolidated, or because the buyer has a number of different operations to which the goods must be used in different forms. Such a logistics centre may also assemble materials supplied into 'kits' so that they are in a form more easily used by the buyer. Most supermarkets use this approach to supply their various-sized outlets with products.

- Supplier-managed delivery to store. This is similar to batch delivery to stock, but instead of the buyer ordering the materials, the supplier determines the range and level of materials to supply. This may mean that the stock is paid for when delivered, or only when it is taken out of stock.

- Supplier-managed store facility. In this approach, the supplier not only determines the amount of material to supply, it also manages and operates the stores facility on the buyer's premises. This is also often referred to as vendor-managed inventory. It is commonly used for lower-value products such as standard electrical components.

- Direct delivery from supplier to buyer's customer. Finally, there may be no store or warehouse at all. Materials go directly from the supplier to the buyer's customers. This would be the case for some fresh produce such as flowers or fresh fruit and vegetables.

In all these cases the introduction of technological improvements has enabled buyers and suppliers to have real-time data on the location of goods in transit. Bar coding, as is now used in most supermarkets, or RFID tags are often used to track material movement both within and beyond these delivery patterns.

In Figure 5.6 the colour-coded triangles represent where the control is. In the case of batch delivered to stock and supplier-managed delivery the green triangle at the buyer's premises identifies the buyer having control. In the direct delivery to production and supplier-managed store (vendor-managed inventory), the blue triangles denote that each is controlled by the supplier, albeit in different locations. Where the supplier uses a warehouse, once again a blue triangle denotes that although the goods are no longer on their premises they are still in control.

We will discuss more about inventory management in Chapter 6.

Fleet management

In order to get materials from suppliers to holding warehouses or directly to process plants the efficient usage of road, rail, or sea transport is required. Rail and sea transport are run by specialist operators, but some organizations will run their own fleet of supply or distribution vehicles and will have to manage the purchasing, maintenance, coordination of supply, and effective operation of these vehicles themselves. For many companies, however, the time and cost involved in this may be prohibitive and they are increasingly looking for specialist companies to take on this responsibility for them. These so-called logistics supply companies (LSCs) take on one or more of these parts of the operation to allow the materials processing company to concentrate on its core activities. One such company in the UK is Eddie Stobart which has an almost fanatical following by devotees of the iconic green lorries which transport goods up and down the motorways of Great Britain and Europe.

Eddie Stobart's green lorries have become iconic. With thanks to Stobart Group, www. stobartgroup.com

Cross-docking

When goods flow in an unbroken sequence from receiving to dispatching, thus eliminating storage time and space, the technique is known as cross-docking. Also called flow-through distribution in some industries, it enables organizations to consolidate and move large quantities of goods via a distribution centre into smaller vehicles loaded with the correct sequencing of orders for onward delivery to businesses further down the chain. This technique is often associated with lean operations and JIT processes, each of which will be discussed in later chapters. Transportation costs and storage costs are reduced by this technique which is used by many retail companies to supply individual stores with goods based on sales demand. Many distribution centres have online links with individual stores to capture electronic point-of-sale (EPOS) data and thereby create shipment plans for each store automatically.

Shipment planning

In order for any operation to be managed effectively it must first be properly planned. Shipments of received raw materials or partially processed goods will be organized either by a 'milk round' pick-up by the materials processor, i.e. they will be picked up by their own vehicles in a route that minimizes waste, or they will be collected via third-party logistics companies who use any available space in their delivery vehicles to service other businesses.

Coordinating this is often now done via computer programme so that each member of the chain is kept up to date with real-time information. This process then continues 'downstream' to ensure that goods are received by the customer on time.

Increasingly due to the distances materials have to travel between suppliers and customers the use of intermodal transport has become essential in keeping costs down. Goods may be consolidated into large shipping containers which can be loaded onto a container ship by crane and then unloaded and put directly onto a lorry or train for onward delivery without disturbing the cargo. In this way it has become possible for a vast array of goods from worldwide locations to be consolidated with other products and sent to customers throughout the world at prices comparable to or even lower than those available locally.

OPERATIONS INSIGHT 5.2
The Box—the BBC's own shipping container

A project to see how containers are used intermodally throughout the global supply chain was started by the BBC in September 2008. It followed a standard 40-foot container as it journeyed around the world with various cargoes using ship, train, and lorry in its travels. As it travelled and stopped in docks throughout the world images were sent back to show how these containers and their associated cargoes are handled. The project found some surprising facts.

The journey lasted 421 days and The Box travelled a total of 51,654 miles of which 47,076 were by ship, 3229 by train and 1349 by road. Amongst its most interesting cargoes were 15,120 bottles of whisky, 4250 bathroom scales and 95,940 tins of cat food!

The Box was able to mirror the global downturn very well as it stood idle at Yokohama docks for four months between April 2009 and July 2009. Statistics gathered by the BBC have estimated that the global container business made a profit of £3 billion in 2008, but made a £20 billion loss in 2009.

Source: compiled from BBC News, Special Report 'The Box', January 2010

Questions

1. What are the advantages and disadvantages of containerized transportation?
2. What ethical issues arise from insights into how containers are used and transported?

Traffic management

Once it has been agreed which method of transport is to be used to collect or deliver goods then it is important for the route to be determined and for accurate time schedules to be produced. This ensures that all parties in the chain are aware of collection and delivery times. Increasing use is now made of satellite navigation systems and real-time computer systems to provide these.

Payment systems

A very important information flow is the payment for goods and services once delivered. These can be vital to ensure a smooth cash flow, especially for small and medium-sized enterprises (SMEs), who often find themselves squeezed by larger suppliers for quick payment, yet cannot get the same terms from their customers. It is not unusual for payments to be requested from large suppliers within 30 days, whereas some large customers do not pay for up to 120 days.

OPERATIONS INSIGHT 5.3
Teesport—port-centric supply chain solutions

In recent years there has been a decline in manufacturing in the UK and a growth in overseas or outsourced production. This means that firms have reorganized their supply chains in order to accommodate the import of goods manufactured elsewhere and imported into the UK. This new supply chain is termed 'port-centric logistics'. Under this model, it is argued that cargo handling, subassembly, storage, and distribution-related activities are best carried out at the port of entry, rather than at inland distribution centres. This may also have benefits relating to deferred duty and VAT (value added tax) payments.

One such provider of port-centric facilities is Teesport, operated by PD Ports. Located on Teesside in northeast England, a major deep-water complex, Teesport combines the ports of Tees and Hartlepool, so that it can take full advantage of the port-centric trend. In 2007, PD Ports invested £300 million on infrastructure, services and equipment, such as nine wide-reach stackers, four Gottwald harbour cranes, a KSR gantry container crane, and numerous terminal tractors and forklifts. This led to the decision by the major retailer ASDA to choose Teesport as the location for its 500,000-square-foot non-food import centre. Renault also chose to operate an import processing and preparation centre there for the pre-delivery inspection (PDI) of vehicles it was importing into the UK. General Motors developed five hectares of storage for vehicles imported from its European distribution centre in Zeebrugge.

Teesport has overcome the historical disadvantages of being located in the northeast of England for a number of reasons. Traffic on the motorway network, and especially around London, is increasingly congested, leading to delayed deliveries. The existing container ports of Felixstowe and Southampton were also operating at near full capacity. Movement of goods by rail in the southeast is restricted by the number of passenger trains needed to transport commuters to and from London. Research showed that Teesport could provide collections and deliveries to all the major centres of population in the UK (except London, Cardiff, and Bristol) in a single one-way driving shift of 4.5 hours.

As well as providing effective transport links, Teesport also offered other advantages for developing 'port-centric' supply chain solutions. These included a plentiful supply of local labour, available development land of over 40 hectares, a well-connected road and rail infrastructure, no congestion at the port, and existing high-productivity container handling. In 2009 it handled over 100,000 containers for the first time, and in 2010 over 150,000. As a result Teesport was the fourth largest port (by volume) in the UK, employing over 1200 people in port services and logistics.

Sources: 'PD Ports, manufacturing gets the green light', The Manufacturer, October 2007; www.pdports.co.uk

Questions

1. How are port-centric logistics different from traditional logistics provision?
2. What do you think are Teesport's order winners?

Supplier relationship management

Efficient supplier relationship management is very important to customers and suppliers alike.

One study (Reid and Reigel 1988) investigated the basis on which American food service organizations selected their suppliers, but most of the features they identify are relevant to a wide range of industry sectors. Respondents were given a list of 20 supplier characteristics and asked to rate their importance. The six most important characteristics, across all types of organization, were:

- Accuracy of fulfilling orders
- Consistent quality level
- On-time delivery
- Willingness to work together to resolve problems
- Willingness to respond in a 'pinch', i.e. respond to emergency or last-minute requests
- Reasonable unit cost.

Institutional food service operators and the larger firms also were concerned about:

- Reasonable minimum orders
- Volume discounts
- Frequency of delivery
- Payment policies.

The least important characteristics tended to be tangential services provided by suppliers such as:

- Ability to source from a single supplier
- Training in product use
- Willingness to break a case, i.e. supply in smaller, non-standard quantities
- Provision of recipe ideas.

Good supplier relations take some time to establish. The survey asked operators how many new suppliers they had added in the past year. All of the organizations, and particularly government food service companies, reported an increase in the use of new suppliers. This is due to a wide range of factors, including the product range and geographical growth of the food service firms themselves. There was also growth in

RESEARCH INSIGHT 5.2

Shepherd, C. and Hannes, G. (2006) Measuring supply chain performance: current research and future directions, *International Journal of Productivity and Performance Management*, 55(3/4), 242–58

In this article, Shepherd and Hannes provide a full and comprehensive list of all the ways in which supply chain performance might be measured. They also discuss the challenges that face practitioners and researchers alike when trying to measure some of these things.

international suppliers, particularly among larger firms and hotel and retail food service organizations. Only the largest food service firms—about 10% of the sample—actually visited more than three-quarters of their suppliers. This practice may not be necessary on an annual basis if firms have long-established relationships with their suppliers.

Trends in supply chain management—third-party logistics, fourth-party logistics, disintermediation, e-procurement

The supply chain is an area of operations management that is hugely dynamic and which has seen a lot of changes over recent years. Some of the trends are as follows.

- Third-party logistics (3PL)—companies that are specialist providers of warehousing, transportation, financial services, and/or distribution services provide their services to organizations as an outsourced resource as part of the overall supply chain.

- Fourth-party logistics (4PL)—companies have now developed levels of expertise such that they can offer organizations a complete package of services to manage their 3PLs. Originally used and trademarked by Accenture, these companies offer a service to organizations which have outsourced their logistics arrangements to two or more third-party logistics companies, by coordinating the whole operation for them. For example one 3PL company might deal with warehousing and transport, whilst another deals with finance and human resources.

- Seventh-party logistics (7PL)—this is a recent innovation whereby one company does the whole job of all of the outsourced logistics companies (i.e. 3PL + 4PL = 7PL).

- **Reverse logistics**—the introduction of returns policies for many products, which also helps to reduce the amount of landfill waste disposal and increase recycling opportunities, has led to the notion of 'reverse logistics'.

- **Disintermediation**—'cutting out the middleman'. Many operations have benefited by removing unwanted stages in their supply chains, thereby reducing overall costs to both themselves and their customers. Airlines, travel agencies, hotels, and many other customer processing operations now operate a direct online service to customers.

- E-procurement—the use of the Internet has allowed goods to be supplied directly to consumers via a distribution warehouse. The customer does not have to physically see any part of the operation. An example of this is Amazon.com who have operated successfully online for a number of years and have increased their product lines from books and DVDs to include many electrical and domestic goods.

- Category mergers—in the fast-moving consumer goods market categories are being merged to try and retain efficiency while reducing information flows and documentation. For example, household and laundry products (such as cleaning products and detergents) are being merged with ambient foods, so that customers (the retailers) can place orders for products from across these product ranges. This allows smaller quantities of each category to be ordered, to keep inventories low, but allows full vehicle deliveries for maximum efficiency.

Reverse logistics the complete supply chain dedicated to the reverse flow of goods for return, repair, or recycling

Disintermediation dealing directly between supplier and customers rather than through intermediaries

OPERATIONS INSIGHT 5.4
Halfords and Unipart—a logistics partnership

Introducing total flexibility into supply chain operations without increasing the logistics overhead has been achieved for Halfords, the UK's leading auto, leisure, and cycling products retailer, with an innovative mix of outsourced logistics and its own operations. However, it has taken two logistics partnerships to make this happen.

In 2002, Halfords realized that its existing two distribution centres could not handle an increasing throughput of products. It decided to enter into a partnership with Unipart Logistics in order to tap into Unipart's resources of flexible warehouse space and a highly effective workforce. As a result of this collaboration between 2005 and 2006 a number of improvements were made to performance, including a 13% increase in lines per man hour, 6.2% reduction in cost per item, and a further 59% reduction in picking errors. Unipart believes that much of this improvement was as a result of its approach to continuous improvement and lean thinking, which it calls the 'Unipart Way'. This is made up of a set of tools and techniques which are used on a daily basis at all levels within the organization in order to improve operational performance. So every member of Unipart staff involved on the Halfords contract would routinely participate in creative problem solving and improvement circles.

Originally, Unipart's logistics centre near Oxford supplied the Halfords distribution centres, but as time went on it became a front-line operation delivering direct to over 400 Halfords stores. As a result it grew from a base operation of 77,000 square feet up to 220,000 square feet. in size. Each distribution centre handled separate types of products. The Unipart logistics centre managed the flow of small parts and general products, ranging from fast-moving products such as mobile phone accessories through to car child seats and roof boxes.

Seasonality can affect the product range; large and bulky roof boxes are mainly a summer item, while winter goods include de-icer, where demand can be unpredictable; and the business needed to be able to respond. The logistics centre was set up with a variety of storage types including block stacking (i.e. storing of pallets one on top of the other in rows or lanes), pallet racking (storing pallets on racks), a secure store for hazardous products such as paints, and a dynamic area which combines storage with conveyors to allow for small-parts picking (i.e. making up an order from many small items). Products were picked throughout the day from individual areas in the warehouse and marshalled at goods out, mainly in roll cages or on pallets, with loading of up to 50 vehicles per day destined for Halfords stores. Joint teams were set up for installation, training, and change management. The new system went in very successfully and was a joint project success with Halfords staff regarding Unipart Logistics staff

Halfords is the UK's leading auto, leisure, and cycling products retailer.

as colleagues working in their supply network, handling their products. The collaboration allowed Halfords to grow the business and add new product ranges.

However, such is the nature of the retail business that five years on this operation and partnership have been superseded by a new collaboration, this time with Manhattan Associates. Halfords needed a new supply chain solution that would reliably support its business as it grew and as it expanded into new areas. The collaboration was not always successful as the sources listed clearly show; however, the result now is a new distribution centre in Coventry which has enabled Halfords to improve availability, cut down lead times, handle peaks in demand, and improve overall supply chain performance in line with its customers' expectations.

Sources: 'Flexible logistics supports business growth', www.supplychainstandard.com; 'Manhattan Associates and Halfords warehouse management case study', www.youtube.com; 'Halfords deliveries grind to a halt', www.thisismoney.co.uk; www.manh.com/

Questions

1. What are the techniques that Halfords has used to enable it to provide a flexible amount of storage capacity and improve its supply lead times by these collaborations?

2. What do you think was the main benefit to Unipart Logistics from the original partnership arrangement as opposed to managing the whole operation for Halfords?

Conclusions

In order to run a successful operation it is necessary to develop links with suppliers, distributors, and customers. These can be very simple and work effectively on a handshake between two small organizations, such as a local greengrocer and a market gardener, or be extremely complex and involve a network of supply and distribution companies under licensed contract to each other to perform at a certain level over the medium to long term, such as would be the case for many suppliers of large supermarkets.

Supply chain management (SCM) is a process and as such it needs to be managed like any other operations management process. The only difference is the degree of complexity which may involve many different organizations in the network and the degree to which the supply network is controlled by any of the participating companies. There are a number of different collaborative arrangements possible between suppliers and customers, namely:

- B2B simple relationship
- Supplier partnerships or alliances
- Virtual integration via computer systems, often over a wide geographical area
- Vertical integration by owning the upstream supply side organizations, the downstream distribution organizations, or both.

Each arrangement requires the skills of negotiation, procurement, and post-delivery evaluation. As supply networks become more complex the amount of technological support increases and this will be dealt with in Chapter 6 on inventory and materials management.

END OF CHAPTER CASE
Diversey UK—both upstream and downstream supply

Diversey is a global manufacturer and supplier of hygiene and cleaning products. It has a broad product range and wide customer base, in markets or sectors such as agriculture, brewing, commercial laundry, contract cleaning, government and education, health care, pharmaceuticals, and retail. For instance, in the agriculture sector the firm has a specific 'hygiene solution' for use in dairies—Deosan Total Hygiene Management—which includes different products to be used by employees working in dairies, for use on cows to ensure udder hygiene, for use on equipment to keep it clean, and for use in the bulk tankers that transport milk. As well as cleaning agents, the company also manufactures equipment that dispenses and applies these agents, and hence it provides its customers with 'cleaning and hygiene solutions and systems'.

Diversey's operation in the UK comprises two main sites—the Cotes Park manufacturing site, and the Amber Park distribution centre. Cotes Park was commissioned in 1996, and occupies a 16-acre site, three miles from J28 of the M1 in Derbyshire. The factory is operated to a high level of automation, with a distributed control system (DCS) managing batch production on a 24-hour-per-day basis. Products are packed into a wide variety of pack size and type from 1.5-litre pouches to bulk road tankers. The site produces approximately 85,000 tonnes of packed liquids and powders, making it the largest Diversey factory in Europe, and a strategic manufacturing base within the company's European supply chain network. Manufacturing is carried out mainly for the UK market, although some product is exported to mainland Europe and the Middle East.

Upstream from its production plant, the firm has over 200 different suppliers which provide it with both the raw materials from which it makes its products, as well as the packaging it needs in order to distribute them. These suppliers are located throughout Europe, with some materials such as iodide being shipped in from Asia. Incoming goods are of various types. Some liquids, such as inorganic chemicals and surfactants (the active ingredient in most cleaning products) are transported in bulk tankers. Approximately 15 tankers a day supply the Cotes Park site, offloading into bulk storage tanks outside the plant. Other liquids, such as dyes, are transported in intermediate bulk containers (IBCs) or 200-litre drums, and offloaded directly into the plant itself. Some raw materials are also transported in powder form (such as sodium carbonate), typically in vats or one-tonne bags. Non-liquid materials such as packaging materials and plastic bottles are transported in bulk on pallets. These pallets are organized so that once unwrapped or 'depalletized' they can be moved directly to the production line on a just-in-time basis.

Some products are used in large quantities. For instance, caustic soda is used in the manufacture of around two-thirds of cleaning products. Others such as iodine, dyes, and perfumes are used in much smaller quantities—either because they are only used in a small proportion of products, or because they are used in small quantities in the making of a product, or both. Commodity products like caustic soda can be bought relatively cheaply from a range of different suppliers, whereas more specialist ingredients, such as perfumes, can be much more expensive and are available from only one or two suppliers. Although Diversey strives to manage its inventory on a just-in-time basis, some hard-to-obtain raw materials, such as proprietary products, are ordered well in advance and held as on-site stock to ensure continuity of supply.

As a global market leader, Diversey is an innovative company—not only in terms of developing new cleaning products, but also the means by which these are applied. This means that some products are patent protected and hence have to be sourced carefully to assure patent compliance.

Most finished product is the result of a mixing process in large vats varying in batch sizes of 2000–16,000 litres. This can then either be left in bulk form, or packed into containers of various sizes and forms, including drums, pouches, and bottles. These products are transported the short distance from Cotes Park to the Amber Park distribution centre every hour, although some bulk product is transported directly in tankers to some corporate clients, notably in the brewing and food processing sectors. Amber Park was completed at the end of 1999 and occupies a 12.5-acre site also near to J28 of the M1. The building has a footprint of 1700 metres squared, with in excess of 18,000 pallet spaces holding over 700 chemical products. The warehouse processes over 280 chemical orders and 200 equipment spares orders per day. There are 16 loading docks plus two external doors for loading and unloading. It not only warehouses products manufactured on the Cotes Park site, but also products manufactured by the firm's plants in other part of Europe. Thus Goods Inwards receives 170 deliveries on average per week, which equates to 2700 pallets.

Both the factory and warehouse are ISO 9001 and 14001 certified, with sound quality, safety, and environmental processes and practices forming an essential part of the firm's operation. In this industry sector all firms have to comply with COMAH (control of major accident hazards) regulations. This means that finished products of different kinds have to be warehoused separately from each other, with specified areas for flammables and for oxidizers.

Diversey used to have its own transportation fleet for downstream distribution to its customer base. Since 2001, this has been outsourced to a logistics company, although the trucks continue to have a Diversey livery. Five years later, the management and administration of Amber Park were also outsourced to the same company. The main reasons that lay behind the outsourcing decision were twofold. First, the logistics company could provide the same level of service as the firm's own in-house fleet, but at a lower cost. This is because the logistics firm is able to take advantage of economies of scale to help keep its costs lower. Second, Diversey outsourced to gain access to the expertise of the logistics company, which it believed was superior to its own in-house expertise. Under this contract Diversey is responsible for taking all the customer orders and agreeing, when appropriate, a delivery schedule with clients, but the logistics company handles the implementation of all deliveries in terms of scheduling vehicles, deciding routes, and assuring safe, on-time delivery. A small number of Diversey planners are located on the Amber Park site, but their main role is to control and oversee inventory.

Downstream delivery is of two main kinds—direct and indirect. Direct delivery is roughly 40% of total goods supplied and it goes from the warehouse to the client. Such clients may have global accounts to supply cleaning materials, such as McDonald's and Hilton, whereas others may be national or regional customers with long-term contracts, such as in the agricultural sector. The other 60% of goods transported go to distributors or wholesalers who then sell products onto retail outlets, or specific client groups, such as the health care sector. Amber Park makes on average 200 loads per week, of which 20% are shipped in bulk tankers.

Source: authors' own research and www.johnsondiversey.com/Cultures/en-GB/default.htm

Questions

1. Identify procurement items that Diversey would regard as 'strategic', 'leverage', 'bottleneck', and 'non-critical'.

2. What mode of delivery and storage has Diversey adopted? Why?

3. Why are downstream logistics organized the way they are for this firm?

Chapter summary

To consolidate your learning, the key points from this chapter are summarized as follows:

- **What is a supply chain?**

  A supply chain is a sequence of business processes and information flows that link the provision of a product or service from its suppliers through its operations and distribution channels to the ultimate customer.

- **Define supply chain management**

  Supply chain management (SCM) can be defined as the planning, design, organization, and control of the flow of information and materials along the supply chain in order to meet customer requirements in an efficient manner.

- **Explain an organization's procurement function**

  Procurement is the function within an organization which relates to selecting, negotiating, purchasing, and managing the supply of essential materials and services necessary to produce a company's products.

- **Explain logistics management**

  Logistics management is that part of SCM that plans, implements and controls the efficient, effective forward and reverse flow and storage of goods, services, and related information between the point of origin and the point of consumption in order to meet customer requirements.

- **Identify and describe key trends in SCM**

  There are a number of key trends in SCM.

  - Outsourcing various components of the supply chain through third-party logistics (3PL) or fourth-party logistics (4PL) companies to allow businesses to concentrate on their core activities.
  - Disintermediation. Cutting out links in the supply network to improve delivery speed and quality of the process.
  - Reverse logistics to manage the return of goods to the manufacturer. Reverse logistics removes waste and creates a 'second customer' for a firm's previously unwanted outputs.
  - Vertical integration. The extent to which a company owns the upstream supply side organizations, the downstream distribution organizations, or both, in its supply network.
  - E-business. Increasing use of online procurement and electronic data interchange (EDI) between suppliers, distributors, and customers.
  - Sustainability issues arise with the distance travelled between suppliers and customers and whether they have a balanced carbon footprint.
  - Ethical issues within SCM and procurement are the ethical standards in the purchasing and tendering process and the degree of 'openness' with which companies or countries are prepared to operate in the global marketplace.

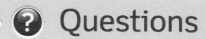
Review questions

1. What are the main components of a supply chain?

2. How many tiers of suppliers should a buyer build relationships with for strategic procurement items? Why?

3. What kind of services are outsourced—in terms of their procurement importance (refer to Figure 5.4)?

4. Which criteria influence an organization to single source?

5. Outline the number of stages in the purchase process for a raw material.

6. Which criteria influence an organization's approach to selecting a mode of delivery?

7. Compare and contrast the logistics operation of a job shop operation (such as a print works) with a mass service operation (such as a supermarket).

8. What is the SCOR® model? Explain how it can be used to improve supply chain efficiency.

9. Explain the impact that containerization has had on global logistics.

10. What are the similarities and major differences between vertical integration and virtual integration?

Discussion questions

1. What are the main differences between the supply chain of a materials processing operation, such as a furniture manufacturer, and those of a customer processing operation, such as a bank?

2. What kind of contractual relationship is a garage repairing cars going to have with its suppliers?

3. What criteria might be used for selecting or evaluating suppliers of components to a large white goods manufacturer?

4. Outline the logistics operation for a hospital.

5. What ethical issues might arise out of managing the supply chain?

Further learning guide

Supply chain management is probably the single most researched area of operations management. This area is now so large that there are a number of academic journals devoted to it, such as the *Journal of Supply Chain Management* and *International Journal of Physical Distribution & Logistics Management*. There are also a number of institutes and associations in this field, each of whom has its own website, such as the Institute for Supply Management (ISM) and Council of Supply Chain Management Professionals (CSCMP). Another source of information, especially with regard to case studies of supply chain management practice, are the major logistics companies such as DHL, Kuehne + Nagel, and Damco. There are also informational websites such as **www.logisticsworld.com**. For more information about the BBC project in Operations insight 5.2, and about containerized shipping in general visit **http://news.bbc.co.uk/1/hi/business/8314116.stm** where there are a number of short video clips which explain intermodal transport very well.

References

Jonsson, P. (2008) *Logistics and Supply Chain Management*, McGraw Hill: London

Kraljic, P. (1983) Purchasing must become supply management, *Harvard Business Review*, September/October, 109–17

Reid, R. and Reigel, C. (1988) Foodservice purchasing: corporate practices, *Cornell HRA Quarterly*, 29(1), 25–9

The Council for Logistics Management (2006) *Physical Distribution & Logistics Management*, CLM: London

Chapter Six

Managing materials and inventory performance

Learning outcomes

After reading this chapter you will be able to:

→ Define inventory management and discuss different types of inventory

→ Identify and discuss different inventory ordering models

→ Understand the nature of demand fluctuation and the bullwhip effect

→ Describe and explain different approaches to production planning and control

→ Identify and explain trends in inventory management

Daval Furniture is based in Huddersfield in the UK and is a leading mid-market manufacturer of household furniture. It originally manufactured bedroom products, but has developed both bespoke bathroom and kitchen installations. Kitchens now represent 25% of turnover. In 2010 it supplied a network of 140 independent retailers throughout the UK. Despite the banking crisis and economic downturn in 2009, Daval grew by 7% in an industry sector that typically suffers badly in such market conditions. It believes that one of the key factors in this growth has been its unique production technology, based on enterprise resource planning (ERP), which it calls Option-i.

The furniture industry is extremely competitive and facing significant cost pressures from manufacturers in the Far East. Many UK companies now outsource to these lower-cost economies. Daval was reluctant to follow this course of action, because it wished to preserve its in-house design capabilities, ability to innovate, and ultimately to protect its market share. It recognized that it had to turn from being a batch producer to a more flexible, agile, and lean manufacturer by reducing as much waste in the process as possible. (The methods used in agile and lean manufacturing programmes are discussed further in Chapter 15.) Daval brought in consultants and an ERP systems vendor to develop its new lean approach. It is now able to produce furniture with just a three-week lead time, outperforming all of its competitors in terms of speed of delivery.

Daval designs its own products, whether for bedroom, bathroom, or kitchen, so that they share a carcass (the basic framework), materials, and fittings. This keeps costs down, but enables customers to select from alternative finishes and price points. A key feature of the ERP system is that it links production to the point of sale in Daval's retail outlets. This enables the manufacturing cells in its factory to work more efficiently. This ensures very low levels of inventory, without the threat of stock-outs or late delivery. Just-in-time inventory also means that the firm can follow the latest design trends, colours, and innovations and incorporate them into production both quickly and efficiently. Whereas most manufacturers introduce a new product range every year, Daval is able to do so every six months. Option-i also ensures there is little or no slow-moving or redundant stock. The next step for Option-i is to develop a web-based online ordering system, so that customers can order their semi-bespoke furniture directly from Daval. This will not only allow them to place their order, but also to track it through manufacture so that they have a clearly identified delivery date.

As well as introducing the ERP system, Daval focused on managing this change and in particular the effect on its workforce. It introduced new and more frequent ways of communicating with staff, and used these to explain the importance and nature of lean manufacturing. It also worked with a number of external agencies to drive this initiative forward. It conducted a lean auditing programme with the Manufacturing Advisory Service (MAS). It also selected 12 high-performing shopfloor workers to take NVQs (National Vocational Qualifications) in lean manufacturing, who qualified for government funding. Another features of Daval's operational model is its commitment to sustaining supplier partnerships. It has deliberately sought to retain the same suppliers for many years, as it believes this enables it to collaborate in new product and process development that is beneficial to both parties.

Sources: www.daval-furniture.co.uk; 'Part of the Furniture', The Manufacturer, April 2010

Questions

1. Why is managing inventory in a furniture manufacturing operation difficult to achieve?

2. How have the changes introduced by Daval helped it to remain competitive?

Introduction

Inventory any quantifiable item that is stored and used in an operation to satisfy a customer demand

Inventory management the planning and controlling of inventory in order to meet the competitive priorities of the operation

In this chapter we build on the concepts and ideas from Chapter 5 on supply chain management to see how materials are stored and controlled within an organization. We begin by considering the nature of **inventory** and the different types of inventory model needed to manage material flow efficiently. This continues to a discussion on supply chain fluctuation and the impact this has on the inventory held by companies at various points in the chain. We then discuss materials management and production planning and control and see how (predominantly) materials processing operations use computerized methods to plan, schedule, and execute their orders, including materials requirements planning (MRP), manufacturing resource planning (MRPII), theory of constraints (TOC), and enterprise resource planning (ERP). We conclude by considering important key performance indicators in this area, along with trends in **inventory management**.

What is inventory?

Inventory is any quantifiable item that is stored and used in an operation to satisfy a customer demand. Hence it is anything that may be used in the process of transforming inputs into outputs. It can refer to both materials processing and customer processing operations. When customers are the inventory stored, we see this as a queue for a particular operation. We will deal with this aspect more fully in Chapter 8.

Very few materials are purchased without a reason or purpose and therefore on receipt there will already be a place for them to be stored and an operations process waiting for them to be used in. In materials processing operations inventory can include raw materials used for manufacturing, semi-finished and finished goods, office and maintenance supplies, and even the fuel to power the vehicles and equipment used by an organization.

Inventory can be one of the most expensive assets owned by an organization, accounting for anything up to 50% of invested capital. Therefore effective inventory management can make a significant improvement to a company's profits. In order to help them control inventory most companies undertake a physical count of their inventory at least once a year and develop systems to record and account for movements in and out of storage areas between these times.

Types of inventory

There are seven main categories of inventory:

- Raw materials. These are the essential ingredients, components, and subassemblies that are needed to make a product. They can be ordered in large quantities to obtain a discount. However, because storage space is also costly, most organizations order these from suppliers in smaller batches, more frequently. Alternative approaches to delivery and storage are identified in Figure 5.6 (see page 128).

- Work in process (WIP) inventory. Also called semi-finished stock. Partially completed products will consist of a combination of raw materials, but as the name implies these are not yet completed. They will be accounted for differently from raw materials as some work (labour, energy, and equipment) has been used to produce them and they will be stored for later use.

- Finished goods inventory. Once completed, products will be booked into finished goods stock. These may then be held separately on racks within the factory or in a warehouse awaiting orders, or more usually consolidated with other orders and dispatched to the customer. They will attract the full amount of raw material, labour, and overhead cost.

- Cycle inventory. If products are produced in batches and more than one type of product is produced from an operation then in order to have sufficient of each type of product available for passing on to the next process or dispatching to the customer, there needs to be a build-up of inventory of each type of product in a 'cycle'. This is a particular feature of batch production and examples can include printing, specialist machining, or bakery products.

- Buffer inventory. Also called safety stock. Due to variation in demand for some products it is common for organizations to call in extra raw materials from some suppliers to enable any additional orders to be satisfied. Safety stocks are also built up if there is uncertainty in the supply chain. Certain materials may be more difficult to make or have specific quality requirements which are difficult to achieve, so it would make good business sense to keep an extra amount.

- Anticipation inventory. In certain industries large requirements for products at certain times of the year can be predicted. Therefore it is wise for operations to build stocks of these in anticipation of large orders. Christmas decorations, Easter eggs, fireworks, and certain seasonal foods are good examples.

- Pipeline inventory. Also known as inventory in transit. When goods have to travel either in their semi-finished or finished state between factories, warehouses, or retail outlets over large distances the inventory then is said to be in the pipeline, and unavailable for use on any other orders. This has become increasingly important as companies have grown to be multinational and operate key parts of their operation in different countries, so many of their inventory items may be in transit for several days or even weeks at a time.

Why keep inventory?

Most organizations keep some inventory because, as we shall see in Chapter 7 when we discuss capacity management, demand is not always predictable so there often needs to be some buffer or safety stock to cater for this variation in demand. Most people also run their household budget along the same lines, by buying food and other regular consumables not just for the current day, but planning ahead and often taking advantage of bulk volume purchase discounts. This is very much the same in business.

Having inventory can lead to competitive advantage and therefore impact positively on the five internal performance objectives we introduced in Chapter 2, namely:

- Cost—buying in bulk can give cost advantages.
- Quality—by always having excess material it is possible to sort it to obtain the best possible material for each operation.

- Flexibility—having raw material or finished goods in stock can help with short-term demands.
- Dependability—ensuing that there is a constant supply of raw materials to process or finished goods in stock will help to get customers' orders delivered on time.
- Speed—the process will flow more smoothly if materials are always available at each work station and therefore a faster throughput rate will result.

Inventories can account for a high proportion of a company's working capital and therefore a high value of inventory can reduce its profitability and return on assets. Many authors agree that too much inventory is a bad thing. Inventory is one of the seven wastes described by Taiichi Ohno (1978) in his book on the Toyota production system, which gave rise to a number of new manufacturing initiatives and philosophies, among them lean manufacturing, which we will discuss in more detail in Chapter 15. This suggests that cost savings can be made from controlling inventory levels.

In addition, there may be a number of logistical or other business reasons for not holding inventory, such as:

- Additional storage or administration costs could be incurred.
- Can become damaged if stored inappropriately or for too long.
- May become obsolete if technology or customers' tastes change.
- May be lost or difficult to recover from warehouse shelves.
- May be hazardous to store, such as flammable products, chemicals, or explosives which require special storage conditions.

Independent or dependent demand

As we stated earlier, demand is not always predictable. Nevertheless operations managers need to be able to plan ahead and control operations. They can do this by firstly determining whether the particular item is independent or dependent. This will determine which of the available methods to use.

- Independent demand. Ordering of this item does not influence any other item, so it can be independently forecast and organized in the most appropriate manner. It is directly influenced by customer demand. Most food items and cosmetics would be in this category. We will discuss some of the inventory order models for independent demand later in this chapter.
- Dependent demand. Here there is a direct link between the ordering of a particular item and other items. This is the basis for materials requirements planning (MRP). A list of linked dependent materials will be set in what is referred to as a bill of material (BOM). This is explained later in this chapter (pages 160–1) when we discuss the manufacture of a table. In this example, orders for the table are independently generated but they will create a dependent order demand for the component parts— the leg subassembly, table top, and screw fixings. These are often planned via computer using a master production schedule (MPS). Most assembled goods follow this pattern.

Actavis Pharmaceuticals—'prescription manufacturing'

Actavis manufactures generic prescription drugs in either tablet or capsule form. In 2011 it was projected that it would produce more than 4100 million tablets, the equivalent of more than 80 million a week. It is a classic batch production process, with between 100,000 and 6 million tablets being made in each batch. A typical drug will have a single active ingredient, which may only weigh a few micrograms. Hence, this core ingredient needs to be mixed with three to six other ingredients, such as maize starch, in order to make a tablet or capsule.

Approximately 60 batches are made each week following a four- or five-stage process. First, raw materials are dispensed, that is to say the ingredients for each tablet are carefully weighed out, to ensure the exact proportions are prepared for each batch. Second, these ingredients are thoroughly mixed to ensure each tablet will contain the right proportion of each ingredient. In some cases, the powders are granulated, by hydration and drying, to ensure this is achieved. Third, the blended ingredients are compressed under force to make a tablet, or enclosed in a capsule shell. Fourth, some tablets may be coated to improve their taste, increase stability or shelf life, or improve their appearance. Some coated tablets may also be polished. Finally, the finished product is packaged, usually in blister packs and boxes, although sometimes in pots.

The factory is laid out in three main areas, of roughly equal size. There is warehousing for raw-materials, and some finished product; production facilities comprising dispensing booths, granulation suites, tableting presses, and coating equipment; and automated packaging lines. In terms of materials, there are roughly 500 different tablet ingredients used. Of these, 25 are purchased in bulk, such as maize starch, whereas the 140 different active ingredients may be in much smaller quantities. In addition, there are 2800 different packaging items in inventory, comprising different types of blister pack bases, printed foil seals for the packs, information sheets to accompany each drug, and the boxes into which each type of drug is placed.

In this industry, it is essential that extremely tight control is exercised over all the materials. If a drug were to be wrongly mixed, labelled, or boxed, it could endanger life. At the same time, batch production has to be scheduled efficiently and meet forecast demand. Actavis therefore carefully monitors inventory levels, sales orders, forecasted sales, safety stocks, minimum order quantities, and lead times. Using this data it produces a forecast of output volume for the next 18 months, as well as a provisional demand schedule for the next two months based on 'make-to-order' principles. Each month an MPS is devised, which specifies start dates and due dates and the production volume. This is linked to a bill of materials list which specifies what raw materials will be required. This also generates a forecast of supply materials and purchase orders to ensure raw materials stock is replenished. Finally work orders (WOs) are produced in order to route each batch through the different stages of manufacture and ensure the optimum use of machinery, equipment, and packing lines. The MPS and WOs are reviewed on a weekly and daily basis by a cross-functional team, so that batches may be re-routed or re-timed if need be in response to circumstances.

Source: author's primary research

Questions

1. Why are materials handling and inventory management so important in this sector?
2. At what stages in the total manufacturing process is inventory actually counted? (Or controlled?)

Tilda Limited supplies basmati rice to consumers and businesses in the UK and Europe. One of the principal features of Tilda's basmati rice, which is harvested from paddy fields at the foot of the Himalayas, is its purity. Rice is cultivated through a 155-day crop cycle. The work of soil preparation, seed broadcasting, removal of saplings and their transplantation, weeding, harvesting, and threshing is all executed by hand. Tilda supports the basmati farmers through specialist technical support and quality rice seeds. After harvesting the crop the farmer takes his produce to the local market (a 'Mandi') to be sold to the highest bidder. Once the rice is procured at the Mandi it is bagged and made ready for shipment. From the moment of purchase Tilda is faced with the challenge of securing the authenticity of the rice as it travels through its international supply chain. Many firms attempt to secure delivery of their product through technologies such as radio frequency identification (RFID). Tilda's drive for quality and authenticity has gone beyond the level of using barcode control to the use of molecular structure monitoring. To ensure the rice that reaches the tables of its consumers is pure basmati, Tilda has engaged the science of DNA analysis. Molecular food authentication is used to assess the purity of the rice. DNA samples are taken and analysed at each stage of the supply chain to ensure authentic supplies of basmati as shown in Figure 6.1. The head of supply chain management at Tilda describes the benefit of DNA in terms of security and authenticity:

Terraces for growing rice In Northern India.
© istock/traveler1116.

> Ensuring the authenticity of the Basmati rice through DNA is a novel but critical part of our supply chain strategy. We use DNA testing to validate what our experts do in the field to ensure the purity of our product. Purity of product is critical for our consumers, customers, the customs authorities and the rice farmers. The integrity of managing our product through such a diverse and traditional international supply chain has been secured through molecular technology.

Source: part of a Surrey University Knowledge Transfer Partnership with the company (led by Dr James Aitken)

Questions

1. Why does Tilda use DNA rather than RFID to secure the authenticity of Basmati rice?
2. What value differences do you think that UK customers and the UK customs authorities place on the purity of Basmati rice?

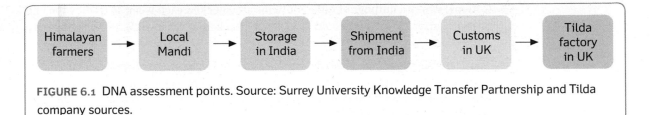

FIGURE 6.1 DNA assessment points. Source: Surrey University Knowledge Transfer Partnership and Tilda company sources.

Inventory management

Inventory management is the planning and controlling of inventories in order to meet the competitive priorities of the operation. It will involve activities both within and outside an organization to ensure that the correct quantity, quality, and type of inventory are delivered to the correct place at the right time and at the right cost.

As a typical manufacturing organization may have several thousand items of inventory which may be worth tens or hundreds of thousands of pounds it is essential that accurate records are kept of stock movements. Individual items of inventory are known as **stock keeping units** (SKUs) and will normally be issued with an identifying code. An organization may well have several thousand SKUs to manage the supply and storage of throughout its supply network. This is usually done by computer and linked to a materials requirements planning system which we will discuss later in this chapter. It is therefore useful to have some means of prioritizing which items to control most closely. A very common inventory classification system is the **ABC classification**.

Stock keeping unit (SKU) an individual item or product held in stock

ABC inventory classification

This looks at inventory items by individual cost and usage and then assigns them to a particular class or category.

ABC classification a method of identifying and categorizing SKUs according to their demand value

- Class A inventory items would be either very high cost relative to other items or those with very high demand. It is usual that these items would account for about 20% of the total quantity of inventory but may constitute up to 80% of the value. In the automotive sector, for example, these could be the engines or gearboxes which cost far more than any other component and would be expensive and difficult to store in large quantities. They would typically be ordered weekly or even daily in some cases. It would be very important therefore for the holding company to know precisely how much value is tied up in these items at all times. They would typically be controlled by a perpetual inventory system which would automatically update the stock record every time a class A item is either booked out of stock or booked back into stock. Each month there would be a physical count and a reconciliation of the value of these items to ensure that no 'slippage' had occurred.

- Class B inventory items would then account for a further 25–30% of the total quantity and be mid-value items accounting for 10–15% of total value. An automotive example here might be wheels, seats, or in-car computer systems. They would not need to be counted as regularly, but would still need to be audited quarterly and physically counted once a year to coincide with the end of the company's financial year. Some companies also use a technique known as cycle counting for these (and for some class

C items) where a number of different items are checked each week so that by the end of the quarter each item would have been checked at least once and any variance reconciled.

- The remaining 50–55% of quantity would be called class C inventory and would be lower-cost items and account for the final 5–10% of total value. Automotive examples here would be cables, fixings, electrical switches, and minor components. As with class B items they would be counted less frequently but physically counted at year end. Due to their relative demand and low cost there would always be plenty of safety stock available of these items.

Increasingly technology is helping many companies' inventory control. The introduction of **radio frequency identification** (RFID) chips embedded in pallets or individual items can track the location of inventory at any location in the supply chain. This is mentioned further when we discuss trends in inventory management later in this chapter.

Radio frequency identification (RFID) a system whereby tracking devices using global position satellite technology are used to identify and locate inventory items

Inventory costs

However, the ordering and controlling of a particular SKU are managed they will incur costs and decisions will have to be made to determine what level of inventory to keep:

- Holding costs. Physically storing any inventory item will take up valuable space and therefore have a cost. In addition there may be further costs due to deterioration, loss, damage, or insurance.

- Ordering costs. To calculate and make out orders and to monitor their progress can involve a high level of clerical and managerial time.

Just-in-time a method for optimizing operations processes by eliminating all forms of extraneous waste

- Set-up costs. Most products require some set-up time from the end of the previous product to the start of the next. This is kept to a minimum in a **just-in-time** (JIT) environment but will still account for some cost.

- Shortage costs. Putting a figure on how much it might cost the organization if there is a shortage of any inventory item can be difficult, but it may result in missed deliveries, poor customer service, and even penalty fines.

As inventory is a major asset in a company it needs to be accounted for as such. There are four main methods available to do this. Each will produce a similar result if the price of the item remains constant over time; however, this is rarely the case so some judgement needs to be made over the likely long-term change in price to select the most appropriate method:

- First in, first out (FIFO). This assumes that the oldest item (first in) is used first and is the most likely method to use in a distribution warehouse.

- Last in, first out (LIFO). This assumes that the latest item (last in) would be used first.

These first two models are also used in queuing management and we will mention them again in Chapter 8.

- Average cost. This method calculates the average amount paid for the item over a period.

- Standard cost. This is the most likely option for inventories as they pass through a manufacturing operation. Costs are determined by taking into account direct material, direct labour, and overhead costs. On a periodic basis variances are then calculated between the standard cost and actual cost and reconciliations made.

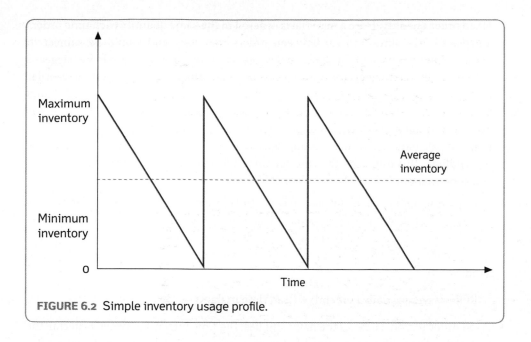

FIGURE 6.2 Simple inventory usage profile.

Inventory usage

Inventory is designed to be used within an operation; therefore the quantity in stock will vary over time. In simple terms the usage profile will look as it does in Figure 6.2.

This simple model is satisfactory to illustrate the general nature of inventory usage and ordering but it has a number of flaws. Firstly as it is drawn it assumes that inventory usage will be at a steady rate. Secondly it assumes that order quantities will be the same each time an order is placed; and thirdly it seems to suggest that orders of new inventory will arrive instantaneously. Clearly these are not realistic assumptions in all cases. In fact inventory usage rates may vary widely and there will be a time delay between placing new orders and the material arriving, which is termed the lead time. Lead times may be days or several weeks depending on location and type of inventory concerned.

Inventory order models

There are a number of different models in regular use by organizations to help calculate how much inventory to order and at what frequency. We will cover these here including some of the calculations used. However, many of these are also associated with statistical and probability theory and involve quite complex mathematical formulae which we believe to be outside the scope of this introductory text, so we will not be recreating these here and will just include a simple explanation of each method.

- Lot for lot. This model, as the name suggests, ensures that no more materials than are necessary are ordered, therefore no safety or buffer is included in the calculation. Exactly the number of parts requested will be ordered each time. This method is the basis for many MRP systems using dependent demand profiles and is often used for JIT operations where inventories are kept as a minimum.

- Fixed order quantity. Here a material is ordered in the same quantity each time orders are placed. The time interval between orders may vary and would be subject to demand fluctuations and the lead time of the material, but orders would be triggered automatically when a certain stock level is reached. This point is termed the reorder point (ROP) and is explained further in the next bullet point. This method would be suitable for class A items of inventory as discussed earlier in this chapter and it is also used in many retail environments where usage is registered electronically from point-of-sale data and where it is appropriate to order complete pallet loads for ease of handling. This might be the case for tinned food or canned drinks, for example, at a supermarket.

- ROP. The inventory level set as a trigger to reorder more of a specific item. This is usually calculated as the expected usage during the supply lead time plus some safety stock to ensure that there is less possibility of running out. In this system the time between reorders will vary as demand varies but the order quantity will remain fixed.

$$ROP = (average\ daily\ demand) \times (lead\ time\ in\ days)$$

- Fixed order period. Here, as the name implies, the time interval between ordering the material is fixed. The time period between orders is calculated using the economic order quantity (EOQ) equation discussed later in the EOQ model and dividing it by the average usage.

$$Order\ period\ (in\ weeks) = \frac{EOQ}{Average\ weekly\ usage}$$

Although the time period is fixed, the quantity ordered can vary significantly with demand. The main advantage of this type of inventory ordering system is that it is simple to operate and the only calculation required is to determine the order quantity. Stocktaking audits are automatically carried out at the fixed order points and this system is sometimes referred to as a periodic review system

- Economic batch quantity (EBQ). This is a calculation which aims to inform the operating company what would be the least cost quantity option to manufacture. This is normally calculated for batch production processes to set output quantities. This may of course result in some short-term or even long-term inventory if demand levels do not match these calculations.

- Economic order quantity (EOQ). This is a calculation which aims to determine the most cost-efficient quantity of a material to purchase and is based on four variables: annual demand in units; annual ordering cost per unit; annual holding cost per unit; and unit cost.

The model has been in use for many years and can be useful in estimating material ordering requirements. The individual components of the economic order quantity model are illustrated in Figures 6.3 and 6.4.

Figure 6.3 shows that in general there is a cost advantage in purchasing a higher quantity of a material.

Figure 6.4 shows that holding costs are roughly proportional to the quantity held, which will negate some of the advantages of buying in large quantities. Therefore a balance needs to be found for each item. This is known as the EOQ and as Figure 6.5 illustrates it occurs at the point when ordering costs and holding costs are the same, i.e. when the total cost is at a minimum.

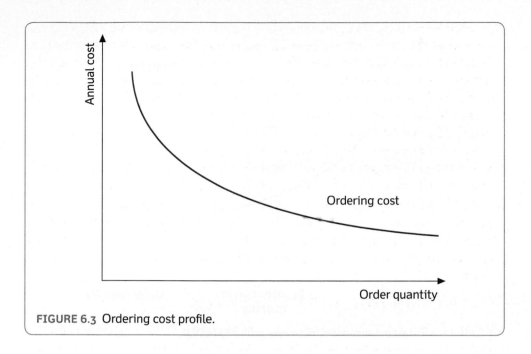

FIGURE 6.3 Ordering cost profile.

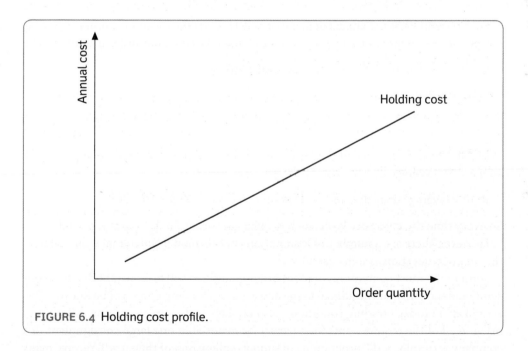

FIGURE 6.4 Holding cost profile.

This relationship is defined by the following word equation:

EOQ = (Square root) of (2 × (Annual demand) × (Order cost) / (Annual holding cost per unit)

This is more usually expressed as the following mathematical formula:

$$Q = \sqrt{((2D \times S) / H)}$$

Where Q = economic order quantity; D = annual demand; S = annual ordering cost per unit; H = annual holding cost per unit.

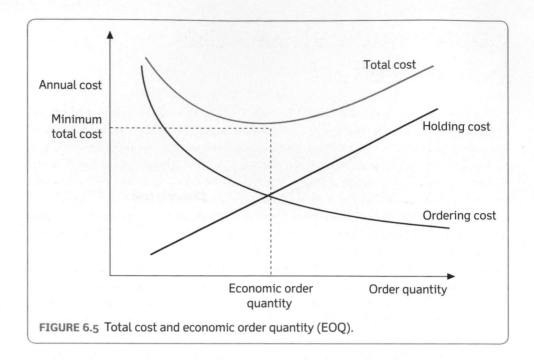

FIGURE 6.5 Total cost and economic order quantity (EOQ).

So, for example, if the annual demand of a SKU is 20,000, the annual ordering cost is £50 per order and the annual holding cost is £20, then the economic order quantity will be

$$Q = \sqrt{((2 \times 20{,}000 \times 50) / 20)} = \sqrt{(2{,}000{,}000 / 20)}$$

$$Q = \sqrt{100{,}000} = 316.2$$

Therefore the most economical batch quantity to order given those conditions would be 316.

The ROP can be calculated if the lead time is known. In this case let us suppose it is 10 days. The average daily demand is 20,000 / 365 = 54.8.

$$ROP = (\text{average daily demand}) \times (\text{lead time in days}) = 54.8 \times 10 = 548$$

So every time the inventory level reaches 548 a new order for 316 parts is placed.

However, there are a number of assumptions in this model which make this calculation open to question as to its usefulness.

Among the most contentious are that order quantities will be constant due to a constant demand and that the annual usage and accurate holding costs will be known. This is unlikely in today's trading conditions; also unlikely is that organizations will want to bring in all of the requirements for a particular material in one large consignment. If a company is running a JIT programme of supply replenishment then it will receive many smaller-quantity deliveries throughout the period. In addition, many sellers offer bulk quantity discounts so this will have an influence on the EOQ calculation where it still might be cheaper to buy in bulk despite higher holding costs.

Due to the fact that demand is not constant over time but follows some kind of normal distribution most companies use either the fixed order quantity or the fixed order period method and include a degree of safety stock in their calculations. This is calculated by determining the effect of a stock shortage of each item and then determining the probability factor that they are prepared to accept of the item not being in stock. For example, many companies will consider a 95% probability of stock availability to be acceptable, so the level of safety stock will be calculated on that basis.

Supply fluctuation—the bullwhip effect

Given that demand is variable and as just discussed may follow some sort of normal distribution over time, it should be possible for companies in a supply network to calculate safety stocks for key items based on expected demand at a certain confidence level to avoid future supply problems. However, life is not that straightforward and supply fluctuation can occur outside these confidence limits, which can have serious consequences further down the supply network. This is known as the **bullwhip effect**.

Identified in 1961, the bullwhip effect, which is also known as the Forrester effect after Jay Forrester, the person who first reported it in an academic context, is the phenomenon whereby there is a disproportionate effect on upstream demand following a relatively small demand change from the customer. Based on the premise that for an even flow of materials through a supply network it is best practice for all parties to agree to hold one order unit's worth of materials in inventory, any change from the customer end to the agreed level will have an increasing knock-on effect, as you travel back along the supply chain.

The bullwhip effect produces a wide fluctuation in demand as shown in Figure 6.6. A change of only 10 or 20 parts per consignment at the customer end can easily lead to

> **Bullwhip effect**
> a disproportionately large fluctuation in demand at the supply end following a minor change at the customer demand end of the supply chain

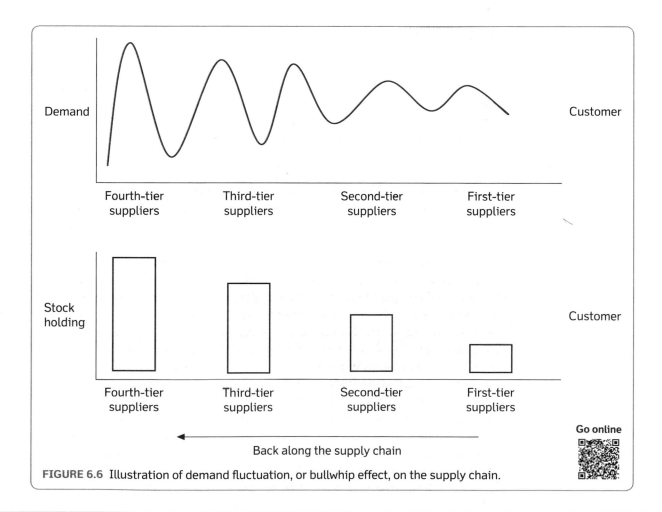

FIGURE 6.6 Illustration of demand fluctuation, or bullwhip effect, on the supply chain.

OPERATIONS INSIGHT 6.3
BAE Systems Regional Aircraft—managing spare parts inventory

Regional Aircraft is a division of BAE Systems that provides aircraft and support services to regional airlines. It has 160 customers, who operate over 1100 aircraft. It also leases and manages 400 aircraft to airlines. In 2007, the company employed 900 people, mainly at its headquarters and engineering/support centre at Prestwick, Ayrshire. It also has facilities in Weybridge (spares and logistics); Hatfield (leasing and portfolio management); Woodford (customer pilot training); and a support facility in Washington DC.

In 2006 it undertook an exercise, Project Oxo, to significantly reduce stock levels and increase efficiency in its spare parts business. Out of a total stockholding of £250 million, it reduced stock by £30 million in 2006 and planned to take another £50 million out in 2007. It found that it was carrying a lot of excess inventory. This was largely because of the build-up of inventory during the production of aircraft that were now no longer needed. By reducing stock, it freed up space in the warehouse which Regional Aircraft planned to market to third parties. Its Weybridge site is strategically positioned, halfway between Heathrow and Gatwick airports, so that airlines can use this space to support their own engineering needs.

Project Oxo was a two-year project designed to cleanse data and discard obsolete parts. Inventory had been accumulated over the years rather than planned. Parts were reviewed to identify if the original manufacturer still existed and had the capability to make the part, in which case only templates of that part were retained. In some cases, there were newer, faster, and better ways to make components, such as machining from a solid block rather than casting from molten metal. So in these cases these parts did not need to be kept in stock.

Linked to this, Regional Aircraft invested £5 million in SAP inventory management software from July 2005 onwards. One capability of this is that it can now sell spares over the Internet, so that it is easier for customers to do business with the company. It is also using SAP Business Warehouse as its management information tool.

To keep up with the needs of customers in this very dynamic and competitive market, the company has organized a spares focus group. This meets twice a year to discuss the Jetspares programme and how well BAE is doing in providing spares. The company also has a technical focus group, which also meets regularly to discuss issues such as cost of ownership and aircraft reliability.

Source: 'Flying to New Heights', The Manufacturer, *May 2007; www.baesystems.com*

Questions

1. Why is managing spare parts inventory a challenge?
2. How does BAE Systems go about managing this inventory?

Materials management, production planning, and control systems

There are many different strategies for manufacturing products and ensuring that the customers get what they ordered in the correct quantity and at the right time.

Three such strategies include:

- Make-to-stock—this involves making products and storing them for future consumption or delivery. This is often driven by a sales forecast.

- Make-to-order—this means making products only when a customer has ordered them. This will require an effective supply network to ensure that there are no undue delays in the processing of these orders.

- Make-to-assembly—this means, for example, making a lot of smaller parts that can later be assembled into a more complex finished product.

Each of these strategies works with dependent demand, which we introduced earlier (page 146). They will require an effective production plan. For most organizations this will be developed by a computerized production planning system. Four such systems are discussed here:

- Materials requirements planning (MRP)
- Manufacturing resource planning (MRPII)
- Theory of constraints (TOC)
- Enterprise resource planning (ERP).

RESEARCH INSIGHT 6.2

Berry, W.L. and Hill, T. (1992) Linking systems to strategy, *International Journal of Operations and Production Management*, 12(10), 3–15

In this article, Berry and Hill discuss the importance of manufacturing planning and control systems. In doing so, they discuss the factors that influence their choice and approaches, which have previously been discussed in this text—market structure (Chapter 2), order qualifiers and order winners (Chapter 2), process choice (Chapter 3), and infrastructure (Chapter 4). Although this article is some years old it is still relevant as it includes a good background to the topic and also a discussion of the reason behind the failure of some companies to realize the expected benefits, even after a large capital investment in these control systems.

Materials requirements planning

Materials requirement planning (MRP) systems were developed in the 1960s and are software-based production planning and inventory control systems. They look at aggregating the demand from customer orders, take into account any existing stock, and then

> **Materials requirements planning (MRP)** a system which aggregates demand from customers, taking into account any existing stock

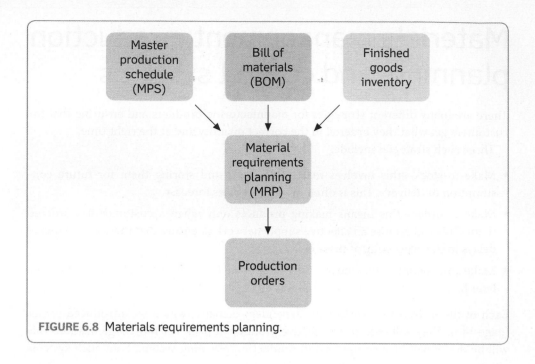

FIGURE 6.8 Materials requirements planning.

create individual works orders to manufacture the required amount of each product. In order to calculate this there will need to be a master production schedule (MPS) detailing all orders required, and each product will require a bill of material (BOM) which will itemize all of its component parts. Figure 6.8 shows how these are interrelated.

An MPS is derived from actual customer orders and forecasts for each product from the sales and marketing function. It will detail all of the products on order and the sequence they are required to be supplied in to the customer. In large organizations the MPS would look to optimize the total capacity of all of the process plant involved by sharing the work between them, where appropriate. It will also show how many additional products will be available at the end of each week to meet future demand. This is a hugely complex task and one which is now generated by computer. However, it provides an excellent look ahead, typically over a two-month horizon and is an invaluable tool for both production and sales staff to help maximize sales opportunities.

The basis for materials requirements planning is the BOM. This is a list of all materials, components, and subassemblies which will be needed in order to make the required quantity of a product. These will be arranged in levels, much like an organization chart. The finished products are in level 0, subassemblies in level 1 and parts for the subassemblies would be in level 2.

Let us consider a simple table as shown in Figure 6.9 to illustrate how a BOM is created. This particular table would be made in a series of operations. First the legs would be individually made and then joined together at the top to a fixing plate. This whole subassembly would then be fixed to the table top by screws.

So the BOM would look like Figure 6.10. The finished product is the table itself, so that would be level 0. The leg subassembly, fixing screws, and the table top unit would then be the next level down, i.e. level 1, and the four legs and the fixing plate would be level 2.

It is easy to see using this very simple example how quickly the levels would build up for more complicated products and how complex the operation to coordinate and control the various subassemblies and final assemblies would be in practice. Again computers

FIGURE 6.9 A simple table. © iStock/Павел Игнатов.

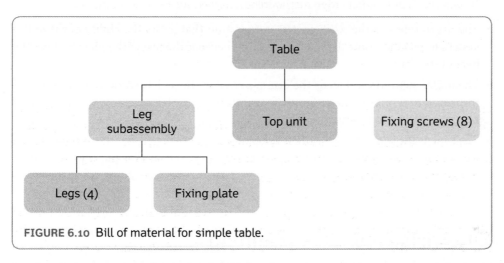

FIGURE 6.10 Bill of material for simple table.

are ideal for this and for consolidating requirements by identifying when particular materials are required in more than one product.

When planning the production and delivery of a finished product the manufacturer has to take into account how long it will take to produce it. It will need accurate estimates for how long each process will take—ordering, manufacturing, assembly, inspection, and packing. Adding all of these process times together will give the lead time, the time required from order receipt to dispatch of the goods. The system can then develop a production plan for how long the product will take to make and therefore when production should start in order to have finished by the required delivery date. This type of scheduling is referred to as backward scheduling as it works back from the required delivery date to determine when the first operation should start.

Manufacturing resource planning (MRPII)

Limitations of MRP systems included inappropriate batch sizes to control inventory and the fact that they only dealt with materials and no account was taken of capacity issues. This led to the development of a new planning system, **MRPII**, in the early 1980s, which extended the original MRP to other areas, such as finance, sales and marketing,

Manufacturing resource planning (MRP II) an extension of materials requirements planning to include finance, sales and marketing, and human resources planning on one database

and human resources all on one database to offer an integrated business solution. This was particularly useful to businesses wishing to account for the real cost of all their operational resources, not just production and raw materials.

Theory of constraints

Theory of constraints (TOC) an operations control system based on the identification of bottlenecks or constraints in the production flow process

The **theory of constraints (TOC)** was originally developed by Goldratt and Cox (1993) in *The Goal: A Process of Ongoing Improvement*. This operations control system is based on the identification of bottlenecks or constraints in the production process flow. A constraint is defined as anything that prevents the system from achieving more of its 'goal' (namely, making money). This could be the physical capacity of a particular machine or a limit placed on the operation by other internal forces, such as a limit on the amount of work in process or finished goods inventory allowed on the premises to keep costs to a minimum.

It uses the drum–buffer–rope methodology, named for its three components.

- The drum refers to the work centre or operation that limits the ability of the entire system to produce more. It is called the drum because the rest of the plant 'follows the beat of the drum'.

- The buffer supports and feeds the drum, so that it always has work to do. Buffers are measured in terms of time rather than quantity of material, such as two days' stock of raw materials or four hours' supply of a component.

- The rope is the way in which work is scheduled through the drum. This is done so that work commences only when an order needs to be met. If work is put into the system earlier than needed, this results in high work-in-process and slows down the entire system.

Enterprise resource planning

Enterprise resource planning (ERP) an extension of business systems integration across different companies in the supply network

The further extension of business systems across boundaries of supply companies, operations and customers has led to the development of **enterprise resource planning (ERP)** systems. Generally using web-enabled software, companies such as SAP and Oracle have developed business-wide solutions to provide real-time data and visibility at all points in the supply network. This relies on very rigid software architecture and strict operating rules to try and ensure that the information is accurate at all levels.

RESEARCH INSIGHT 6.3

Hawking, P. (2007) Implementing ERP systems globally: Challenges and lessons learned for Asian countries, *Journal of Business Systems, Governance, and Ethics*, 2(1), 21–32

In this article, Paul Hawking considers the difficulties facing operations managers seeking to operate an ERP system internationally, especially in Asia. Of great interest in this article is his identification of the critical success factors for successful implementation. He identifies these as organizational fit, skill mix, management structure and strategy, software systems design, user involvement and training, technology planning, and project management.

Integration is very complex and therefore ERP systems are very expensive to purchase and also expensive to implement. However, many large organizations in the UK, such as DIY retail stores, major chemical companies, and some county councils are already benefiting from the extra visibility and the faster information exchange that have become possible. On the other hand, a third of manufacturers in Western Europe see no measurable benefit from their ERP system, according to research carried out by IDC Manufacturing Insights in conjunction with ERP vendor Infor (Wheatley 2010). This is partly due to the rigid operating procedures which tend to make them less user friendly and the change to ERP systems are often not accepted readily by staff.

Hence, Wheatley (2010) identifies four features that should ensure the successful adoption and implementation of an ERP solution.

The first is to select a system that fits the industry sector. Many ERP vendors now offer 'industry templates', i.e. systems that are preconfigured with industry-leading best practice. For instance, KK Fine Foods has grown 700% over the last six years, due in large part to adopting a sector-specific ERP solution that understands features of food manufacturing—such as recipes, multiple units of measure, and 'disassembly', i.e. manufacturing a variety of different products from a single raw material such as a chicken.

The second key feature is the availability of actionable information. ERP systems routinely produce a huge amount of information, which can lead to a number of problems including the fact that there is too much information, it is not timely, and managers do not action it. One way that this can be addressed is by adapting the system so that routine data is screened and users only see exceptional information in the form of 'alerts'.

Although ERP systems need to be designed to meet the specific needs of the operation, they also need to be adaptable. This is because, as we have seen, operations are adapting and changing all the time. ERP vendors therefore often design systems in a modular way, so that additional features can be added if needed in the future. An example of this is shown in Figure 6.11 which illustrates the relationship between ERP and MRP systems.

Finally, firms need to consider alternative approaches to the information technology (IT) infrastructure supporting the ERP system. The conventional approach has been for the operator to host it on a main server, which is very expensive and prohibitive for many companies. However, it is now possible to use other methods to reduce the cost. This makes use of 'cloud computing' and is sometimes referred to as 'software as a service' (SaaS). In simple terms this means the outsourcing of ERP. The systems and the computer rooms that run them are moved off site. This relieves operations of owning, updating, and maintaining their own systems, along with all of the associated skill, labour, and expense involved. This enables SMEs to gain the benefits of large-scale business applications without the cost of a large IT infrastructure. A number of major vendors offer SaaS solutions—SAP has Business by Design and NetSuite, while Oracle has Oracle on Demand.

Key performance indicators

Stock turn a method of measuring inventory and supply chain management efficiency

Inventory turnover or **stock turn** is a key performance indicator for many companies. It is a measure of supply chain efficiency and is calculated by dividing the total cost of

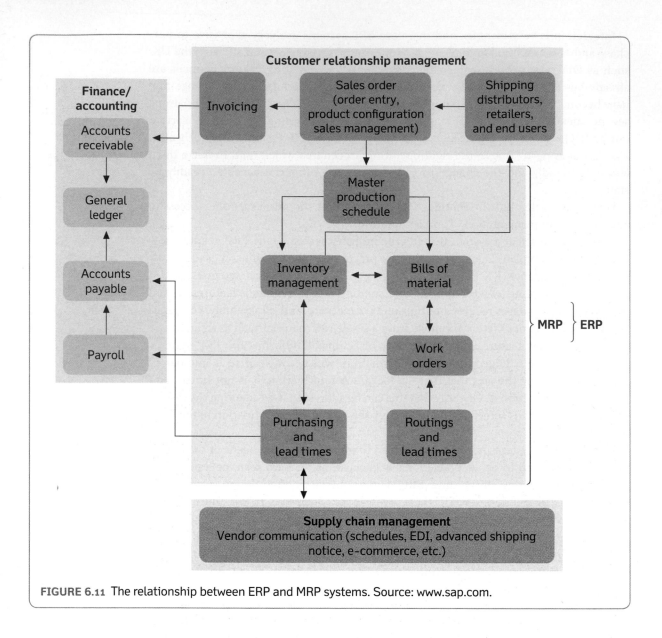

FIGURE 6.11 The relationship between ERP and MRP systems. Source: www.sap.com.

goods sold over a period (typically a month or financial quarter) by the average aggregate inventory value over that period. Values for this ratio vary widely between industries and between types of organization. Many supermarkets or fast food restaurants may have stock turns of up to 100, whereas for more traditional manufacturing companies stock turns of seven or eight may be considered acceptable.

By increasing this ratio, companies can generate more revenue from less inventory-holding cost and therefore increase profits. Dell has improved profitability by increasing its stock turns to 60 or more.

The inverse of inventory turnover is the number of weeks of supply, or the number of weeks' worth of inventory a company has. Therefore a high inventory turnover would result in a low value for this, i.e. the company would have very little of its costs tied up as inventory.

Trends in inventory management

There are three major trends in this area—JIT, RFID, and **electronic data interchange** (EDI).

Electronic data interchange (EDI) the transfer of information using the Internet or secure network

- JIT—this is a method for optimizing manufacturing processes by eliminating all extraneous waste, such as excess material, excess inventory, or excess movement of personnel or materials (Ohno 1988). Deliveries are made in correct quantities and in the correct sequence as a result of pull planning systems and sent directly to the production line. This type of operation is widely used in the automotive industry where component or systems suppliers work in close long-term relationships to put together consignments based on order schedules supplied by the customer, and deliver them straight to the assembly line so that they can be fitted directly to the models being assembled. Orders are pulled through the system only when required, thereby not building unnecessary inventory, using signals called Kanbans which can be a physical or electronic ticket or an empty container or a marked space on the factory floor requiring filling. This has the added advantage of providing flexibility so that different component modules can be added to adjacent vehicles without adding cost, thereby achieving mass customization. These methods will be discussed further in Chapter 15 when we discuss lean and agile manufacturing.

- RFIDs—these refer to tracking devices which enable suppliers, operations, and customers to know precisely where their shipment of goods are, and therefore increase the accuracy of raw material supply forecasting and ultimately customer service of the final product. They have an advantage over bar coding because they can use global positioning satellite (GPS) technology, can hold much more data, do not need a line of sight to work, and can be used in much harsher conditions than would be possible for bar code labels. According to *The Manufacturer* (2010), major retailers, such as Tesco and Wal-Mart, use RFID to manage inventory, United Biscuits uses RFID to control movement of raw materials, and pharmaceutical firms such as Astra Zeneca use RFID to identify counterfeit products and protect brands. It also reported that BMW, Ford, Airbus, BAE Systems, Unilever, Nestlé, and Allied Domecq were also about to adopt this technology.

- EDI—information transfer between suppliers, operations, and customers needs to be instantaneous in today's digital landscape. One method for doing this is by EDI, using the Internet or secure computer networks to reduce the time taken in the procurement process to input material requirements and create shipping documents. The automotive industry has its own EDI standard called ODETTE and many other industry sectors are also developing similar platforms.

- JIT II—this is a concept, originally developed by the Bose Corporation, which has been implemented widely in the USA. Instead of the client having a traditional buying team and the vendor having a traditional sales team, these have been replaced by a supplier's employee located in the client factory. This vendor representative is empowered to place purchase orders on behalf of the client to the supplier he works for. As well as place orders, this representative can walk around wherever he chooses, attend production status meetings, and have access to the client's computers. He may also engage in improvement activities such as concurrent engineering with the client's engineering department. So the key features of JIT II are 'vendor-managed inventory', which was discussed in Chapter 5 and 'automatic material replenishment'.

to consolidate stock from different printers before shipment to the UK. The UK distribution centre is in Kettering, Lincolnshire. It holds around 33,000 SKUs. This facility is managed by the Inventory Department, which is responsible for distributing books throughout the UK and internationally.

Orders for books are placed with Customer Services using a variety of different channels—telephone, the Internet, and electronic data interchange (EDI). Such orders may be of three main kinds. First, chains of books stores such as Waterstones may place orders, in which case books will be transported to these chains' own warehouses. Second, books may be ordered by individual retail stores or schools. And finally, books may be ordered online by individual customers. Picking and packing in the distribution centre are aided by the bar coding on each book, which will also be used by retailers at the point of sale.

The most dynamic of OUP's markets is the demand for ELT books. Here inventory forecasting and planning are much more reliant on the market intelligence being gathered by sales representatives. They routinely visit major customers and language schools throughout the world to establish likely future orders. These are consolidated into large orders which are placed with printers, but the 'call off', i.e. number of books to be shipped, is spread over a number of months. For instance, a printer may be given an order for 100,000 books, but delivery is to be 20,000 over five months. This shifts the EOQ decision to the printer, who has to decide whether to print all the order and hold stock for five months, or have several shorter print runs to avoid stockholding.

Sources: author's primary research and www.sap. com

Questions

1. What type of inventory does OUP hold and why? What class (A, B, or C) of inventory is it?

2. What factors influence the economic order quantity for a title reprint?

3. How did SAP demand planning facilitate its adoption and implementation within OUP, based on Wheatley's (2010) criteria?

Chapter summary

To consolidate your learning, the key points from this chapter are summarized as follows:

- **Define inventory management and explain different types of inventory**

  Inventory management can be defined as the planning and controlling of activities both within and outside an organization to ensure that the correct quantity and type of inventory are delivered to the correct place at the right time and at the right cost.

  - Raw materials. These are the essential items needed to make a product.
  - Work in process (WIP) inventory. Also called semi-finished stock. Partially completed products will consist of a combination of raw materials, but as the name implies, not yet completed.
  - Finished goods inventory. Once completed, products will be booked into finished goods stock.

– Cycle inventory. If products are produced in batches and more than one type of product is produced from an operation then in order to have sufficient of each type of product available for passing on to the next process or dispatching to the customer, there needs to be a build-up of inventory of each type of product in a 'cycle'.

– Buffer inventory. Also called safety stock. Due to variation in demand for some products it is common for organizations to call in extra raw materials from some suppliers to enable any additional orders to be satisfied.

– Anticipation inventory. In certain industries large requirements for products at certain times of the year can be predicted.

– Pipeline inventory. Also known as inventory in transit. When goods have to travel either in a semi-finished or finished state between factories, warehouses, or retail outlets over large distances the inventory then is in the pipeline, and unavailable for use on any other orders.

- **Explain three different approaches to calculating inventory order quantities**

   Three different inventory models are

   1. Fixed order quantity—a material is ordered in the same quantity each time orders are placed. The time interval between orders may vary and would be subject to demand fluctuations but orders would be triggered automatically when a certain stock level is reached, known as the reorder point (ROP).

   2. Fixed order period—here the time interval between ordering the material is fixed. However, the quantity ordered can vary significantly with demand.

   3. Economic order quantity (EOQ)—this is a calculation which aims to determine the most cost-efficient quantity of a material to purchase.

- **What is the major performance indicator in materials and inventory management?**

   The main performance indicator is stock turn. It is a measure of supply chain efficiency and is calculated by dividing the total cost of goods sold over a period (typically a month or financial quarter) by the average aggregate inventory value over that period. By increasing this ratio companies can generate more revenue from less inventory-holding cost and therefore increase their profits.

- **Identify and differentiate between alternative approaches to production planning and control**

   There are three main approaches—MRP, MRPII, and ERP. MRP systems are software-based production planning and inventory control systems. They look at aggregating the demand from customer orders, take into account any existing stock and then create individual works orders to manufacture the required amount of each product.

   MRPII systems extended the original MRP to other areas, such as finance, sales and marketing, and human resources, all on one database to offer an integrated business solution.

   ERP systems generally use web-enabled software to provide real-time data and visibility at all points in the supply network. This relies on very rigid software architecture and strict operating rules to try and ensure that the information is accurate at all levels. ERP systems can be very expensive to install and due in part to their rigid operating rules are not easily accepted by employees so do not have a very high success rate.

- **Identify and describe key trends in inventory management**

  These are:

  - Just-in-time (JIT). This is a method for optimizing manufacturing processes by eliminating all extraneous waste, such as excess material, excess inventory, or excess movement of personnel or materials.
  - Radio frequency identification (RFID). This refers to tracking devices which enable suppliers, operations, and customers to know precisely where their shipment of goods are, and therefore increase the accuracy of raw material supply forecasting and ultimately customer service of the final product.
  - Electronic data interchange (EDI). Information transfer between suppliers, operations, and customers using the Internet or secure computer networks to reduce the time taken in the procurement process to input material requirements and create shipping documents.
  - Just-in-time II (JIT II). This relates to the vendor having a representative in the client's manufacturing plant, engaged in ordering the right amount or materials to fit with the client's production schedules.

? Questions

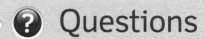

Review questions

1. What is inventory?

2. What are the different categories of inventory?

3. What are the main differences between the inventory held by a materials processing operation, such as a domestic oven manufacturer, and those of a customer processing operation, such as a cinema?

4. What are the main inventory order models used by operations?

5. Explain what is meant by the reorder point (ROP) and show how it is used to calculate order quantities.

6. What are the main benefits and drawbacks of the economic order quantity (EOQ) model?

7. Explain the bullwhip effect and suggest some ways of minimizing it within the supply chain.

8. What is a master production schedule (MPS) and what information does it provide?

9. What are the main constituents of a materials requirements planning (MRP) system?

10. What criteria influence an organization's adoption of an enterprise resource planning (ERP) system?

Discussion questions

1. Discuss the importance of accurate forecasting in materials and production planning systems.

2. Discuss how operations managers may reconcile the need to minimize inventory and yet be flexible enough to support customers who are adopting JIT practices.

3. What are the main factors an operations manager needs to take into account before they can decide whether to implement an ERP system?

4. How might ERP be implemented in a hospital to improve efficiency or effectiveness?

5. What are the ethical and sustainability implications of managing inventory?

Further learning guide

A useful source of up-to-date news is the magazine *The Manufacturer* or its website **www.themanufacturer.com**. This has articles and case studies not only on inventory management, but also on many other aspects of operations management. The other obvious web-based sources of information are the websites of vendors such as Oracle and SAP. These too often have case studies of firms that have implemented their ERP solutions.

References

Berry, W.L. and Hill, T. (1992) Linking systems to strategy, *International Journal of Operations and Production Management*, 12(10), 3–15

Hawking, P. (2007) Implementing ERP systems globally: Challenges and lessons learned for Asian countries, *Journal of Business Systems, Governance, and Ethics*, 2(1), 21–32

Goldratt, E.M. and Cox, J. (1993) *The Goal: A Process of Ongoing Improvement*, (2nd ed.), Gower Publishing: Aldershot

Ohno, T. (1978) *The Toyota Production System: Beyond Large Scale Production*, Productivity Press: Portland, OR

The Manufacturer (2010) Is warehouse management tagging along? *The Manufacturer*, August [online] www.themanufacturer.com

Wheatley, M. (2010) Five top tips for successful ERP selection, *The Manufacturer*, posted 21 Sep 2010 [online] www.themanufacturer.com

Introduction

Materials processing operations (MPOs) depend on a supply chain or network of suppliers if they are to operate smoothly and efficiently, as we have seen in the last two chapters. In the same way, customer processing operations (CPOs) try to manage their supply of customers, since it is they that flow through the system. We will discuss how customers are managed more fully in Chapter 8. Whichever type of operation they are engaged in, operations managers will need to understand the likely demand for their product or service and ensure that there is sufficient **capacity** made available in their operation to supply this demand on time and in the correct quantity. This is not easy to achieve. Even with products which are only required at a particular time of year, such as Christmas decorations or Easter eggs, which we mentioned in Chapter 6 as examples of anticipation inventory, the operation still needs to know how many of each type to make. The total requirement must be planned as it cannot all be made in the last few weeks before the start of the Christmas or Easter period. One way to estimate demand is by looking at several years' demand figures and making an estimate for the coming year. However, this is not always a good indicator so more sophisticated methods are often required, such as causal modelling or scenario planning. These will be dealt with later in this chapter.

> **Capacity** the maximum possible output in a given time

In this chapter we will define capacity and consider how companies reconcile capacity and demand. Having too little capacity will result in customers not getting their orders or not being served on time, having too much capacity will result in staff or machines being idle some of the time and therefore costing the company in lost revenue. We will look at how capacity is measured and managed by both MPOs and CPOs and discuss why managing capacity is such a challenge in customer processing operations and go on to compare and contrast three alternative strategies for managing capacity—level capacity, chase demand, and demand management. In doing so we identify and explain some key concepts: machine utilization and efficiency, labour flexibility and its various forms, and revenue management.

Capacity management in materials processing operations

Capacity can be defined as the maximum possible output of an operation or process in a given time. In a continuous flow process, such as oil refining, the capacity is relatively easy to establish. Since a refinery operates on a continuous basis non-stop, the rate of production is fixed by the capacity of the 'columns' that distil, crack, and blend the oil, as well as the pipes, pumps, and valves that transport the materials through the system. The whole refinery will be designed and built to process specific types of crude oil with a highly predictable level of output.

Likewise in a properly designed assembly line operation, the flow of materials through the system will be highly predictable and the rate of flow through the system will be directly controlled by the speed of the line itself. In this type of operation, the challenge is not so much the capacity of the system, but the sheer number of different components and parts that the manufacturing process may require, at different stages in the process.

However, the challenge in measuring and understanding capacity does arise in batch production and job shops. This is because materials are being used in a variety of different ways and in different-size production runs. Changing from the production of one product to another typically involves 'downtime', whilst machines are cleaned or reset or retooled. Hence a batch producer may have one day when there is little downtime because they have one or two long production runs, and another day when there is considerable downtime resulting from many short production runs. In addition, all operations will have downtime due to planned maintenance, breakdowns, or other unforeseen circumstances. Hence there is a difference between what an operation might theoretically produce and what it is actually able to do.

Design capacity

The theoretical maximum capacity of an operation is called its design capacity. This assumes that the operation is used up to its full capacity, not allowing for any downtime. In most cases design capacity, by definition, cannot be exceeded. However, there are only a few systems where routinely such capacity is exceeded, most notably with regard to crowded rush-hour trains. In most cases, it is accepted that design capacity is rarely met, and managers seek to achieve an 'effective' capacity.

Effective capacity

The effective capacity of an operation is the potential capacity that can be achieved on a typical day. For instance, most factories do not run all of their machines for the full design capacity. They have times allocated for planned maintenance and for product changeovers.

Achieved capacity

On any given day the actual output of an operation may be less than the effective capacity as there may be further avoidable downtime due to unplanned events such as machinery breakdowns or staff shortages. This is then referred to as the achieved capacity.

This leads to two different measures of performance, termed '**utilization**' and '**efficiency**'. Utilization compares achieved capacity, i.e. the actual output, against design capacity, whereas efficiency is a measure of achieved capacity against effective capacity. Both of these are usually expressed as a percentage (as shown in the worked example that follows). This is illustrated in Figure 7.1.

To illustrate this consider that a food canning machine is designed to operate 24 hours a day, seven days a week, but has planned downtime of 28 hours due to product changeovers and maintenance. In addition, there is a further loss of output due to quality concerns and material shortages totalling a further 40 hours. The utilization and the efficiency of the operation are calculated as follows:

> **Utilization** the proportion of design capacity that is actually achieved

> **Efficiency** the proportion of effective capacity that is achieved

Design capacity = 24 × 7 = 168 hours

Effective capacity = Design capacity − Planned downtime
                   = (168 − 28) = 140 hours

Achieved capacity = Effective capacity − Avoidable downtime
                  = (140 − 40) = 100 hours

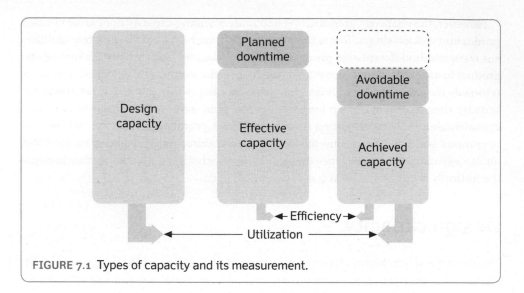

FIGURE 7.1 Types of capacity and its measurement.

Go online

Therefore:

Machine utilization = Achieved capacity / Design capacity
= (100 / 168) × 100% = 59.5%

Efficiency = Achieved capacity / Effective capacity
= (100 / 140) × 100% = 71.4%

Operations managers always seek to ensure that their operations are efficient on a day-to-day basis, and in the longer term plan to maximize utilization. One of the keys to managing efficiency in materials processing operations is inventory management, as was discussed in Chapter 6. The others are ensuring that the equipment is used effectively and also that labour is allocated and managed appropriately.

Whilst utilization and efficiency are good measures they do not take into account the quality of the output. In many organizations this added dimension is required which has led to more sophisticated measures, one of which is **overall equipment effectiveness** (OEE).

Overall equipment effectiveness (OEE) a measure of a machine's utilization, speed, and reliability

Overall equipment effectiveness

This measure includes an assessment of the quality aspects of an operation in addition to those traditionally used to calculate efficiency, to provide an effectiveness value. This is seen as more representative for many materials processing operations since it is possible to be either highly efficient or have high utilization of equipment to keep costs per unit low and yet not produce quality products. Moreover it takes into account the speed at which machinery can be operated—the so-called 'run rate'. Whereas utilization and efficiency are measured in time (typically hours), OEE is measured in output per hour (i.e. speed), so the run rate can be slow or fast.

Hence the overall equipment effectiveness of a process is normally expressed as a percentage and is measured as follows:

OEE = Availability × Performance × Quality

Availability is the ratio of achieved capacity to design capacity (in other words the same as machine utilization). A measure of 100% availability means the process has been operating continuously. Downtime losses which will reduce availability include equipment failures, material shortages, and changeover time.

Performance is the ratio of actual run rate to ideal run rate. A measure of 100% performance means the process has been consistently running at its theoretical maximum speed. Speed losses which will reduce performance include machine wear and tear.

Quality is the ratio of good production output to total pieces made. A measure of 100% quality means there have been no reject or rework pieces. Quality losses which will reduce quality include any produced parts that do not meet the required quality standards.

OPERATIONS INSIGHT 7.1
Chocolate box packaging—OEE in practice

Factories that make boxes of chocolates also have machines that package the chocolates into boxes. Such machines take pre-cut printed sheets of cardboard, one for the bottom and one for the top of the box, fold them and glue them. This is done on a short production line involving three main pieces of equipment—a machine that applies the glue, another that folds the box into shape, and a third that optically checks the box to check it has been made correctly. If it has not,

Pre-cut sheets of cardboard are folded and glued by machines to form boxes. © istock/Nancy Louie.

the faulty box is removed automatically from the line into a reject bin. Let's take an example of a line which is designed to produce 3600 boxes an hour, which is an average run rate of one box every second. However, it has been found that operating the line at design capacity results in a significant number of defective boxes, as many as 2% of the total. By operating the machine at the lower run rate of 3200 boxes per hour the defects fall to 0.5% of output, so this is normal practice.

On one typical working shift of eight hours, there were three occasions when there was downtime. The first occurred when a fault developed in the glue applicator, which required the onsite engineer to attend. He took ten minutes to arrive and another 15 minutes to fix the problem, which was a blocked nozzle on the dispenser. Later in the morning, there was a brief power cut, and although the factory's own generators cut in, there was a five-minute delay at this time. Finally, the line was due to have its three-monthly maintenance service, so it was stopped early by 30 minutes so that the engineer could carry this out. At the end of the shift the operator checked the reject bin and found 140 unusable lids and 127 unusable bases.

Questions

1. What are the levels of utilization and efficiency during this shift?
2. What is the overall equipment efficiency during this shift?

Capacity management in customer processing operations

Customer processing operations have two main ways of estimating the arrival rate of customers—through a reservations system or forecasting. The advantages and disadvantages of these two approaches are compared later in the chapter. But unlike the supply chain, in most cases customers are 'disaggregated'—that is to say there is no one single source of customers. Each individual customer chooses where and when they will use the service operation. Hence to manage this flow of customers a great deal of effort has to go into influencing these individual choices. This is why some operators are very happy to offer group discounts, as it not only ensures volume of traffic through the business but also reduces the cost of 'acquiring' customers. Moreover groups of customers can be required to arrive and depart at specific times, significantly reducing uncertainty with regard to customer flows.

Why capacity in customer processing operations is a challenge

The ideal operation is one in which a single input is transformed by a simple process, operating at a standard rate, to produce a single output. In other words, volume is constant, variety is non-existent, and variability negligible (see pages 14–15). In this hypothetical example, demand matches supply and everything operates as smoothly and efficiently as possible. Unfortunately, no operation is ever this simple, and most are considerably more complex. Matching supply and demand in CPOs is especially problematic because:

- Most CPOs are in a fixed location—hence customers have to come to them rather than the operation go to the customer.

- Most CPOs produce services that are consumed at the same time as they are produced (simultaneity).

- The infrastructure of the CPO, i.e. buildings, fixtures, fittings, and equipment, are very inflexible so that capacity is fixed.

- Demand for CPO services is difficult to predict.

- Most CPOs will offer a variety of services for which the service time may vary, thereby making it difficult to predict the flow through the system.

In Chapter 1 we discussed the four Vs—volume, variety, variability, and variation. Each of these has implications for capacity management. With regard to volume, it is very likely that this will change over time. Hence there is an issue when a service operation is first established as to what level of volume to build it for—current level of trade, peak level of demand, or future predicted levels of demand? Because the infrastructure is fixed and places constraints on the number of customers that can be served, establishing the right-size infrastructure in the first instance is a key issue. If demand does increase it may then be difficult to expand capacity to accommodate this. Constraints on expansion include the UK's planning laws, regulations concerning the use of buildings, availability of space adjacent to the site, and so on. Accor Hotels builds its budget hotel brand Formule 1 using prefabricated bedrooms that fit together like toy bricks. As well as keeping the building cost down, another advantage of this approach is that it is possible to expand the hotel relatively easily with additional bedrooms should the volume of business warrant it.

Most CPOs also provide a variety of different services. Such variety may be in different forms. It may be the range of products and services available. It may also be the extent to which a service is customized. Hairdressers provide a single service, but each customer gets a unique haircut and hence predicting the time a haircut will take is not straightforward. And some CPOs may require a high level of customer involvement. This also makes predicting transaction time a challenge, as new users typically take longer to serve themselves than repeat customers, who already know how the system works.

The third 'V' is variation—how total demand changes over time. Such fluctuations can be over a relatively short time frame or much longer, such as:

- Daily—demand varies during the day in many CPOs because of the work/eating pattern of most people's day. Most people arrive at work between 8.00 and 9.00 am, they take a break for lunch between 12.00 noon and 2.00 pm, and finish work around 5.00 pm. Hence shops, bars, restaurants, and banks tend to have peaks in demand between 12.00 noon and 2.00 pm, and again immediately after people finish work.

- Weekly—demand fluctuates during the week because most people work Monday to Friday so that there is a peak in demand for some services at weekends.

- Monthly—some services experience more demand at the beginning of the month than towards the end. This is because more and more employees are being paid on a monthly basis, so that people tend to spend more just after they have been paid, and then put off spending later in the month until they are paid again.

- Seasonality—the different seasons clearly influence the demand for some services, such as theme parks, holiday accommodation, and so on.

- Cyclical—in some cases there are routinely peaks and troughs in demand based on a wide range of factors. For instance, due to the motor licensing system in the UK most cars are bought in April and October. This means that the demand for licences and MOT tests also follows this pattern. Cyclical patterns may also be linked with the product or service firm life cycle (see pages 70–5).

In addition to these patterns of demand, there may be random variations due to a wide range of extraneous causes—such as the state of the economy, social well-being or unrest, terrorist activity, and weather-related phenomena (such as hurricanes, floods, etc.).

Finally variability refers to how the demand for different aspects of service provision can vary within the total pattern of demand. Often this is driven by different customer segments or by the product/service range. A simple example of this would be a hairdresser that serves both men and women. Whereas it may take around ten minutes to cut a man's hair, it takes around 40 minutes to cut a woman's. Clearly the pace and throughput of the operation will be very different on a day when mainly men seek haircuts, compared with a day when most of the customers are women. In a supermarket there may be as many as 40,000 separate items on sale, so variability could be huge in this context, having significant implications for stocking the shelves, ordering supplies, and so on. Some of this variability can be very unpredictable. In periods of wet weather there are stories of shops running out of umbrellas, and in hot weather of theme parks running out of ice cream.

Reservations versus forecasting

Given that there can be variability and variation, operations managers seek to predict as accurately as they can, or to control, what the demand will be for the operation overall, and for the different products and services that they offer.

Reservation systems

The best way to plan and manage demand is to have a reservations system. This requires customers to book, and sometimes pay, in advance. Not only does this enable the manager to know how many customers are expected (i.e. volume), it also enables the flow of customers through the operation to be managed (i.e. it controls variation). Hence to make an appointment to see a doctor, to reserve a table in a restaurant, or book a hairdressing appointment, customers are given a time when they are to turn up. This is designed to ensure that the flow of customers into the operation is as smooth as possible—thereby causing no delays for the customer and utilizing the time of the service employees as efficiently as possible. In some cases, the arrival rate is not spread over time; the system requires all customers to arrive by a specified time. In these instances, tickets are sold in advance, as for instance in a theatre, by an airline, or an event.

A problem with any reservations system is 'no shows', i.e. customers that make a booking or buy a ticket and do not turn up. In 2009, many upmarket restaurateurs in London complained that business people were booking tables in their restaurants weeks and months in advance 'just in case' they had a client to entertain, and then cancelling them at the last minute. They therefore began to instigate a system whereby customers were billed for a meal if they did not show up. In many sectors, customers are required to pay in advance. Not only does this remove the concern about no shows (because you have the revenue from that sale anyway) but it also provides positive cash flow for the business, i.e. money is flowing into the business before it has to be spent on paying costs.

Forecasting

In many customer processing operations, such as retailing, however, it is not possible to have a reservations system. In these cases, operations managers adopt forecasting methods in order to predict as accurately as they can what demand will be. In most cases, demand will follow the kinds of pattern discussed earlier in his section. But no forecasting method can cope with random variation, which is why managers always need to use their knowledge of current and future possible events to inform their interpretation of any forecast.

Before selecting a specific forecasting technique, organizations need to be clear about what to forecast and how far into the future the forecast will go. In the last chapter, we saw how materials processing operations measure and monitor inventory by stock-keeping units (SKUs). The SKU then becomes the item for which forecast demand is calculated (see page 149). In CPOs, the unit of measurement is usually the number of customers (passengers on an airline, patients in a hospital, or visitors to a theme park). However, simply forecasting total volume for the next year may be helpful, but only in the broadest terms. Most organizations need forecasts that break down demand by market segment and/or products and services, as well as forecasts for the short (next few days), medium (next few months), and long term (next few years). For instance, a schedule airline will have forecasts for each of its seat classes (first, business, and economy), each of its route networks (short haul and long haul), and even for individual routes on these networks (such as London–New York or Glasgow–Amsterdam). These forecasts will also be for different time periods. Those for the near future (short term) are very likely to be more accurate than those for the longer term. This is largely because of ticket sales, which make predicting volume more reliable.

Given the complexity of forecasting most organizations then have to select and use some kind of forecasting system. This is partly because many parts of the organization need access to the data—not just operations. Sales and marketing need the information to help their planning, human resources need it to help plan recruitment and off-the-job training programmes, and finance need forecasts to project cash flows. Often the information is also used as the basis for budgeting by every division or department within the organization. An integrated system is also required because the data needs to be collected from a wide range of sources. One of the most valuable sources is sales data, often collected at the point of sale through electronic point-of-sale (EPOS) systems. Retailers have such forecasting systems as part of their supply chain management system. For instance Wal-Mart use an Internet-based system called CPFR (Collaborative Planning, Forecasting and Replenishment).

There are a wide range of different forecasting techniques, each designed to provide different levels of accuracy and different contexts. Time series analysis takes historical data, such as the number of customers served or tickets sold, and projects this into the future. The use of this method is made easier by the fact that it can be automated, as the data needed to make such projections can be routinely collected through point-of-sale devices or reservations systems. Alternative techniques include:

- Simple moving averages—this method forecasts future demand for the next time period, say a week, by taking an average of the last few weeks, say four weeks.

- Weighted moving averages—this method is similar to simple moving averages, except rather than assume each time period is equally important it weights the different periods. Usually the most recent period is weighted higher than preceding weeks. So in a four-week model, the most recent week might be weighted 0.4, the second most recent 0.3, the week before that 0.2, and the fourth week back 0.1.

- Exponential smoothing—this is often used as it is simpler than most other methods and requires the least amount of data. It averages the last week's forecast and actual demand for this week, adjusted by 'alpha', which is a smoothing parameter (a number between 0 and 1) applied to actual demand (and 1—alpha applied to the forecast), so that the actual is weighted more heavily than the forecast.

Table 7.1 shows how a forecast may vary according to which of these methods has been used. The forecast is 425 using the simple moving average approach. It is 432 using weighted moving average, largely because last week's high demand is the most heavily weighted. And it is 466 using the exponential smoothing approach. Given that different methods produce different forecasts, most managers initially use different methods and then adopt the method that proves to be the most accurate.

Causal modelling methods are more sophisticated quantitative approaches to forecasting. They tend to be used for fairly long-range forecasts and to predict when changes are likely to occur. This is because they take into account not simply historical data, but also the factors that may affect performance. Some of these factors may be generated by

TABLE 7.1 Comparison of time series forecasting methods

	Simple moving average	Weighted moving average	Exponential smoothing
Week 4	400	$400 \times 0.1 = 40$	
Week 3	450	$450 \times 0.2 = 90$	
Week 2	380	$380 \times 0.3 = 114$	
Week 1 (last week)	470	$470 \times 0.4 = 188$	470
Last week's forecast	N/a	N/a	450
Alpha	N/a	N/a	0.8
Forecast (this week)	425	432	466

N/a: not applicable

the organization, such as promotional sales campaigns, or externally, such as changes in interest rates or number of tourists to the UK.

One of the most common methods used is regression analysis—this models the variable you are interested in, i.e. the dependent variable, against one or more factors that may affect it, i.e. the independent variables. In terms of forecasting, the dependent variable is likely to be the number of customers expected or some other measure of volume. The independent variables will be those that are specifically relevant to the business you are in. One of the advantages of this approach is that an organization can use projections or forecasts developed by other organizations in order to forecast what will happen in its business. For instance, most experts agree that there is a strong link between gross domestic product (GDP) and air travel. Hence airlines can use governments' or consultants' forecasts of GDP in order to predict demand for their flights.

Subjective methods are qualitative approaches to forecasting. These tend to be used for looking forward in the long term rather than the short term. Hence a bus company might adopt this approach in order to plan what its fleet size might need to be five or ten years in the future. Likewise, theme park operators adopt this approach to plan their investment in new rides and infrastructure.

- Expert panel approach—a group of experts meet to determine their best guess to predict demand.
- Delphi—uses a questionnaire to gain information from a greater number of experts. The experts each work independently and do not know who else is providing an opinion. Once the information is collected and collated, it is circulated again in an effort to gain consensus among the experts as to the most likely outcome.
- Scenario planning—involves a group of experts looking at various possible scenarios and gauging the associated risks before coming up with a predicted demand.

It should be noted that in some circumstances, neither reservations nor forecasting are essential, because the operator knows that the operation will be at full capacity. This is because demand exceeds supply. In this instance tickets may still be issued, but not to control capacity, rather to ration those that wish to attend the event or use the service. Examples of this include major sports or entertainment events and demand for rail services on some rail lines at peak periods. Where tickets cannot be sold in advance, another sign that demand exceeds supply is when queues form. Queuing is discussed in Chapter 8.

RESEARCH INSIGHT 7.1

Ernst, A.T., Jiang, H., Krishnamoorthy, M., and Sier, D. (2004) Staff scheduling and rostering: A review of applications, methods and models, *European Journal of Operational Research*, 153(1), 3–27

One of the major reasons for engaging in forecasting is in order to determine how many staff might be needed. Indeed one of the major things that most operations managers would engage in is labour scheduling or rostering. And yet this is rarely talked about in the textbooks. What makes this article so interesting is that it reviews a whole range of different industries and identifies the specific scheduling issues in each one. As we shall see in a moment, using labour flexibly is a key aspect of capacity management.

OPERATIONS INSIGHT 7.2
Club 18–30—planning the summer season

This tour operator specializes in providing low-cost holidays in resorts that appeal to a specific age group. In 2011, it offered air travel from six different UK airports to ten summer holiday destinations, with a choice of up to 80 different hotels to stay in. In order to do this, the company has to forecast demand one year ahead for the following season and then negotiate contracts with airlines for airline seats, coach companies for transportation to and from the resort, and hotels in which its customers will stay. The forecasts have to be very detailed. Demand will vary over the course of a summer season, with July and August being the peak demand, and other months being periods of lower demand. The company also has to estimate the strength of demand in different regions of the UK, as most holidaymakers prefer to fly out from the airport nearest to them. Finally, it has to estimate the relative popularity of each resort and within each resort the demand for the different types of accommodation that it provides. For instance, in 2011, it offered nine different hotels in Magaluf, on the Spanish island of Majorca, that varied in size, facilities, and distance from the beach or nightlife.

The basis for forecasting next year's demand is clearly the level of demand in the current year, and perhaps the year before, to show general trends. However, simply knowing the number of customers that stayed in a particular hotel in a particular resort may not be enough. The company needs to know how many people made enquiries about staying there, in order to fully understand the potential demand for bed spaces. For instance, Club 18–30 may have had 100 bed spaces available in the Martinique Apartments throughout July 2010. In the first two weeks it may have had only 90 bookings, but in the second two weeks it may have been

Nightlife venues which are popular one year may go out of fashion the next. © istock/Abel Mitja Varela.

100% full and have turned away a further 20 customers. Hence for the coming year it may wish to adjust its inventory to reflect this by negotiation with the hotel, or alternatively seek to manage demand by offering a slightly lower price for the first two weeks of July and a higher price for the second two weeks.

As well as forecasting demand for flights and hotels based on customer data, Club 18–30 also takes into account other factors that may affect demand. Eighteen-to-30-year-olds are fashion conscious and holiday resorts come into and go out of fashion for all kinds of reasons. So whilst Ibiza may be the place to party this year, Majorca or another resort may come into fashion the next year. What makes a resort popular or less popular is complex, but largely derives from media reports and word of mouth. Such reports may either be positive about aspects of a destination (such as visited by celebrities, great weather, new attractions) or negative (such as reports of serious crime, a food poisoning outbreak, or industrial disputes by airport workers).

Having taken all of these factors into account Club 18–30 puts together a brochure for the season which specifies exactly which hotels and flights are available at specified prices. It also signs contracts with the airlines, coach companies, and hotels to ensure that transportation and bed spaces will be available. At this point its inventory is largely fixed and it hopes that its forecasts have been accurate so that no inventory is unsold. If it is, the company's fall-back position is that it can offer discounted holidays and last-minute deals that are designed to fill unsold space.

Sources: www.club18-30.com and authors' primary research

Questions

1. What are the specific challenges facing Club 18–30 in determining its capacity?

2. What methods of forecasting will be the most effective in helping Club 18–30 plan its brochure? How accurate are these likely to be?

Alternative strategies to manage capacity

So far we have only discussed how managers seek to know how busy they will be at any given time. We have not identified how they manage their operation based on this knowledge. There are three ways of doing so (Sasser et al. 1978)—the **level capacity strategy**, the chase demand strategy, and the demand management strategy. These are equally applicable to materials processing operations or customer processing operations.

> **Level capacity strategy** keeping inputs constant during periods of low demand to create inventory to meet periods of high demand

Level capacity strategy

This strategy is adopted where the operation can really only operate at one level or rate. It ignores any variation in demand, as illustrated in Figure 7.2. This is usually because

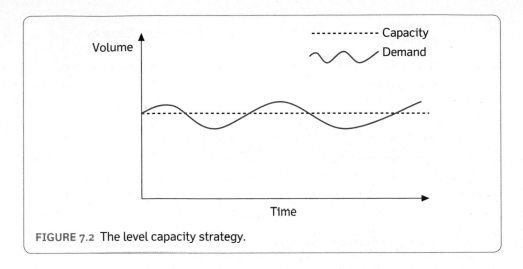

FIGURE 7.2 The level capacity strategy.

Go online

the provision is based on fixed capacity that cannot be changed, except in the long term. So hotels have a fixed number of bedrooms, theatres a fixed number of seats, and hospitals a certain number of X-ray machines. In effect, if demand exceeds this limited supply, customers are 'put into inventory', i.e. stored up until they can be processed. What this means is that for CPOs that have a reservations system, the booking is scheduled for a long time in the future. And for operations where customers just turn up, a queue forms.

This inflexible approach to managing capacity is great from an operations perspective, since it means that work is easily planned and managed, as there is always a relatively smooth flow of customers through the process. It obviously works best in situations where there is little or no variation, although such situations are extremely rare. For instance, there are some health services for which demand is constant and relatively stable—such as cancer treatment—but there many conditions which have seasonal fluctuations—such as influenza (prevalent in the winter), and even heart attacks (twice as many in January as in summer months). In addition this strategy's inflexibility may not please customers, because the service may not be available when they want it. So customers are more likely to accept this situation if it is one where they can appreciate the need to wait. For instance, theatre-goers in London know they have to book months in advance to see popular West End shows.

Chase demand strategy

The **chase demand strategy** adopts a completely different approach to capacity. In this instance, operators seek to match supply as closely to demand as possible. This is illustrated in Figure 7.3.

In order to do this well, the organization either needs a highly effective forecasting or reservation system. The main elements of the operation that can be made flexible in this way are the equipment and the workforce, and there are various ways in which managers can approach this.

Additional machinery can be made available or turned off to suit the demand. This is not always practical within a company and in some cases the additional equipment may come from outsourcing to subcontractors who are able to manufacture the required products.

Chase demand strategy
adjusting inputs so that outputs match demand

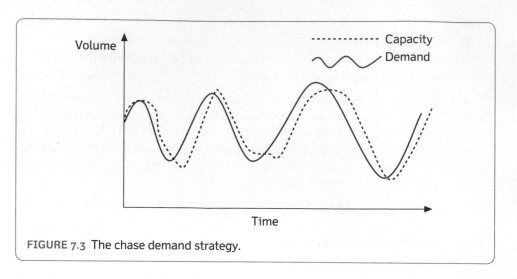

FIGURE 7.3 The chase demand strategy.

Go online

Compared with equipment, it is relatively easy to flex the workforce in a variety of ways. The seminal analysis of labour flexibility is given by Atkinson (1986), who identifies four types, as follows.

External numerical flexibility refers to adjusting the number of workers by recruiting more from the external labour market. This can be done by employing workers on temporary work or fixed-term contracts, subcontracting, or outsourcing work. This is typically done in order to cope with peaks in demand. For instance, the Royal Mail routinely employs extra postal workers at Christmas to cope with the greetings cards and parcels sent at this time of year. In the construction industry it is common to subcontract work to cope with peaks in demand for building works. The main advantage of this approach is that it is not too disruptive to the organization; the existing workforce is able to get on with their normal workload. The disadvantage of this approach is that there is a loss of control over processes, either to inexperienced workers or to other organizations, and as a result quality may suffer. In addition, it may be more costly to use external labour, although this would depend on the rates of pay and overtime existing workers are entitled to.

Internal numerical flexibility is sometimes known as working time flexibility or temporal flexibility. It is achieved by adjusting full-time employees' hours or schedules. This includes:

- Requiring full-time staff to work 'flexitime' or flexible working hours and shifts (including night shifts and weekend shifts). This enables the scheduling of staff so that they are at work specifically when they are needed. Many fast food restaurants schedule staff to start not just on the hour but on the half hour or quarter hour, and shifts may also be for multiples of 15 minutes (e.g. six and half hours, or seven and a quarter hours). The disadvantage of this from the manager's point of view is the complexity of scheduling, whilst employees may not like it because they are not sure when they are working from one week to the next. Many employees have social circumstances such as child care which do not fit easily with changing shift patterns.

- Employing workers on annualized hours. This is designed to cope with seasonal variation. Employees are guaranteed an average number of hours per week, but during the off season they may work fewer than this and during the high season work more.

- Hiring part-time workers. The advantage of this is there is a core of full-time employees who have set hours or shifts to work, and the part-time workers may not want, or be able to work, more hours. For instance, overseas students on visas are only allowed by law to work up to 20 hours per week. The downside of this approach is that part-timers may be less well trained and experienced than full-timers, and also be less committed to their employer.

- Arranging holiday and leave entitlements. Employees may be restricted as to when they take holidays to ensure they are available to cope with peak periods of demand.
- Paying overtime. To cope with peaks, full-time staff may be asked to work extra hours in return for which they are paid overtime. This is often the quickest and simplest way to resolve an unexpected surge in demand, so long as staff are willing to work the extra hours. Different sectors have different rates of pay for this, which are between one and half to twice normal hourly rates. The clear disadvantage of this approach is that it is increases labour cost significantly.

Functional flexibility or **multiskilling** is the extent to which employees can be transferred to different tasks or roles within the organization. Thus in CPOs that have relatively simple tasks, such as fast food, every employee might be expected to be able to work anywhere. In practice there may be limitations on how flexible people can be. Some occupations require a period of training that cannot be incorporated into a multiskilling scheme. Moreover if the industry has traditional ways of doing things, it also has well-established job titles. Employees therefore have an 'occupational identity'—they think of themselves in this job or role. Hence one of the first questions you ask a stranger is 'What do you do?' as this tells you a lot about that person (supposedly). This becomes a barrier to flexibility, as people are reluctant to shift from this identity and move out of their 'safety zone'.

> **Multiskilling** training employees to do a variety of tasks

Functional flexibility clearly enables a manager to move staff to where they are most needed. It therefore increases efficiency. But research has also identified a number of other benefits:

- Job satisfaction is increased, as multiskilled workers have more interesting work, greater confidence, and are encouraged to learn and develop.
- Increased staff retention, especially amongst part-time employees.
- Improved team working, as workers begin to appreciate the work their colleagues do in other parts of the organization.
- Improved work processes, as multiskill employees approach their second role with experience of the organization but objective insights towards their new department.
- Lower induction training costs, as multiskilled staff need only be inducted into the organization once.
- Better coordination and collaboration between heads of department because they have to jointly schedule multiskilled staff.

On the other hand there is an argument that increasing job complexity and work intensity promotes stress, which might lead to higher labour turnover rather than staff retention due to job satisfaction.

Not all multiskilling schemes are the same. Management have a number of choices to make. First, there are choices about the breadth of the scheme—the extent to which it will be applied across the operation and whether it will apply to all or only some of the workforce. Second, there is the issue of how to select staff for the scheme. In some organizations employee are asked to volunteer to be multiskilled, in others they are required to be. Third, there is the question of depth, the level of skill the employee will need to perform other roles. Will staff be expected to perform all, or just a selected number, of the tasks in their second (or subsequent) roles? Finally on a day-to-day basis it needs to be decided if staff will be moved between departments within a shift, or only on separate shifts.

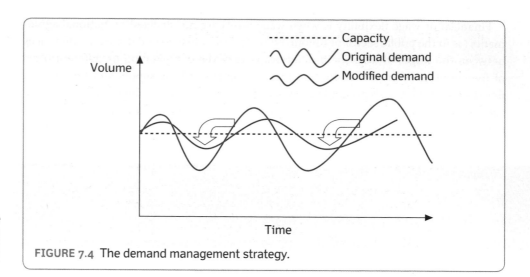

FIGURE 7.4 The demand management strategy.

Go online

The main way in which demand is shifted is through changes to the marketing mix, or four Ps, as follows:

- Price—this can be adjusted to encourage customers to come, usually through discounting, or discourage purchase, by adding a surcharge. Many nightclubs sell cheap drinks on quiet evenings of the week, like Tuesday, but put on an entrance fee on busy nights, such as Friday and Saturday.

- Promotion—linked to price there may be a variety of promotions such as buy-one-get-one-free, free wine with a meal, and so on. Happy hours in pubs and clubs are usually in the early evening in order to get customers arriving earlier than they might normally do.

- Product—the product or service itself may be modified so that it appeals to the off-peak market. Fast food chains have a different menu in the early morning from their standard menu, in order to attract breakfast customers.

- Place—different channels of distribution can be used to target specific market segments whose usage pattern is typically in off-peak periods. Theatres and cinemas specifically advertise to senior citizens their matinee or afternoon performances, for instance.

Depending on the nature of the business, shifting demand may be aimed at all customers, or specific segments of the market.

Strategy integration

Many organizations do not adopt one or other of these strategies, but use them in combination with each other. Three examples of how firms do this are given in Table 7.3.

Revenue management

Revenue management a system for managing advanced reservations through pricing and other mechanisms to maximize profitability

A major trend in many customer processing operations is so-called '**revenue management**' (RM). It is also known as 'yield management' by some authors, such as those in

TABLE 7.3 Integration of capacity management strategies

	Level capacity	Chase demand	Demand management
Airline	Maximum load as often as possible	Reservations staffing flex to meet booking patterns	Promote off-peak Manage revenue on seat by seat basis
Insurance	Protect back office experts from demand variation	Call centres scheduled for call patterns	Influence selling cycle and policy renewal peaks
Restaurant	Basics produced to stock	Staff rotas Use of part-time and casual staff On-call staff	Two-for-one offers Happy hour

Research insight 7.3 later in this chapter. Originating in the airline industry it is now commonly used in many other sectors that have fixed capacity, for example, hotels, golf clubs, and theatres. There are many definitions of RM. It has been defined as 'a method that can help a firm sell the right inventory unit to the right customer at the right time'. This definition is widely used in the industry. But prior to RM systems it seems unlikely that organizations were deliberately selling the 'wrong' inventory, to the 'wrong' customer, at the 'wrong' price. So if organizations have always tried to make as much money as they could out of their fixed capacity, how is RM different from what organizations have always done?

The major differences between a straightforward reservations system and a revenue management system are as follows:

- RM is supported by sophisticated IT systems specifically designed for this purpose.
- The RM system analyses data to produce very accurate forecasts of demand for any given day in the future.
- The system also analyses demand from a wide range of distribution channels so that different prices can be set for each channel.
- The system not only advises what price to charge but whether or not to take the booking. Reservations can be denied if the system forecasts a 'better' booking might be made later. A 'better' booking might be one that can be at a higher price or for a longer period of time (in a hotel).

So Jones (1999) defines revenue management as 'a system for [operators] to maximize profitability through their senior management in [operations] identifying the profitability of market segments, establishing value, setting prices, creating discount and displacement rules for application to the advanced reservations process, and monitoring the effectiveness of these rules and their implementation'.

Revenue management practice is not the same across all sectors. Unlike the airline business, in the hotel business a single reservation can have a 'displacement' effect. This is because instead of an airline customer reserving a seat on a specific flight, the hotel customer reserves a room for one or more nights. Hence a hotel reservation may span time periods for which demand is high and a high rate can be quoted (such as mid week in a business hotel), along with slack periods when the room rate would be lower (such as weekends in a business hotel). Moreover, in the airline industry RM is particularly

- **Name three different methods for forecasting demand**

  The three main approaches are time series forecasting (such as weighted average and exponential smoothing), causal modelling (such as regression analysis), and qualitative techniques (such as Delphi and expert panel).

- **Compare and contrast reservations systems with forecasting**

  Reservation systems enable operations managers to control both the volume and arrival rate of customers into a customer processing operation, which helps ensure the most efficient use of resources and no delays for customers. Forecasting is used when a reservations system cannot be used, to predict the likely volume of customers for any given period in advance.

- **Name the alternative strategies for managing capacity**

  There are three main approaches to managing capacity—level capacity, chase demand, and demand management.

- **Name the different forms of labour flexibility**

  There are four different forms of labour flexibility—external labour flexibility, temporal flexibility, functional flexibility, and financial flexibility.

- **Explain revenue management**

  Revenue management is 'a system for [operators] to maximize profitability through their senior management in [operations] identifying the profitability of market segments, establishing value, setting prices, creating discount and displacement rules for application to the advanced reservations process, and monitoring the effectiveness of these rules and their implementation' (Jones, 1999).

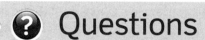 **Questions**

Review questions

1. What is the design capacity of an operation?

2. What is effective capacity of an operation?

3. What is the difference between efficiency and effectiveness?

4. Why is overall equipment effectiveness a better operations output measure than machine utilization?

5. What are the key differences between a level capacity strategy and a chase demand strategy?

6. Compare and contrast two different time series forecasting methods.

7. How does causal modelling help operations managers predict demand?

8. Identify some of the challenges that face an operations manager engaging in demand management.

9. What are the benefits and disadvantages of different forms of flexible working?

10. In what way is revenue management in the airline business different from the hotel business?

Discussion questions

1. Consider the capacity of a college or university. What are its design capacity, effective capacity, and achieved capacity?

2. How do different parts of a hospital (such as accident and emergency, the X-ray department, and surgical admissions) go about managing capacity?

3. How does a visitor attraction, such as Alton Towers, go about forecasting demand?

4. How do alternative demand management practices relate to market segmentation?

5. What forms of flexible working are most likely to be used in a mass service operation (such as a supermarket)?

Further learning guide

For an overview of forecasting and more detailed explanations of specific forecasting methods and techniques go to **www.statisticalforecasting.com**.

The Institute for Operations Research and Management Sciences (INFORMS) has a section devoted to revenue management (**http://revenue-mgt.section.informs.org**). This website provides an overview of the subject and links to a specialist journal and to suppliers of revenue management systems.

For further information on all kinds of flexible working, the UK government website (www.direct.gov.uk) has a great deal of information. It also outlines relevant legislation and regulations with regard to such employment practices.

References

Atkinson J. (1986) Employment flexibility in internal and external labour markets, in Dahrendorf, R., Kohler, E., and Piotet, F. (eds.), *New forms of work and activity*, European Foundation for the Improvement of Living and Working Conditions: Dublin

Jones, P. (1999) Yield management in UK hotels: A systems analysis, *Journal of Operational Research Society*, 50(11), 1111–19

Sasser, W.E., Wyckoff, D.D., and Olsen, M. (1978) *The management of service operations*, Allyn & Bacon: Boston, MA

Chapter Eight

Managing queuing and customer satisfaction

Learning outcomes

After reading this chapter you will be able to:

→ Explain the concept of the 'service encounter' and how it should be managed

→ Explain the principles of queuing theory and the psychology of waiting lines

→ Identify the reasons for service failure and explain alternative approaches to service recovery

→ Explain the concept of 'prosumption' and the different roles that customers may play in service operations

National Health Service waiting lists—patience wearing thin

With a change of UK Government in 1997, there was a pledge to reduce waiting times and waiting lists for National Health Service (NHS) inpatients and out-patients. This was operationalized in the NHS Plan (Department of Health 2001) and has largely been successful with the average wait for treatment for patients admitted to hospital falling to 8.6 weeks and outpatient waits at an average of 4.6 weeks in January 2009 (from 7.4 weeks at August 2007) (Department of Health 2009). A clear approach has been documented for reducing waiting lists and it involves a number of different approaches (Hensher and Edwards 2002) including buying extra capacity, avoiding inappropriate admission, providing alternatives to hospital admission, and accelerating discharge.

In terms of checking the appropriateness of admission, it is argued that most patients attending hospital have no appropriate alternative. One way to avoid inappropriate hospital admission is to manage patients in primary care. This allows certain patients to be seen in their home or community setting, thereby never actually reaching the hospital. The NHS is also introducing a referral management system which seeks to filter referrals to hospitals, even though many patients will have already been seen by their general practitioner. This system ensures that these generalist generated referrals are appropriate for a hospital setting. The NHS is also finding ways of providing specialist care outside a hospital, thereby again reducing waiting times. For instance, orthopaedic surgeons are running clinics within general practice clinics and there are minor injury clinics and independent sector-run treatment centres. The NHS has also started providing 'intermediate' care which includes community hospitals and care homes as a way of redirecting patients and reducing the waiting time for hospital care.

One other approach is to avoid hospital admission by undertaking some procedures as a day case operation, where the patient is not admitted to a ward. This increases the throughput of the hospital, again reducing the waiting list (Hensher and Edwards 2002). Between 1982 and 1999 inpatient cases

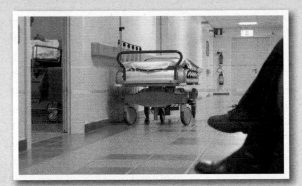

The NHS has adopted various approaches to ensure waiting list times have fallen. © istock/LdF.

increased by 48% but day cases increased by 344% (Hensher and Edwards 1999).

The final approach to reducing waiting lists is by increasing hospital throughput by accelerating hospital discharge. Considerable attention has been paid to improving planning discharge from hospitals. In the past this has not been well addressed and patients have remained in hospital blocking beds. The range of approaches include planning and implementing clear patient care pathways which focus on ensuring the patient leaves hospital at the appropriate time; that TTO (to-take-out) medication is waiting for the patient when he or she is ready to leave hospital (rather than the other way round); and making sure that there is liaison with social services so that patients have care and support on leaving hospitals. Using these techniques to increase capacity, speed throughput, and ensure that only appropriate patients are admitted to hospitals, waiting lists and times have been significantly reduced.

Sources: Hensher and Edwards 1999, 2002; Department of Health 2001

Questions

1. What are the main ways the NHS has reduced the waiting time for admission to hospital for routine treatment?

2. In what ways have these alternative approaches impacted on patients? Has this made their 'service experience' better?

Introduction

In a manufacturing organization it is usually only a few staff, mainly sales-related, that meet customers on a face-to-face basis. But in service organizations, often processing thousands of customers a week, it is the majority of employees who are customer-facing. This means that managing such interaction is extremely challenging. Managers cannot be present all the time. Therefore they have to rely on employees to deal with customers in the appropriate way. Exactly how this is done will vary from one type of customer processing operations—service shop, service factory, or mass service—to another (see page 68). We have also seen in Chapter 1, that in self-serve situations customers themselves 'become' employees (see page 23).

Service encounter the interaction between the customer and service provider

Customer processing is based around the management of the so-called 'service encounter'. A service encounter is that period of time during which the customer and the service organization interact face-to-face, over the telephone, or through any other media. These contact points are frequently called 'moments of truth' (Gronroos 1988), in other words events where the customer evaluates whether the business has or has not met expectations. Three key players shape the outcome of any encounter: the service organization that sets policies and guidelines on how to process and deal with customers; the employees who follows these policies and guidelines (or not!); and the customer, who has needs and wants to be satisfied.

This chapter begins by looking at the concept of the service encounter and the factors that need to be considered to make it successful. It goes on to identify that many processes are made up of a series of encounters. These are often separated by customers waiting in queues, either as part of the process or because the operation has a bottleneck at some stage. The role that technology can play in processing customers is then reviewed. Finally the issues of service failure and service recovery are discussed.

The service encounter

Seven key characteristics of a service encounter were identified over 20 years ago by Czepiel and his colleagues (1985). These characteristics are:

- Specific roles for both the service employee and customer.
- Goal orientation—both parties are seeking something from the event.
- Mostly task oriented—the encounter is defined by the specific process in which the customers is engaged.
- Undertaken as part of work activities—the relationship is therefore not social; although normal 'rules' of society may be observed.
- Primarily a stranger relationship—customers and employees have not met before (although loyal customers may well establish relationships with long-serving employees that have served them before).
- Narrow in scope—only surface topics of conversation.
- Mostly follow a predefined set of rules to facilitate the interaction, in some cases the employee may even follow a predetermined script.

A number of factors influence the success, or otherwise, of the service encounter. These are:

Staff attitude/service predisposition: research has suggested some people have a predisposition towards customer service. This customer-oriented approach tends to be demonstrated by employees who can communicate effectively, be effective team workers, understand customers' emotional demands, and understand the importance of serving customers well within the broader context of the organization. Varca (2004) summarized such a predisposition as comprising skills, personality, and attitudes, specifically in terms of oral communication skills, empathy, stress tolerance, social sensitivity, and behavioural flexibility. So some organizations now use personality or psychometric tests in order to recruit employees with the 'right' disposition.

Recruitment and selection of suitable employees: if skills, personality, and attitudes are important, service organizations need to ensure that recruitment advertising identifies these characteristics and that selection processes are designed to identify and measure these. Some service organizations now use competency based interviewing in order to select staff, since it requires applicants to give examples of how they have behaved in the past to show their level of competency in relevant aspects of the job.

Appropriate induction and training of employees: even if employees are selected on the basis of their pre-dispositions, customer service skills can be further enhanced by the correct training. Organization interested in how to do this can always follows the British Standard code of practice on customer service.

Empowering front-line workers: empowerment refers to giving front-line staff the latitude in decision-making to provide satisfying service to the customer (see Operations insight 8.3 about Ritz-Carlton later in this chapter). McColl-Kennedy and Sparks (2003) showed that the ability of frontline personnel to think about alternatives was a key factor in determining customers' satisfaction with the organization, and hence may lead to more examples of 'peak performance' (discussed later in this section).

Systems for optimizing the service encounter: managers need to ensure there are good systems in place to facilitate the offering of service to customers. This requires undertaking various analyses of the service delivery processes. In Chapter 4 we considered the servicescape, and how this can positively influence customers. But in addition to the interior design and ambiance of an outlet, we also have to consider the flow of customers through the service process. Service blueprints or flow charts provide insight into overall service delivery and identify any points in the process that may be susceptible to error. In Chapter 10 we look at process design in more detail.

Monitoring service encounter performance: managers typically monitor performance through various mechanisms including mystery shoppers, observation by supervisors, and the development of rating criteria. Much of this information can be used to provide ongoing feedback to service staff. However, research suggests that most service personnel are not informed about the day-to-day quality of their job performance.

Culture: as we have already noted, service encounter interactions between customers and frontline staff have a social dimension, which may well vary from one culture to another. So it is not surprising that a customer's cultural orientation can influence how the service encounter is experienced and evaluated. This issue is further discussed in Chapter 17 on globalization.

Communication: communication effectiveness is vital to the service encounter as it ensures the process is followed correctly. Moreover, communication, especially the interpersonal interactions between providers and customers, forms the basis of many service quality evaluations. Early work by Parasuraman and colleagues (1988) highlighted the importance of responsiveness, courtesy, empathy, and communicative aspects of the service provider's behaviour in terms of how consumers make evaluations about service purchases. In a service interaction there is a complex language of communication that takes place, which involves not only the spoken word but a range of non-verbal behaviours. Non-verbal communication can actually make a significant difference as to how a customer might perceive an otherwise identical event. For instance, British army personnel are trained to remove sun glasses when meeting civilians, because direct eye contact is an important part of talking to people.

Control and efficiency: an issue for many customer processing operations is how to control the encounter and ensure it is efficient. Bateson (2000) characterizes the service encounter as a 'three cornered' struggle for control, with the customer, the front-line employee, and the organization all vying to control the encounter. A simple study by Nightingale (1985) into the provision of beverages during conferences, showed that customers, employees, and managers all had a very different view as to what constituted a good 'beverage break'. The customer focused on speed, the employee on the quality of coffee, and the management on the cleanliness of the equipment. This issue of ensuring standards will be discussed in more detail when we look at how quality is managed in operations (see Chapter 9).

Although often thought of as a single event, in many customer processing operations, there are a chain of service encounters, during which the customer may come into contact with a number of service personnel. Verhoef et al. (2004) researched how individual events contribute to customers' overall evaluation with a process. They found that while the average performance during the encounter is important, satisfaction typically arises from 'peak performances', i.e. occasions when employees performed at a very high level, sometimes above the expectations of the customer. Other research (Hansen and Danaher, 1999) suggests that the performance trend—that is, whether positive or negative performances are first or last in the sequence—also significantly impact customer evaluations. It has also been suggested that a service encounter in one service organization affects the perceived quality of another encounter provided by a different service organization.

OPERATIONS INSIGHT 8.1
T.G.I. Friday's restaurants—making memorable service encounters

This restaurant chain has always had a very clear approach to how it recruits and trains its staff. Firstly it is clear that it is looking for a particular kind of person—outgoing, friendly, and enthusiastic. In order to ensure such people are recruited, applicants are typically invited (in their own time and at their own expense) to spend some time in the restaurant to see for themselves what it is like—to get a 'feel' for the place. Applicants will also go through at least two and sometimes three interviews—first with a supervisor, then with an assistant manager and finally with the general manager. In other words T.G.I. Friday's make it difficult for applicants to get the job—so that those that do tend to be highly committed to the organization from day one.

Second, the restaurant chain has a rigorous training programme that systematically takes employees through all the operational standards. Employees are then tested on their product knowledge through a series of quizzes. All of this is done in the context of what the chain calls 'positive management'—praising good performance rather than finding fault with employees.

Third, T.G.I. Friday's has a very distinctive organizational culture which is designed to reinforce their strategy. Every employee knows that the goal of the firm is to win the loyalty of their customers so that they will revisit the restaurant. To do this employees understand that they have to 'wow' the customer—give them a really good experience, or in TGIF-speak an 'A-plus experience'. This culture manifests itself in a number of ways—through language, dress code, 'heroes', and organizational rituals. The chain has its own jargon that has grown up over the years—for instance, wait staff are 'dub-dubs' and team members in general 'Fridoids'—all of which reinforces the team ethos and gives employees a sense of 'belonging' to the group. Dub-dubs wear a uniform, but are then expected to customize this by the extravagant display of badges and pins, as well as unusual headgear. This is all part of the fun image of the restaurant. The company also recognizes excellent employees as 'heroes' and writes about them on the Fridoid blog (www.fridoids.co.uk/blog). Finally, one example of an organizational ritual is that the management team have a 15-minute team briefing before the restaurant opens to ensure the team is 'ready for action'. This briefing is the opportunity to reinforce standards, continuously train staff, and identify any specific features of the service that day.

Sources: www.fridoids.co.uk; www.tgifridays.co.uk; BBC 'Business Matters' video 'Front Line Managers'

Questions

1. What impacts—both positive and negative—might the approach adopted by T.G.I. Friday's have on the customer experience?

2. In what other types of service operation might this approach be desirable? In what settings might it be undesirable?

Queuing

Often a key part of a customer process or chain of encounters is queuing. A queue is a situation in which the customer is passively engaged with the process, waiting for action to be taken in some way. Queuing theory was developed in the early 1900s by A.K. Erlang to study fluctuating demands in telephone traffic. After World War II, Erlang's work was extended to general business applications, and today it is used extensively in both materials and customer processing operations. As we saw in Chapter 7, operations management frequently applies scheduling, simulation, forecasting, and process design to manage materials flow. Similar techniques can be used to manager customer flow and queues, although waiting time can rarely be eliminated completely.

The key characteristics of a **queuing system** in a customer processing operations are:

Queuing system the organization of customers for processing through a service experience

- Population of customers—this can be either limited or unlimited. An unlimited population represents a system with a large number of possible customers (a store in a shopping mall or a motorway petrol station). Whereas a limited population may be a process where the number of customers is predetermined or known, such as the number of guests staying in a hotel.

- Arrival pattern—this refers to how users enter the system. Typically arrivals follow no pattern with random intervals between each one.

- Queue—this specifically refers to the number of customers waiting in line. Someone being served is not usually included in the queue. In some operations customers form a physical queue (people waiting in a line in a supermarket), but sometimes the queue is hidden or 'virtual' (telephone callers waiting to speak to a call centre operative).

- System capacity—this is the maximum number of users waiting in the queue and being served.

- Queuing discipline—this refers to how the queue is managed (based around rules allowing customer to join or leave the queue). There are a number of alternatives:

  - FIFO (first in, first out) or FCFS (first come, first serve). This is what most customers expect.

  - LIFO (last in, first out) also called LCFS (last come, first serve). In poorly organized systems this might occur, but it is likely to lead to a high level of customer complaints about the 'unfairness' of the system.

  - SPF (shortest processed first). This is a queuing system in which brief transactions with sooner—as in a six-items-only queue in a supermarket. This can work well but only if users understand it and respect the concept.

  - SIRO (serve in random order). This occurs in especially busy areas where there is no obvious queue—for instance, in bars and clubs on Saturday nights.

- Service—this is what customers are waiting for. The service transaction can be relatively simple and brief (as in a fast food restaurant) or complex and lengthy (as in the accident and emergency department of a hospital). Lengthy service processes are often broken up into a series of encounters with different employers. However, there is evidence from at least one study that customers do not like this. For example, Dube and colleagues (1991) found customers preferred to wait eight minutes at once rather than to wait five minutes in one line and three minutes in a second line. Therefore, they suggested that service providers should minimize waiting time before and after service, and should integrate a series of short waiting steps into a longer waiting period, if possible.

- Output—this refers to the way customers leave the system.

There are a number of alternative queuing systems, depending on the number of waiting lines or 'channels' and service points. These are:

- Single line queue—this entails all customers lining up one behind the other, usually on the basis of when they arrive. This is typically found in banks and post offices. Customers appreciate this system because they consider it to be fair.

- Multiple channels—this is the typical arrangement in fast food outlets and supermarkets. There are a number of individual queues, with no filtering of customers so that they search for and join the shortest queue. If transaction times vary from one customer to another, customers may end up waiting for more than the average service time and as a consequence become resentful, stressed, or anxious. Whilst this form of queue makes good use of space, it is really only appropriate for low-value transactions, with a relatively low level of service expected by customers.

- Diffuse queue—the best example of this is the 'take-a-ticket' queuing model. There is no actual line but customers register their place in the process with a ticket. Supermarkets often do this at their delicatessen counter. The great advantage of this is that customers can browse if they want to while they are waiting. The disadvantage of this system is that customers find it difficult to estimate when they will be served, so they are continually monitoring the ticket number being served. To overcome this, more sophisticated versions provide zoned service or display expected time for service information. Customers should be encouraged to browse so that they move away from the ticket dispenser, which allows other customers to see and use the ticket dispenser. This approach is the most appropriate for transactions that vary widely in their duration.

- Priority queue—this involves a number of different queues for various types of customer. For instance, airports often have 'fast track' channels for first and business class passengers and supermarkets have priority queues for customers paying cash.

Queuing theory is a variety of mathematical models of different queuing systems that combine features such as arrival pattern, queue length, and system capacity in order to design more efficient and effective queues. Such modelling is typically a trade-off between reducing the length of time that customers wait (in order to increase customer satisfaction) and the cost of doing so. Where multiple queues are used, simulation is used to design the best system.

RESEARCH INSIGHT 8.1

Sheu, C., McHaney, R., and Babbar, S. (2003) Service process design flexibility and customer waiting time, *International Journal of Operations & Production Management*, 23(8), 901–17

This article has been selected because it ties together a number of topics—process design, queuing theory, wait time, and simulation. Sheu and colleagues run a number of computer simulations for two different processes—order taking and order preparation. These simulations show no one queue design outperforms the others at all levels of demand. What this suggests is that queue design needs to be flexible—adopting one approach when demand is relatively low and steady, and a different approach when it gets busier.

Queuing behaviours

Good queue management requires managers to observe customer behaviour. All customers are initially attracted to a service operation and therefore move towards it. Often this involves joining a queue. The sight of a queue may be enough to deter some customers and they 'reject' the service and avoid waiting in line. In some instances there may be a maximum number that can safely queue for a service and so the system would

FIGURE 8.1 Queuing behaviours. Adapted from *Operations Management*, Slack et al., Pearson Education Limited. Copyright 2010.

then reject additional customers. When customers join a queue initially but then almost immediately leave it believing that the queue will take too long to disperse, the behaviour is known as 'balking'.

A sign that customers are unhappy with the system is 'reneging' behaviour i.e. customers leaving the queue after they have joined it for some time. However, people may be deterred from leaving the queue by its length. Zhou and Soman (2003) found that as the number of people behind in the queue increases the consumer is less likely to renege, largely because they felt better relative to those behind them, who were seen as less fortunate than themselves. Figure 8.1 illustrates these behaviour types.

Managers should also clearly identify the start and end points of any queue so that customers can see clearly where they go to join it. Ideally the direction of the queue and where it ends should also be visible, so that people queuing know they are travelling in the right direction and can find their way out after service. Where there are several queues in operation, perhaps for different types of service or goods, it must be made clear to consumers what each queue is for. Clear signage that is easy to understand is essential for this.

OPERATIONS INSIGHT 8.2
Heathrow Terminal 5—flying without tears

Anyone travelling by air goes through a series of 'service encounters' when they arrive at an airport to board their flight. For some passengers this experience can be a nightmare, especially in large, very busy airports. Even before they arrive at the airport passengers are likely to be stressed—they do not want to miss their flight, so they are very conscious of time, and they may be concerned about the actual flight itself, as some passengers do not like flying. In addition, they have suitcases and hand luggage to carry or wheel on a trolley. So they are physically encumbered, which makes moving around difficult, and stressed because they are concerned about the security of their belongings in such a busy space.

The stereotypical airport experience comprises a long wait at the check-in desk to obtain a boarding pass and check in bags, a queue to go through immigration, and an even longer queue to go through security. Once in the departure lounge there are then queues in the coffee shops and restaurants, queues at the duty free check out, and even (on a

Increased space between the entrance doors and the check-in desks at Heathrow's Terminal 5. © istock/Alan Crawford.

bad day) queues to use the toilets. Then when the flight is called there are further queues to get into the gate lounge and another to get on the aircraft. The whole process might take more than two hours of which more than half can be spent waiting in line.

Of course, it need not be like this. Modern airports can be designed to considerably improve the passenger experience. The new terminal at London Heathrow airport illustrates this. As British Airways (BA) states 'The creation of Terminal 5 was a once-in-a-lifetime opportunity for us to redefine air travel. Our aim was to replace the queues, the crowds and the stress with space, light and calm'. All reports suggest that, after initial teething problems, they have succeeded in doing so. BA believe that the average passenger now takes less than 10 minutes in getting from their entry into the terminal to sitting down in the departure lounge. To achieve this they have done a number of things:

- Increased the space between the entrance doors and the check-in desks.
- Increased the number of check-in desks to 96 in total.
- Encouraged their passengers to go online up to 24 hours before their flight in order to select their seat and print off their boarding pass.
- Installed a large number of self-service check-in machines.
- Provided customer service agents to guide and assist passengers through the process.
- Separated the process of getting a boarding pass from that of dropping off bags, so that there are now 'fast bag drops'.
- Installed the most modern equipment at immigration desks.
- Increased the number of channels and staff at security.

Source: various newspaper reports and websites

Questions

1. What are the factors that influence customer satisfaction with their airport experience?
2. What can airport management do to improve this experience?

the market segments that may be using these vehicles, to ensure that the services on board are able to cope with the different demands of these segments. Most tourist passengers adopt a very similar behaviour. Upon leaving the car decks, they secure a place on the seating decks and 'nest'—that is to say they select the specific seats they plan to occupy for the 90-minute crossing. If the passengers plan to have a main meal they will nest in the restaurant or food court, if not they will select one of the bars or lounges. Having done this, one of the family or group is sent out to 'scout' the ship in order to locate the service areas that they plan to use. These are the toilets, the food and beverage outlets, the shop, and the foreign exchange kiosk.

P&O Ferries tries to reduce this scouting behaviour because it increases the level of congestion and prevents customers arriving from the car decks finding a space easily. To do this they provide 'pre-awareness' materials designed to familiarize travellers with the ship's layout. Such material includes brochures, emails, and promotional flyers that show what facilities are on board and where they are located on the ship. This is also done in order to promote buying behaviour. At stair wells, each ferry also has large plans of the vessel showing the location of different types of facility.

Having done the scouting, 'expeditions' are sent out from the nest to buy drinks or food, shop, and exchange currency. And despite the fact that passengers could be on the ferry for 90 minutes or more, they try to do all of this in the first 30 minutes on board. There are a number of reasons for this. First, having travelled to the port they may be very thirsty or hungry. Second, they know the crossing is short, so want to be sure they do everything they need to well ahead of arrival. And third, they see everyone else doing it, and hence queues building up, so they adopt the same behaviour.

P&O Ferries organize these queues in a variety of ways. The largest restaurant facility is designed as a food court, made up of a variety of separate food counters serving different style of food—starters, salads, main courses, chilled items, beverages, and desserts. So that this does not get too crowded, customers queue in a single zig-zag line before taking a tray and having access to the counters. They then 'free flow' around the food court and queue again at tills before exiting to the seating area. In the shop there are multiple queues at multiple tills, but at the foreign exchange and in the coffee shops there is a single line. Bar service is first come, first served at any point along the counter.

Whilst most tourists and families follow the common behaviour described above, there are clearly identifiable subgroups who do not. For instance, lorry drivers have their own cafeteria, shop, and drivers' lounge, so that they rarely if ever come into contact with other passengers. Most ferries also provide showers for such drivers, since on long trans-European trips, drivers may sleep in their lorries. Coach parties also exhibit specific behaviours. Around Easter there are many school parties, whose spending pattern is quite different to parties of over 50s. Moreover their queuing behaviour is different, with older groups forming elegantly ordered lines, whilst younger people clump together and jostle. Some groups, such as sports clubs and university students go direct to the bars and stay there the whole time.

Aware that onboard behaviour and spending can vary widely, P&O Ferries carefully forecasts these patterns of demand and the likely segment mix so that the different retail areas of the ship can be staffed appropriately. Such forecasting ensures that sufficient service points and tills are open to optimize the flow of passengers. The result of this highly efficient and well-organized system is that in 2009, the company's Dover–Calais ferries carried a total of 7.1 million people, 61,300 coaches, 1.4 million tourist vehicles, and 1.1 million HGVs.

Source: author's primary research

Questions

1. What makes it challenging for P&O Ferries to process customers on the Dover–Calais crossing?

2. How does the company manage queues at the port? And how does it manage queues on board the ferry?

3. How might the servicescape of a ferry be designed to manage queues?

Chapter summary

To consolidate your learning, the key points from this chapter are summarized as follows:

- **Explain the concept of the 'service encounter' and how it should be managed**

  A service encounter is that period of time during which the customer and the service organization interact face-to-face, over the telephone, or through other media. Many customer processing operations involve a series of such encounters. Blueprinting or flow charting the process and specifically identifying the employee/customer interfaces enables the process to be designed efficiently and employees trained appropriately.

- **Explain the principles of queuing theory and the psychology of waiting lines**

  A queue is a situation in which the customer is passively engaged with the process, waiting for action to be taken in some way. Queuing theory comprises mathematical models of various queuing systems that analyse data such as arrival pattern, queue length, system capacity, and queuing discipline in order to design more efficient and effective queues. Such modelling is typically a trade-off between reducing the length of time that customers wait (in order to increase customer satisfaction) and the cost of doing so.

  Customers typically believe they have waited longer in a queue than they actually have. This is more likely to happen if customers spend time in the queue unoccupied, pre-process, uncertain, without explanation, unfairly, on their own, or uncomfortably. Customers are also happy to wait longer if the service is valuable to them or they are experienced users of the service.

- **Identify the reasons for service failure and explain alternative approaches to service recovery**

  There are three main reasons for service failure—new or untrained employees, technological breakdown, or first-time customers of the operation. The main ways of recovering from a service failure are to offer an apology, put the error right, explain the cause of the error, or compensate the customer in some way.

- **Explain the concept of 'prosumption' and the different roles that customer may play in service operations**

  Prosumption refers to the role that customers play in the co-creation and co-production of services. This means that customers play a significant role in the operation and can have roles such as end user, co-producer, co-consumer, and inspector.

Questions

Review questions

1. What are the seven key characteristics of a service encounter?
2. What makes a 'good' service encounter?
3. What is the difference between queuing discipline and queuing system?

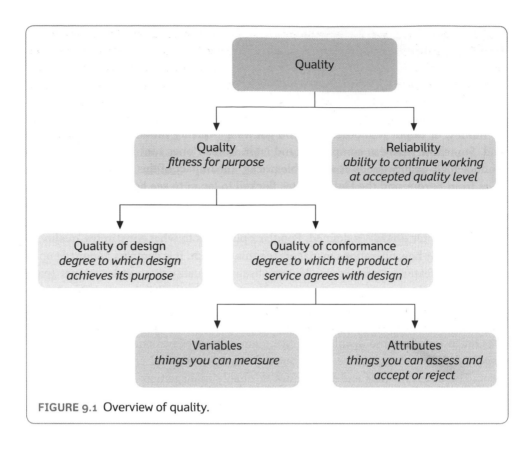

FIGURE 9.1 Overview of quality.

able to do so consistently over time (be reliable). Second, they have to make products or deliver services in such a way that meets these design criteria. It is no good having a brilliantly designed light bulb, if it is made so badly that it fails shortly after purchase.

There are two kinds of conformance criteria, i.e. the specifications or standards laid down. Variables are features that can be measured on a scale of some kind. Whereas attributes are features that are either present or not present. For example, a light bulb may have a bayonet fitting or not (attribute) and give out a specified amount of light in lumens (variable). This discussion of what is meant by quality is illustrated in Figure 9.1.

The quality challenge

Quality is both central to successful operations and difficult to achieve. It is fundamental because customers make quality judgements all the time. Indeed a whole industry has grown up that enables and facilitates consumers to make choices based on thorough testing and evaluations of products and services. Most notable amongst these is *Which?* magazine, but all kinds of media do consumer testing and advice—from car shows on television to specialist magazines such as *Angling Times*. Indeed, with the growth of the Internet, quality rating is no longer just done by critics or experts, customers themselves can go online and rate products and service themselves through a huge variety of websites. For instance, www.airlinemeals.net has photographs and reviews of thousands of airline meals from over 150 different airlines throughout the world.

The second challenge for operations managers is conformance. In assembly line operations, many thousands of parts may be processed to make hundreds of finished products in a day. Every single component has to work. Likewise, in mass service operations there can be thousands of service encounters every day, each of which also has to meet customer expectations. What every organization would like to have is 'zero defects'—a term originally coined by one of the gurus of quality management, Phil Crosby (1979). Zero defects literally means no mistakes or errors at all, irrespective of how many products are made or customers served. In other words, it means perfection. How organizations seek to achieve this nirvana is the subject of the rest of this chapter.

The quality gap model

Since zero defects is a very high level of performance it helps to understand how and why defects or errors can occur. The quality gap model, as shown in Figure 9.2, identifies five main ways in which quality may be lower than desired. Originally developed with customer processing operations in mind, it is equally valid for materials processing.

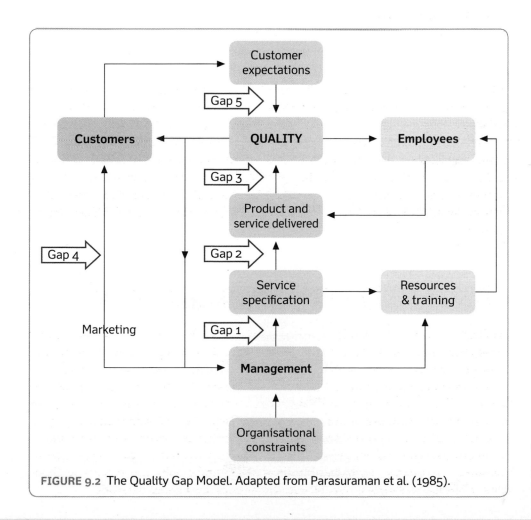

FIGURE 9.2 The Quality Gap Model. Adapted from Parasuraman et al. (1985).

Go online

The positioning gap develops if the product or service concept diverges from customer requirements. This may happen if fashion or demographic change affects the marketplace. Long-term control of the positioning gap can be achieved by regular top-level reviews of the established product or service. This is usually done through both qualitative and quantitative market research, aimed at identifying customers' current wants and needs. The product concept should also take account of competitors' activities and the differentiating 'edge'—the distinctive skills, assets, and know-how of the organization.

The specification gap refers to the difference between actual standards set by management compared with managers' understanding of customer needs. If this occurs, it is usual that managers specify a standard lower than that expected by customers. It may seem strange for managers to do this, but they do so for a number of reasons:

- A belief that customers' expectations are unrealistic or unachievable.
- A view that failure to deliver on one feature of a product or service can be more than compensated by other features.
- A concern that overdelivery of features will erode margins and reduce the return on investment.

The delivery gap develops where employees do not, or cannot, make a product or deliver a service to the standard required. This tends to be where most managers focus their attention. This is because their day-to-day activity is centred on managing processes, but perhaps also because they fail to recognize the existence of the other gaps.

The fourth gap relates to promotional communication. This has an important influence upon customer perceptions of quality, because for many operations it is the basis upon which customers build their expectations. Therefore, organizations need to ensure that marketing, advertising, and promotion does not make a 'promise' that they cannot keep.

The perception gap is the only one of the five gaps over which the operations manager has little or no direct control. It is the gap between what the customer expected and what they perceived they got. We have already seen that customers' perceptions may be different from reality when we looked at queuing and the perception of waiting times (page 208). This same kind of perceptual difference can also apply to product features and other elements of service. These five gaps are summarized in Table 9.1.

TABLE 9.1 The 'Five Gap Model' of quality.

Gap	Name	Definition
1	Positioning	Between management perceptions of customer expectations and the expectations themselves
2	Specification	Between management perceptions of customer expectations and the actual product/service specified
3	Delivery	Between the product/service promised and that actually delivered
4	Communication	Between the product/service actually delivered and that externally communicated to customers (e.g. through advertising)
5	Perception	Between the product/service quality perceived and that expected by the customer

New Coke—quality gaps at work

On 23 April 1985 Coca-Cola changed the formulation of their soft drink and relaunched it onto the market with one of the most expensive global marketing campaigns ever. The reaction was not what they expected. Market research, and in particular blind tastings of their original product and Pepsi, showed that customers preferred the taste of their major competitors. Coke was too sweet. New Coke was therefore designed to more closely match customer expectations by changing the formula. So con-

Fuss and media coverage of the launch led to great sales for Coca-Cola. © istock/Liv Friis-Larsen

fident was the company that they would meet their customers' expectations, not only did they launch new Coke, but they announced that the old style Coke would no longer be available. But within days of the launch protests groups began to spring up demanding that old style Coke be reinstated, especially in the Southern states of the USA where Coca Cola was originally from. Bottles and cans of new Coke were being opened in the streets and poured down the drain. Protesters with placards were walking up and down outside Coca-Cola's headquarters in Atlanta. The situation became even more serious when companies that bottled the drink started legal proceedings against the company. These bottlers feared a decline in revenue if the new product sold in lower volumes. On 10 July, less than three months later, Coca-Cola climbed down and announced that the old formula Coke would be reintroduced to the market and sold as Coke Classic.

Despite often being referred to as the worst product launch of all time, Coca-Cola did very well out of it. First, some consumers did like new Coke and it sold reasonably well. But more importantly, all the fuss and media coverage meant that when Coke Classic was relaunched, it had really great sales. By the end of 1985, Cokes sales were increasing at double the rate of Pepsi.

Sources: numerous newspaper reports

Questions

1. Which of the quality gaps led to new Coke being perceived as a failure?
2. If consumers were buying old Coke even though they thought it too sweet, what attributes of the product were they buying?

The cost of quality

If an organization tries to ensure quality but fails to do so, this may lead to extra costs. Such 'quality costs' fall into four main categories:

- Prevention—costs of setting up standards and a system to maintain them, e.g. training staff, preparing purchase specifications, developing standards, monitoring, and documentation procedures.

- Assurance—cost of actually maintaining standards, e.g. resources required for inspection, measurement, and documentation cost of surveys and audits.

- Internal failure—costs due to waste or losses before the product reaches the customer, e.g. rejection of raw materials, losses due to faulty storage, downtime, scrap, rework.

- External failure—costs due to defective items reaching the customer, e.g. warranty costs, poor word-of-mouth, ultimately marketing costs and loss of repeat business.

The four types of quality cost are shown in Figure 9.3. This also illustrates how the total cost of quality can change over time, if greater emphasis is placed on prevention and assurance. Total cost falls because internal and external failure costs decline. This is the argument that underpins the adoption of more sophisticated approaches to quality management—which are discussed in the next section.

Phil Crosby (1979) has identified what he calls the 'price of non-conformance' (PONC). This is the cost to management of not getting it right first time and every time. In other words, the cost of internal and external failure. Calculating the cost of quality in this way is, of course, difficult because the value of lost repeat business and customer dissatisfaction, for example, is not easy to assess. However, many companies in the manufacturing sector already assign such costs to their service operations. The normal procedure is to decide standard costs for specific failure events and to multiply them by the number of such failure events. PONC calculations are usually carried out department by department, and individual mangers are consulted as to what constitutes a 'non-conformance'. Even today, Phil Crosby Associates estimate PONC to be 25–40% of operating cost (www.philipcrosby.com/pca/B.FAQ.html).

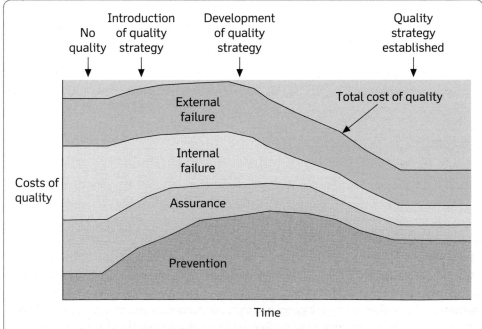

FIGURE 9.3 The costs of quality. Adapted from *Operations Management*, Slack et al., Pearson Education Limited. Copyright 2010.

Alternative strategies for managing quality

There are five basic approaches to quality management. These are not mutually exclusive but range from very straightforward and simple approaches (such as quality inspection (QI) and **quality control** (QC)) up to more sophisticated approaches (such as total quality management (TQM)) as shown in Figure 9.4.

Quality inspection

The simplest way to manage quality is to inspect the product before it is sold to the customer. Therefore the goals of a QI system are very simple: set up a specification of the product, cost it, and detect any defects before delivering it or selling it to the end user. It is very much a 'shop-floor' activity, involving only those employees directly concerned with the making of the product or delivery of the service, and their superiors. This means QI takes place after the product has been produced.

The problems with this approach are:

- In materials processing operations there are the costs of rework and scrap—once a fault or error is detected it is too late to do anything about it.

- It is not really workable in customer processing operations because production and consumption happen at the same time. In a QI-based system the customer becomes the inspector and hence experiences poor service.

- It does little for staff motivation as it tends to accentuate negative feedback in terms performance.

- The system can only be improved by increased inspection, thus increasing cost. Because of this, there is often a trade-off between quality and cost.

In view of this, most organizations try to exercise more control over processes. However, this approach is still used in relatively simple contexts. For instance, the housekeeping department in a hotel usually has QI. After the room attendant has cleaned the room, a floor supervisor goes round to check if the room meets the required standard.

Quality control

In this control model of quality management, after designing the quality level and setting standards, the principal role of the manager is checking on conformance, at several stages in the total process. Two features can be monitored—the actual outcomes and the process of working practices employed. But even though the outputs of sub-processes are checked, this system has some of the problems associated with QI. Errors and faults are likely to be detected earlier in the total process, there may still be scrap and rework costs. In this approach, quality can be measured internally or by an external auditor. Typically a number of approaches are adopted, such as internal inspection by

Quality control processes designed to monitor production or operations in order to maintain quality

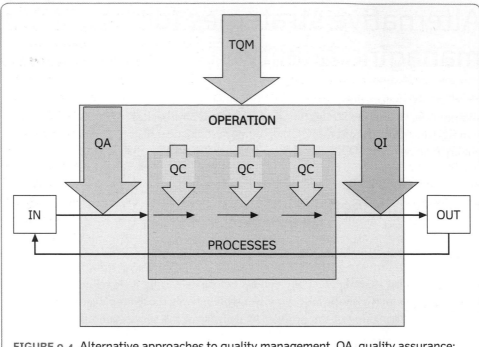

FIGURE 9.4 Alternative approaches to quality management. QA, quality assurance; QC, quality control; QI, quality inspection; TQM, total quality management.

Go online

quality inspectors, quality audits by management, and mystery shopper or mystery guest programmes.

Quality assurance

The essential difference between control and assurance is that the assurance concept is designed to ensure that errors and faults do not occur in the first place. This is often referred to as 'get it right first time every time'. This is particularly important where there is face-to-face contact with customers, as badly handled service encounters are very difficult to correct. Some of the tools and techniques that support **quality assurance** (QA) are discussed in the next part of the chapter.

In a QA-based operation, the whole operational context and management style is likely to be different to that in a QC-based system. For instance, management and staff help to set standards by behaving as role models, thereby contributing to the cultural climate. This means management and supervisory staff must clearly express opinions and display behaviour that is quality conscious, and staff who are particularly adept must be seen to be highly regarded. Such members of staff become 'heroes' to whom other members of staff can relate and look up to, they make success human and attainable, and potentially they can motivate their fellow workers. This can further be supported by the organization's 'rites' and 'rituals' that arise in any organization. They might include the manager buying a drink after work for the employee who has been the most quality conscious worker of the week, or the informal presentation of awards to staff during a training session.

Quality assurance the design of production or operations in order to maintain quality

Another approach to assuring the quality of service is to adopt 'internal marketing'. Internal marketing recognizes the central role that employees make to the effective provision of services. This involves recognizing that staff, as well as customers, experience the organization's media advertising. Internal communications with staff should reinforce and build on the message(s) of this advertising. Research has found that well-conceived advertising has a positive impact on employees. For instance, the campaign of one American bank about 'person-to-person' banking using bank employees to explain the idea resulted in 9% recall by employees, over 80% agreeing that the advertisement set a job performance standard for them to follow, and nearly 75% stating that they had become more concerned with customer care. The same impact of advertising has also been seen in airline organizations, railways, and travel and hotel companies. Similarly, approaches that increase sales, such as sales promotions, can equally be applied to staff. For instance, just as it is possible to 'reward' loyal customers with gold charge cards, it is possible to reward loyal staff with a badge or insignia of 'rank'.

Total quality management

A significant development of the 1980s was the emergence of the concept of **total quality management (TQM)**. The strategy is entirely customer-driven and its holistic approach is adopted with an almost missionary zeal. TQM involves the whole organization, every department, every activity, every single person at every level.

> **Total quality management**
> the adoption of quality assurance at all levels of the organization

Whilst this includes some of the features of the QC and QA strategies, TQM differs from these in a number of ways. First, it is holistic and involves the whole organization. Second, senior executives play a key role in leading the quality drive and communicating the quality message. Third, a key aspect is employee empowerment which enables employees to make decisions, within clearly defined parameters, in order to address quality issues and problems.

Lascelles and Dale (1991) suggested that there are six kinds of organizations that claim to be working towards TQM. They define these as:

- Uncommitted—those organizations which have not yet started the formal process of quality improvement.

- Drifters—those which will probably have been engaged in a process of quality improvement for between 18–36 months and, in general, have followed the available advice on TQM.

- Tool Pushers—those with more operating experiences of TQM than a Drifter, say, three to five years.

- Improvers—involved for five to eight years and made important advances in terms of cultural change and recognition of continuous quality improvement.

- Award Winners—winning, say, British, Scottish, Irish, European Quality Awards which allows companies to use recognition as a competitive tool.

- World Class—characterized by the total integration of quality improvement and business strategy to creatively delight the customer.

Although the number of world-class companies has grown since they wrote about this, it is still a relatively small number of organizations. Contemporary organizations are tending to focus on a slightly different concept—continuous improvement (CI).

Continuous improvement

In services especially, TQM has tended to become enshrined as the 'best practice' in quality management, partly through accreditation schemes, such as EFQM (European Foundation for Quality Management), and recognition schemes, such as the Malcolm Baldrige Award. However, many firms, notably in manufacturing, are highly effective in managing their quality, without adopting TQM, through CI. CI has many similarities to TQM, but is more flexible in its philosophy and approach. Originating in Japan as kaizan, CI is a strategy to continuously, and incrementally change and improve all aspects of the operation—equipment, processes, competencies—over time. This is discussed in full in Chapter 16.

RESEARCH INSIGHT 9.1

Sousa, R. and Voss, C.A. (2002) Quality management revisited: a reflective review and agenda for future research, *Journal of Operations Management*, 20, 91–109

This article 'does what it says on the tin', in other words it reflects on over 20 years of research into quality management. In doing so, it addresses a number of issues:

- How quality can be defined.

- How quality might be measured.

- Whether or not quality has led to improved operational and organizational performance.

- How quality management relates to management in general and the concept of 'best practice' specifically.

- The implementation of quality management, both in terms of what to do and how to do it.

In doing this, it reviews and summarizes the most significant research studies into quality management that took place in the 1980s and 1990s—when quality management changed from being the newest way in which to compete, into something that everyone did as a matter of course. Sousa and Voss (2002) end by being somewhat critical of both researchers and practitioners. They suggest that research has not fully explained how quality management implementation should reflect the specific context of each firm. Whilst practitioners, including those making awards, have tended to expand quality management into business improvement in general—by adding concepts, tools, and techniques that are not specific to quality.

Quality tools and techniques

Tools and techniques for managing quality can be divided into two major groups—enabling tools and measurement tools. In addition, both kinds of tool can be integrated into a specific approach to the management of quality, as, for example, in the case of statistical process control or Six Sigma (discussed later in this section).

Enabling tools

Poka-yokes

Poka-yoke is Japanese for a fail-safe device. An early example of this concept is the 'deadman's handle', the lever which a train driver has to hold on to in order for it to go forward. Should the driver become unconscious, this lever is released and the train will come to a halt. The same idea is seen on electric lawn mowers. In materials process settings there are several types of poka yoke—control, warning, and shut-down.

Poka-yoke
Japanese term
for a fail safe
device

- Control poka-yokes take the response to a specific type of error out of the hands of the operator and do not permit the process to commence or continue after an error has occurred. Simple examples of control poka-yokes could be a machine jig designed with a sensing device that does not allow the process to continue unless the right part is correctly inserted, or the timer in the car that will turn off the lights automatically when the engine is off to prevent a dead battery. This type of poka-yoke is beneficial in mass production situations where material is processed rapidly, since the device prevents mass production of material that will be scrapped or reworked.

- Warning poka-yokes simply alert the operator that an error has occurred or is about to occur, but allows processing to proceed. A simple illustration is the warning light in a car which alerts the driver of potential problems (e.g. door ajar, washer fluid, etc.). Another example of a warning poka-yoke is an obstruction detector in the material loading or feeding areas of a machine to detect the blockage and warn the operator.

- Shut-down poka-yokes bring the process to a halt under specific conditions. They are typically found in maintenance applications. So a machine may be designed to operate for 400 hours using a simple tool, and a meter can be designed into the machine to count how long it has been operating for and shut the machine down after this time, if the tool has not been changed and the timer reset.

This concept has also been extended into customer processing operations. In this instance, there are poka-yokes designed for the service provider and for the customer. Service provider poka-yokes have been termed task, treatment, and tangibles.

- Task poka-yokes focus on common mistakes the server makes while performing the service/task for the customer. For instance, keys on tills and other point-of-sale devices are colour coded to assist staff in recording the right items; and trays in hospital operating theatres are indented to take specific instruments to ensure all are accounted for when the operation is over.

- Treatment poka-yokes focus on the social interaction between the server and customer such as eye contact and greeting. Thus some shops have an audible signal when a customer enters the shop to ensure they are greeted straight away.

- Tangibles poka-yokes are designed to improve the tangible, physical impression, and experience for the customer. Examples of this include thermostats to control room temperatures and spell checkers on word processors.

Since so much of customer processing is now done by the customer themselves, poka-yokes have also been designed to ensure that they do things right too. These have been termed preparation, encounter, and resolution poka-yokes.

- Preparation poka-yokes attempt to prepare the customer before they even enter the service environment. An example is the notice letter that a university sends to students prior to registration for the next semester, detailing the modules that need to be completed. We also saw in the IKEA End of chapter case in Chapter 4 that many IKEA customer consult the IKEA catalogue or website before actually shopping in the store.

- Encounter poka-yokes are used to fail-safe a customer who may misunderstand, ignore, or forget the nature of the service encounter or their role in it. Examples include height bars in theme parks to ensure that only those permitted on the ride are allowed on and barriers to ensure that cars only enter or exit car parks from one direction. ATMs feature a number of poka-yokes to ensure that customers use them correctly—each key stroke when entering the pin number is accompanied by an audible signal as well as display on screen to confirm it has been keyed in, and there are further audible signals to remind users to remove their card and take their money.

- Resolution poka-yokes remind customers of how they can contribute to the continuous improvement of a service. Fairfield Inn hotels use of 'scorecard' is an example. This was a keyboard and screen set up near the front desk on which guests completed a short survey when checking out.

Quality circles or teams

A quality circle is typically a group of four to ten employees, probably working for the same line manager, who meet once a week, for an hour or so, under the leadership of their manager, to identify, analyse, and solve their own work-related problems. The typical features of such circles are that they are entirely voluntary, intensely practical, and unbureaucratic. But there is widespread confusion about both the objectives and appropriate format of quality circles in the USA and UK. Originally modelled on circles developed in Japan, certain features of Japanese work ethics and culture do not exist in the West. For instance, Japanese workers are very loyal, expect to work for the same employer for their lifetime, share a team-based work ethic, and enjoy joining in various company organized activities, including quality circles, outside their normal working hours.

Since the basis of quality circles is to identify and solve problems, a typically circle will receive training in how to do this. Such training will identify the typical approach to their role, such as:

- Originate list of problems by brainstorming
- Reject those problems outside own work area
- Select those problems that are possible to solve
- Rank problems in priority order
- Analyse the problem
- Collect relevant data
- Solve the problem
- Sell this solution to management.

For this concept to be effective it is essential that some guiding principles are followed. Much of the criticism of quality circles has come from organizations who have implemented the idea without fully adopting these principles.

First, membership of the circle is entirely voluntary. Thus management cannot even set up the first circle, they can only explain the idea to supervisors and workforce and then hope that their staff will take up the idea. Since there is no obligation to return every week, quality circles will only continue if the workforce continue to volunteer. Second, particularly in the early stages, circles should only aim to solve problems within their own work area. It is usually the case that poor performance is blamed on other sections of the workforce, but this is not the concern of the members of a quality circle. Third, the circle itself will determine its mode of operation, although the organization can provide support with regard to training and expertise in techniques such as brainstorming, data analysis, and process mapping. Problem-solving requires staff to become experts in a very difficult area of expertise, so that they may also need to be introduced to techniques such as Pareto analysis, flow charting, and fishbone analysis (discussed in Chapter 10). Fourth, the circle will only be effective if it is accepted by management and given any information that it thinks it requires to solve problems. Companies and management are often reluctant to divulge information which they regard as confidential, partly because it gives them authority over others, but facts and figures are necessary if problem-solving techniques are to be applied. Finally, the organization must have a realistic time perspective with regards to how long it will take for the idea and the groups to be effective. It is likely that at least two years are needed before quality circles might start to consider problems at the interface between themselves and other employees.

The reported benefits of quality circles are numerous. Most importantly they change attitudes within the organization: staff are better motivated, line managers gain confidence, problem-solving is more competent, communication at all levels is improved, and there is the creation of a can-do culture rather than blame-shifting and lack of engagement. As well as these unquantifiable results, organizations have found that the solutions that circles generate can in some cases save them thousands of pounds per year. And a better motivated workforce has resulted in less absenteeism and lower rates of staff turnover, which also cuts costs. These reported benefits have also caused some confusion as to the role that circles play. In Japan and as described earlier, quality circles are all about solving problems and issues related to quality. Outcomes relating to improved work relations are largely taken for granted. In the UK, however, quality circles have sometimes been formed with the intention of simply improving work relationships. Such objectives should be viewed as possible, but quite separate and distinct from the quality issue.

OPERATIONS INSIGHT 9.2
Morgan Motor Cars—quality automobiles

Morgan Motor Cars Ltd is situated in Malvern Link in Worcestershire, in premises comprising ten workshops built on a hill. It manufactures around 1100 cars a year and exports most of its output. Quality is synonymous with the Morgan brand as cars are literally hand-built to order. The two main model types, the Classic and Aero, have different assembly processes but the company's size means that products can move from one work station to another, when orders favour one model more than another. Quality is managed in a number of different ways—through working with suppliers and dealers, through quality controls at key stages in production, through quality assurance in production areas, and the firm's overall culture and values.

Morgan's relatively small size means that it does not have much buying power. However, it addresses this by having a team of supply chain managers that work very closely with suppliers to assure the quality of components purchased, as well as a fair price. They deliberately set out to establish a long-term working relationship, and keep suppliers well informed of their production targets, new product developments, and forecasts through presentations and suppliers forums. As a result, their supplier of sheet metal has been supplying them for many years, as has their paint supplier and supplier of aluminium panels.

The AeroMax. At Morgan all cars are hand-built to order.

There are six main stages in building a Morgan car. These are chassis, assembly, sheet metal, wood, machine, paint, and trim (i.e. upholstery). At the bare chassis stage, everything is configured in the car—axles with wheels and the engine have been fitted to the main frame of the vehicle. This means that by linking a laptop to the car, it can be started and driven away. So at this stage a 'full configuration' check is made—checks for fuel leaks, drivetrain, and engine checks. If there is found to be a defect it is much easier to resolve at this stage than once the car is completed.

As the vehicle moves through the six stages of assembly it is accompanied by a 'build book', which starts with the high-level BoM (bill of materials). This book not only governs and drives stocking procedures and practices, it also ensures good quality control. The standard time required for each production task is specified as well as the standard operating procedure. If, at any time, one of the operators is not happy with something on the car, he can raise it with the supervisor. Together they will undertake a root cause analysis, in order to identify the cause of the problem and prevent it from reoccurring. Morgan has also been an ISO 9001-accredited company since 2009.

At the back of the book is the PDI (pre-delivery inspection) sheet. Upon completion of the build process the cars are all road tested, they then go through a full technical PDI before having an underbody protection. When this process is complete the car then receives a full PDI in preparation for despatch to either the customer or dealer. The dealers themselves also identify any points they encounter and alert Morgan.

Morgan is a relatively small company with a very loyal workforce of around 185 people, many of whom have worked for the company for many years. The company is still led by a member of the Morgan family, and hence there is a strong organizational culture devoted to producing high-quality, traditional sports cars. Although the company has had many ups and downs in its 100-year history, the Morgan family are most proud of the fact that they have never made an employee redundant. This approach to employee relations helps underpin the quality strategy. This strategy is also underpinned by an unusual feature for most car factories, namely that it is a 'visitor attraction'. Roughly 500 visitors a week pay for a factory tour, anxious to see how this iconic motor car is made. Being 'on show' in this way helps to ensure operators work to the highest standards.

Sources: The Manufacturer, *August 2009 and May 2011;* Handmade 2 – Into the 21st century DVD, *Morgan*

Questions

1. What formal systems does Morgan employ to manage quality, and what informal systems support this?

2. Explain the link between Morgan's operations strategy, their order winners, and how they manage quality.

Measurement techniques

Quality audit

An audit is an evaluation of quality to determine its fitness for purpose and conformance to specifications. They can be used either to assess specific issues or concerns about quality, or they can be used as part of a total quality programme. The auditor may be someone from within the organization who has this specific role, or they may be employed from outside. The benefit of an audit approach is that it is independent from the organization and conducted by experts.

Prior to any such audit taking place, management and auditor discuss and agree the objectives, methodology, scheduling, and reporting procedures of the study.

There are two main methodologies, both of which are usually used. The first involves the auditor observing the process, and the second is for the auditor to participate in the process in some way. In some cases the auditor is introduced to employees and his or her role explained, in other cases not. It is difficult to do the latter as typically an audit requires a detailed recording of the process, which can involve note-taking, tape-recording, photographs, checklists, and chatting to employees (and customers in a service setting).

The supposed advantages of quality audits are:

- They are process orientated.
- Auditors take a operator's or customer's perspective but can explain themselves to management in a way that management can understand.
- The audit is independent and therefore objective.
- It provides a wealth of detail.
- The data collected is actionable, that is to say, management can act to correct below-standard performance.

The disadvantages are:

- In terms of statistical sampling an audit is not a reliable sample.
- There may be bias on the part of the auditor.

so that it can receive monthly or quarterly reports on performance within that market segment or industry sector.

- Sector or industry—as well as comparison between firms in the same sector, comparison between sectors or within an industry can also be very revealing. Such 'league tables' of operational performance allow operators to position themselves and may reveal that they are more effective at controlling certain costs or carrying out certain tasks.

- Generic—this leads then to the view that benchmarking, particularly of processes, should be done with any operation in any industry in any part of the world that can demonstrate world-class performance. For instance, there are some processes that are common to a wide range of different industry sectors—call centres, for example.

Approaches that integrate measurement and implementation

Statistical process control

Statistical process control (SPC) is a quality technique based on statistics. It was developed by Shewhart, Dodge, and Roming in the Bell Telephone Laboratories in the 1930s. The British Standard Institute describes SPC as 'The in-process application of statistical data analysis to identify out of tolerance conditions for a specific production process and to notify the operator of the current or impending problem' (BSI 1994). The approach aims to eradicate the special causes of variation, by measuring, revising, and controlling process performance. SPC achieves this by the use of control charts, check sheets, histograms, scatter diagrams, Pareto analysis, cause and effect diagrams, and graphs.

Six Sigma

Six Sigma a disciplined methodology that uses data and statistical analysis to measure and improve a company's operational performance by identifying and eliminating 'defects' in manufacturing and service-related processes

Six Sigma is not new—it originated in the 1980s and is mostly associated with Motorola where it was developed. The name derives from the statistical term used to describe three standard deviations from the mean. This represents the idea that 99.99966% of products manufactured are expected to be free of defects (i.e. only 3.4 defects per million). For all intents and purposes this represents the idea of zero defects as proposed by Phil Crosby, the quality guru. This is achieved by Six Sigma's fully integrated principles and practices, supported by a specific organizational approach of quality champions and implementers, named after martial arts rankings (e.g. black belt and green belt). Key features of this approach are using accurate data for making process improvement decisions and focusing on clearly identifiable and measurable performance improvement goals. Quality initiatives follow a precise project methodology, which for existing processes is 'DMAIC'—define, measure, analyse, improve, and control. The tools used to conduct such measurement and analysis include process mapping, Pareto analysis, the five whys and Ishikawa diagrams (all of which are explained in Chapter 10). One of the most distinctive features of Six Sigma is that it creates a 'quality career path' for any employee within the organization. Whatever their job role, an employee can start as a green belt, and then develop through training to become a black belt and master black belt, as described in Operations insight 9.3.

OPERATIONS INSIGHT 9.3
Starwood Hotels and Six Sigma

Starwood Hotels is one of the largest hotel companies in the world. At the end of 2010, their chain comprised 1027 hotels with approximately 302,000 rooms in nearly 100 countries. The hotels were either owned or leased (62 properties), managed on a hotel management contract (463), or franchised hotels (502 properties). Over half their hotels are in North America and the Caribbean and one-quarter in Europe, Middle East, and Africa (EMEA). Most of their brands are in the upper end of the market, and include St. Regis, W Hotels, Westin, Le Méridien, and Sheraton. This market position means that the chain has focused on quality and was an early adopter of Six Sigma amongst service firms in 2001. Between 2001 and 2006 the company reported that it had delivered $100 million of extra profit from its Six Sigma initiative and that this explained why its net margin was 15% higher than its two main rivals—Hilton and Marriott.

Managers and employees trained in Six Sigma work at all levels of the organization—in hotels, area management, divisions, and corporate head office. Green Belts have full-time job positions, but spend a proportion of their time working on Six Sigma projects. They will mostly be engaged in collecting and analysing data for projects and monitoring improvements. By 2010, over 50% of all Starwood's managers had been trained to this level at least. At the next level up, Black Belts work only on Six Sigma projects. When Starwood first began the programme, it sent Black Belts to every one of its hotels with the specific task of introducing the initiative to the workforce, training some employees to be Green Belts, and identify improvement projects. By 2010, all hotels had a Six Sigma Council led by a Black Belt. Master Black Belts are the next level up the Six Sigma hierarchy. They are fully trained in all the principles and tools of Six Sigma, and have the specific role of ensuring consistent practices across Six Sigma projects. In Starwood, they work full-time overseeing a portfolio of different projects in an area, region, or division. Because Black Belts and Master Black Belts work full-time on improvement projects, some have been recruited and appointed who have no experience of the hotel industry. This means that they may be able to look at hotel processes with fresh eyes, and bring into the chain new ideas from other sectors of industry that long-term hotel employees might not have thought of. In 2009 Starwood was named the No. 1 best place to work for Six Sigma practitioners by iSix Sigma magazine.

One example of a Six Sigma project is one conducted in 2004 to improve employee safety and reduce claims for compensation. A Six Sigma team analysed the incidence of accidents and conducted root cause analysis to identify why these occurred. It was found that slips and falls were the main type of accident, whilst housekeeping staff had particular problems with back strains due to lifting. A number of improvements were made in order to address these issues, including equipping housekeeping staff with longer-handled cleaning tools and requiring them to do a stretching routine before commencing work. As a result the accident rate went from 12 to two for every 200,000 work hours.

Source: authors' primary research

Questions

1. Using the four costs of quality to illustrate your answer, how has Starwood cut cost and improved its profit margin?

2. How might Six Sigma be used for other aspects of operations management, other than managing quality?

Quality recognition and accreditation

Whichever of the quality strategies a firm adopts, it may also seek to gain recognition or accreditation of quality through any one of a number of schemes. In many cases, firms use these schemes as one of the ways to upgrade and improve their approach to quality, since they provide a specific objective for management and employees to work towards. Some of the major schemes include ISO 9000, the Customer Service Excellence scheme, and the EFQM scheme.

ISO 9000

ISO 9000 is based on the British Standard BS 5750 which was initially published in 1979 to define to suppliers and manufacturers what is required for a quality-orientated system. The standard was originally devised for manufacturing industry, and has now been adopted in service sector organizations, including financial services, catering, health care, and educational establishments. The standard is very process orientated, relying heavily on fully documenting and controlling all aspects of 'production processes.'

RESEARCH INSIGHT 9.2

Terziovski, M., Power, D., and Sohal, A.S. (2003) The longitudinal effects of the ISO 9000 certification process on business performance, *European Journal of Operational Research*, 146(3), 580–95

This study of manufacturing firms in Australia sought to identify if business performance improved as a result of ISO 9000 certification. This research suggests that managers believe that it does. It should be noted that not all studies that have researched this have found the same results (for instance, Naveh and Marcus, 2005).

Customer Service Excellence

In 2008 the government introduced a new Customer Service Excellence (CES) standard, which replaced the previous Charter Mark scheme. CES is described as 'a practical tool to support and drive public services so that they are more responsive to people's needs'. CES is supposed to measure those things that are a priority for customers, with particular focus on delivery, timeliness, information, professionalism, and staff attitude, and the scheme also encourages adopters to develop customer insight, understand the user's experience, and measure service satisfaction.

European Foundation for Quality Management scheme

The EFQM was formed in 1988. A TQM model for self-appraisal was issued in 1992. The scheme allows institutions to introduce a TQM scheme which is self-assessed for the purposes of obtaining a quality award. However, a representative of the Foundation may request a site visit to validate the information given in the self-assessment. The scheme is not focused on products, customers, or services but is a total quality scheme which attempts to address all aspects of quality within an organization.

The cost of introducing such quality standards is hard to quantify. Quality systems generally result in considerable savings in staff time and wastage. The cost of running a quality programme in monetary terms has been shown, for instance, to be typically of the order of £50,000–60,000 per annum for organizations introducing ISO 9000. There is usually an ongoing requirement of at least one high-level full-time quality manger with administrative support, and time will have to be allocated by many other staff to operate this system.

In general, in the long term the benefits would outweigh the costs. Figure 9.5 summarizes the benefits of managing quality effectively.

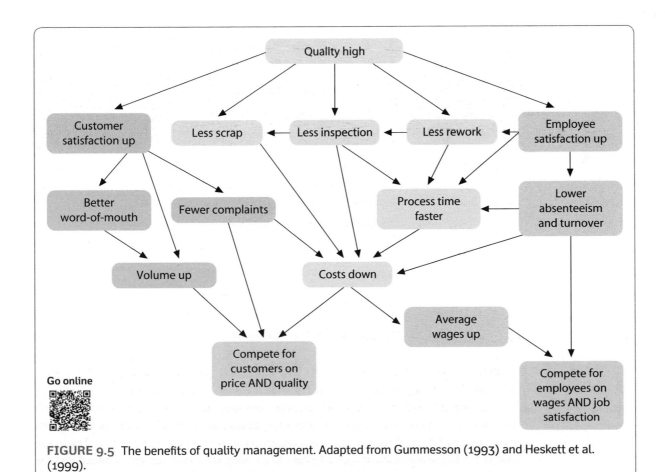

Go online

FIGURE 9.5 The benefits of quality management. Adapted from Gummesson (1993) and Heskett et al. (1999).

Conclusions

In world-leading organizations—manufacturers such as Toyota and service firms such as Disney—quality has become second nature. It is so built into their organizational philosophy and ways of working that not to have quality would be almost impossible. But they are not complacent. They continue to seek ways of becoming even better. However, the proportion of organizations that are truly world leading is relatively small, so there are many thousands who still have a great deal to do in the area of quality. Developing and managing quality requires management to be fully committed. Moreover, applying quality management is potentially becoming more challenging with the changes in the way in which firms do business. For instance, how is quality to be managed across fully integrated supply chains; and how is quality managed in relation to outsourcing?

Regrettably many firms think, or claim, that they are better than they really are. Such firms delight when their customer satisfaction scores go up from 68% to 69%, believing that satisfying the 31% who are not satisfied is unattainable. It is true that moving from this kind of average position to one based on zero defects is hugely challenging. It cannot be achieved in less than several years. But as the Operations insight 9.3 about Starwood Hotels showed, unless top management commit themselves and their organization to this goal, it will never be achievable. And quality will continue to be a hit and miss affair, rather than the perfection that some managers seek—and all customers would like. The End of chapter case on Ashford Colour Press illustrates how quality can truly be integrated into organizational and operational practices.

END OF CHAPTER CASE
Ashford Colour Press—quality in practice

Ashford Colour Press (ACP) specializes in printing soft-cover books of all kinds—paperbacks, textbooks, manuals, and other printed materials. Their customers include many of the UK's major publishers, such as Oxford University Press. They print over 10,000 titles a year, with print runs varying from just a few hundred up to 20,000 or more. To do this they operate 24 hours a day, seven days a week, thereby utilizing their equipment and machinery to its maximum. Such heavy usage means that the lifetime of a machine might be only three or four years. But printing technology is advancing so rapidly, this means that old machines can be replaced by state-of-the-art equipment that performs to an even higher standard and speed.

In order to manage quality, ACP has a quality manager who is specifically responsible for this area. His role is to oversee all aspects of the quality management processes explained in this case study. To further support quality, ACP has been accredited for nearly 20 years, first of all with BS 5750 and now by ISO 9001. And as a company concerned about the environment, ACP also has ISO 14001, FSC and PEFC accreditation.

The ten main operational processes of the firm are shown in Figure 9.6, which also shows the critical control points at each stage in the total process. As well as the main stages and critical control points (CCPs), the specific procedure for managing each control point is identified down the left-hand side, and the relevant documentation needed at stage is identified down the right-hand side. The first five stages are concerned with the processing of raw materials, i.e. specification, supplier selection, purchasing, goods

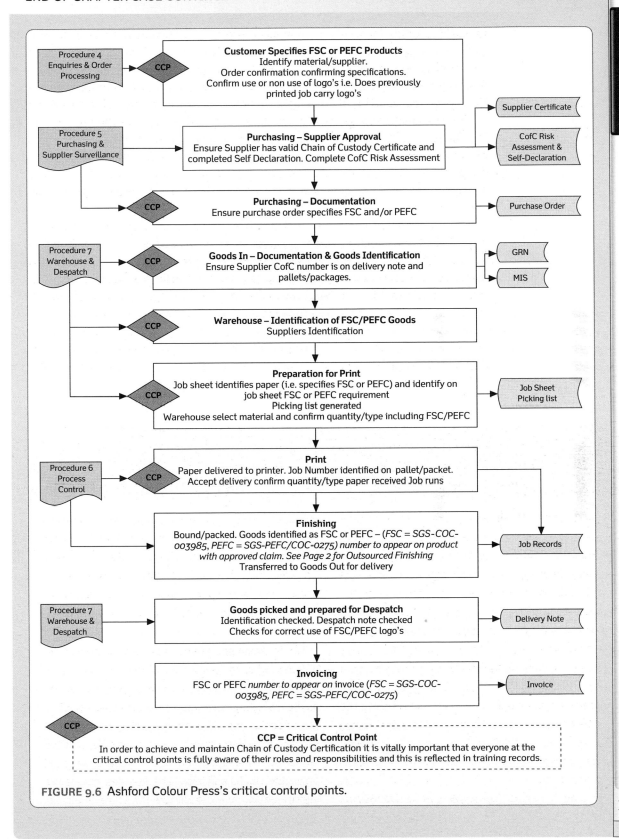

FIGURE 9.6 Ashford Colour Press's critical control points.

inwards, and warehousing. The next four stages are concerned with the production process itself, i.e. preparation for print, print, finishing, and preparation for despatch, whilst the final process is concerned with invoicing the customer for the work done.

At the beginning of each job (such as a book), a job sheet is prepared which has six different coloured copies. Each goes to a different department of the organization:

- Blue—Production
- Yellow—Print (text)
- Orange—Print (cover)
- Green—Planning (cover)
- White—Planning (text)
- Pink—Accounts.

The job sheet contains all the key information needed to process the book, such as the job number, publisher details, book title, quantity, paper type and size, planning, print, finishing, and delivery instructions.

It is the publisher's responsibility to ensure that this text has no errors in it. They typically do this by having it proof read either by a professional proof reader, or by the author, or both. ACP's responsibility for quality starts at the point when it receives a PDF of the text from a publisher. Books are printed not on to individual sheets of paper, but typically onto B0 and B1 size sheets. This size of paper means that 32 pages of a typical paperback, or 16 pages of a typical textbook are printed at a time. Since these sheets are subsequently folded and cut, the pages are not laid out in numerical order but in a print order designed to allow for this process. ACP uses specific software to enable them to do this, which has a variety of templates that can be used for ensuring the correct layout is adopted. As well as this, additional information is added in the margin of each sheet comprising the job number, the customer, the planner, and the section number. This is so the work can be monitored all the way through the printing and binding process. There is also a barcode put in the margin so that when the book is bound a barcode reader can check

to see that sections are being bound in the correct order. All of this additional data is subsequently lost after binding, when the margins are cut and removed.

Once the pages have been laid out in print order digitally, the next stage is to transfer this onto the aluminium metal plate that will be used in the lithographic printing process. This is a largely automated process, so that there is very little likelihood of error at this stage. These plates are then transported to the litho machines that do the actual printing. The system is designed so that this coincides with the picking and delivery of the specific type of paper needed for that particular print run.

At ACP there are a variety of slightly different machines, the largest of which can process 10,000 sheets of paper an hour. With colour printing there are basically four inks used, each of which is transferred onto the paper by rollers at different points within the print machine. These four base colours can be overlaid on each other in order to produce the full range of different colours. To ensure the right amount of ink is used, there are 42 'keys' which can be adjusted across each Duct roller. In some cases, this is done automatically by a machine that scans the printed sheet, but it can also be done manually by the printer. It is standard practice to have a short test run, in order for the print quality to be checked, before undertaking the full print run. This allows for minor adjustments to be made to the keys, if necessary. The process for printing the cover of each book is also similar, except that the density of the paper is greater and this may have additional processing such as lamination, varnishing, and embossing.

After printing the sheets have to be folded and cut. In most cases, the pages are not completely separated from each other but are left in 'sections' which are then assembled into the right order when the book is bound. There are three types of binding process— 'stitching', 'burst binding' (which involves gluing sections of the book together inside the cover), and PUR binding which involves gluing individual sheets into the cover. You can tell which method has been used by seeing if the book stays open easily when reading it. Burst bound books do not stay open, whereas PUR bound ones do. After the book has been bound, they are cut and trimmed so that the pages fit exactly inside the cover. At this point, the books are boxed up and stored on pallets ready for delivery to the publisher. As speed to market for these books is critical, the finished product is despatched as soon as possible after it has been produced.

Although the quality manager spends a fair amount of his time managing quality issues on the shop floor, he is responsible for quality across the whole organization. This includes a range of processes that support production such as administration, sales, accounting, human resources, and buildings maintenance. In order to do this, ACP has adopted a Business Improvement Report (BIR) system which documents every kind of error, incident, or suggestion that might be identified anywhere in the organization. In any month, up to 40 BIRs might be created. These could arise from a customer complaint, a problem with a supplier or subcontractor, an incident recorded under health and safety legislation, an internal or external audit, a revision to procedures resulting from the introduction of new technology, or just a simple suggestion from an employee. For instance, ISO 9001 requires that the premises and processes are externally audited every six months, and internally various procedures are audited each month.

BIRs can vary from simple things like there being no soap in the washrooms up to major incidents such as a large batch of books being rejected by the publisher due to a printing error. However large or small, a BIR is raised and the issue or suggestion recorded. All of these go to the quality manager who logs them in the BIR register and then allocates a person or department to be responsible for taking action to resolve the issue or evaluate the suggestion. The quality manager then monitors this to ensure resolution and if necessary ensures senior management buy in. The action is then recorded on the BIR and the register is updated. The originator of the BIR is then informed of the outcome. This is always important, but especially so with regards to issues raised by external auditors. The BIR register is then reviewed by management on a monthly basis in order to see what kinds of issues have been raised and what kinds of actions have been taken.

A casual tour of the shop floor would highlight that all kinds of poka-yoke are in place. Most of the large items of equipment have control, warning, and shut-down poka-yokes. For instance, the large printing machines are similar to photocopiers in terms of stopping when there is a paper jam and identifying where the blockage is. There are also control poka-yokes in use during the book binding process to ensure that books dry properly after they have been glued and do not become creased or unstuck. There are also task poka-yokes in place designed to minimize operator error. For instance, procedure flowcharts to identify key operations, trip switches on machines to prevent paper jams, smoother plates to hold down covers to stop curling, safety light sensors on guillotines to prevent injury, and limiter switches on delivery vehicles to prevent speeding.

Overall, ACP has developed an organizational culture that encourages employees to take responsibility for what they do and make suggestions about how to improve it. Errors and mistakes are seen as an opportunity to improve, rather than something to blame someone for. Systems and processes are now so well designed that the quality manager does not routinely monitor waste. This is so small as to be relatively insignificant. One gets the sense that not only do the printing and binding machines run smoothly and efficiently, but the whole organization does likewise.

Source: authors' primary research

Questions

1. What is ACPs' overall approach to quality management?

2. Identify specific stages in the printing process where QI or QC is conducted.

3. What is the evidence for suggesting that ACP has reduced its total cost of quality, by adjusting the four different costs of quality?

✱ Chapter summary

To consolidate your learning, the key points from this chapter are summarized as follows:

- **Explain what is meant by 'quality' and why it is so challenging**

  Quality is often explained as 'the best'. But in operations management the right way to define it is as 'fit for purpose'. Quality is challenging because consumers evaluate products and services all the time and ensuring every single product or service encounter is to standard is extremely difficult. It requires so-called 'zero defects'.

- **Explain quality 'gaps' and costs**

  There are five quality gaps. These are the positioning gap, specification gap, delivery gap, communication gap, and perception gap. There are four quality costs. These are prevention, appraisal, internal failure and external failure costs.

- **Differentiate between quality inspection (QI), quality control (QC), quality assurance (QA), total quality management (TQM), and continuous improvement (CI)**

  QI is based on inspecting the finished product before delivering it or selling it to the end user. QC involves inspecting work-in-progress, as well as the finished product. QA seeks to do things right first time, every time, so that the focus is on prevention rather than inspection. TQM is holistic and involves the whole organization; senior executives play a key role in leading the quality drive and communicating the quality message; and a key aspect is employee empowerment which enables employees to make decisions, within clearly defined parameters, in order to address quality issues and problems. CI is more flexible than TQM although it has many similar features.

- **Explain some of the major tools and techniques for managing quality**

  Tools and techniques for managing quality can be divided into three major groups—enabling tools, measurement techniques, and integrated approaches. Examples of enabling tools are poka-yokes and quality circles. Alternative approaches to measuring quality are quality audits, mystery shoppers, customer satisfaction surveys, and benchmarking. Integrated approaches include statistical process control and Six Sigma.

- **Compare and contrast alternative approaches to the external accreditation of quality**

  There are a wide range of accreditation bodies and recognition schemes. Amongst the most significant are ISO 9000, European Foundation for Quality Management, and the Malcolm Baldrige Award.

❓ Questions

Review questions

1. What are the five so-called 'quality gaps'?

2. What are the key differences between quality control and quality assurance?

3. What are the key challenges that face the operations manager in engaging in TQM?

4. How do the four costs of quality relate to alternative approaches to quality management?

5. What is Six Sigma?

6. What different types of poka-yokes are there?

7. How are quality circles or quality teams organized?

8. What is benchmarking and why is it used?

9. In what ways can quality be accredited or recognized?

Discussion questions

1. How can an organization measure each of its quality gaps?

2. In what way does process type (job shop, batch production, mass production) affect the adoption of quality assurance?

3. How might the four costs of quality be different for manufacturing firms and service organizations?

4. In which strategy (QC, QA, TQM, or CI) would quality circles be most appropriate and why?

5. Why is it more difficult to manage the quality of customer processing operations than materials processing operations?

6. What are the disadvantages of a mystery shopper or mystery guest programme?

7. Quality is an order winner (see page 36). Do the features of quality that an organization is competing on affect which quality strategy it adopts?

8. How is quality management consistent with ethical and sustainable practices?

Further learning guide

Quality is a topic that has been extensively researched and written about over the last 30 years. It is probably a good idea to look at the websites of those bodies responsible for accrediting quality such as the British Standards Institute (BSI) and the European Foundation for Quality Management (EFQM). For an example of how quality may be managed and accredited in the public sector, the UK government's scheme is explained at **www.customerservicexcellence. uk.com**. Further insight into QM can be gained by exploring the life and works of some the gurus of quality management, such as Phil Crosby, Joseph Juran, and W. Edwards Deming. There is also a professional association dedicated to quality management—namely the Chartered Quality Institute (**www.thecqi.org**).

References

British Standards Institute (1979) *BS5750: Quality systems. Specification for manufacture and installation*, BSI: London

Crosby, P. (1979) *Quality is free*, McGraw Hill: New York

Gummesson, E. (1993) Service productivity, service quality, and service profitability, *Proceedings of the 8th International Conference of the Operations Management Association*, Warwick, UK

Heskett. J.L., Sasser, W.E. and Schlesinger, L.A. (1997) *The service profit chain: How leading companies link profit and growth to loyalty, satisfaction, and value*, The Free Press: New York

Lascelles, D.M. and Dale, B.G. (1991) Levelling out the future, *The TQM Magazine*, 3(2), 125–8

Naveh, E. and Marcus, A. (2005) Achieving competitive advantage through implementing a replicable management standard: Installing and using ISO 9000, *Journal of Operations Management*, 24(1), 1–26

Parasuraman, A., Zeithaml, V.A. and Berry, L.L. (1985) A conceptual model of service quality and its implications for future research, *Journal of Marketing*, 49, 41–50

Part C

Designing and developing operations

Chapter Ten

Designing processes and using technology

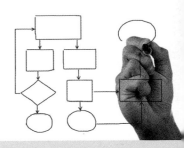

Learning outcomes

After reading this chapter you will be able to:

→ Outline the principles of process design using different types of process chart

→ Discuss alternative approaches to process improvement

→ Discuss the role of technology in materials processing operations

→ Discuss the role of technology in customer processing operations

Stepchange and improving the police response process

Stepchange is a consulting and technology company that specializes in process improvement for public sector organizations. They have worked with numerous health authorities, police forces, and local authorities throughout the UK looking at a wide range of different processes. For instance, in one NHS Trust they reviewed and revised the staff selection process, which had been taking 18 weeks to complete. Following their work, the Trust now recruits within 11 weeks and as a result is saving £700,000 per annum.

Mike Tresise, Director of Stepchange, explains that an important part of their work includes the use of one of the world's leading process mapping and analysis software tools—iGrafx. Business process tools such as iGrafx are used extensively in the US, Europe, and Asia and are a vital tool in for a manager in any operational role in these countries. However, in the UK, the take up of these tools and techniques has been slow which may explain why study after study has shown that UK productivity, across a range of industry sectors, is lower than it is in these other countries.

One of processes Stepchange has analysed is the 'police response process', as shown in Figure 10.1. This analysis was not done to redesign the process, since many of the steps in the process are followed by the police in order to ensure they comply with legal and regulatory requirements. The study was done to improve the response times, by ensuring resources were allocated in the right way at the right time.

Figure 10.1 shows the iGrafx printout that maps the basic process. There are four stakeholders in the process—the police sergeant who takes the emergency call, the police officer who is sent out in response to the call, the custody officer who processes prisoners, and the Crown Prosecution Service (CPS) who advise on whether to charge the prisoner or not. The process flow chart assigns a number to each stage in the process. In this case, it is a 20-stage process that begins with the receipt of an emergency call (stage 1) and ends with the police officer being ready for redeployment. The chart also identifies the time each stage might take, either as a standard time or as a range of times. For instance, booking the prisoner into custody (stage 10) should take 15 minutes, whereas the travel time for the officers attending can be from 0 minutes up to 11 minutes. Such times can either derive from time and motion studies, and/or from targets set by the Police Authority.

The process flow chart also identifies a number decision points (shown as diamonds on the chart) where there can be different outcomes. For instance, at stage 6 no further action might be taken or the detained person might be arrested, at which point they become a prisoner. There are other decision points at stage 11 and stage 17.

This process flow chart can be used in a number of ways. First it helps to identify the relative roles of different stakeholders. In this example, 13 of the 20 stages are carried out by the police officer; hence this person is central to ensuring the process is performed correctly. Second, it enables the total process time to be established. Such analysis shows that the police officer may spend anything between a few minutes (if no further action is taken) up to more than two hours if the prisoner is charged.

But more importantly, iGrafx is dynamic and hence it can be used to simulate flow through this process, and thereby identify bottlenecks and delays. Figure 10.2 shows a typical 24-hour period with the number of emergency calls that a police station might receive. This shows very few calls around noon, and a peak in calls between 6 pm and 10 pm. The police service also knows that at stage 6, nine out of ten incidents will not lead to an arrest; that at stage 11 only four out of ten prisoners will be detained; and that at stage 17, only 50% of prisoners will be

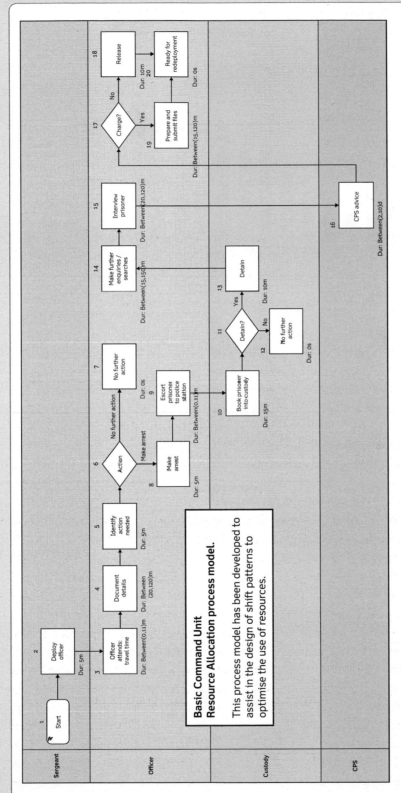

**Basic Command Unit
Resource Allocation process model.**

This process model has been developed to assist in the design of shift patterns to optimise the use of resources.

FIGURE 10.1 The police response process. Mike Tresise (2011) www.stepchange.co.uk.

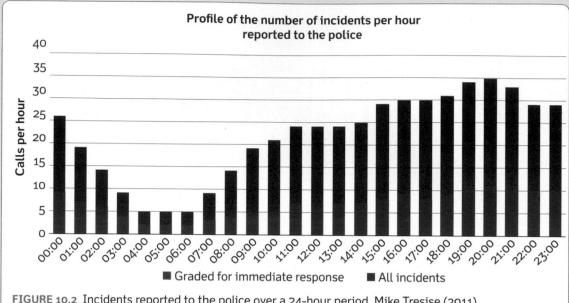

FIGURE 10.2 Incidents reported to the police over a 24-hour period. Mike Tresise (2011) ww.stepchange.co.uk.

charged. Using this data, iGrafx can simulate a 24-hour period using different levels of resource, such as the number of police officers, sergeants, and custody officers.

The analysis is visually displayed by the colour of each box (stage) on the chart in Figure 10.3. A blue box denotes work taking place, green an activity moving, yellow is an activity that is delayed by a lack of resource and red an activity that is blocked. Grey indicates a delay where the process is suspended, for instance outside working hours. In this example, it

was found that stage 13 was a bottleneck during the peak evening period highlighted in yellow, indicating the lack of resource available to respond to the calls during that period.

Questions

1. What different uses can a process flow chart be put to?

2. Using Figure 10.2, identify the total number of emergency calls received in a typical day. Then, using the information provided in the case, identify how many prisoners might be charged every 24 hours.

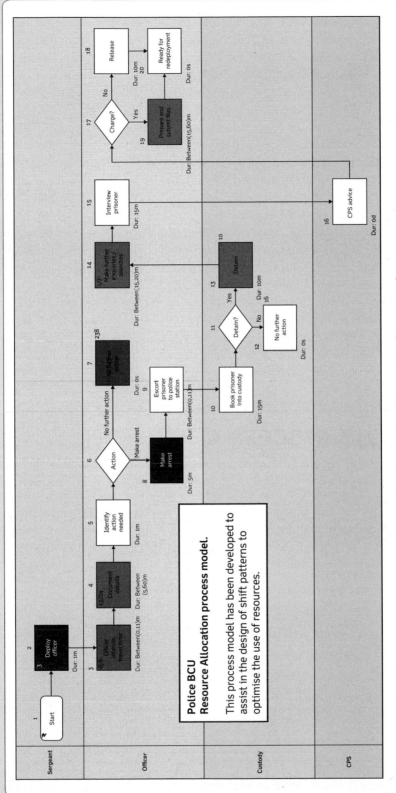

FIGURE 10.3 The police response process—analysis. Mike Tresise (2011) www.stepchange.co.uk.

Introduction

Process a systematic arrangement of actions design to achieve specific outcomes

As we have seen, processes are at the heart of operations management. We discussed in Chapter 3 the basic types of **process** that exist in manufacturing (project, job, shop, batch, assembly line, and continuous) and services (professional, service shop, and mass service), and in Chapter 4, the different kinds of layout each of these is likely to have. But we have not yet examined in detail exactly what a process is and how it can be designed to be effective (do what it is meant to do) and efficient (using the minimum of resources), as in the Stepchange Case insight.

A review of any organization's processes typically identifies areas for improvement. Poorly designed processes frequently create employee frustration, which derives from either having too much to do because the process is too complicated or bureaucratic, or because there are unnecessary delays due to a bottleneck in the system. For instance, the government has appointed a 'Reducing Bureaucracy in Policing Advocate' to look at policing in the UK because it is reported that police officers typically spend up to half their shifts sitting in an office filling out forms, when they should out patrolling the streets. This investigation has found that one way to overcome this problem is to equip police officers with hand-held computers. This illustrates another aspect of process design, namely how processes need to be constantly reviewed in order to identify opportunities to introduce new technologies into the process.

Technology the use of technical means to achieve process outcomes

In this chapter we begin by reviewing the principles of good process design, before going on to discuss the various ways in which organizations go about improving processes. We conclude by examining the role that **technology** can play in both materials and customer processing operations.

The process challenge

Given that we are surrounded by processes and that work is organized in this way, it might be assumed that processes are generally well designed and work well. In fact most, if not all, processes can be improved. So how can you tell if a process is not working as well as it might? According to Value Creation Partners (www.valuecreationpartners.com), there are 15 telltale symptoms that processes are not working.

These are as follows:

- Customers (either internal or external) are unhappy.
- Some operations take too long.
- The process produces too many errors, scrap, or rework (i.e. not right first time).
- Management assigns people to resolve the problem, but it does not improve.
- Employees report high levels of frustration with the process.
- Processes cross many departments and a blame culture develops between them.
- Processes are not measured or controlled effectively.
- Inventory and expensive assets sit idle.
- Data errors and data redundancy are common.
- There are too many process reviews and changes.
- Complexity, exceptions, and special cases are common.

- Established procedures are not followed in order to get work done.
- No one manages the total process.
- Management has invested in trying to solve problems, but they are not resolved.
- Managers spend a great deal of their time 'firefighting'.

As you can see, having any two or more of these symptoms present in a process can seriously impede progress, lower process efficiency, as well as lowering staff morale and customer confidence.

So it is important to design processes well for many different reasons. The characteristics of a well-designed process are:

- Each element is consistent with the overall purpose of the operating system.
- The whole process is user friendly, with easy to understand steps.
- The whole process is robust (i.e. can take small variations without affecting delivery).
- Consistency is easily maintained at every stage.
- There are effective links with other processes within the operating system.
- The whole process is cost-effective.

OPERATIONS INSIGHT 10.1
Apex Linvar—redesigning their processes

Apex Linvar (formerly LINPAC Storage Systems) designs, manufactures, and installs pallet racking and shelving storage systems. Its clients include Amazon, Dunlop-Goodyear, P&O Ferries, Matalan, Marks & Spencer, Argos, and TNT. Based in Milton Keynes their manufacturing plant incorporates steel forming presses, specialist steel rolling mills, automatic welding machines, and one of the largest epoxy polyester coating paint lines in Europe. Since 2006, the company has engaged in important technological investments to help improve production efficiency, so that output has increased tenfold. New technology has included a new bracing line, which produces both horizontal and diagonal braces on one production line, increasing productivity by 50%; an automatic welder, which can weld five times quicker than manual welding; and a rolling mill, specializing in rolling, forming, and boxing the two-part boxed section beam.

Another investment in technology was in two rapid colour change powder paint booths. These provide significant improvements in application control of powder to steel components manufactured on the two large conveyor lines. The control of the application equipment and movement of the paint guns are regulated at central touch screens, ensuring optimum settings are maintained allowing the operator to devote more time to checking and controlling both quality and costs. This £300,000 investment has led to a 60% reduction in raw materials and a significant reduction in colour changeover times, from six hours to under ten minutes, with only one operator. Both booths are now fed by 600-kilogram bulk feed systems, replacing manually fed 20-kilogram powder boxes. These bulk systems eliminate manual handling issues and reduce labour costs. Overall this technology saved £150,000 per year, giving a payback of under two years.

Apex Linvar has adopted its own lean management and process improvement programme —known within the company as LPOS (LINPAC Production Operating System). Yearly strategies are set up for each department, with goals, objectives, and measures reviewed monthly. The LPOS programme has played a major role in ensuring the organization survived the recession by operating leanly and keeping costs to a minimum. As part of the programme, all operators are responsible for quality and regularly raise issues via daily meetings. These issues are acted upon using different tools and techniques. Continuous improvement techniques including 5S, single minute of exchange of die (SMED), time-based management (TBM), total productive maintenance (TPM), and statistical process control (SPC) were all being implemented from 2009 onwards.

A number of process improvements have taken place. The SMED exercise carried out on the main rolling mill reduced change over times from 4 to 1.5 hours. This resulted in improved lead times, planning, and productivity. Other improvements have included changing the four-stage pre-treatment process to a three-stage process, saving chemicals, gas, and electricity; decreasing powder usage; and reducing oven temperatures.

These changes have also led to environmental improvement. The company is implementing activities throughout its operations to reduce the use of materials and energy, increase recycling, and minimize emissions and wastes to air, water, and soil. The management team also takes the environment into account when updating operation practices, ensuring the company employs any available technological advancement which may assist in reducing its environmental impact.

Sources: 'Progressive manufacturing', The Manufacturer, September 2010 and www.linpacstorage.com

Questions

1. What problems did Apex Linvar have with their process design?
2. What features of good process design have Apex Linvar adopted?

Principles of process design

Processes can be described and analysed by some kind of process 'map', sometimes called process maps, blueprints, flow diagrams, or relationship diagrams. There are three basic types of such map, each which presents the information in different ways for different purposes. The most basic is a relationship map, which generally is a diagram showing each stage of the process labelled in a box, connected to other stages by arrows. Figure 10.4 is an example of a relationship map. The second type is the cross-functional map, which is similar to the relationship, but organized so that each stage is put into its relevant 'stream', or 'swim lane', as shown in Figure 10.5. These two figures show the same process but provide different insights into the nature and design of the process. The third type of process map is the process **flow chart**. This uses specific shapes of boxes to denote a range of different activities, as explained in the following sections.

Flow chart a diagram of stages in a process

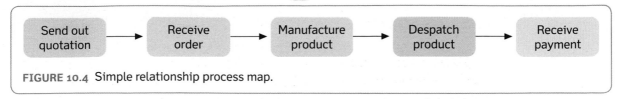

FIGURE 10.4 Simple relationship process map.

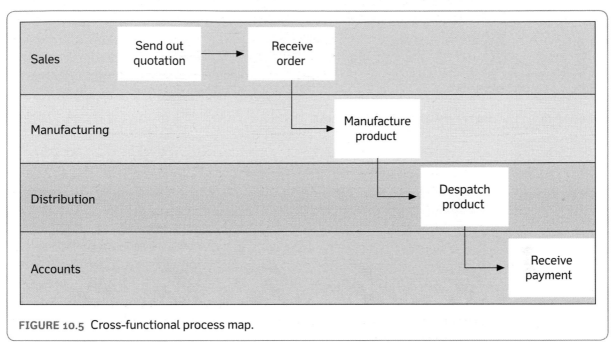

FIGURE 10.5 Cross-functional process map.

Process flow charting

Go online

A flowchart is the way in which processes are mapped and analysed. The conventional way of drawing a flowchart is to use symbols to identify differentiate between activities in the process. The most typical ones are as follows:

○ = **operation**—any activity that adds to, changes, or removes from the product/ service. Examples are drilling a metal component, moulding plastic parts, printing a page of a book, or serving a customer.

⇨ = **transportation**—any movement of the product or customer through the process. Examples might be wheeling a trolley of parts to a new location, a passenger walking through an airport terminal, or shipping components in a container.

▭ = **inspection**—any check or verification of the product or service. Examples might include a simple visual check by an employee, checking the weight of an item, or using lasers to precisely measure a machine part.

◗ = **delay**—waiting for no reason. This refers to any time that the product or customer spends without being operated on, transported, inspected, or deliberately stored.

▽ = **storage**—deliberate and planned delay in the process. As we saw when discussing materials processing (in chapter 6), modern manufacturing tries to eliminate unnecessary storage and minimize stock levels. But some storage is inevitable in most materials processing operations.

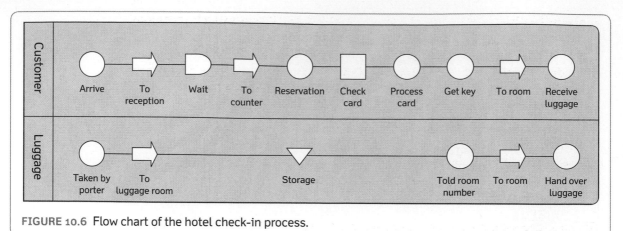

FIGURE 10.6 Flow chart of the hotel check-in process.

TABLE 10.1 Process chart of the hotel check-in process

Step	Time (secs)	Distance (metres)	◯	⇨	▢	D	▽	Description
1	20		X					At front door—luggage to porter
2	20	10		X				Walk to reception desk
3	30					X		Wait in line
4	5	2		X				Move forward to counter
5	30		X					Confirm details of reservation
6	5				X			Hand over credit card
7	15		X					Process credit card details
8	20		X					Receive room key and information
9	120	60		X				Take elevator to room

A straightforward flowchart using these symbols is shown in Figure 10.6.

An alternative way of charting this process is shown in Table 10.1. As Table 10.1 illustrates, various the types of information can be captured in a process chart:

- Communication—showing the relationship between task owners, usually depicted by a line or arrow connection.
- Activity—typically considered as operation, transport, inspection, storage, or delay.
- Time—e.g. cycle time, process time, and wait time.
- Distance—the physical distance between operations and the distance workers need to move between individual steps in the process.

This approach provides more detail with regards performance, but is more difficult to interpret that the first example.

In analysing and improving processes, there are three levels of process mapping:

- Macro-level—this is the least detailed of the three but depicts the critical elements of the process. Usually consisting of between three and seven steps, it depicts a whole process, typically using a relationship map.

- Functional-activity level—this is the second level of detail. It shows which operations will be carried and shows the job titles of the people involved in the process. So in Figure 10.5, above those involved at the quotation stage will be sales executives, sales administrative staff, and technical staff. At the manufacturing stage, production planning, production supervision, and operations staff will be involved, and at the payment stage sales and accounting staff will be involved.

- Task and procedural level—this is the third and most detailed level. Each of the activities from the functional-activity level flowchart will be exploded to create precise detailed activities so that any person can carry out the activity. This is particularly useful during the trialling of process change activities and in new personnel training. Flow charts are typically used in this situation.

For any process it is possible to frame some basic questions about its design, such as:

- Are the steps arranged in a logical sequence?
- Are the capacities of each step balanced?
- How much flexibility is available at each step?
- Can steps be combined or should parallel steps be considered?
- Have customer-process interactions been considered at each step?

So process maps can help both the process designer and the process users in managing processes.

There are five main advantages to process mapping. The first is that there is an overview of the whole process, which is particularly important if the process spans across boundaries within an organization, i.e. different departments of sections. Second, the map will highlight where most of the work is being performed, and hence enable improvement to be focused where it could have the most impact. Third, each stage in the process can be reviewed in terms of how much value it adds. It is not unknown for new technology to make one or more stages in a process unnecessary, but these continue because no one has recognized that they can be removed. Fourthly, the map or chart will identify actual or potential problem areas. Finally, controls can be designed into the process to avoid delays and errors.

Rigid versus flexible processes

In many situations, a process is designed so that there is only one way in which it can be done. The police response process discussed in the opening Case insight was an example of this. This is typically the case if the process is simple and straightforward, or highly automated, or if the output is very specifically prescribed. So, for instance, a customer using an ATM has a very rigid process to follow. If they do not follow it they will not succeed in making a transaction, and may even lose their bank card. Workers on production lines also follow rigid processes. On the other hand, especially in customer processing operations, the process may be designed to be flexible. Indeed the exact nature of the process may vary from one situation to another. For instance, in a table service restaurant the exact sequence of service will depend entirely on what each diner orders from the menu. The difference between rigid and flexible processes is summarized in Table 10.2.

TABLE 10.2 Comparison of rigid and flexible processes

	Rigid	Flexible
Volume of materials or customers through process	High	Low
Level of task variety	Low	High
Technical skill of process user	Low	High
Level of discretion by process user	Low	High
Arrival rate of work into the process	Predictable	Unpredictable
Rate of work flowing through process	Certain	Uncertain
Need for information search during process	Low	High
Level of information exchange within the process	Low	High

Process improvement

In order to improve processes, three concepts need to be understood. These are:

- The 'problem'—an opportunity for improvement, an undesired condition, can be measured.
- The 'cause'—the situation that creates the problem, eliminating the cause should prevent problems recurring.
- The 'solution'—an action taken to eliminate a cause.

It is commonly agreed that there is a danger that many managers go directly from identifying a problem to proposing a solution without analysing the cause. This often means that the symptoms of the problem may go away, at least in the short term. But the problem will continue or re-emerge in a different form, because the root cause of the problem has not been diagnosed or remedied.

Problem identification and prioritization

There are a number of different tools and techniques that can be adopted in order to identify and prioritize problems.

- Flow chart—as we have discussed earlier, by mapping processes it is possible to identify problem areas.
- Error or fault analysis—most organizations have information on or collect data on errors or faults. In manufacturing companies this is in the form of number of rejected parts or final products, whereas in service organizations it may take the form of collecting on information on customer complaints. The main function of statistical process control is to detect and identify deviations from standard.

Pareto analysis
a statistical technique designed to identify a limited number of causes with the greatest effect

- **Pareto analysis**—is a way to 'separate the vital few from the trivial many' and hence prioritize problems. It is named after the Italian economist Vilfredo Pareto, who observed in 1906 that 80% of the land in Italy was owned by 20% of the population. This helped to establish the so-called 80/20 rule. Hence using this approach it is possible to improve a process by reducing a large problem rather than eliminating a small one. Pareto analysis involves listing faults or problems in the process, recording the frequency of their occurrence, calculating the percentage frequency for each, and showing this on a chart such as that in Operations insight 10.2.

- Pairs comparison—this is a method to prioritize which problems to tackle by generating consensus on the relative importance of items in a list. All the items are listed and then item 1 is compared with item 2, the preferred option is identified, and then each item with each other, until it is possible to total the scores for each items. This creates a list in order of preference.

Problem analysis

Once the problem has been selected it is then necessary to apply appropriate tools and techniques to understanding the problem and identify root causes. Such tools include soft systems analysis and failure mode and effect analysis.

- **Soft systems analysis**—this was developed by Peter Checkland (1999). It is based on a qualitative approach to analysing problems based around the development of 'rich pictures', as illustrated in Figure 10.7. The idea of using drawings or pictures to

Soft systems the social, political, or organizational aspects of any operational process

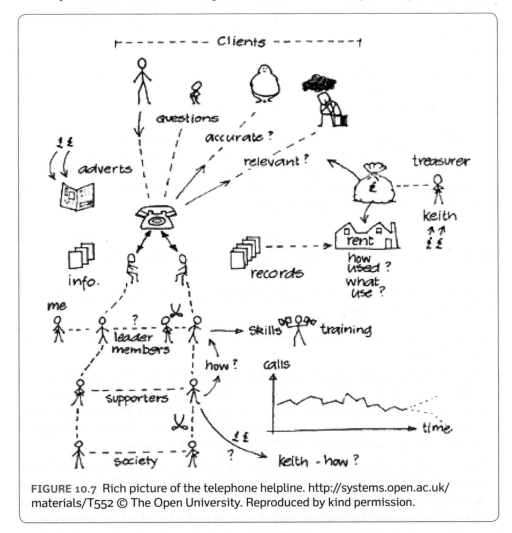

FIGURE 10.7 Rich picture of the telephone helpline. http://systems.open.ac.uk/materials/T552 © The Open University. Reproduced by kind permission.

think about issues is common to several problem solving or creative thinking methods. It can be argued that our intuitive consciousness communicates more easily in impressions and symbols than in words. Drawings can both evoke and record insight into a situation. In Chapter 1, we identified that inputs into a process can be of two kinds—inputs that are transformed through processes, and so-called 'transformational inputs' or 'structures' that do the transformation (Figure 1.5b, page 22). Rich pictures are drawn to clarify what should best be regarded as process and which as structure. In the example of the telephone helpline, shown in Figure 10.7, the process involves customers telephoning operatives, whilst the structure is represented by data records and buildings. Not only can relationships be established in a rich picture, but problem areas can be identified. These are typically annotated as 'conflict' and represented by crossed swords. For instance, in Figure 10.7 there are two examples of this—conflict between society and supporters, and conflict amongst leader members.

RESEARCH INSIGHT 10.1

Mingers, J., and Taylor S. (1992) The use of soft systems methodology in practice, *The Journal of the Operational Research Society*, 43(4), 321–32

There is no better way to understand a technique than to hear from the people that use it. This article reports on a survey of managers and others that actively and enthusiastically engaged in soft systems analysis.

Failure mode and effect analysis (FMEA) technique for analysing potential failure modes within a system

- **Failure mode and effect analysis (FMEA)**—is a technique initially used in materials processing operations for analysing potential failure modes within a system. It is now increasingly finding use in customer processing operations. Failure modes are any errors or defects in a process, design, or product, especially those that affect the customer. Effect analysis refers to investigating and understanding the consequences of such failures. FMEA was originally introduced in the late 1940s by the US Armed Forces. Later it was used for aerospace development to pinpoint problems in the manufacture of small components being used in rocket technology. In the late 1970s the Ford Motor Company introduced FMEA to the automotive industry to help ensure it complied with safety regulations, and to improve production and design. FMEA methodology is now used across a wide range of different industry sectors including semiconductor processing, plastics, software, and health care.

Problem solution

Once the problem has been analysed, it is necessary to think of ways in which to remove the root cause of the problem. For instance, at its largest bottling plant in Europe, Coca Cola reduced by 29% over five years the complaints per million units by using root cause analysis. There are now only 1.7 complaints for every million cans produced (Anon 2010). Tools and techniques for conducting root cause analysis include

- Brainstorming—a way of using a group of people to generate, clarify, and evaluate a large list of ideas. This requires the group to generate lots of ideas and record for everyone to see. This means there should be no criticism, evaluation, or judgement of ideas in the early stages of the process. Everyone should take a turn—one idea per turn or pass.

- Ishikawa analysis—named after the Japanese engineer Kaoru Ishikawa, this is sometimes called fishbone analysis or cause and effect analysis. It is based around a diagram which resembles a fishbone, as illustrated in Operations insight 10.2 where the technique begins by stating a problem in the form of a question, such as 'Why does it take two hours for the IT help desk to respond to a fault?'. The question is then written in a box at the 'head' of the fishbone. The rest of the fishbone then consists of one line drawn across the page, attached to the problem statement, and several lines, or 'bones', coming out vertically from this line. Each of these lines are labelled with different categories, such as the five Ms (manpower, materials, machinery, methods, markets) or the four Ps (policies, procedures, people, plant/technology).

- 'Five whys?' analysis—this is an extension of the technique explained earlier for the cause and effect analysis and is a simple tool to get to the root cause of a problem. Used by many leading organizations, such as Toyota, this technique looks at a problem and asks the question 'Why?' five times, each time peeling off layers of the symptoms of the problem until eventually the root cause is revealed.

OPERATIONS INSIGHT 10.2
Process analysis of a quality problem

In the manufacture of a plastic children's garden slide a considerable amount of the production was being rejected at the quality inspection stage as a result of flaws in the edges of the plastic. The production cycle was observed over a shift and 82 pieces were rejected. An analysis of the causes of rejection were recorded, as shown in Figure 10.8a. A Pareto chart of the analysis, as shown in Figure 10.8b highlighted that 50% of the direct cause of flaws was down to three areas, the largest being errors directly attributable to a lack of training of the operators. Although the job does not require a high level of skill, insufficient training and the motivation of the operators to hit production targets in attempting to achieve bonuses was resulting in considerable wasted time and production materials.

A fishbone diagram was prepared (Figure 10.9) using a Transactional Cause and Effect diagram type. The central arrow—Edge Flaws—is the effect being analysed. Each of the arrows leading into the central arrow represents a cause of edge flaws in the product. These causes are further broken down into sub-causes, like Stamping, Moulding, and Trimming. The key influences on production were established as Machines, Methods, Operators, and Materials.

A modest training programme was implemented and a change to the bonus formula, to take account of production lost to quality, was agreed to allow operators to achieve higher bonuses providing production levels and quality targets were met. The training also revealed opportunities to improve the mixing technique. The immediate result was a reduction in errors to 41 per shift and that the focus for future improvement should be in looking at the machinery, in particular the stamping equipment.

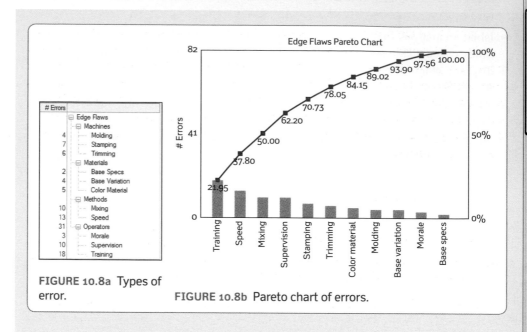

FIGURE 10.8a Types of error.

FIGURE 10.8b Pareto chart of errors.

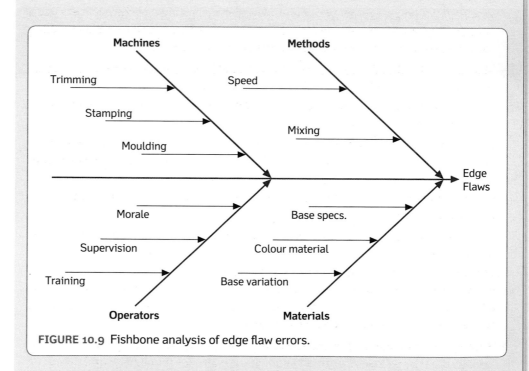

FIGURE 10.9 Fishbone analysis of edge flaw errors.

Questions

1. What are the advantages and disadvantages of using Ishikawa (cause and effect) diagrams and Pareto charts?

2. In this instance, if training is successful what should the error rate per shift fall to?

Using technology

In Chapter 1 we discussed the 'servicescape'. This illustrated that there were two major ways in which operations could change. The first was to shift process stages from back of house to front of house, or vice versa. The second was to shift process performance from employees to technology. Indeed, one of the ways that processes are being continually modified and revised is use to the advance of technology and the introduction of new equipment or software systems. In this section we take a closer look at the kinds of technology that are used in materials processing (or manufacturing) and customer processing (services)

Technology in materials processing

There does not appear to be a classification or typology of technology used in manufacturing. Given that processes are about operation, transport, storage, and inspection we could suggest the following types of 'materials processing technology':

- Moulding—either hot or cold depending on the material to be moulded. This typically involves material being placed or injected between two metal plates with the desired final profile and the resultant moulded article removed after a set moulding time. Hot moulding would be carried out for plastic or rubber articles, such as plastic household goods like buckets, bowls or brushes, or a rubber car tyre. Cold moulding could be used to make tablets or pills in the pharmaceutical industry.

- Machining—i.e. drilling, cutting, etc. These would be secondary operations in a typical wood, metal, or plastic manufacturing process. Once the initial shape has been formed, for example, by moulding, then bolt holes could be drilled or the component could be cut to a special shape.

- Fabricating—this may include bending or shaping metal or other material components so that they will fit together in a later process, or could be the major part of the manufacturing operation as with the production of woven fabric for making into clothing, which would be made on a loom with many individual fibres being woven together in an automated process.

- Assembling or fitting together—here pre-made components will be assembled, often in a mass production or assembly line. These components will be put together in a predefined order with operators being responsible for one or two components only before passing the unit on to the next work station for further components to be added. Examples of this type of manufacturing process would be white goods such as cookers, washing machines, and refrigerators.

- Printing—many components and finished products require printing. This can be to identify them by part number or material type but also location marks or lines can be added to enable fitting to occur correctly in subsequent processes. In addition many foodstuffs we purchase nowadays have printed information telling us of the manufacturing date and the date they should be consumed by. This is printed on to the container at the filling stage.

- Canning, bottling, and packaging—many foodstuffs are sold in cans or in glass or plastic bottles. These containers will be made in a mass production line and then will be filled and sealed using an automated filling process. As explained earlier, they will be printed with the safe consumption date during the closure operation. Often these goods are then packaged for safe transport to the wholesaler, retailer, or customer, usually in cardboard boxes which have also been printed to identify the product.

- Oven curing—many plastic or rubber components require an oven curing process following moulding. In addition, products such as car bodies which need layers of paint added will need to go through an oven to dry and cure the paint before they can safely continue to the next process.

- Finishing—painting, polishing, etc. Often products need to be given a final coating or polish to give them extra environmental protection and to make them more appealing to customers. Cars, for example, are manufactured with many layers of paint but then coated with a layer of grease to protect them during delivery to the car showroom. Before display in the showroom or supply to the customer the car is polished to a high-gloss finish.

As well as technology to process materials, there are different types of 'transport technology' to move materials before, during, and after the manufacturing process. These are:

- Moving assembly line, e.g. conveyor belt, tracks, and moving floors. These are used in many automated production lines and also in despatching operations.

- Forklift trucks. These are widely used throughout industry to help carry palletized loads and can be ride-on or battery powered assisted trucks.

- By hand. Manual handling is covered by Health and Safety legislation. A maximum of 25 kilograms can be carried safely by a man and a maximum of 16 kilograms by a woman. However, these limits reduce dramatically if the weight is carried at arms length, so best practice advice suggests carrying loads close in to the body for maximum lifting effect and to minimize harm to the body.

- Automated guided vehicles (AGVs). These can be unmanned vehicles which collect and deliver goods within factory premises. These run on tracks within the factory, often between storage areas and production lines.

- Hanging systems. When goods require an air drying or oven curing process, for example, painted or sprayed articles such as car body shells, they make use of suspended conveyor systems. In addition, where there may be large distances between operations within the same building, companies often make use of otherwise wasted space by installing overhead hanging conveyor systems.

As well as being processed and moved, materials also have to be stored, hence there are also different types of 'storage technology'.

- Pallets. By far the most common unit of storage within most factories is the so called Euro pallet. Measuring 1200 mm × 800 mm it is normally manufactured in wood allowing forklift access on either side. This standardization has enabled swift transfer of raw materials, semi-finished, and finished products both within factories and to and from suppliers and customers without unnecessary additional handling. Pallets are stored on racking within factories or distribution warehouses for ease of retrieval and also to best utilize high ceiling areas.

- Ambient conditions. Most raw materials can be stored under 'normal' ambient conditions without fear of deterioration. However, some foodstuffs and other sensitive materials are more prone to deterioration and must be kept in temperature-controlled environments or environments where they will not absorb moisture.

- Chilled or frozen storage. Many fresh foods require low temperature storage prior to delivery to retail or catering establishments, who will have their own chilled cabinets to keep them in to ensure that they are fresh at the point of sale. When goods are frozen then they can be stored and then transported in specially adapted vehicles at temperatures below freezing before reaching their destination.

Finally, technology is also used to inspect materials and products. Some types of 'inspection technology' are:

- Visual. Some products are safety critical, such as seals to prevent leakage of dangerous or toxic substances. In these instances it would be normal practice to visually inspect all finished product. However not all products need 100% checking and excessive handling may damage some products. In these instances a system of statistical sampling based on data collected from previous batches would be instigated. So long as there were no abnormalities in the products chosen for inspection the whole production batch would be allowed to go to the customer. If problems were found then more samples would be taken and the batch would be quarantined until the result of these tests was known.

- Automated. Where appropriate some critical dimensions or surface appearance of products can be checked automatically by photo imaging. Any out-of-specification product is then quarantined as per the visual inspection and the batch is quarantined until more samples from the batch are checked. Coating processes, such as those adding a waterproofing coating to material to be made into outer garments, may use radioactive sources to control and inspect the final thickness of the product.

- Three-dimensional (3D) inspection. Some very complex shaped products require more sophisticated inspection. Use is then made of 3D inspection, often by the use of a coordinate measuring machine. This machine checks the spatial arrangement of the product against a specification to ensure that it will be suitable.

OPERATIONS INSIGHT 10.3
Plastic moulding—understanding this technology

Many household items are the product of a moulding process. This includes parts of electrical appliances such as kettles, irons, and vacuum cleaners as well as plastic buckets, bowls, dustpans, and brushes. All of these moulded items need designing. However, it is not sufficient to just consider the final product in the design, it is very important to design the process by which the product or its constituent parts are to be produced. Most plastic products are made by injection moulding using machines much like the one shown in Figure 10.10. This consists of a hopper where plastic granules are added, a screw extruder to heat the plastic and make it more viscous, and a metal mould into which the molten plastic is injected. The mould will be in two or more pieces depending on the complexity of the moulded shape. For a simple plastic bucket, for example, it will be a two-piece mould and the finished article will simply fall out after moulding due to gravity. More complex parts need moulds to be designed so that the finished part can still be removed easily. This can be achieved by having

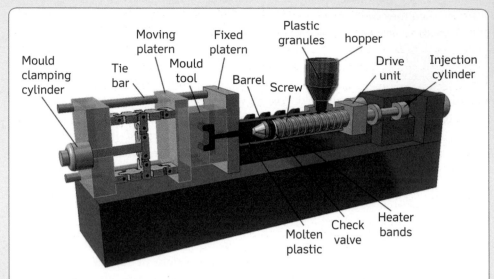

FIGURE 10.10 Plastic injection moulding machine. Used with kind permission of Rutland Plastics Ltd.

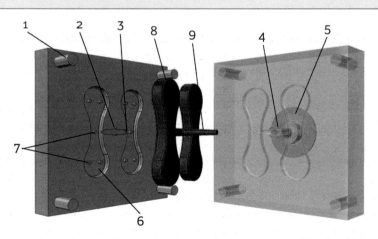

FIGURE 10.11 Injection mould tool. Used with kind permission of Rutland Plastics Ltd.

Key: 1. Guide pins—fixed to one half of the mould and align the two halves by entering the holes in the other half.
2. Runner—passageways in the mould connecting the cavities to the sprue bush.
3. Gate—frequently the runner narrows as it enters the mould cavity. This is called a gate and produces a weak point enabling the moulding to be easily broken or cut from the runner.
4. Sprue bush—tapered hole in the centre of the mould into which the molten plastic is first injected.
5. Locating ring—positions the mould on the fixed platen so that the injection nozzle lines up with the sprue bush.
6. Mould cavity—the space in the mould shaped to produce the finished component(s).
7. Ejector pins—these pins push the moulding and sprue/runner out of the mould.
8. The shot—total amount of plastic injected into mould.
9. Sprue—material which sets in the sprue bush.

removable cores or ejector pins included in the mould tool. Careful design will also ensure that the finished moulded article has very little extraneous material (called sprue) which would otherwise have to be cut or buffed off in a subsequent finishing process, adding further cost and potentially affecting the quality appearance of the product.

A typical mould tool is shown in Figure 10.11. It also identifies the key components of the tool. By paying attention to the moulding and de-moulding process product designers are able to design products which can be manufactured in a mass process with very little human intervention.

Questions

1. Draw a simple process flow chart of how a plastic product would be made using the machine shown in Figure 10.10.

2. Identify the poka-yokes incorporated into the moulding machine and the mould tool.

Technology in customer processing

We considered the servuction system in Chapter 1. This identified key features of customer processing, one of which was the balance between using technology or employees to serve the customers. Whilst in Chapter 8 we identified 'prosumption', the idea that customers become co-workers in an operation by directly using an organization's technology. But we have discussed service encounters by focusing on the interpersonal and human dynamics of encounters, rather than technology. However, advances in technology have been altering various aspects of customer processing. Indeed technology can now be thought of as a fourth element in the service encounter, along with management, employees, and customers. So in this section we consider the different ways that technology can be used in processes involving the customer.

It has been suggested that technology can improve such interactions in three ways, largely through customizing the encounter, facilitating an effective service recovery following a service failure, or as a means of delighting customers.

There are five specific ways in which technology might be used. These are:

- Customer and employee interaction with technology—this refers to a technology that is used by both customers and employees during the service encounter. The most frequently used example of this is the hand-held credit card reader. It is used by the customer to pay their bill and requires them to enter their pin number, and it is used by the employee to record the transaction and issue a receipt.

- Employee-only interaction with technology—in this setting the employee is provided with a technology that simplifies or speeds up the process, but the customer interacts with the employee not the technology. An example of this is when guests check into hotels. The receptionist has all the details on their computer screen and allocates a room to the guest.

- Self-service—in this instance the customer only interacts with technology. There is usually some employee interaction with the technology in order to support its effective functioning. For instance, customers are able to serve themselves from vending machines, but an employee has to restock the machine, remove the cash, and make sure it is working properly.

- Passive self-service—this technology is used by customers but with the minimum of interaction. It is usually signage or displays of some kind, that smooth the flow of the customer through the process, almost without them being aware of it. Menu display boards in cafeterias and quick service restaurants are examples of this.

- 'Hidden' technology interaction—in some cases there is a technology that the customer is probably unaware of but which serves to monitor the process in some way. Such a technology is closed circuit television (CCTV), which many organizations use to assure security and monitor both customer and employee behaviour.

These are illustrated in Figure 10.12.

As we saw in Chapter 1, self-service has been a major trends in customer processing operations, leading to the idea of 'customers as employees'. But as Figure 10.12 illustrates, 'self-service' is more complex than it might appear. Customers may serve themselves, as in Figure 10.12 examples (a) and (c) but they do not necessarily have to actively interact with technology. It can be used by employees to facilitate the process (b) or it can passively influence customer behaviour (d) and (e).

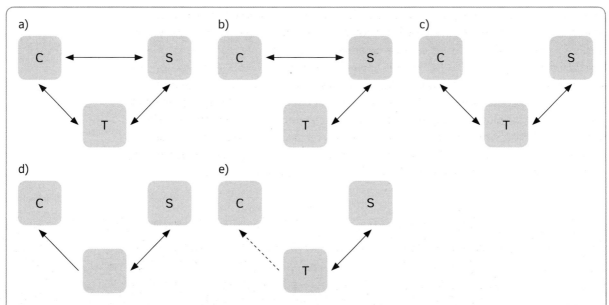

FIGURE 10.12 Alternative roles for technology in customer processing. a) Customer and employee interaction with technology (e.g. supermarket check-out). b) No customer interaction with technology (e.g. hotel check-in). c) Self service approach (e.g. vending machine). d) Passive 'self-service' (e.g. service display boards). e) 'Hidden' technology interaction (e.g. CCTV surveillance of public areas). C = customer; S = staff; T = technology.

RESEARCH INSIGHT 10.2

Biazzo, S. (2002) Process mapping techniques and organizational analysis: lessons from sociotechnical system theory, *Business Process Management Journal*, 8(1), 42–52

Having discussed technology in some detail, it is worth reminding ourselves of the importance of human beings in most systems. In this article, Biazzo compares and contrasts three different approaches to process mapping commonly adopted in the 1990s. He then goes on to critique these by comparing them with the earlier concept of sociotechnical analysis, originally developed in the 1960s. As a result he suggest that the more modern approaches to process mapping focus too much on technology and not enough on the social aspects of any process. As we have already seen in this book, operations are concerned with transactions, relationships, and resources (for instance, see Chapter 2). In this Insight Biazza suggests similar aspects of processes, namely 'personality disposition, power relationships, status structure, attitudes, commitment, etc.'.

Conclusions

As we have seen in this chapter, careful attention to detail and correct choice of process design can make the difference between success and failure of operations. Many companies have adopted continuous improvement techniques as we saw in Chapter 9 when discussing Six Sigma and other quality-related improvements. Some of the process improvement tools discussed in this chapter are also useful in improving quality, such as cause and effect diagrams and failure mode and effect analysis. Managing the whole process is the key to removing inefficiencies and making operations much easier to understand. Customers and suppliers will benefit from this attention to detail also.

Process mapping is one way of taking a close look at process operations before they are put into practice and are also useful in the process improvement cycle.

END OF CHAPTER CASE
iGrafx and Xchanging—managing millions of transactions daily

Xchanging was founded in 1999 and specializes delivering procurement, accounting and settlement, customer administration, and human resources (HR) services to a range of clients. It became a public listed company (plc) eight years later, and by 2010 it was a FTSE 250 company employing more than 8800 staff in Europe, the USA, and Asia, with a customer base in 37 countries. The company is relatively unique in business process outsourcing as it focuses on transforming large organizations' back offices. These are often considered to be the 'Cinderellas of business' because they are the part the customer never sees.

The kind of back office services it specializes in are in financial services, insurance claims, and HR. In 2010 the company settled more than £60 billion of insurance transactions between more than 200 companies and managed over 250,000 claims a year, totalling £8 billion for the London Insurance Market alone. It settled 2.5 million securities trades daily, totalling EUR 500 billion annually for the banking industry, sourced £200 million of spend, and provided HR services to over 250,000 customer employees and dependants. It won this level of business because it is more efficient in managing such processes than its clients are, for instance, by bringing to the financial services sector the ability to achieve process performance standards more commonly found in world-class manufacturers (i.e. less than 1% error rate). Moreover, the shift to outsourcing was made swift and easy, along with providing sustained improvements to cost savings. To achieve this Xchanging focuses on seven key features of their business—service, people, process, technology, environment, sourcing, and implementation.

In order to understand how its clients' businesses work, Xchanging needed process design software that would enable it to map multiple levels of processes, as well as to simulate how changes to process design would impact performance. After going through a detailed selection process, Xchanging chose iGrafx FlowCharter to be the mapping tool it would use for its process improvement initiatives. It selected FlowCharter because it enabled Xchanging's teams to quickly and easily understand the highest-level processes of a customer's business and its interaction with functions, departments, customers, and suppliers—all mapped in 'swimlanes'—which is the vital first step in identifying key process improvement opportunities. These high-level tasks are then mapped to the level of detail to show re-work processes and non value-added work. It is at this level that projects are developed and delivered in order to ensure sustained process improvement.

Most companies already have their own in-house business process improvement team. But often these in-house experts have only been using drawing tools to map processes. iGrafx FlowCharter and similar products are more sophisticated than this in that each element of the process flow chart can contain data, such as time, cost, and utilization. This data is then used to create simulations of process flow, thereby enabling the speed of the process to be identified, along with any problem areas, levels of utilization, and operating costs.

When a company like Xchanging decides to adopt the iGrafx software, it buys a user licence and puts its existing business process improvement team members through a one-day training workshop. The ease of use of the software then allows the team to get on with whatever project they are working on. Projects typically take three months to complete, in three stages. The first stage is to collect data from each of the business units about the nature of the process. Often this is done through a series of workshops wherein users are brought together to describe and discuss the processes they are engaged in and visually map these using post-it notes, white boards, or flip charts. The second stage is for the technical members of the team to take this information and transfer it to FlowCharter. Finally, process experts take the process maps and analyse these to run simulations and see how the process might be improved. Such experts are typically trained in lean thinking and may be Master Black Belts in Six Sigma. The first stage typically takes up 30% of the project time, mapping onto FlowCharter up to 15%, with the majority of the time spent on process analysis and improvement.

iGrafx believe that the 80/20 rule applies when their software is adopted. That is to say, that 80% of the potential process improvement is achieved very soon after adoption and implementation of the software. Hence initially there may be a team of 10–20 people working on a project like the Xchanging example discussed earlier. But within about three months, this team will have done most of its work, and only one or team process managers will need to monitor ongoing process issues. Most flow charts are designed with a number of different levels, so that an overview flow chart would have charts of its subprocesses, and so on. iGrafx recommend no more than three levels, although more are possible. In most cases, subsequent process monitoring focuses on these subprocesses by following-up on glitches, complaints, and breakdowns and identifying the issues that have caused these.

For instance, when Deutsche Bank outsourced its global equities (GE) business to Xchanging the first step was to create an end-to-end map of the entire process, showing the interaction with Xchanging Transaction Bank (Xtb). This helps to identify the largest opportunities for improvement as often these lie at the boundary between one department and another, or between one functional area and another. Examples of such boundary-spanning problems include manual fax interfaces, redundant reconciliation, and breaks in trade processing, all of which can lead to waste and errors. Such an 'industry map' sets out the key steps in a logical flow, detailing who carries out each process step, what interfaces exist between different areas, and what databases

are used. Prior to this, the GE business only had internal process maps that only covered some stages of the process, across suppliers, service providers, and customers. This was the first time there was a top-level picture of how this part of the bank's business operated. The process improvements that resulted from this mapping eventually yielded total savings of more than EUR 400,000 per year and a touch-time reduction of 60%. Furthermore, the department has eliminated the handling of about 150,000 paper-based dividend advices and 100,000 credit advices annually and has been able to cut external supplier costs.

Source: authors' primary research and www.igraf. com

Questions

1. What different kinds of process are mapped by Xchanging when taking on a client contract?

2. What are Xchanging's order winners and how does process improvement help deliver these?

3. What are the benefits of being able to simulate processes?

Chapter summary

To consolidate your learning, the key points from this chapter are summarized as follows:

- **Outline the principles of good process design using different types of process chart**

  Processes should be designed with the following characteristics:
  - Each element is consistent with the overall purpose of the operating system.
  - The whole process is user friendly, with easy to understand steps.
  - The whole process is robust (i.e. can take small variations without affecting delivery).
  - Consistency is easily maintained at every stage.
  - There are effective links with other processes within the operating system.
  - The whole process is cost-effective.

  There are three basic types of process chart—relationship chart, cross-functional chart, and process flow chart.

- **Discuss alternative approaches to process improvement**

  Process improvement can be achieved through a number of techniques such as soft system analysis, failure mode and effect analysis (FMEA), cause and effect (fishbone) diagrams, or the 'Five whys' approach.

- **Discuss the role of technology in materials processing operations**

  The factors that influence materials processing operations include the operation itself (e.g. moulding, fabricating, printing, etc.), transport and movement systems technology, storage, and inspection technologies.

- **Discuss the role of technology in customer processing**

  There are five ways in which technology can be introduced into the service encounter—both customers and employees interact with the technology; only the employee interacts with it; only the customer interacts with it; the customer interacts passively with it; or there is a 'hidden' interaction.

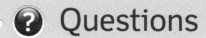 Questions

Review questions

1. What are the key challenges in designing processes?

2. What are the main differences between a rigid and a flexible process?

3. What kinds of process map are there and how do they differ?

4. What techniques enable problems to be identified?

5. What techniques enable problems to be prioritized?

6. What techniques enable problems to be analysed?

7. What techniques enable problems to be solved?

8. What are the key technological developments that have impacted on materials processing?

9. What are the five ways in which customers may interact with a service organization's technology?

10. Which types of technology give the customers the most control over their experience?

Discussion questions

1. Why do so many processes remain unimproved?

2. Are there any major differences between technology used in manufacturing and the technology used in services?

3. What impact does technology have on the kind of work that operatives do?

4. What are the ethics of using CCTV cameras in the workplace?

5. What other ethical issues might arise from the nature of processes in different industry settings?

Further learning guide

There are a number of consulting firms, like Stepchange, that specialize in process improvement. Many of their websites have examples or case studies of how they went about improving their client's processes. Similarly, there are software companies, like iGrafx, that have developed process mapping tools. Their websites, too, may have interesting case studies. For an understanding of how technology may affect operations and business in general, check out **www.technologyreview.com** or the *BT Technology Journal*, which focuses on information and communications technologies.

References

Anon (2010) Coca Cola Enterprises: the coke side of life, *The Manufacturer*, October

Biazzo, S. (2002) Process mapping techniques and organizational analysis: lessons from sociotechnical system theory, *Business Process Management Journal*, 8(1), 42–52

Checkland, P. (1999) *Soft Systems Methodology in Action*, John Wiley and Sons Ltd: Chichester

Mingers, J. and Taylor, S. (1992) The use of soft systems methodology in practice, *The Journal of the Operational Research Society*, 43(4), 321–32

Chapter Eleven

Designing jobs and managing people

Learning outcomes

After reading this chapter you will be able to:

→ Understand how labour structures affect managing people in operations

→ Explain job design and the alternative approaches to this

→ Review alternative approaches to rewarding employees

→ Explain job enlargement and job enrichment

→ Discuss empowerment in the workplace

→ Compare and contrast different types of organizational culture

This company was founded in 1985 and in 2011 had 78 UK stores and a home shopping channel. It has been described as a 'charming lifestyle boutique selling lovely clothes for lovely people'. The staff are described as a 'chilled out bunch' who had one the lowest levels of reported stress of any company entering the Times 'Best Companies to Work For' competition in 2009. This very much stems from the philosophy of the firm's two founders—Sean Thomas and George Treves—who started the company by selling T-shirts in the French Alps so they could prolong their skiing trip. It may also be due to the fact that the average age of employees in 2009 was 26 years old. They are also pretty upfront when it comes to their values and approach to work, as illustrated in Figure 11.1 by a screen shot from their 2010 website.

When it came to managing people, White Stuff had some unique policies. In addition to standard holiday entitlement, staff based in the London Head Office could have two 'duvet days' or 'afternoon naps' every year. The staff were also treated to free massages and subsidised yoga sessions. Reiki and beauty treatments were also available in the therapy rooms. The company organized lots of events for their employees, such as two day surfing trips to Cornwall, trips to theme parks, their own fancy-dress Olympics, and even karaoke nights. As a result employees were reported to spend a lot of time together outside work, which contributed to making White Stuff a fun company to work for.

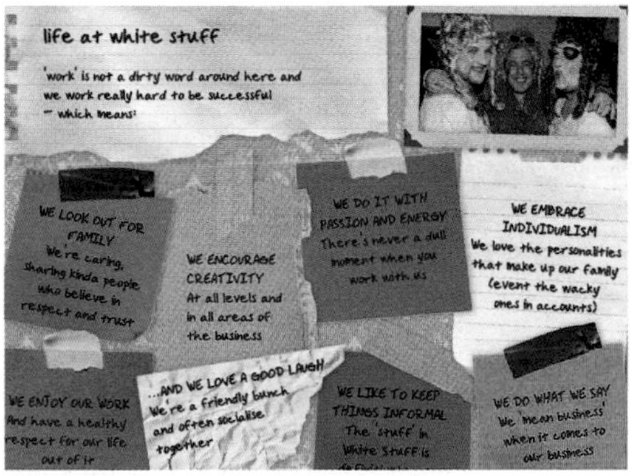

There is clearly a strong organisational culture that underpins the company's strategy of being design led and innovative. Their website in 2010 recounted the story of how Thomas and Treaves set up the company and recruited two employees in 1993, Ivy and Lil, to make their clothing. Ivy and Lil still worked for the company seventeen years later and represented many of the White Stuff's cultural norms espoused in Figure 11.1—hard work, 'family', and having a good laugh. As a result employees reported in the 2009 Times competition that they really cared for each other and had a real sense of teamwork.

Source: http://business.timesonline.co.uk/tol/ business/career_and_jobs/best_100_companies/ article5717426.ece and www.whitestuff.com (accessed in 2010)

FIGURE 11.1 Working for White Stuff
Source: http://www.whitestuff.com/cid/ 8OQPIF3YN6oCJWDGLKO9MVBGK9F7UKTC/ life-at-white-stuff-Acs_life_at_WS/

Questions

1. What appears to be distinctive about the people who work at White Stuff?

2. What is done to ensure employees enjoy working for the firm? Why?

Introduction

As we identified in Chapter 1, 60–70% of employees in most organization work in operations. Operational success therefore depends on people. More specifically it depends on how people are fitted into the processes of the organization—the tasks they are given, their level of control over their work, how they are communicated with and treated by the organization, and ultimately their level of job satisfaction. And in UK organizations we do not seem to do this very well. Strikes, industrial action, high staff turnover, and absenteeism are all symptoms of poor employee management practices. In 2009, the Office of National Statistics reported 'the 2008 total of 758,900 working days lost [through labour disputes] is lower than the 2007 total (1,041,100). But the total is higher than the average number of working days lost per year in the 1990s (660,000)'. Whilst the Health and Safety Executive estimated that in 2008/2009 nearly 30 million days were lost due to workplace injury and illness.

If you talk to many managers (and management students) you will hear them say that the problem with employees is motivation, employees are not committed enough, or they do not have the right work ethic. But we would argue that this is the wrong place to start. There are three major questions that should be asked first before we worry about motivating employees. These are:

- Have we designed a job that is doable?
- Have we got the 'right' person? Are they able to do the job we expect them to—physically, mentally, and emotionally?
- Have we communicated to the employee what standard of performance is expected of them?

This is because it is possible to highly motivate someone and still not get the desired performance, if they are the wrong person, or in a job that is not doable, or they do not know what level of performance they are expected to achieve.

In this chapter, we begin by considering an organization's external environment from the perspective of its labour market—this places a major constraint on what an organization is able to do with regard to employing people in its operations. We go on to consider jobs, how these are designed and the tasks that employees are asked to do. We then consider the role that operations managers play in specifying, recruiting, and selecting employees to work in these jobs, before looking at how staff are paid and rewarded. Having considered individual workers, we then explore the nature of teams and teamwork in operations and how these should be managed. We conclude by looking at the concept of organizational culture and the significant impact this can have on operational performance. In doing all of this, we shall clearly touch on issues that in many organizations are often the responsibility of the human resource function. But at the end of the day, it is operations managers who have direct line responsibility for the majority of employees and operations managers who have responsibility for managing the cost, productivity, and performance of the key workforce.

Labour structure issues

Before we can look at managing employees in operations we need to understand that 'employees' are not a homogeneous group. Employees can be classified into different groups, each of which may need to be managed differently. These classifications include:

- Managers and operatives—enables roles and responsibilities to be defined and reporting relationships established. This is usually captured on the typical organization chart.

- Fixed- and variable-cost staff—as we saw in Chapter 7 in operations with wide and unpredictable levels of demand, it is more cost-effective to employ hourly-paid employees, whose hours can be adjusted to match demand—so-called temporal flexibility.

- Full-time, part-time, and casual staff—these categories are defined by UK legislation, and has implications for National Insurance, contracts of employment, and other employer responsibilities.

- Core, opportunist, and peripheral staff—this stems largely from the fundamental review of business practice that has gone on since the late 1980s which emphasizes that very large, diverse companies may not be the most effective. This has led to the breaking up of firms into smaller business units, the contracting out of some activities, and a focus on the core business, along with the core workforce needed to support it.

The precise numbers of staff to be found in each group, for example, the number of managers and operatives, will depend upon a host of variables ranging from company policies to the time of day. Different operations will be staffed with different mixes of each group. This makes managing employees highly complex—both in terms of selecting the right approach and measuring performance.

Moreover, a manager's ability to staff an operation with exactly the right kind of staff may be constrained by local labour market conditions. These can vary greatly from one place to another in terms of:

- Size of the local population.
- Demographic profile such as number of men and women, different age groups, etc.
- Proportion of people employed and unemployed.
- Skills and expertise of the available workforce.
- Qualifications of the available workforce.

In order to assist organizations, the Office for National Statistics provides a website, called Nomis, which provides details of employment in different areas of the UK. This is organized by parliamentary constituency, local authority, and by wards within constituencies. Table 11.1 shows unemployment in the Aston ward in Birmingham for October 2009. It compares those on Job Seekers Allowance in the ward, with the city and the country. So the proportion of unemployed workers in this ward (13.8%) is considerably higher than the city overall (8.1%), which in turn is higher than Great Britain in general (4.1%). Within this group the proportion of younger people aged 18–24 years is slightly lower than the national average (29% compared with 30.3%), and the proportion of older people (over 50) much lower (10.4% compared with 15.2%). The statistics also show that the proportion of unemployed people that have been on job seekers allowance for more than 12 months is also much more than the national average (28.5% compared with 11.5%).

Hence an organization with operations in different parts of the UK may face very different challenges in one place compared with another. At an operational level, this has implications for how it recruits staff, what level and type of training is required, and the rates of pay that may need to be offered. And at a strategic level, it may influence decisions about where to locate an operation, as we saw when discussing the location decision in Chapter 4. Moreover, regions with weak economic and employment conditions may be designated as development areas, in which incentives are offered for organizations to locate there.

over and over again. Workers in foundries, steel mills, or on oil rigs work in conditions that can be very unpleasant. Some jobs—such as nursing, firefighting, and policing—place employees in positions that can be emotionally and mentally stressful. So jobs have to be designed, within the limits of the tasks that have to be done, with the employees in mind.

As far back as the late 18th century job design has been a topic for discussion and debate as to how best to carry out work activities. Prior to that time the supply and demand of most goods and services was relatively balanced. With the coming of the Industrial Revolution more products were required as the population increased.

The development of job design approaches from the 18th century to the present day is shown in Figure 11.2. We can see a general trend from an emphasis on managerial control where employees are seen as a cost to one where commitment and engagement of staff is preferred, where employees are considered a key resource. There have been certain key developments, as follows:

- Division of labour. Adam Smith is credited with the idea of division of labour which seeks to separate individuals or groups of individuals by the tasks they are carrying out. This helped to develop key skills, save time in operations through repetition, and gave the opportunity to develop specialized tools and equipment for jobs. This type of process is still in use today in many mass production operations, as we saw in Chapter 3 when we discussed automobile assembly and Henry Ford.

- Scientific Management. Frederick W. Taylor brought in the idea of scientific measurement of work in the late 1800s. He developed ideas on work design and work measurement. Together with Frank and Gillian Gilbreth in the early 1900s, they pioneered method study and the standardization of processes. In 1911 Taylor authored his book *Principles of Scientific Management.*

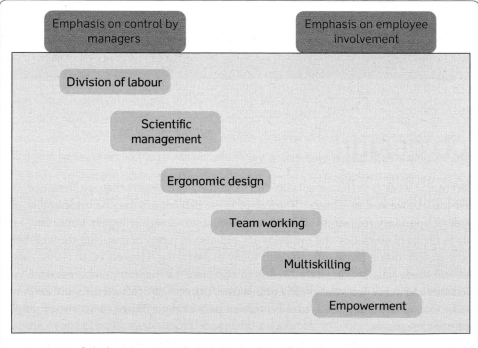

Go online

FIGURE 11.2 Job design approaches. Adapted from *Operations Management*, Slack et al., Pearson Education Limited. Copyright 2004.

- Behavioural school. This was sparked by research conducted by Elton Mayo at the Western Electric factory in the USA. He articulated this approach in his 1933 book *The Human Problems of an Industrial Civilization*.

There are number of different tools that enable work to be analysed and hence tasks to be specified and jobs designed. They include:

- Work simplification
- Work sampling
- Ergonomic analysis
- Methods analysis
- Time and motion study
- Simulation modelling
- Job enrichment programming.

Generally all these tools are grouped together under the concept of work study.

Work study consists of a range of techniques which are associated with either method study—to determine the best ways of doing things in order to make improvement—or work measurement—to determine the time required for a suitably qualified worker to perform a task to prescribed standards. Such techniques can measure not only what employees are doing, but also the frequency of use of plant and equipment. Such techniques may be of value in identifying opportunities for productivity improvement in an operation if they can cut down on 'unproductive time'. That is to say, the length of time employees spend in unnecessary waiting, or movement from one part of the operation to another.

Method study

Method study is normally limited to the study of operations and materials handling methods and is often used when new technology is introduced. The main objectives of method study are, first, to improve productivity by reducing costs whilst maintaining output, or to improve the value of outputs; and secondly, to improve working conditions. These can be achieved by:

- Improving product/service or system design.
- Improving the use of resources.
- Better layout of facilities.
- Reducing physical effort or energy required to perform work.
- Utilizing existing skills fully and developing new skills.
- Creating better physical working conditions, otherwise known as ergonomics.

Method study comprises a series of steps. Because of the complexities it would be impossible to study the total operation. The first step is therefore to select the activity or process to be studied. Second, all the relevant facts about the present work process are recorded or charted. The third step is to analyse the facts critically and carefully, followed by the development of an improved way of carrying out the activity as the fourth step. Fifth, new methods are recorded and then re-examined to ensure that it is practical. Finally, the new method is installed and maintained.

Selecting employees

From an operations perspective it is essential to match the employee to the job. This match may be in three areas—intellectual, physical, and social, or any combination of these.

From the intellectual perspective does the potential employee have the required qualifications and mental skills to carry out the task? For example, an inventory controller may need mathematical ability, whilst a delivery person will need driving skills. Physically, some jobs, such as many of those required by the armed forces or security services require physical fitness. Also some jobs require heavy lifting or considerable physical effort to perform, such as working in a steel works or the mining industry. Finally, the social and interpersonal abilities of employees may need to be considered. Many customer-facing jobs, such as receptionist or nurse, can be very stressful. As we have seen previously, service workers are often engaged in so-called emotional labour, therefore it is important to consider whether applicants can handle stress.

There are various stages during the recruitment process when such matching can be assured.

Firstly, the job must be advertised so that the demands of the job are made clear and/or the type of person being recruited is explained. There can be made easier by the use of industry magazines or newspapers, and specialist recruitment companies or websites. Second, applications should be screened to ensure only suitably qualified people are invited to the selection process. Finally the right approach to selection must be used. This may be by face-to-face or panel interview, or using some form of psychometric test which will indicate whether the candidate has the appropriate skills for the job. Operations managers' roles in selection vary from organization to organization, but often they will be involved in the screening and interviewing processes.

Job communication

When new employees are recruited to a company they need to understand the role they are going to be doing and how this relates to the organization. The way this is communicated will depend to some extent on the size of the organization and the culture within it. However, every company is likely to have three main approaches—induction, training, and appraisal.

Induction is carried out as close to the new employee's starting date as possible. It typically includes a tour of the premises, noting important health and safety aspects and fire evacuation procedures. It will also include an overview of the role and where this fits in to the whole organization. Specific health and safety procedures should be explained and any protective clothing provided before work is started.

Training can take a number of forms. On-the-job training typically would involve initial instruction by a supervisor or co-worker and then ongoing supervision to ensure performance to standard. One-to-one training is based on learning from someone who already knows how to carry out the tasks involved and who passes on all of the key skills before the employee performs the job on their own. Some jobs can be learnt by multimedia training. This could include sales and customer service techniques or complex data entry tasks. It is also the case that operating manuals or standards of performance manuals are provided for operations which have many detailed stages to enable employees to learn how and in which order to carry them out. In addition, as a pre-requisite for some quality management standards, such as ISO 9000, detailed procedural instructions should be made available to all staff.

Employee appraisal systems provide employees with regular feedback on their performance. These are typically carried out annually on a one-to-one basis between the employee and their manager. They are used to clarify goals and set new targets, as well as being used as a motivational tool for the effective management of employees. Some organizations have taken this concept further and encourage 360° appraisals through which employees appraise their manager.

Job content

As part of work study the amount of work expected to be produced by an employee or group of employees has been determined. This leads to the concepts of efficient and effective work output. These were discussed in the context of equipment in Chapter 7 when we reviewed capacity management. It is no different with an employee's output. This can be measured against a standard or expected output and an efficiency percentage or effective output rate can be determined. This allows comparisons to be made between employees and also helps the job designer to ensure that work allocation is fair and that a continuous work flow is obtained.

When employees have demonstrated a satisfactory level of skill within set tasks then supervisors often look for ways to develop their skills. There are two main ways to do this, as shown in Figure 11.4, and discussed as follows:

- **Job enlargement** (or job rotation)—this is when the employee is given more tasks of the same type, thereby increasing their flexibility and value to the organization.

- **Job enrichment**—this is when an employee is given more tasks with increased responsibility, autonomy, or decision-making. This has been proven to increase motivation and also improve output and reduce staff turnover. One example of this is multiskilling, which was discussed in Chapter 7 and illustrated by Operations insight 7.3 (see page 188).

> **Job enlargement** increasing the scale of a job by adding more tasks of the same type

> **Job enrichment** increasing the scope of a job by assigning more responsibility for the work done

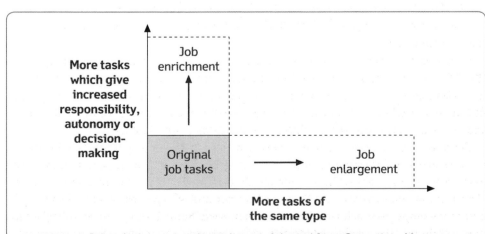

FIGURE 11.4 Job enlargement and enrichment. Adapted from *Operations Management*, Slack et al., Pearson Education Limited. Copyright 2010.

Go online

Michelin Tyres have two UK manufacturing plants. One is in Northern Ireland making bus and truck tyres, of which 70% are exported, mainly to the USA. The second is in Dundee, Scotland making 7 million car tyres for export all over the world. Both plants have faced strong competition from low-cost manufacturers in Asia, and have therefore had to significantly improve productivity year on year.

The company believes that one way to achieve this is through a strong organizational culture. It has very explicit corporate values, which it explains on its website, as follows:

> One of the leading values is Respect for Facts. This means not being superficial, but getting to the heart of the matter so as to take the initiatives that will yield results. The second major value is Respect for People. This is reflected in support through career management, the possibility of changing within the occupational field and within the company, and the desire to develop our people's skills. There is also Respect for Customers. The company is focused on satisfying the needs of its customers, who are its real purpose.

Reflecting this culture the Michelin Tyre bus and truck tyre facility in Ballymena, Northern Ireland, has been set specific productivity targets of 6% per year. To achieve this it has invested in new machinery and in its workforce, by enabling employees to work more efficiently by developing and adopting new processes. In term of technological investment, Michelin Ballymena invested £7 million each year since 2000 on new equipment and machinery. And in terms of process improvement, the firm implemented its own lean system, named the 'Michelin Manufacturing Way'.

Michelin seeks therefore to maintain a balance between increasing efficiency and taking good care of its 1000-strong workforce. To this end there is the Michelin Performance and Responsibility Charter. This sets out the values of the company and how these are implemented in an operational way. The Charter is on the Internet and is available to the whole workforce. Consistent with this, the firm has very a structured and focused way of improving the efficiency of processes by maximizing the potential of employees through good training, adequate and professional target-setting, daily reviews, and monitoring of performance. It also has systems in place to listen to any problems raised by employees and to resolve these as soon as possible. Consequently staff attrition is low, at around 2% per year.

Part of Michelin's Charter is to have a social responsibility programme designed to help people and companies in the local community. This obviously helps to foster a positive commitment amongst the workforce. In Northern Ireland, a subsidiary of the firm, Michelin Development, provides expert support and subsidized loans to local small businesses to allow them to grow and develop. Over the past three years, Michelin has been able to help create 150-plus jobs at such firms in the local area by way of this scheme. Michelin Development has also provided the expertise of its specialists to smaller businesses in areas such as environmental management, marketing, and finance. Michelin are also closely linked to the community through employee training. The firm physically relocated its apprenticeship school into a local college of further education. So they not only train their own employees, but also people from other companies. In this way they are providing a service to the community by providing engineering apprenticeships and training. In 2008 an adult apprenticeship was set up in order to up-skill existing workers. This is a two-year course, and employees will come away with a full qualification in maintenance engineering, NVQ (National Vocational Qualification) level three.

In Scotland, Michelin Dundee faced an uncertain future due to the banking crisis in 2008 and subsequent economic downturn. It survived this by having a highly committed workforce that ensured it was ahead of target in 2010. There are four basic production lines at the plant running simultaneously, and the plant is currently operating at full capacity with an output of 22,000 tyres a day. Management in Dundee, consistent with the Michelin culture, had always been open and honest with the workforce and communicated the good, the bad, and everything in between. As a result, employees have been exposed to uncertainty, but the company believes that this helps them to understand why performance needed to be improved and changes implemented.

Michelin Dundee dedicates around 6% of its time and resources on training and development to get the understanding, ability, and business literate workforce that the company has become known for. With 24-hour operation, managers are not always on site, so employees need to be able to manage themselves. Employee training is therefore focused on work methods, flexibility between posts, operational management, and on the empowerment of self-managed teams. Managers believe that eight out of ten problems are routinely resolved by such teams, and managers only step in when a big issue emerges.

Sources: 'You reap what you sow', The Manufacturer *September 2008; www.michelin.co.uk; 'Treading ahead',* The Manufacturer *November 2010; 'Modernism in motion—Michelin makes way for innovation',* The Manufacturer *April 2011*

Questions

1. What are the formal systems Michelin has in place to develop its workforce?
2. What are the informal systems?

Control versus involvement

There are two basic schools of thought with regard to managing employees—the control model and the involvement model. This was illustrated in Figure 11.2.

Many organizations traditionally adopted the 'command and control' model of management as used by the armed forces. In this model, decisions are passed down through the ranks, e.g. from General to Major and through to Sergeant, Corporal, and finally to Private. In this way the Private simply acts on the information given to him by his immediate superior, namely the Corporal. In a company context instructions are sent down through layers of management. Directors inform senior managers who then inform managers, who in turn inform supervisors and then, finally, the employees hear of their decisions.

This has two main drawbacks. Firstly the time delay in getting the information to the lowest levels where it can be acted upon, and secondly the remoteness felt by employees at the end of the chain and to a lesser extent of the middle managers in the chain. It can also lead to mis-information, either knowingly or unknowingly, as information passes between many people before it reaches those who have to implement it.

In the 1970s, Theodore Levitt, an academic at Harvard Business School, looked at operations and suggested that customer processing operations could learn a lot from traditional materials processing companies. He suggested that simplification of processes, the use of technology, equipment, and appropriate systems would help to improve productivity. He recognized that materials processing companies, such as automotive manufacturers, were using standardized, tightly controlled procedures to improve throughput and reduce variability in the process. This approach was adopted by many customer processing operations and was a key element in the growth of the fast food service industry among others.

The second approach is the involvement model. This emerged out of behavioural approaches to job design whereby organizations wanted more from their staff than merely carrying out predetermined tasks and instructions. Work by many researchers, including Hackman and Oldham in 1976 (see Figure 11.5), had supported earlier work by Maslow (1943) and Herzberg (1959) showing that employees were motivated by the work itself rather than just the monetary reward. This had the effect of 'turning the front line loose' meaning that employees in these types of customer-facing roles were able to exercise initiative and come up with innovative solutions to problems without having to seek approval from senior management. This has been adopted by many organizations including most leading hotel groups and results in quicker resolution of problems, greater customer satisfaction, increased employee satisfaction, and reduced employee turnover.

Hackman and Oldham's research led them to conclude that five key characteristics could be used to describe the motivating potential of a job:

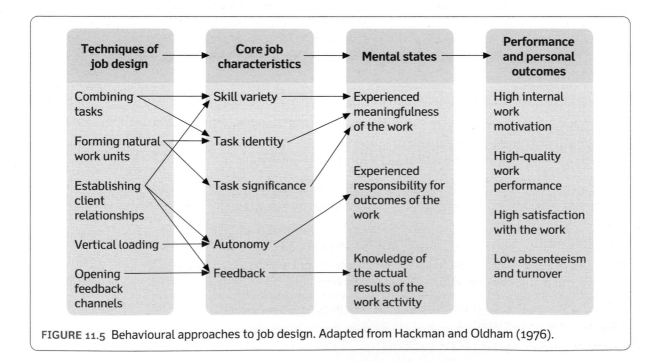

FIGURE 11.5 Behavioural approaches to job design. Adapted from Hackman and Oldham (1976).

- Skill variety—the degree to which a job requires a number of different skills to be exercised.

- Task identity—the extent to which a job requires completion of a whole and identifiable piece of work.

- Task significance—refers to the importance of the job, i.e. how it relates to other tasks within the organization, other people or society at large.

- Autonomy for the task—the degree to which the job holder is able to schedule the pace of the work and determine the procedures to be used.

- Feedback—the degree to which the individual doing the job obtains information about the effectiveness of their performance. This does not only involve management feedback, but also the ability to see the results of their own work.

They then proposed that high motivation is related to three psychological states whilst working:

- Meaningfulness of work—i.e. that the work has some 'meaning' or relevance and not just a series of tasks.

- Responsibility—i.e. that the job holder would have been given the opportunity to succeed or fail by virtue of being allowed to decide how the job should be carried out.

- Knowledge of outcomes—i.e. that the job holder be informed as to the success or failure of their work and therefore be able to learn from their mistakes. In addition this gives the job holder the notion of the customer value chain, so that they are more likely to do a good job if they are aware that the next person in the chain is taking note of their output.

Empowerment

In the 1990s, a particular approach to employee management emerged based on the concept of **empowerment**. Empowering employees to take decisions and create their own procedures for making goods or delivering services seems an ideal situation for busy operations managers. The advantages of doing this can be summarized as follows:

> **Empowerment** authorizing employees to make critical decisions about how their work should be done

- Greater employee autonomy and decision-making authority.

- Increased job satisfaction from self-direction and using skills and knowledge to the full.

- Management released from the role of procedure implementation.

- More time for strategic planning and customer responsiveness.

- Access to previously untapped employee resourcefulness, energy, enthusiasm, and creativity.

However, in practice this may not always happen. Many companies on pay 'lip service' to the idea of empowerment and many managers find it difficult to relinquish control. This may lead to one or more of the following situations:

- Often associated with unrealistic expectations as a universal panacea, therefore expectations are not realized.

- Increased autonomy = increased workload.

- Often preceded by cost-based rationalization programmes, therefore it is effectively empowerment by de-layering.
- Conflict arises between the previous structured management programmes and the newer, more flexible empowered employee programmes.

Teams

Many organizations have found that team working and particularly self-managed work teams are very effective ways to improve efficiency and improve morale. Organizations are typically broken down into groups, each managed by separate layers of management, much as the command and control structures present in the military. However, groups are not same as teams. Groups are often within departments whereas teams are more often created to fulfil a need that crosses departmental boundaries. The concept of team infers greater individual commitment and trust using a complementarity of skills and expertise.

Cross functional teams are often used to help implement change throughout an organization, such as a new computer system, since the team may consist of members of each of the user departments. In this example, if the change were to be implemented by a group of information technology (IT) specialists with little negotiation with user departments then it may well be difficult to get the necessary 'buy-in'. Technology transfer issues and user non-acceptance of change are two of the main reasons why many IT system installations fail.

RESEARCH INSIGHT 11.2

Mickan, S. and Rodger, S. (2000) Characteristics of effective teams: A literature review, *Australian Health Review*, 23(3), 201–8

In this short paper, Mickan and Rodger identify 18 factors that research has suggested contribute to effective teamwork. They group theses into three main areas—organizational structure, team processes, and individual contribution. Although they are talking about this from the perspective of health care professionals, their review covers a wide range of different organizational settings.

Organizational culture

Organizational culture can be defined as the way things get done in an organization through the values, behaviours, and traditions of the employees—rather than through plans, policies, and procedures. The culture represents the identity of the organization and provides 'organizational meaning'. Hence it influences employee attitudes and behaviour, either positively in terms of supporting the organization's goals and objectives, or negatively.

The way to identify a culture is through organizational symbols, heroes, stories, jargon, and rituals. Because many organizations are now aware of how important culture is, many of these things are now made explicit—on websites, through in-house publications, and forms of communication. The Case insight on White Stuff, at the beginning of this chapter, is a very good example of this.

There has been a great deal of research into organizational culture. This has revealed that there tend to be four different types of culture, although different authors call them by different names and give different emphases to the features of each type. In this book we shall refer the four types as 'power', 'role', 'task', and 'person' (based on the work of Deal and Kennedy in the 1980s).

Power culture

In organizations with a power culture it is likely that there is a central power source, who may often be the founder of the company. In such organizations power is centred on individuals and relationships rather than expertise. It is who you know, rather than what you know, that is important. This means such organizations can be abrasive and highly results-oriented. There are few rules and procedures, decisions are made on the basis of precedent, i.e. what did we do the last time? This is similar to the so-called 'tough guy' or 'macho' culture. It can be found in any sector with strong leadership, but is particularly evident in sports organizations such as Formula 1 motor racing teams.

Role culture

Another name for a role culture is 'process culture'. It tends to be highly bureaucratic, logical, and rational. Managers and employees are very careful to follow procedures and rules. There is likely to be a highly structured organization, with clear lines of responsibility. Such organizations tend to be found in industries that are relatively stable and predictable, which is just as well as managers in them tend to be change resistant and conservative. Examples of such organizations may be found in the health services, retail banking, and higher education sector.

Task culture

An alternative way of thinking about this type of culture is as a 'bet-your-company culture'. This is because task cultures tend to be found in sectors that are high risk. Decisions that are made may not have any payback for months or event years. Examples would be in sectors that depend heavily on exploration, such as oil and gas companies, or on research and development, such as pharmaceuticals. Work is often project- or assignment-based, so is carried out by project teams or task forces. This makes the organization structure complex, as these teams may well be cross-functional. It is also flexible, as one project ends and another, with a different team, starts up. Resources are allocated to the project, so management is exerted through project leadership.

Person culture

This type of culture is almost not a culture at all, in that it is the individuals within the organization that dominate. In many respects employees feel that the organization is

physiotherapy, acupuncture, and counselling. This is reflected in how employees rated the company for this aspect of the Awards scheme. In 2009, it achieved the second highest score of any UK firm for 'well-being', with 88% of respondents reporting they had no stress-related symptoms in the past 12 months. In 2010, the company was the third-highest ranked company of those competing for an Award in terms of employees not 'feeling exhausted when they come home from work'.

It might be thought that the role of human re-source (HR) director is important in this company, but in fact no such role exists. The HR function is very small and responsible only for basic personnel administration such as keeping records to ensure that the firm complies with all its statutory and regulatory obligations, in areas such as contracts of employ-ment, working hours, and health and safety. Other aspects of the conventional HR department such as recruitment and selection of new employees are the responsibility of line managers.

Work is organized and scheduled as in most project-based companies, with trade operatives assigned to specific jobs on a project-by-project basis. With regard to managerial staff, their work hours are more conventional, with head office operating from 8.00 am to 5.00 pm Monday to Friday. However, un-like many construction companies, Lindum provides flexible working. Such options include job sharing, home working, term-time-only and school-hour con-tracts, in addition to sabbaticals and career breaks. This is unusual in the construction sector and reflects Lindum's business model. Whereas most medium- to large-scale construction firms subcontract work to smaller, specialist companies, Lindum has a full-time workforce. This potentially has two downsides—first it makes them less flexible in an industry that is no-toriously cyclical and seasonal, and second, as a con-sequence, their labour cost may be higher than the industry average. However, David Chambers believes that this is more than offset by his company's ability to deliver a project on time and to a very high stand-ard. This level of dependability and quality is only possible with a highly committed in-house workforce. In periods of slack demand, the firm tries hard not to lay workers off, but reassigns them to tasks outside

their trade. For instance, the firm has its own security team guarding construction sites and stores, so if an electrician or plumber if not needed for a short period of time, he may be redeployed to this area to cover for staff who are on holiday or unwell.

As part of this commitment to Lindum's future workforce, the company organizes an annual National Construction event which offers a 'taster' in different construction related skills to over 500 local school children during the course of the week. Employees are encouraged to participate and give up their time to attend the event and offer their support and exper-tise. The company is committed to developing young people and in 2011 had 26 apprentices working for it, 50% of all the apprenticeships in Lincolnshire. Staff have also expressed pride in the firm's community and charity work. Lindum matches employees' fund-raising and supports a nominated charity annually. The company has taken on two special projects, using its own expertise and workforce. One involved buying and converting a commercial property that was to be used to house young homeless people, whilst the second was the conversion of a derelict building into a training facility for a local special needs school. Lindum also supports environmental initiatives. For instance, it has invested £1 million in a waste recycling station. As a consequence, 71% of the employees do not feel that profit is the only thing driving the organization, according to the 2010 survey—making Lindum a top 20 score nationally. Likewise the company achieved top ten scores with regards to putting a lot back into the local commu-nity and working hard to protect the environment.

Sources: author's primary research; http://www.best-companiesguide.co.uk/; 'Lindum Group: Construction & development', Times Online, 7 March 2010; 'Lindum Group: Construction, Development & Housing', Times Online, 8 March 2009; www.lindum group.com

Questions

1. How does Lindum organize and schedule work?

2. How are Lindum's employees rewarded and incentivized?

3. What impact does Lindum's organizational culture have on its performance?

Chapter summary

To consolidate your learning, the key points from this chapter are summarized as follows:

- **Explain how labour structures affect managing people in operations**

  Local labour markets affect the number of people that may be available for work, as well as the skills and expertise that they may have. In a favourable labour market, an operation will find it easy to recruit staff that have the right skills and expertise; in an unfavourable one it may have to take special measures to recruit staff (such as offer higher wages or on-site accommodation), as well as provide more training to new employees.

- **Explain different approaches to job design**

  The two main approaches to job design are work study and methods study.

- **Review alternative approaches to rewarding employees**

  There are two basic ways in which to reward employees—financial and non-financial. Financial rewards refers to pay, wages, and salaries which can be paid in a variety of ways (hourly, weekly, etc.) for a 'standard' amount of work, but may also be paid in a variety of ways for specific performance of work (such as bonuses, incentive payments, and profit sharing). Non-financial rewards refer to ways in which an organization may recognize employee's performance, through recognition schemes.

- **Explain the difference between job enlargement and job enrichment**

  Job enlargement involves additional tasks of the same type whereas job enrichment involves more tasks which give increased responsibility, autonomy, or decision-making.

- **Explain empowerment**

  Empowerment is the devolvement of decision-making to the lowest possible level in order to improve customer service, staff involvement, and morale.

- **Compare and contrast different types of organizational culture**

  There are four types of organizational culture identified by Deal and Kennedy. Power culture, where there is a central power source, such as a media organization. Role culture organizations are highly bureaucratic, such as banks or civil service. Task culture is often found in businesses where there is high risk, such as oil exploration, research and development, or pharmaceuticals. Person culture is where 'professionals' dominate and the organization is perceived to serve the employees, such as a university.

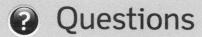

Questions

Review questions

1. How does the local labour market affect operations management?

2. What are the key features of job design?

3. What are the advantages of different forms of remuneration system?

4. Why do some firms use non-financial reward systems?

5. What are the main differences between a control culture and an involvement culture?

6. What is meant by the term 'empowerment' and what forms of empowerment are there?

7. How should teams be managed?

8. What different types of organizational culture are there and how do they differ?

Discussion questions

1. Why is true employee empowerment often difficult to achieve?

2. What are the key challenges that face the operations manager when managing teams as opposed to straightforward groups of employees?

3. What would be the best way to implement a change in working practice at a multi-site operation?

4. What are the challenges for operations managers working in an organization with a mixed culture?

5. What ethical issues face employers?

 # Further learning guide

The UK government has for many years been concerned about productivity levels in the UK and the extent to which the UK is able to compete in a global economy. This concern has identified that a key element of competitiveness is the flexibility of the labour market. As a result there are a number of studies that explore this. A good example of such a report is *Managing Change: Practical Ways to Reduce Long Hours and Reform Working Practices* (**www.bis.gov.uk/files/file14239.pdf**). The report has a number of case studies of British firms and looks at issues such as training, rewards, empowerment, and leadership. Another valuable government report is called *Human resource management practices, organizational outcomes and performance: An analysis of WERS 2004 data* (**www.bis.gov.uk/files/file44947.pdf**). The basic finding of this report is that the more sophisticated the approach to managing human resources, the higher the level of productivity within the organization. In view of this and other research, during the 2000s there was considerable debate around the idea that firms should have to report on their human resource policies, just as they explain their financial performance in their annual reports. In 2003, Denise Kingsmill produced a report *Accounting for People* that addressed this issue. It remains an issue of concern today—see **www. accountingforpeople.org**.

References

Deal, T. and Kennedy, A. (1982) *Corporate Cultures: The rites and rituals of corporate life*, Addison-Wesley: New York

Hackman, J.R. and Oldham, G.R. (1976) *Motivation through the design of work: Test of a theory*, Academic Press: New York

Health and Safety Executive (2009) *Health and safety: Statistics 2008/9*, published October 2009, http://www.hse.gov.uk/statistics/overall/hssh0809.pdf

Herzberg, F. (1959) *The Motivation to Work*, Wiley/Chapman & Hall: New York/London

Heskett, J.L., Sasser, W.E., and Schlesinger, L.A. (1997) *The service profit chain: How leading companies link profit and growth to loyalty, satisfaction, and value*, Free Press: New York

Levitt, T. (1976) The industrialization of service, *Harvard Business Review*, 50, 41–52

Mackay, H. (1997) The changing nature of work, *Management, the Journal of the Australian Institute of Management*, July, 5–7

Maslow, A. (1943) A theory of human motivation, *Psychological Review*, 50, 370–96

Mayo, E. (1933) *The Human Problems of an Industrial Civilization*, Macmillan: New York

Office for National Statistics (D. Hale, ed.) (2009) Labour disputes in 2008, *Economic & Labour Market Review*, 3(6), 26–38.

Pfeffer, J. (1998) Six dangerous myths about pay, *Harvard Business Review*, 76(3), 109–19

Prentice, G., Burgess, S., and Propper, C. (2007) *Performance Pay in the Public Sector: a review of the issues and evidence*, Office of Manpower Economics: London

Slack, N., Chambers, S. and Johnston, R. (2004) *Operations Management* (4th ed.), Prentice Hall: Harlow

Taylor, F.W. (1911) *The Principles of Scientific Management*, Harper & Brothers: New York

Chapter Twelve

Developing new products and services

Learning outcomes

After reading this chapter you will be able to:

→ Understand the different levels of novelty in developing new products or services

→ Outline the new product development (NPD) and new service development (NSD) process

→ Identify the factors that affect the NPD and NSD process

→ Compare and contrast informal and formal approaches to NPD/NSD

Purbeck Ice Cream is an award-winning manufacturer of premium ice creams located on a farm near Dorset's Jurassic coast. The founders of the company have a strong commitment to ethics and sustainability. This means that all their products are free of genetically modified organisms (GMOs), artificial flavouring, artificial colours, preservatives, and gluten. This makes producing their frozen products a challenge, since all the ingredients have to be carefully sourced locally to ensure they comply with their 'all-natural' and sustainable criteria. It also means that compared with other ice cream manufacturers, the Purbeck range looks less colourful than many others. So Purbeck have to actively promote their ethical credentials and natural ingredients to customers, as well as ensure that their product tastes great.

The company also promotes its innovativeness. And they have to, since there are over 1000 ice cream manufacturers in the UK. This is largely because the Ministry of Agriculture throughout the 1990s actively encouraged farmers to diversify their operations. Hence many dairy farmers, like Purbek's owners, set up small-scale ice cream manufacturing plants in order to use up their European Union milk quotas. To differentiate themselves from the competition, Purbeck have developed a range of flavours and products that are distinctive. One example is their Spice Rack range of ice creams that includes a chilli ice cream that they recommend be served with seafood, a cracked black pepper flavour that can be served with steak, and a green tea ice that is a great favourite with Chinese restaurants.

Purbeck Ice Cream's market is 60% the food service sector (restaurants, pubs, cruise ships, and airlines) and 40% retail (farm shops, corner stores, and supermarkets) throughout the south of England. They therefore produce ice creams and sorbets in two- and four-litre tubs for scooping (mainly for their food service customers), and in 500-millilitre take-

All Purbeck products are free from GMOs, artificial flavouring, artificial colours, preservatives, and gluten.

home and 125-millilitre individual tubs (for retailers). They produce a brochure in February each year that lists their full range of products for that year, as well as making limited edition flavours that are sold for shorter periods of time. For instance, in the winter of 2010 they developed a 'chrimbo pud' ice cream.

Clearly new product development is an important part of the Purbeck operation, and everyone that works there is involved in the NPD process. Ideas for new products come from a variety of sources, most notably employees (and their families and friends) and customers. In particular, Purbeck's sales staff routinely talk to their restaurant customers in London to find out the latest food fashions and trends. One year pomegranates were all the rage, so Purbeck developed an ice cream with this fruit's flavour. They also keep an eye on their competitor's product range, although they prefer to lead the market rather than follow others. There are four basic ice cream mixes that can be flavoured—vanilla, chocolate, double cream, and clotted cream—as well as a basic sorbet mix. Towards the end of the summer the Purbeck team start to think about the next year's product range and select the ideas that they are going to develop. Once ingredients have been sourced, prototype ice creams are made in relatively small batches in a machine that can produce between two to 14 litres at a time. These are then tested (i.e. tasted) by any or all of the Purbeck team, along with anyone else (such as the postman) who happens to be around at the time. Products that fail this initial screening are not thrown away, but put in a freezer for any employee to take home with them. They then get further feedback from that employee's family as to what is good and not so good about the prototype. If the team thinks they have got the product right, a larger quantity is produced and other people, particularly restaurant chefs, are asked to test it.

The whole NPD process can take anything from a few days up to two years. When they developed their chrimbo pub product the first batch met with everyone's approval, whereas it took many trials with different ingredients to get a cherry-flavoured ice cream that they were happy with. Moreover, repeat trials may be needed in order to adjust the ingredient mix for cost reasons. Finally, new ice creams and sorbets are launched in the product list brochure, typically by highlighting them as 'new'. How long that product then stays on the list then depends on how well it sells.

Source: author's primary research

Questions

1. Why does Purbeck Ice Cream develop new products every year?

2. Identify the steps Purbeck go through in developing a new product.

Introduction

All organizations need to develop new products or new services. The pressures to do so are many, including changing consumer tastes, competitors' actions, or the availability of new technologies. In this chapter we consider new product development (NPD) and new service development (NSD). Both NPD and NSD are specific types of **innovation** and most organizations regard themselves as innovative. A glance through any company's annual report show that most chief executive officers believe a key to future success will be new products or new services. In reality, most firms are not as innovative as they think they are—for instance, many innovations are not 'new to the world' (10% according to some estimates) but just new for that organization.

> **Innovation** putting into practice anything new that an organization has not done before

In this chapter we look at the process of NPD and NSD and review whether it is the rational and logical process that some people would suggest. Although a number of structured models of innovation have been proposed, we suggest that most innovation is not carried out in a structured way—nor, as this chapter illustrates, need it be. Innovation requires creativity and this thrives in unstructured environments, that some might call chaotic, risk-taking, and boundary-pushing. IDEO, the innovative industrial design company, advocates this and is being asked to advise companies on how to create such an environment (see Operations insight 12.1).

> **Invention** the development of a novel idea

This chapter begins by differentiating between **invention** and innovation, before proposing a typical 15-stage process for developing new products and services. It then examines the extent to which industry practice actually reflects this. Often organizations follow such a systematic process—more or less—but many do not knowingly do so. Even when they are clear about their process, they do not always follow all its stages. This is because NPD and NSD is highly *contingent*, that is to say it depends on the circumstances and context of the innovation as to what process should be followed. On this basis, the management of innovation can range from being a highly systematic research and development process through to a somewhat chaotic, but exciting, activity designed to beat competitors to the market. The chapter concludes by identifying the factors that influence the choice of NPD or NSD process.

Innovation

NPD and NSD are specific examples of innovation. Hence before looking at these in some detail it is important to understand what is meant by 'innovation', especially since it is often misunderstood. One way in which it is misunderstood is that it is confused with invention. But innovation is not the same as invention. Invention is the development of an idea that is new to the world, whereas innovation is putting into practice anything new that an organization has not done before. This is illustrated in Figure 12.1.

Figure 12.1 identifies two kinds of innovation, depending on the nature of the new idea and its 'impact'. **Incremental innovation** refers to innovations that may be small scale and have a limited impact individually. It may also be that the innovation is not new to the world and the organization is adopting something new that others have already done. However, if the organization systematically encourages incremental innovations, together these many small ideas and changes can have a big impact. This in effect is the operations strategy of 'continuous improvement', which is discussed in detail in Chapter 16. On the other hand, the innovation may be 'radical' or 'disruptive' because it has a significant impact on the organization. Such disruption is often a result of invention. For instance, the invention of digital cameras had a hugely disruptive effect on firms that manufactured photographic film, such as Kodak.

Incremental innovation changes made to existing products or technologies to improve performance

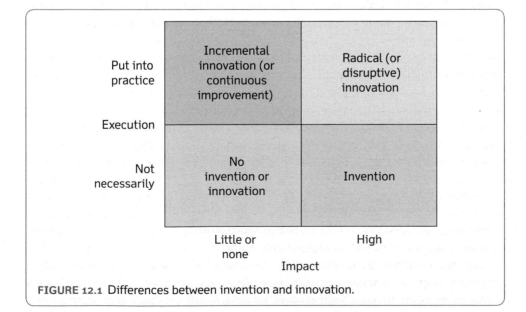

FIGURE 12.1 Differences between invention and innovation.

Go online

Innovation is often described as a 'funnel', that is to say many ideas are generated about new ways of doing things but only a small number of these are ever executed. However the funnel metaphor can be misleading. This is because it is really describing **radical innovation** based on invention. As the TV programme *Dragons' Den* illustrates, there are many inventors and innovators but only a small number of these will succeed in developing their idea into a commercial success. Whilst there are examples of innovation in firms that have gone through this narrowing down and filtering of alternatives, there are also examples of innovation where one basic idea has led to many different outcomes. So that rather than innovation being a filtering process, it can also be seen as a 'flowering' process. Indeed the whole thrust of this chapter is that there is no one single 'right way' to engage in NPD or NSD. The process varies widely from one setting to another.

Radical innovation the commercialization of products or services that have a big impact on both the market and the company

RESEARCH INSIGHT 12.1

Christensen, C.M., Johnson, M.W., and Rigby, D.K. (2002) Foundations for growth: How to identify and build disruptive new businesses, *Sloan Management Review*, 43(3), 22–31

As we have just discussed, some innovation can be radical or 'disruptive', potentially requiring the firm to rethink almost everything that it does. In this article, Christensen at al. argue that companies can see the advantage of disruptive innovation (it leads to competitive advantage) but are concerned about how to do it and the effect it may have on their performance. They therefore present a 'blueprint' to help managers understand if the conditions are right for disruption—and how to pull it off again and again.

What is 'new'?

It might seem that it is fairly obvious if something is 'new' or not. However, it is not as straightforward as that. For instance, take something as simple as baked beans. Is it new if the beans are sold in a different size can, or sold in a plastic sachet instead of a tin? Is it new if flavours are added to the beans to create 'Mexican' beans or 'tikka' beans? Think about all the different types of beans that Heinz produce, including regular, vegetarian, salt free, 'weight watchers', Mexican flavour, and in 'snap pots'.

From this it is fairly obvious that there are different levels of 'newness', or novelty, involved in developing new products and services. It ranges from making some fairly small changes to existing products up to creating completely new ones. Six levels of novelty can be identified, as follows:

- Modifications—this means taking an existing product and changing it in some way. An example of this would be low-salt or low-fat baked beans.

- Restaging—this means modifying the product so that it can be used on different occasions, or by new market segments, or some other factor. Heinz selling beans in snack pots is an example of this.

- Line extensions—this refers to a product variation of an existing brand. Heinz flavouring baked beans with chilli to make Mexican beans is an example.

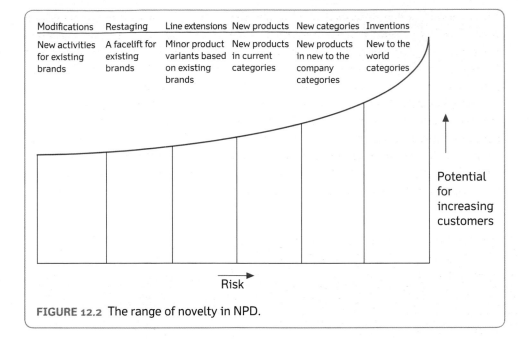

Modifications	Restaging	Line extensions	New products	New categories	Inventions
New activities for existing brands	A facelift for existing brands	Minor product variants based on existing brands	New products in current categories	New products in new to the company categories	New to the world categories

Risk

Potential for increasing customers

FIGURE 12.2 The range of novelty in NPD.

- New products in existing categories—this refers to developing a new product as part of an existing range of products. An example would be if Heinz developed a new tinned vegetable product.

- New categories—this relates to the firm developing an entirely new product or product range that they had not previously produced before, although other firms may have done so. This would be the case if Heinz started making and selling crisps—maybe with baked bean flavours!

- Inventions—this refers to a product that is entirely new to the world, as we saw in Figure 12.1. In the food industry, many companies are developing what are known as functional foods, i.e. food products that have health and medical benefits over and above simple nutrition. Currently there are some yogurts and drinks that are said to have these properties.

These alternatives are shown in Figure 12.2. This shows that the potential for increasing sales is more as the firm moves from simple modifications towards invention, but risk increases also. One of the reasons that successful movies are followed by sequels (or even prequels) is that the audience for the follow-up movies are more predictable than those for completely new films, and hence there is much less risk. Hence many films come in threes—such as *Toy Story*, *Shrek*, and *Spider Man*.

NPD versus NSD

There is a reasonably well-established approach to new product development. But there is a huge difference in terms of developing a new motor car compared with a toothbrush. So any NPD process has to be flexible. In addition, many new 'products' are not simply products, they have service implications too. These service implications may mean modification to the processes carried out back of house, or directly affect the way in which customers are served. So NPD has to accommodate service development too.

TABLE 12.1 New product or service development process

Formulate ideas	1. Objectives and strategy
	2. Structure
	3. Idea generation and screening
Decide on whether to proceed	4. Concept development
	5. Concept testing
	6. Business analysis
	7. Project authorization
Test the design	8. Service design and testing
	9. Process and system design and testing
	10. Marketing programme design and testing
	11. Personnel training
Evaluate the outcome	12. Service testing
	13. Test marketing
	14. Launch
	15. Post launch review

Source: Jones (1996)

For instance, libraries have been transformed over the last 20 years by the development of computers and the Internet. As a result librarians have had to 'reskill and retool' in order to deliver to their users what they expect and need. When libraries consisted largely of written texts, librarians were skilled in cataloguing, filing, and issuing. Today librarians routinely use information technologies and have skills related to their use.

When it comes to service development, some have argued that services are more complex to develop for some of the reasons we have previously discussed (see page 16)—intangibility, simultaneity, and inseparability. They therefore suggest that additional stages in the development process may be needed to accommodate these issues. But just like there may be simple and complex products, not all services are complex to develop, so the NSD process needs to be as flexible as the NPD process.

In view of this, considering products and services separately does not make sense. Although this chapter talks about both NPD and NSD, we shall propose a single, but flexible, development process (Jones 1996) that is adapted according to whether a simple or complex product or service is being developed, as shown in Table 12.1. For an innovation that involves a significant service development, all 15 steps of the process may need to be followed, although not necessarily in the sequence shown. But for a simple product-based development, many of the steps may be partially or totally excluded.

Stages in the development process

The fifteen steps outlined in Table 12.1 can be considered as four main stages:

- Formulating ideas
- Deciding on whether to proceed
- Testing the design
- Evaluating the outcome of the process.

We will now consider each of these in more detail.

Formulate ideas

The first stage of successful innovation focuses on how new ideas are generated and developed (steps one to three). These typically apply to both new product and new service development.

Objectives and strategy

The development process typically begins in the context of an organization's operations strategy and objectives concerning innovation. In some organizations, especially large multinationals, a strategy drives and directs the entire development process and managers seek to assure it is both effective and efficient. Within the strategy, organizations may then set specific objectives with regards to the number and nature of new products or services they will develop over the forthcoming months or years. The extent to which these objectives may be realized will depend very much on the environment in which the organization operates. Pharmaceutical companies are often engaged in ground-breaking research into genetics and biochemistry, the outcomes of which are often difficult to predict. Book and music publishers on the other hand are reasonably confident that they can publish new works on a fairly regular basis, as authors and musicians produce more new works than are actually published.

Structure

As well as having a clear strategy for NPD/NSD, organizations also ensure that they have structured themselves so that they are able to support innovation. In large companies, this may be a Research and Development (R&D) department. However, research in service firms (Jones et al. 1998; Ottenbacher et al. 2006) suggests that only a small number of companies—as low as 10%—have a specific department responsible for research and development. In organizations without R&D departments, it is likely to be the sales and marketing people who have responsibility for generating new ideas, largely because they are likely to be doing market research. Organizations may also create a structure to elicit good ideas from a wide range of sources—employees, customers, and suppliers. Some organizations encourage, through their websites, their customers to suggest new ideas. The Purbeck Ice Cream Case insight illustrated the role customers played in their NPD process, but also that of employees. With regards to employees, Center Parcs created the job of 'Bright Ideas Manager', whose role was to organize and manage a scheme for employees to make suggestions for improving existing products and services, as well as new ones.

Idea generation and screening

Given the variety of 'structures' that might exist, it is clear that new ideas can be drawn from external sources, internal research programmes, consultation, and brainstorming with employees. Tidd and Bodley (2002), in Research insight 12.2, discuss some of these 'tools', whilst Operations insight 12.1 is about a firm that specializes in idea generation. Given the wide range of these, ideas are likely to be generated in an ad hoc way, no one ever being entirely sure when someone will have a 'brain wave'. This is especially true of many smaller organizations. So in general terms, innovative organizations encourage as many new ideas as possible. Quantity is considered to be more important than quality, because once there are lots of ideas, it is possible to review or screen these in order to identify those that have the most potential to improve the organization's performance.

As well as there being many tools to create ideas, there are many ways to screen out the best ones. The criteria for screening ideas vary greatly from one industry sector to another, and from one organization to another. Some criteria that might be considered include:

- Level of investment needed
- Ease of implementation
- Demand from customers
- Fit with existing product/service range.

OPERATIONS INSIGHT 12.1
IDEO—creativity at work

IDEO is an industrial design company founded in Palo Alto, California by Dave Kelley and Bill Moggridge. Beginning in 1991, IDEO topped *BusinessWeek*'s list of design award winners for fourteen years. Between 2005 and 2008, the Boston Consulting Group identified IDEO as one of the most innovative companies in the world. The company has contributed to the design and development of many ground-breaking innovations, such as the first keyboard mouse (for Apple Computer) and the world's first notebook computer (for GRiD Computer). It now has expertise in 13 discrete areas. Some are clearly product-related, such as 'engineering' (especially electrical and electronic goods) and 'play' (the design of new toys and electronic games). Some are service-based, such as financial services, education, and the public sector. Whilst a third area relates to designing organizations—for instance, it advised the UK's National Health Service (NHS) when it set up its Institute for Innovation and Improvement.

In 2011, IDEO employed more than 550 people from a wide range of backgrounds—design, engineering, social science, food science, software engineering, and business strategy. IDEO's approach is to put together multidisciplinary teams when working on a project. In addition, Kelley and Moggridge developed a specific process for developing innovations which they called the 'Deep Dive'.

The Deep Dive is a 12-stage process which was featured in an ABC television programme, when an IDEO team was challenged to redesign the traditional supermarket shopping trolley in five days. The first step in the Deep Dive is to define the design challenge. This is to make sure everyone in the team knows what the objective is and are working to the same outcome. The second step is to build the right team. IDEO's multidisciplinary approach means that teams will typically be diverse—employees of different ages, gender, culture, and expertise. Some of these may have specific expertise that will obviously be needed on the project, but some will not. Some team members will be selected because they are highly creative, but others because they are highly effective in working in a team or because they are good at meeting deadlines.

'Get the room right' is the third step. This is because IDEO believe that having the right venue can help stimulate both creativity and effective team working. Step Four is to 'set the stage', in other words kick off the day in the right way. This involves the team getting to know each other and the team leader setting the ground rules as to how the team will work together. After this, the next step is to 'visit the experts', that is to say, to identify all the issues and display these in the design venue so every team member can see these. In the case of the trolley, team members visited a supermarket to observe a shopper using the trolley, took photographs, and talked to supermarket employees.

Step Six is to brainstorm possible solutions, followed by Step Seven which involves each team member voting for the best ideas. The brainstorming generates lots of solutions, the voting screens these. At this point two or more alternative solutions may be developed and the next step is to create subteams to build these into 'rapid prototypes'. Prototypes can be simple models of the real thing made from paper or Plasticine, or real-size mockups. Step Nine is called 'Frenzy'. This is when the different prototypes are presented to the full team and criticized. The subteams may then go back and repeat the cycle (brainstorm, prototype, frenzy), which leads to the penultimate step, which is to construct the final prototype. In the case of the shopping trolley, the final design was a wheeled frame in which four separate shopping baskets could sit. The final step is to review the whole Deep Dive process.

Sources: IDEO Fact Sheet 2008, www.ideo.com and 'The Deep Dive: One Company's Secret Weapon for Innovation', ABC News 1999

Questions

1. What are the features of the Deep Dive that encourage innovation?
2. What are the features of the Deep Dive that assure project completion?

Decide on go/no go

The idea formulation stage is followed by four stages that enable the company to decide if it will proceed with the new development (steps 4 to 7). In most cases, some kind of business analysis and project authorization process will be followed. But the other two stages tend to be associated with just NSD.

Concept development

This requires that the ideas which are not screened out are expanded into fully fledged concepts, especially if there is a significant service element. A typical concept statement would include a description of the problem, the reasons why the new product or service is to be offered, an outline of its features and benefits, and the rationale for its continued development and/or purchase. In the case of NSD this step normally involves the organization's own customer contact personnel, since these front-line staff are a valuable source of knowledge regarding customer needs and wants.

Concept testing

This next stage in the development process is a research technique designed to evaluate whether a prospective user understands the idea of the proposed product or service, reacts favourably to it, and feels it offers benefits that answer unmet needs. This can be done by talking directly to the users or to those closest to the user—sales staff or service providers. For instance, Purbeck Ice Cream were unsure about the idea of making an ice cream flavoured with the ingredients of a Christmas pudding, so they talked to a variety of people to see if they thought it was a good idea.

Business analysis

This usually involves a comprehensive investigation into the business implications of each concept. It can include a complete market assessment and the drafting of a budget for the development and introduction of each proposed new product/service.

Each industry goes about this in slightly different ways. For instance, we saw in Chapter 4 that hotel companies use feasibility studies in order to decide where to build new hotels (pages 88, 93), whereas Purbeck Ice Cream conduct simple product trials to ensure production costs are within pre-established targets.

Project authorization

This step occurs when top management commits corporate resources to the implementation of a new idea. In small companies, it is likely that there is just one person in the company, often the founder or owner, who authorizes all innovative projects. In larger organizations there may regular meetings of cross-functional managers, i.e. operations, marketing, finance, and specialist functions, for this purpose.

Test the design

Once the project has been authorized, the detailed design and implementation of the innovation can be carried out (steps eight to 11). Some of these steps may not be necessary or very much simplified in new product development, namely process and system design and testing, marketing programme design and testing, and personnel training.

Design and testing

This step is the conversion of the new concept into an operational entity or prototype. This is then tested and specific issues or faults identified. The product is then redesigned and another prototype developed. James Dyson talks about having 5000 prototypes of his vacuum cleaner before it actually went into production. For products, testing may largely be conducted by a specialist team. But for services this activity is likely to involve both the input of potential customers and the active cooperation of the operations personnel who will ultimately be delivering the service. This was very evident in the Purbeck Ice Cream case study.

Process and system design and testing

This stage is applicable to both products and services. For products this may vary from large-scale developments, such as designing new production processes, to relatively straightforward activities such as making new dies or mouldings. For services, this stage refers to all aspects of the operation, both back of house and front of house.

Marketing programme design and testing

The introductory marketing programme should be formulated and tested on customers. Especially with services, it is common for the marketing programme to be devised in conjunction with the service development, given that service workers can engage in direct selling to customers. In product development, the marketing programme may be developed entirely separate from the development process.

Personnel training

This applies mainly to service development, but may apply to manufacturers who are starting up or engaged in a major shift in process type or technology. To complete the design phase, all employees should be familiarized with the nature and operational details of the new product or service.

Evaluating the innovation

The evaluation of a new innovation may involve a four-step process (steps 12 to 15). These stages could be used for either products or services.

Product/service testing

Testing is typically carried out to determine potential customers' acceptance of the new product or service, while a pilot run ensures its smooth functioning. Once developed, nearly all companies carry out 'pilot runs' to test new products/services. This can either be carried out internally, using in-house personnel, or by trialling the new product or service in the marketplace. For instance, Rowntree trialled its Yorkie chocolate bar in the northeast of England before launching it nationally. In service operations, there may be what is a termed a 'soft opening' before the new service is officially launched. For instance, new hotels typically have guests stay during a period of four or five weeks before the property officially opens, so that systems and technologies can be tested, and staff be fully trained. The guests are often employees of the hotel chain or loyal customers, who know that they are there for the testing phase and therefore stay for free or at a very low rate.

Test marketing

This examines the saleability of the new product or service. Often field tests are carried out with a limited sample of customers. The aim is to understand the reaction of

Understanding that there is no one 'right' way of innovating is important. But even companies such as IDEO that specialize in NPD have specific ways of going about their business, such as their Deep Dive process. Equally important is the need to manage the process in the way that fits together the new product or service, with the organization and its competitive environment. Management also needs to be proactive in ensuring new ideas are surfaced and developed.

END OF CHAPTER CASE
Quodpod—thinking inside the box

Developing new products takes time, in this case more than two years. The Quodpod is the brainchild of Katie Davidson, a young industrial designer and entrepreneur. It is a 'pod' designed to replace the conventional airline meal tray. Davidson hoped that it would significantly improve food quality, enable more food choice, simplify cabin crew procedures, minimize environmental impact, and appeal to passengers.

The original concept was based on using induction ovens in aircraft galleys and thereby enabling hot meals to be cooked by steam from raw ingredients. This was to be achieved by having separate dishes of meat and vegetables stacked on one side of an oven-able plastic 'pod'. The base of the box would contain ice, thereby keeping the food safely chilled during loading and transportation. The ice would then be melted to form steam by a ferrous metal plate in a reservoir at the base of the pod when put into the oven. A small hole in the lid enables the steam to be safely vented. This steam would cook the food items in one half of the pod, whilst the two dishes in the other half remain chilled, as induction ovens do not become hot but only heat ferrous materials Davidson got this idea from a Chinese bamboo steam basket. She even bought one of these to experiment with in her kitchen at home in order to see how food cooked under these conditions.

The concept also simplified cabin crew service, since rather than have to put hot items into an oven separate from the rest of the meal tray and then put these hot items onto it during service, the pod could be taken directly from the oven and given to the passenger. Even cutlery was designed to be incorporated into the pod system and the clip that held it when undone served to stabilize the pod on the passenger's drop down table.

The pod concept reduced waste since every component of the pod was reusable—such equipment is referred to as 'rotable' by the flight catering industry. Flight catering kitchens are routinely equipped with wash-up facilities that process such rotable items. Davidson arranged to visit such a kitchen at Heathrow in order to see to how this process worked. She realized that the pod would have to be demountable so that its separate parts could be washed. The original design had around ten parts, plus the cutlery. In addition the 'bean shape' of each pod facilitated the packing density of pods into standard airline trolleys, so that up to 50% more pods could be put in a trolley compared with the standard meal tray. This would significantly save on both space and weight onboard aircraft.

Davidson also designed it so that 'it would bring a smile to the customers' face'. Passengers were not faced with the entire meal in one go, they could 'swivel out courses' as they preferred. The swivel mechanism is a key feature of the design and features in the pod's patent. The upper lid did not move. The pod was kept stable via a ratcheted footing which was deployed before eating. The footing had a second use as storage device for the curvy cutlery which wrapped around the front. The lid design incorporated visual cues—four circles each larger than the next—to suggest the rotational opening process. Two small sections of the lid were also transparent so that the user could see the dishes underneath. It was also envisaged that passengers would find the pod aesthetically appealing, since it could be manufactured in a variety of colours and surface textures. Davidson even experimented with the cutlery, which to fit the pod had to be curvilinear in shape, but still ergonomic to use.

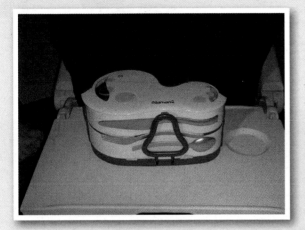

First Prototype of the Quodpod: the 'Original'.

From this original design the Quodpod subsequently went through three further design stages. Industry feedback on the prototype identified some fundamental issues which needed addressing. The complexity of the pod, with around ten separate parts some of which were complex to tool up for, would make the manufacturing process challenging and hence the cost prohibitively high. Second, further research with induction oven manufacturers identified that to achieve acceptable pattern densities only dishes to be heated could be put in the oven, rather than the whole pod. Third, only two out of the four spaces for food had insertable dishes and caterers indicated they wanted all four spaces to have a separate dish insert which would help them to pack dishes in bulk, prior to loading into the pod. Finally, Davidson was not happy with the stabilizer, especially with regards having the top layer swivelled out. She therefore decided that only the bottom layer should swivel, and the top layer could be accessed by an opening, hinged lid.

This led to the development of Prototype 2, which Davidson describes as the 'Ugly Duckling'. Davidson spent roughly six months working on this. The reser-

voir was removed from the base and made into a communal reservoir for five pods. The top layer was made static in order to eliminate the stability issue, and also the cumbersome ratcheted clip. This meant that a solution to how the cutlery would be presented was unresolved in this model. The hinged lid had large cut outs to reduce weight and increase visibility of the food underneath. A new feature was the incorporation of a handle in order to assist with service.

However, when the prototype was made from the computer-aided drawings the handle proved to be too flimsy. Thus a number of issues remained unresolved and new issues emerged. Although the design of the component parts of the pod had been simplified, thereby reducing potential manufacturing costs, there was still potential to reduce the complexity of the build further. Second, this prototype was still working on the premise of heating the whole pod—though it soon became clear that this was an inefficient use of an oven, since half the pod would not be heated. Finally, compared with the original design, Davidson found this prototype much less pleasing to the eye—'functionality had overridden personality'.

Feeling somewhat dissatisfied with the 'ugly duckling', Davidson began work almost immediately on a third prototype. This pod was designed so that the dishes are removed and heated separately in an induction steam box. The large and small hot dish from each pod stack on top of each other inside a heating box and steam is channelled up though both of them from a semi-pressurized reservoir. Trials of this approach showed that the oven manufacturers required their existing equipment to be used, and this did not allow for pressurized steam, so Davidson had to go to back to the drawing board with regards to how the dishes were to be heated.

In prototype 3 there was a deployable handle though the lid for easy handling. The overall footprint dimensions and the dishes were made bigger, using the maximum area available while still tessellating three pods to one tray. At this time, Davidson decided to enter her innovation in the Mercurys, the International Travel Catering Association's annual

- **Compare and contrast informal and formal approaches to NPD/NSD**

  Informal approaches to NPD/NSD are most likely when simple modifications are made to existing products or services; innovation is not part of a major change programe; there is no licence or patent protection; competitors are actively innovating; and the 'new' product is largely a copy of a competitor's product. Formal systems are likely to be in place when new products, with major process impact, are developed; number of interrelated innovations are being developed simultaneously; the new product is protected by a licence or patent; product life cycles are long; competitors are unlikely to enter the market with a similar product/service; and the innovation is original or 'new-to-the-world'.

- **Consider the ethics of NPD and NSD**

  Organizations need to protect the time and investment they have put into research and development and developing their brand name. They can do this through patents, design rights, copyright, and trademarks.

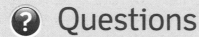

Questions

Review questions

1. What are the differences between invention and innovation?
2. What are the six levels of novelty?
3. Why are there more stages in the NSD process than in the NPD process?
4. What are the key challenges that face the operations manager in engaging in NPD or NSD?
5. What stages of the NPD or NSD process are essential?
6. What factors influence the nature of the NPD/NSD process?
7. What was the innovation process followed by Katie Davidson in developing the Quodpod?

Discussion questions

1. What is the range of novelty in the bicycle market?
2. Are there some sectors of industry in which radical (or disruptive) innovation is the norm?
3. According to Tidd and Bodley (2002), some of the most frequently used tools in the NPD process are perceived as being the least useful. Why might this be the case?
4. Why are there different forms of legal protection for an organization's innovations?

Further learning guide

The International Society for Professional Innovation Management (ISPIM) website (**http://www.ispim.org**) provides many interesting links, notably to its own academic journal the *International Journal of Innovation Management*. The UK government has on its website a report by Swann and Birke (2005) called *How do Creativity and Design Enhance Business Performance? A Framework for Interpreting the Evidence* (**www.bis.gov.uk/files/file14794.**

pdf). This reviews research which has shown many different linkages between creativity, R&D, design, innovation, productivity, creative culture or creative climate, and performance, with some of these linkages operating in two directions. The UK government Business Link website (**http://www.businesslink.gov.uk**) also has a large number of case studies about innovation and NPD. Insight can also be found by looking at websites featuring high-profile inventors or innovators, such as Trevor Bayliss or James Dyson, and organizations such as IDEO. To understand the role of teams and the characteristics of creative individuals, visit **www.belbin.com**.

References

Belbin R.M. (2010) *Management Teams: Why They Succeed or Fail*, (3rd ed.), Butterworth Heinemann: Oxford

Hsieh, L.-F. and Chen, S.K. (2007) A study of cross functional collaboration in new production development, *International Journal of Productivity and Quality Management*, 2(1), 23–40

Jones, P. (1996) Managing hospitality innovation, *Cornell HRA Quarterly*, 37(5), 86–95

Jones, P., Hudson, S., and Costis, P. (1998) New product development in the U.K. tour operating industry, *Progress in Hospitality and Tourism Research*, 3(4), 283–94

Ottenbacher, M. Gnoth, A., and Jones, P. (2006) Identifying determinants of success in development of new high–contact services: Insights from the hospitality industry, *International Journal of Service Industry Management*, 17(4), 344–56

Petersen, K.J., Handfield, R.B., and Ragatz, G.L. (2004) Coordinating product design, process design and supply chain design decisions, *Journal of Operations Management*, 23(4), 371–88

Swann, P. and Birke, D. (2005) *How do Creativity and Design Enhance Business Performance? A Framework for Interpreting the Evidence*, Department of Trade and Industry Think Piece: University of Nottingham Business School

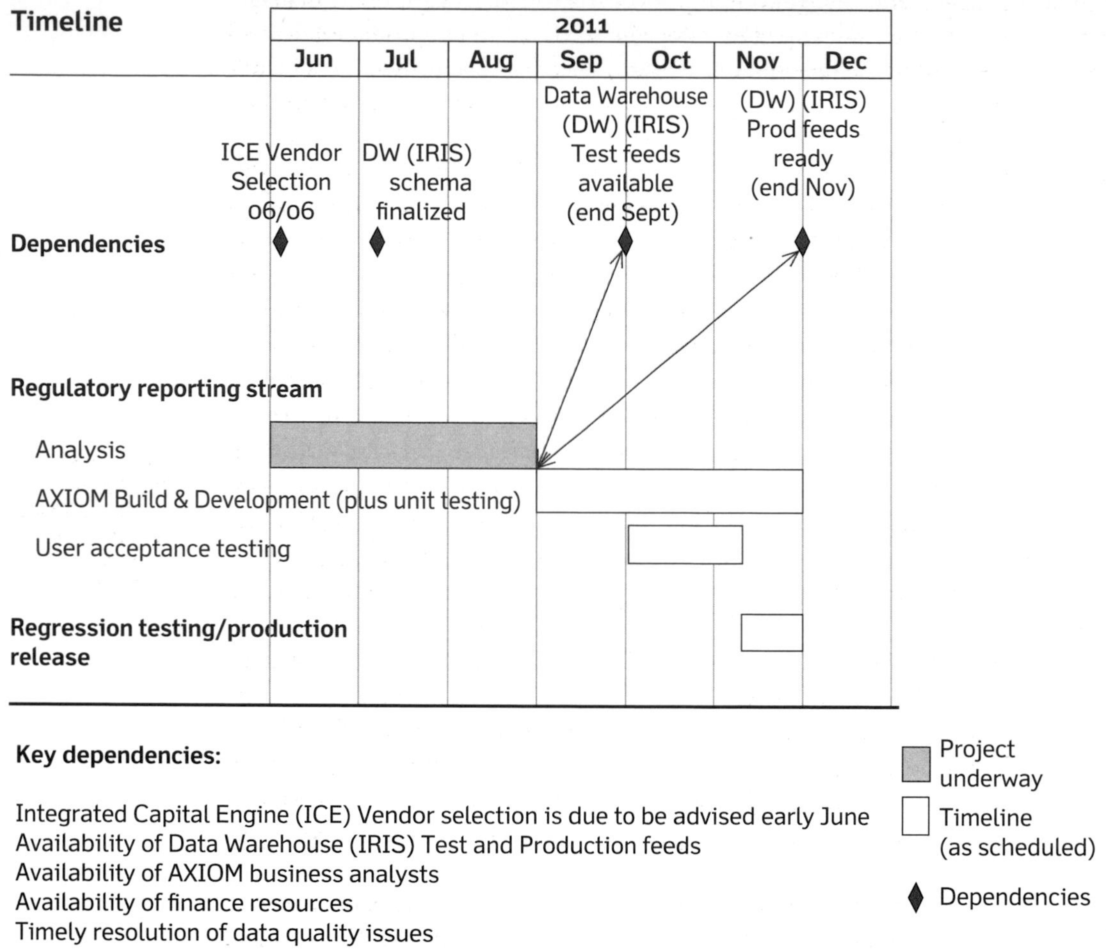

Timeline

Timeline		2011						
		Jun	Jul	Aug	Sep	Oct	Nov	Dec
Dependencies		ICE Vendor Selection 06/06 ◆	DW (IRIS) schema finalized ◆		Data Warehouse (DW) (IRIS) Test feeds available (end Sept)		(DW) (IRIS) Prod feeds ready (end Nov)	

Regulatory reporting stream

Analysis

AXIOM Build & Development (plus unit testing)

User acceptance testing

Regression testing/production release

Key dependencies:

Integrated Capital Engine (ICE) Vendor selection is due to be advised early June
Availability of Data Warehouse (IRIS) Test and Production feeds
Availability of AXIOM business analysts
Availability of finance resources
Timely resolution of data quality issues

■ Project underway

□ Timeline (as scheduled)

◆ Dependencies

FIGURE 13.1 Gantt chart of the project.

tasks as necessary, sometimes in increments as small as one hour. The overall project was planned for implementation in a six-month timeline commencing June 2011.

Source: authors' primary research

Questions

1. What are the advantages of separating the project plan into an initiation stage and a delivery/implementation stage?

2. What are the main challenges the project manager faces in this project?

Introduction

At first sight it might seem strange to link project management with crisis management. A project consists of a unique set of tasks which are created to produce a defined outcome as is illustrated in the opening Case insight, where a specific need was identified to meet financial industry regulations. However, projects can vary widely in their complexity, for example, getting up and going to your first lecture at university is a project, as you will not have carried out this precise set of tasks before. Initially this could be very risky as there are many unknowns which might mean that you are unable to find the lecture room in time. As you become more used to your surroundings these unknowns reduce and therefore you perceive the risks involved as less. In fact your subconscious mind has taken over and enabled you to get to your lecture on 'autopilot'. The risks are just as great that something will go wrong, but you are not so aware of them. This is much the same in business. Having regard to the risks involved in an activity and being mindful of those risks is often the difference between a successful project outcome and a **crisis** or disaster occurring. A crisis is an extreme negative situation where the outcome has not been anticipated. It is not surprising that most traffic accidents happen to and from work as routine-like behaviour makes us less receptive and less able to adapt to unfamiliar circumstances. Managing projects and managing a crisis both require the same degree of skill in planning, organizing, and effectively delivering a solution.

> **Crisis** the breakdown of order in a process leading to an extreme condition

In Chapter 3, illustrated in Figure 3.3, we identified a project as a specific operations process. In Hayes and Wheelwright's (1979) matrix it is explained as being of very low volume and very high variety. In other words projects are generally one-offs and vary enormously in their characteristics. Hence certain sectors tend to specialize in project management, such as shipbuilding, infrastructure construction (roads, railways, and buildings), IT (hardware and software development, systems development, and installation), oil exploration, and consulting.

Despite the widespread use of projects and project management in many business sectors, industry surveys and research alike often draw a picture of failure. For example, losses totalling over $100 million, due to poorly managed projects in the IT industry have been reported (Nelson 2007). Due to these and other highly publicized failures (particularly in the construction industry due to overspend and late completion of buildings and transport infrastructure), it is not surprising that many organizations have developed techniques to effectively manage projects. The Project Management Institute (PMI) in the USA who publish *A Guide to the Project Management Body of Knowledge* (PMBOK® Guide) and the Association for Project Management (APM) in the UK are examples of such organizations who advocate a rule-based approach to the project management process.

This chapter provides you with an insight into the rules of project management and the concepts of **risk management** and crisis management. Whilst 'processes' need to have their place in managing these criteria, in order to be effective in managing uncertainty, appropriate human thinking and intelligent application of these processes have to be applied. At the end of the chapter we discuss the ways in which companies try to avoid crises having a negative effect on their operations and explore the concept of business continuity planning.

> **Risk management** the process whereby organizations methodically address the risks attached to their activities with the goal of achieving sustained benefit within each activity and across the portfolio of all activities

Project management

Project management the planning, organizing, directing, and controlling of resources to complete the specific goals and objectives of a project

Project management, in its modern form, began to develop only a few decades ago. Prior to the 1960s, projects were managed on an ad hoc basis using informal techniques and tools. From the early 1960s, organizations began to deliberately organize work on a project basis, and to understand the importance of communication and integration across multiple departments and professions. Project standards were created by the PMI and APM and best practice methods began to be used in projects in many different industries and these have continued to be developed to the present day. Kerzner (2006) defines project management as 'the planning, organizing, directing, and controlling of company resources for a relatively short-term objective that has been established to complete specific goals and objectives'.

What is a project?

Project a temporary endeavour with a definite beginning and end in which the delivery of outcomes is constrained by a clearly defined scope statement

A **project** is a temporary endeavour. It has a definite beginning and end and the delivery of the project outcomes is constrained by certain criteria which need to be delivered to a certain quality standard in a certain time at an agreed cost. So, creating a new flavour of ice cream or designing a brochure for the launch of a new motor car are projects. The trade-off between quality, time, and cost is sometimes referred to as the 'iron triangle' and some compromise is necessary in most cases.

In whatever job you embark on after leaving university it is very likely that in addition to carrying out your own functional role you will also be involved in some sort of project with people from other functions or even other companies. For example, most companies use external consultants to help with change management or new IT system implementation projects. Therefore if you are involved in either of these projects you will work with people from different sectors of your own business and also with the external consultants.

We mentioned earlier that a project is a particular type of operation. There are two distinct differences between a project and an operation:

1. Uniqueness. In contrast to a 'pure' operation, a project includes a certain degree of uniqueness, dissimilarity, and risk from what has gone before.

2. The other difference is that operations are typically managed in a hierarchical structure (see page 6), whilst by their very nature projects are cross-functional, i.e. they will include employees from different functional areas, such as finance, sales and marketing, and technical development, as well as from operations. The project manager will have to manage each of these personnel differently as they will each have their own line manager and have other responsibilities to be undertaken in addition to the tasks allocated by the project itself.

Project stages

Projects are often medium- to long-term undertakings and are best managed in a number of stages, namely scoping, planning, implementation, and evaluation as shown in Figure 13.2. Each of these stages will require resources, namely time, equipment, and people to carry them out. The extent of the resources required for each stage will depend on the specific project and the outcomes required.

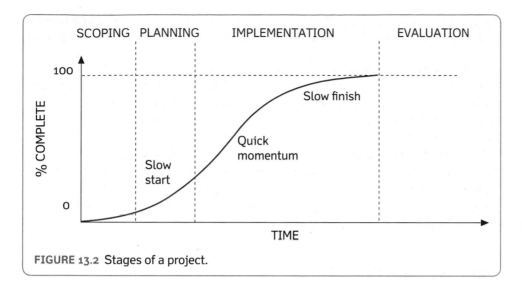

FIGURE 13.2 Stages of a project.

Go online

Project scope

At the outset of a project it is important for everyone concerned, i.e. the '**stakeholders**' in the project (those people or organizations who will be affected in any way by the project), that the scope of the project is defined, communicated, and understood by all. The project **scope statement** will consist of the following:

- The project objectives
- Main outputs or deliverables
- Milestones or significant events
- Any technical requirements
- Any limits and exclusions
- How the project will be evaluated and approved by the customer.

The objectives will be specific and measurable and include any quantity or quality requirements. The scope of a project is very important to the project manager and the client as it is their agreed contract. However, due to the nature of projects, over time these requirements may change, for any number of reasons, which can lead to uncertainty and less clarity in the project. This 'scope creep' as it is called can be very damaging to both parties unless proper change controls are put in place to take account of the resource implications of any changes.

Planning phase

During this phase managers will be discussing the feasibility of the project, for instance, can it be achieved with the resources allocated to it and is there a clear benefit or 'business case'. They will also agree the specific outcomes and plan all the activities necessary to allow the project to be delivered on time. To ensure that time and costs are estimated as accurately as possible during this phase one technique employed would be the creation of a work breakdown structure (WBS) to identify the areas of activity involved. As its name implies, this breaks down the work involved into individual work packages which can then be allocated certain resources, namely labour, time and cost. WBSs are

Stakeholders
those people or organizations affected in any way by the project

Scope statement
a definition of the purpose of a project, usually including project objectives, deliverables, milestones, specifications, limitations, and exclusions

often represented diagrammatically and resemble an organization chart in a series of levels. The highest level is the project itself and lower levels are the functions and activities required of them to carry out the project. A worked example is shown later in this chapter in Table 13.1.

Once the WBS has been set then it is usual to instigate a computer-based planning tool to create a series of steps to be followed throughout the project. The two most common planning tools are the Gantt chart and the network diagram.

- Gantt chart—a Gantt chart is similar to a computer spreadsheet with horizontal bars reflecting the amount of time and resources that will be necessary to carry out each process. It also shows the earliest start date and latest finish date for each step and whether any steps can be carried out at the same time. This also helps to show which tasks are critical to the completion of the project on time and whether there is any free (or slack) time available in any of the activities. The key tasks with no slack are designated as being on the 'critical path', which is the shortest time needed to complete all of the required tasks in the project. Examples of Gantt charts are shown in Figures 13.1 and 13.4.

- Network diagram—a network diagram is an alternative method for evaluating and viewing the project activities. It consists of a network of linked activities, each with a certain amount of resources assigned to them. It is often associated with the programme evaluation review technique (PERT). Originally designed for use by the US Navy, PERT diagrams have become a very important tool in planning projects. Each task may be assigned an optimistic, most likely or pessimistic time for completion. By using probability theory (as was mentioned for inventory demand modelling in Chapter 6), estimates for completion of the project can be determined for these three levels. Project managers can then use these estimates combined with their own experience to keep stakeholders aware of the likely completion times and the probability of achieving a better time or failing to meet that time. Network diagrams are also a good way to demonstrate the critical path. An example is shown later in Figure 13.5.

Implementation phase

Once the plan has been set then it is the responsibility of project managers and team leaders to action the plan. In order to assist them they will often set milestones along the way to help ensure the timely and successful delivery of each specific outcome. By doing this they help to set up a control mechanism and the necessary levels of communication to be able to respond to situations as they arise.

Evaluation phase

This is the formal acceptance stage of the project. As in any process, continuous improvement is also an essential part. This helps to provide a mechanism to correct any defects and to learn for next time. Despite projects being a series of unique events there are still lessons to be learnt and best practices to follow in the future. Many of these have been written up as standards and guidelines and are contained in a number of key reference texts on the subject of Project Management, such as the PMI's 'A Guide to the Project Management Body of Knowledge (PMBOK® Guide), referred to earlier.

TABLE 13.1 Example of a 'Typical Project's' Set of Activities

Item	Activity	Pre-activity	Time (weeks)
1	Design drawing	—	2
2.1	Design acceptance	1	4
2.2	Marketing brochures	1	11
3.1	Design advertising	2.1	8
3.2	Manufacture prototypes	2.1	5
4	Prototype testing	2.2, 3.1	2
5	Manufacture product	3.1, 3.2	4
6	Product testing	3.2	5
7	Product launch	4, 5, 6	4

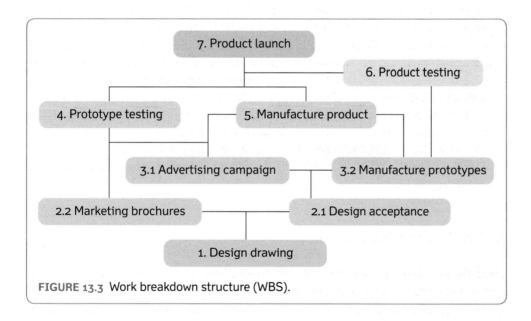

FIGURE 13.3 Work breakdown structure (WBS).

If we look at the set of activities in Table 13.1 which could be a 'typical project' for the launch of a new product, such as a new design of mobile phone.

The first thing to do is to create a WBS to show the relationship of the various activities, as illustrated in Figure 13.3.

We can see that the WBS is in different levels with the product launch as the highest level. Each of these activities will have a number of individual steps which can be managed separately, for example, product testing can include adherence to technical specifications, health and safety requirements, and physical robustness of the product itself.

In order to show how long each individual activity takes and when each can be started a Gantt chart can be created. In this example, Microsoft Project has been used. It has been recreated here as a screen shot in Figure 13.4.

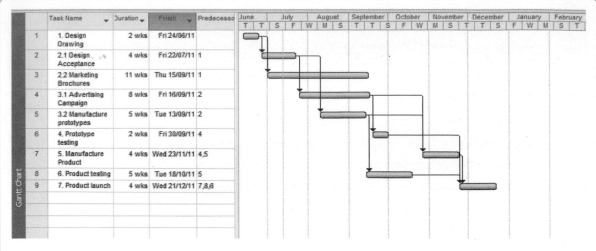

FIGURE 13.4 Gantt chart of our 'typical project'.

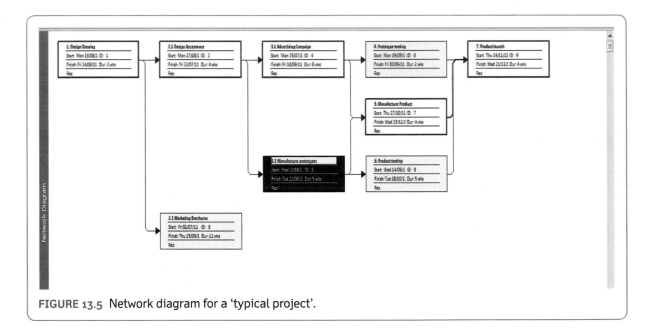

FIGURE 13.5 Network diagram for a 'typical project'.

The Gantt chart shows clearly the interdependencies of the tasks (designated by the arrows) and it also helps us to calculate the critical path for the project, i.e. the shortest time to complete all of the required activities in the project, calculated as follows:

$$\text{Critical path} = \text{Tasks } 1 + 2.1 + 3.1 + 5 + 7$$
$$= (2 + 4 + 8 + 4 + 4) \text{ weeks} = 22 \text{ weeks}$$

The Gantt chart can also be reproduced as a network diagram (as shown in Figure 13.5), which is similar to a process flow chart. Again the dependencies between the different tasks are shown by the arrows and the critical tasks are shown in red. As before the critical path can be calculated at 22 weeks. In this case the project is quite straightforward so the network is simple. However, with more complex projects the network diagram gets very large and can be difficult to use. In these cases a series of individual Gantt charts are often preferred.

Project standards

Most dominant amongst the number of project standards available are the best practice standards of the Project Management Institute (PMI). The PMI standard *A Guide to the Project Management Body of Knowledge* (PMBOK® Guide), (Project Management Institute 2004) includes nine areas of project management knowledge:

- Integration management—ensuring that the project plans are coordinated.
- Scope management—concerning what is and what is not included in the project.
- Time management—estimates of the time to carry out each activity.
- Cost management—including cost estimating, budgeting, and controlling.
- Quality management—ensures adherence to quality standards.
- Human resource management—effective planning of the use of human capital in the project.
- Communications management—provides processes to ensure effective communication to deliver a successful project.
- Procurement management—processes to determine what to buy for the project, how much, and from where.

Each of these areas has specific standards or 'rules' which should be followed in order to manage projects in the best possible way. Refer to the PMI website for more detailed information of each of these (www.pmi.org).

Project success

There are three dimensions of success in a typical project.:

- Implementation of the project. This relates to project efficiency and includes criteria such as meeting cost and time targets, technical specifications, and other pre-stated project objectives.
- Stakeholder satisfaction should also be considered. Key stakeholders in a typical project are the project manager, the customer or client, the organization that carries out the work of the project, project team members, the owner or sponsor of the project, and anyone else affected by the process or outcome.
- Perceived value of the project. This relates to whether the purpose and benefits of the project were achieved or not. The achievement of the purpose addresses the direct impact of the project on the organization; for example, in the Case insight the implementation of the new IT system was to reduce risk by eliminating the errors that occurred from having a manual system. As well as meeting the specific purpose, a project may lead to other benefits. For instance, by installing new IT system it may be possible to build on this and automate other systems, or the organization may learn things from the project that help it improve in other areas.

RESEARCH INSIGHT 13.1

Gary, L. (2003) Dealing with a project's fuzzy front end, *Harvard Management Update*, 8(6), 3

In this very short briefing, Gary identifies that project management used to be about driving out uncertainty. The deliverables were agreed right at the outset and all the issues of project scale, size, and sequence were thought through. As Gary says 'There were always a few surprises, but in general, you could pretty much predict what you were in for'. However, Gary goes on to identify that due to the complexity of information management, uncertainty cannot simply be eliminated and that the initial phase of a complex project has a disproportionately large impact on the end result. He then proposes ways in which to manage this 'fuzzy front end' of a project.

Many projects nowadays are mega-programmes with interconnected projects and portfolios. For example, the quest to put a man on the moon was finally achieved by the United States in 1969. The race to put a man on the moon was a very complex mega-programme with many hundreds of individual projects coming together on that successful day. However, at the time many issues were still not fully understood within the programme making it a very high-risk activity. This was demonstrated very dramatically some years later when a near-miss occurred with the Apollo 13 mission, when a component failed, leading to an explosion.

As Operations insight 13.1 illustrates, large-scale projects often require collaboration between public and private institutions in order to firstly fund them adequately and also to ensure that all of the stakeholders' views and needs are properly taken into account. They can also take a huge amount of time to complete.

OPERATIONS INSIGHT 13.1
Heathrow T5 underground extension—public private partnership in action

With the capacity to handle over 30 million passengers per annum, London Heathrow Airport's new Terminal 5 building was officially opened by Her Majesty the Queen on 14 March 2008. The building project itself was a vast undertaking costing an estimated £4.3 billion, Terminal 5 becoming the largest single-span building in the UK. In conjunction with this was the need to swiftly and safely carry passengers and staff to and from the Terminal building and also to any of the other four Terminals at Heathrow. There was already a fast rail link between London and Heathrow's other Terminals (the Heathrow Express) and an Underground link via the Piccadilly line. However, to serve Terminal 5 a new Piccadilly line underground extension would need to be constructed. The job of making this happen fell to a public private partnership (PPP), a consortium of local businesses as well as local and national government departments.

A new underground extension was needed to serve Heathrow's Terminal 5. © istock/David Joyner.

The partnership was between Heathrow Airport Limited, a subsidiary of British Airports Authority (BAA), who owned the land the airport was on, London Underground Limited (LUL), Department for Transport (DfT), and Her Majesty's Treasury, plus close working relationships with other companies such as Balfour Beatty, Mott MacDonald, Tube Lines, and EDF. With so much public interest it was not surprising that this project took many years and a public inquiry to complete. The original proposal for the project was put forward in November 1994 after feasibility studies were carried out jointly between BAA and LUL from as early as 1991. The business case for the project was a public sector service benefit (a desire by BAA and LUL to increase the public transport share of air passengers getting to the new Heathrow Terminal from 30% to 50%) and a value for money and guaranteed rate of return for each participating business. In order for these to become a reality the new Piccadilly Extension would need to be able to handle up to 12 trains per hour at peak times. An agreement was made between BAA and LUL in late 1996 on how the scheme would be funded, provided it gained acceptance by the government. This was given in the House of Commons in March 1998. However, it would not be until August 2004 following a successful public inquiry that a finally signed agreement was made between all parties. A government directive in 2002 stated that the new Terminal 5 building could not be opened before the Piccadilly extension was ready.

The Piccadilly line extension required 2.5 kilometres of rail track fitted into new tunnels dug deep under the Terminal 5 building and extensive collaboration, negotiation, and compromise between the parties involved together with a successful public inquiry to ensure that all stakeholder needs were satisfied. It was certainly a success but was more than 10 years from initial offer to finally signing the agreement for the PPP. The result is a cheaper journey for passengers and staff into central London from the new Terminal.

Sources: Dr Mark Gannon, 'The tube flies to T5. Development of a public private partnership to fund the Piccadilly line extension to Heathrow Terminal 5'; Chartered Institute of Logistics and Transport (CILT) magazine article (2008): www.tfl.gov.uk; www.baa.com

Questions

1. Who do you think are the major stakeholders in this project?

2. Consider the eight project standards mentioned in the text (page 341) and determine which ones were the most challenging in his project.

Project risk management and agile project management

Project risk management is a systematic process which includes the identification, analysis, and response to project uncertainties. The recognition of uncertainty by scholars and practitioners has led to new approaches in project management that can be seen in contrast to traditional approaches to the management of risk advocated by organizations such as PMI or APM. A new type of project management approach has emerged. It can be defined as 'agile' project management. For example, in software development, prominent approaches of this type are the so-called Scrum, Extreme Programming (XP) and Adaptive Software Development (ASD). In contrast to traditional methods, agile project management philosophies offer a higher degree of flexibility; for a project to be successful in an inherently uncertain environment, flexibility is assumed to be of major importance.

Uncertainty and risk management

The purpose of project management is to manage tasks, requirements, and objectives (and their associated risks) in advance; and is often reliant on hindsight as a predicator for future changes. Project outcomes have become more uncertain over time, whether it is due to increases in cost or time, or due to changes outside the direct influence of the project management team, such as regulatory or environmental changes, or increased customer demands. Project management organizations continue to extend their project services and offer new ways of delivering them. Business change as a project outcome is more uncertain and more difficult to deliver given the high number of inter-related factors that may change over time. Given that most people are resistant to change this makes it even more difficult to achieve. The challenge for the project manager lies in the rate of change of many projects and the lack of certainty that this brings with it.

Uncertainty is a commonly occurring phenomenon in projects, since each one is a unique event, yet project managers have difficulty managing it. Partly because most project team members have a direct line manager as well as a project manager there is often uncertainty about priorities and chains of command. One of the major causes of dispute amongst project team members is due to unclear communication, often as a result of an unclear scope statement. In addition uncertainty can also occur in the product or process itself as there may be previously unforeseen consequences, for example, with some prescription drugs or the use of some optical equipment for long periods of time.

In academic terms, uncertainties can be described as being either aleatory or epistemic. Aleatory uncertainty refers to chance and describes a random process. For example, it is possible to calculate the probability of a number on a standard dice being thrown due to how many sides it has. Whilst it is not possible to predict exactly what number will come up every time the dice is thrown, we know that on average any one number has a one in six chance of being thrown. So whilst there is some uncertainty about which specific number will be thrown, there is no uncertainty as to the probability of the number coming up—it is random but not completely uncertain. Epistemic

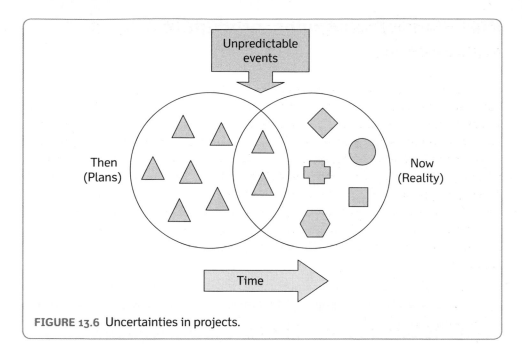

FIGURE 13.6 Uncertainties in projects.

uncertainty results from gaps in knowledge. For example, we may be uncertain of an outcome because there is no basis on which to calculate or foresee probabilities. However, once we have collected sufficient data then the outcome becomes predictable. In a business context this means that managers remain uncertain of future outcomes until they have experienced them through future events. This is shown in Figure 13.6 which depicts the known 'planned' outcomes as triangles, whereas the actual future reality may be completely different (a random set of shapes in this instance). No amount of previous knowledge can help us to predict this future reality.

Unpredictable events may significantly impact on project performance. In the extreme, these risks may turn into a crisis that may threaten the success of the project itself. If it remains unmanaged then a crisis may develop into a disaster from which a recovery is not possible. A crisis is often perceived as sudden. Yet, in many projects, a 'snowball effect' can be identified that remained undetected until it emerged as a sudden crisis. The 'snowball effect' is a term for a process of events, each of small significance, which then build upon themselves, becoming larger and perhaps potentially disastrous.

In order to prevent a crisis in a project from happening and to manage a crisis effectively there are three barriers of defence:

1. Risk management rules, procedures, and processes

2. Individual and collective mindfulness

3. Crisis management.

Each of these is described in more detail later in the chapter.

In many project organizations, particular emphasis is placed on the implementation and application of risk management rules, procedures, and processes. However, the focus on rules, procedures, and processes in isolation only provides limited protection from uncertainties becoming an uncomfortable reality Frosdick (1997).

Risk management rules, procedures, and processes

In order to prevent risks from happening and building into a crisis and in order to recover from crisis situations, project management standards have been defined with the purpose of planning, organizing, and controlling project performance, despite all uncertainties. The Institute of Risk Management (2002) defines risk management as 'the process whereby organizations methodically address the risks attaching to their activities with the goal of achieving sustained benefit within each activity and across the portfolio of all activities'.

Risk assessment is now mandatory in most activities. The management of risk plays an important role in preventing crises from occurring. A risk includes four components, namely threats, resources, consequences, and modifying factors. A threat (a source of danger) may be, for example, turbulence dynamic environment (i.e. constantly changing, highly uncertain, and ambiguous), which could have adverse effects on resources. Resources are components of a project such as the budget, personnel, and material that could be affected by these threats. The term 'consequences', relates to the potential a particular risk has to negatively influence the project outcome. Modifying factors can define how risk aversion responses increase or decrease the likelihood of the threat becoming a reality or the probable consequence of such a reality.

A project manager may modify or change risk by reducing the likelihood of a threat materializing or the severity of its consequences, or both. This is the basis for the use of project risk management.

Risk management processes

In summary, 'best practice' risk management processes can be organized in five stages: planning, identification, analysis, response, and monitoring and control.

1. Firstly, a project manager can apply risk management planning to define which activities should be taken in response to project uncertainties and to decide what risk impact areas are most significant in assessing and prioritizing risk.

2. Secondly, risk identification requires project managers to identify the specific uncertainties that may affect objectives.

3. Thirdly, by using risk analysis a project manager evaluates quantitatively or qualitatively the likely consequences of these uncertainties, as well as the likelihood of them occurring.

4. Fourthly, risk response enables the project manager to keep track of defined risks, to identify new risks during the project and to develop procedures and techniques to avoid, transfer, and avoid risks. Four fundamental responses help managers to address risks: avoid, reduce, transfer, and accept. The avoidance of risk is associated with actions to lower the probability of an adverse event happening. The avoidance and reduction of risks implies adapting the project management plan so that risks can be isolated through lowering the probability or impact of a possible adverse event. The transfer of risk involves a shift of the impact of risk on to a third party. Project managers may also choose to accept the risk under the consideration of resource constraints.

5. Lastly, all of these processes stress the importance of keeping the process alive and learning lessons to build knowledge for the future.

Unfortunately, despite the widely accepted use of risk management rules, processes, and procedures, crises are actually the norm rather than the exception, as the following examples illustrate.

- In 2006, the Airbus President Christian Streiff announced a further significant delay in the delivery of the Airbus 380. One of the problems that contributed to the delay in that project was the incompatibility of software packages. Part of the information system was delivered by German contractors, other parts by their French counterparts. Unfortunately, both systems refused to talk to each other. The Airbus issue highlighted a problem that is not uncommon but yet seriously impacted the project.

- In 2004, the implementation of a £456 million information system in the UK led to the taxpayer ultimately picking up a bill for over a billion pounds and led to a backlog of unpaid bills to single parents. The new information system somehow managed to overpay 1.9 million people and underpay around 700,000. Ultimately, the problems led to the termination of the customer itself, the Child Support Agency (CSA). The reason for the system underperforming was a lack of stability and flexibility in the system due to the imposition of rigid ways of working with the software.

- In 1999, NASA lost its $125 million Mars Climate orbiter. The problem occurred when a navigational error led to the probe entering the Mars atmosphere at too low an angle. The cause of its destruction was the indiscriminate use of both metric and imperial measurement systems.

In all these examples risk management rules, procedures, and processes have been applied. However, a crisis still occurred, fortunately not incurring any loss of life, but each project had irrecoverable losses. In light of such failure it is unsurprising that an answer to the question of how to meet the demands of an unpredictable environment remains elusive.

It is imperative that managers engaging with projects prepare themselves for the unexpected, not just by complying and conforming to risk management standards. Unfortunately, most project managers are hugely unprepared for the unpredictable. The imposition of ever greater rule-based controls in order to assure project success is often counter-productive since simply sticking to the rules can create 'blindness' to some of the unwelcome situations that may occur.

RESEARCH INSIGHT 13.2

Coutu, D.L. (2003) Sense and reliability: A conversation with celebrated psychologist Karl E. Weick, *Harvard Business Review*, 81(4), 84–90

This is an interview conducted by Diane Coutu, *Harvard Business Review*'s senior editor, with the organizational behaviourist Karl Weick. In it they discuss the extent to which the world is a predictable place and whether this is more an illusion than fact: 'Indeed, in an ever-changing, rough-and-tumble business environment, the assumption that the corporation is something stable and secure becomes dangerous' (Weick, in Coutu 2003). They then go on to discuss high reliability organizations (HROs) which are able to cope with unpredictability and achieve high reliability, such as nuclear power plants and fire and rescue services. Weick identifies the key principles of high reliability as follows:

- Preoccupation with failure
- Reluctance to simplify
- Sensitivity to operations
- Commitment to resilience
- Deference to expertise.

HROs react to even very weak signals that some kind of change or danger is approaching. They are fixated on failure and focus on detail. Managers in HROs do not simplify reality but deliberately develop through broad work experiences. Rather than expect the world to be orderly, they expect it to be chaotic and have learnt to deal with that.

Individual and collective judgement to avoid the 'snowball effect'

The prevention of crisis situations in projects is built on three assumptions:

- Project managers are alert to their environment and to potential threats which might affect the project.
- Project managers are able to put these potential threats into the context of the project's strategic objectives.
- Project managers will take swift action to engage with the threat.

However, this may not always be the case as project managers tend to portray themselves and their competencies to deliver a project on time, on budget, and according to the required quality in the best possible way. At the bidding stage of a project, key stakeholders need to be convinced that the project manager is able to successfully deliver the project. During the execution phase of the project, the project manager wants to be perceived to be in control of the project. This optimistic view on his management may be fuelled by his experience and previous success in projects. Hence, there should be no indication that something could go wrong. A long list of successes may breed complacency and self-satisfaction. When coupled with an unawareness of threats, questions about whether the project will actually deliver on time and at budgeted costs are suppressed.

Project managers need to develop a 'mindful' approach where they are alert and have an appreciation of the impact a small change can have and its ability to develop into the 'snowball effect'. This is the escalation of problems which if gone undetected will increase rapidly to a situation of crisis within an organization. The expression 'no smoke without fire' is helpful in understanding this phenomenon. Whilst there might be the first signs of a problem (the smoke) this could quite easily be addressed if quickly dealt with. However, if left unattended this could lead to a crisis (the fire) which could lead to more catastrophic problems for the organization.

Taking action is the ultimate goal to deal with the unexpected. If risks remain unmanaged and if project managers do not attack risk, risk will surely attack them. Managing the unexpected and averting a crisis can only work if managers are open to the unexpected and develop the right mindset which enables them to effectively apply rules, procedures, and processes.

Crisis management

Despite all efforts to anticipate and prevent a crisis from happening in projects, it is not the 'if' but rather the 'when' a crisis situation occurs. Preparations have to be made to soften the blow of such extreme conditions. A lot of attention has been paid to how projects react to a crisis. Individuals and groups of project managers tend to behave rigidly in threatening crises. While individuals react in different ways to a crisis, a number of models have been developed, although they overlap substantially.

A typical model is suggested by Fink et al. (1971) as shown in Table 13.2. They propose the theory that initially, individuals go through a 'shock' phase. Threats are perceived as overwhelming and 'panic' sets in. This phase is followed by denying that the threat exists and despite evidence of disruptions old patterns are maintained. Subsequently, individuals cope with crisis by acknowledging the 'realism' of threats resulting in bitterness about the status quo and finally, attempts are made to recover from the crisis. However, this view of crisis management is more the exception rather than the norm. Although a crisis does not need to be planned for in detail, project managers need to prepare themselves in a methodological manner for the possible effects.

By looking at an example of the BP Deepwater Horizon oil spill (Operations insight 13.2), we can see how decisions taken by individuals and groups of individuals can have a devastating effect both in creating a crisis and in finding ways to resolve it.

TABLE 13.2 Crisis behaviour

Phase	Self-experience	Reality perception	Emotional experience	Cognitive structure
Shock	Threat to existing structure	Perceived as overwhelming	Panic, helplessness	Disorganization, inability to plan, reason or understand situation
Defensive retreat	Attempt to maintain old order	Avoidance of reality	Indifference, euphoria, or anger	Defensive re-organization Resistance to change
Acknowledgement	Giving up existing structure, self-depreciation	Facing reality	Depression, bitterness	Defensive breakdown Reorganization in terms of altered perceptions
Adoption and change	Establishing new structure, sense of worth	New reality testing	Gradual increase in satisfying experiences	Re-organization in terms of present resources and abilities

Source: Fink et al. (1971)

OPERATIONS INSIGHT 13.2
BP's Deepwater Horizon oil spill

On 20 April 2010 there was an explosion and fire on the Deepwater Horizon oil rig, run by a consortium of BP, Halliburton, and Transocean, which killed 11 workers and injured another 17. A blowout preventer, which was meant to prevent the release of crude oil, failed and oil began pouring out of the well into the Gulf of Mexico. Three days later the rig sank. A US homeland security department risk analysis stated that the incident 'poses a negligible risk to regional oil supply markets and will not cause significant national economic impacts'. It was only on 24 April that oil was found to be leaking from the well. US coast guard remote underwater cameras reported this as 1000 barrels of crude oil per day (bpd). At this point it was assumed that remote underwater vehicles could be used to activate the blowout preventer and stop the leak.

Fifteen thousand US gallons (56,700 litres) of oil dispersant and 21,000 feet (6400 metres) of containment material were taken to the spill site and the US coast guard proposed setting fire to the leaking crude to slow the spread of oil in the Gulf, and plans were approved to drill two relief wells. By this time the risk analysis centre had changed its assessment, reporting that the 'release of crude oil, natural gas and diesel fuel poses a high risk of environmental contamination in the Gulf of Mexico'.

On 28 April, the US coast guard stated that the flow of oil was five times greater than first estimated at 5000 bpd, after a third leak was discovered. BP attempted unsuccessfully to repair a hydraulic leak on the blowout preventer valve, so oil continued to be burned in an effort to prevent the spill reaching the coastline. As the oil slick approached, Louisiana declared a state of emergency. One day later, President Obama intervened and pledged 'every single available resource', including the US military, to contain the spreading oil spill. He also stated that BP was responsible for the clean-up.

In an effort to reassure public opinion, BP chairman Tony Hayward said that the company would take full responsibility for the spill, paying for all legitimate claims and the cost of the clean-up. However, the coast guard announced that the leak would definitely affect the Gulf shore and environmentalists were warned of impending disaster for wildlife. By 5 May, BP had managed to attach a valve to the end of the broken drilling pipe at the Macondo well. Whilst this shut off one of the three leaks, it did not reduce the amount of oil gushing out. One day earlier, the White House backed a Senate proposal to increase the limit on liability pay-outs from $75 million to $10 billion (£6.5 billion) for the cost of the spill.

Tony Hayward told the BBC that the blowout preventer owned by Transocean was at fault for the leak. The cost of the spill for BP was then estimated to be at £15 billion. Before a Senate committee meeting on 11 May, representatives of

An aerial view of the Deepwater Horizon oil spill.
© istock/Michael Watkins.

the three oil companies—BP, Halliburton, and Transocean—involved in the deep water drilling blamed each other for the accident. With oil still spilling into the Gulf, on 11 July BP made another attempt to seal the leak, by installing a replacement containment system using robots. Four days later BP the flow of oil stopped for the first time in 87 days.

On 26 July it was announced that the BP chief executive, Tony Hayward, was to leave the company, to be replaced by Bob Dudley, the BP executive overseeing the clean-up. The day after that, Greenpeace activists closed 46 BP garages in central London in protest at what had occurred. It was only on 19 September, that BP finally sealed off the ruptured well, five months after the explosion. Scientists estimated that a total of 4.4 million barrels of oil were released into the Gulf of Mexico. On 1 October, Tony Hayward left his position as chief executive of BP.

Sources: numerous media sources, including the BBC and the Guardian

Questions

1. How well was risk understood and managed?
2. How well did the company respond to the various stakeholders as the crisis unfolded?

Business continuity planning

Business continuity planning (BCP) refers to ways in which organizations can ensure that their operations and business activities can continue in the event of some kind of crisis. The British Standards Institution (BSI) has a standard for BCP published in 2007, BS 25999-2 'Specification for Business Continuity Management'. This specifies requirements for implementing, operating, and improving a documented Business Continuity Management System (BCMS). The international equivalent of this is ISO 17799/27001.

The development of a business continuity plan can have five main phases:

1. Analysis
2. Solution design
3. Implementation
4. Testing and organization acceptance
5. Maintenance.

At the analysis stage, the full range of potential crises that might affect the business are considered, ranging from natural disasters such as earthquake and flood, to man-made events such as bomb damage or arson. The degree of risk is evaluated and the impact on the business identified, both in terms of the organization's physical infrastructure and its employee base. All kinds of solutions may be developed as a result of this analysis. In some cases, a replica infrastructure is developed some distance from the existing operation that can be moved into if this becomes unusable. For instance, concern that a 'dirty bomb' (one that contaminates an area with radiation) might be detonated by terrorists in the City of London, has led to City trading firms setting up identical, but unused, trading floors in a number of UK locations. In other instances, large firms may be able to switch production from one of their facilities to others that they operate. For instance, Northern Foods have a number of food manufacturing plants and should any one of these become unusable, the other plants have the capability, in terms of equipment and expertise, to take over that plant's production.

These solutions are then implemented. This may mean designing and building duplicate infrastructure, or drawing up plans with regards to how production may be re-allocated. Once in place, these contingencies are tested, to see if they are effective and achieve their goal. For instance, in 2009 many universities developed a continuity plan in response to the possible effect of the swine flu outbreak. So that students would not be brought into physical contact with others, such plans envisaged normal classes being suspended, and being switched to the university's virtual classroom environment. When this was tested, it was found that whilst the virtual infrastructure was robust enough to support teaching normally, many universities need to invest in more technical infrastructure if all teaching were to be conducted virtually. Finally, facilities and plans are regularly reviewed and maintained in order to ensure they can be implemented in response to any crisis that occurs.

Conclusions

Many projects are organized with no contingency plan to manage the unexpected. It is not surprising therefore that despite the development of sophisticated, sensible processes—project failure is still more likely than success. Effective project management requires a careful application of these processes as well as risk management and preparation for the unexpected. The first step towards successful risk management is an acknowledgement that we cannot accurately predict the future. Risks need to be identified and then mechanisms need to be put in place to deal with issues and potential crises, not just on a procedural level but also on a behavioural level. Many organizations spend an enormous amount of resources making sure that managers adhere to rules, processes, and procedures and very little on the human aspects of managing people and managing risk. The number of project failures means that there should be a shift of emphasis to these criteria. A mindset of 'prevention rather than cure' as is the case in many repetitive operations should be put to the test.

Nonetheless there will always be circumstances, which may be outside the control of the organization, that lead to crises. So crisis plans and business continuity plans need to be established and managed to ensure the response is effective and efficient.

END OF CHAPTER CASE
touraid—opening up opportunities for children across the world

touraid was set up in 2006 by Andy Berry. It is a registered children's charity that seeks to establish long-term, sustainable relationships between schools and clubs in the UK with similar organizations around the world to support disadvantaged children. Since its launch in October 2006 touraid has organized 55 tours to the UK for 850 children aged between 11–14 from 27 countries across four continents. It does this by inviting schools to host visiting parties from countries such as India, Pakistan, Botswana, Ghana, and Kenya.

Designing and developing each tour is a project. touraid has to organize the travel arrangements for each group, whilst each school engages in fundraising to pay for the tour, organizes host families to accommodate the children, and devises a programme of activities. Although originally based around rugby, touraid has expanded into facilitating any popular sport and cultural activity for boys or girls, such as netball and the performing arts.

In 2011, touraid had expressions of interest from 43 potential host schools. This significant expansion in activity has meant that Andy and the small management team that runs the charity has had to analyse in depth the process of setting up and organizing a tour. This process is complex as it involves a large number of different stakeholders, spans two or more countries often thousands of miles apart, and necessitates overcoming significant obstacles. For instance, nearly all of the disadvantaged children are orphans and often do not know the names of their parents or their date of birth. This means that obtaining documentation such as passports and visas for them is challenging.

Each touraid project has at least a six-month lead in before the tour commences so that effective planning can take place. To help illustrate the project planning process, Andy and his team developed the planning chart shown in Figure 13.7, which shows

the typical tasks that need to be organized in the UK. Partners in the different countries touraid work with plan and organize the groups that come to the UK.

Projects begin by initiating a marketing promotion, or responding to an invitation to send information, to a specific school. This is then followed up by one or more visits to the school in order to discuss the project with relevant stakeholders—head, teachers, parents, and students. If the tour is agreed, then a formal agreement is signed. This requires the host school to engage in fundraising to meet the travel and ancillary costs of the visiting children—touraid have a pack that helps schools identify ways of going about this. Each visiting student is accommodated with a host family, so these have to be identified and agreed upon. For legal reasons, a check is made on the family members' suitability to do this. With financing in place and host accommodation agreed, touraid then organize the travel documents and air tickets of the visiting party. At the same, they engage in discussion with the school about the nature and timing of the activities the tour party will take part in. touraid also arrange media coverage of the tour in order to ensure publicity and hence further promotion of the charity's work. Finally, the charity's staff assist in meeting the tour party on its arrival in the UK and transfer to the school, as well as monitoring the tour whilst it is taking place.

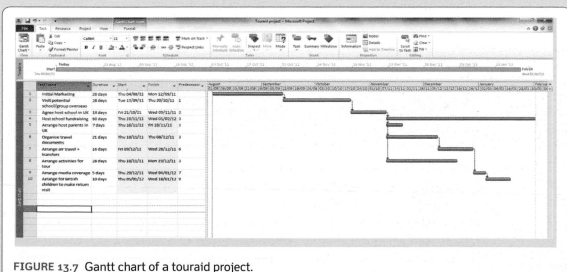

FIGURE 13.7 Gantt chart of a touraid project.

The tour in the UK can be hugely benificial for all children involved.

touraid seeks to establish relationships between schools and clubs in the UK with those around the world.

Given the charity was set up from scratch, it has taken some time for Andy and his very small team to create a standard way of tackling each tour project. In the early days all kinds of crises emerged which were unexpected. For instance, on one occasion Andy feared that a tour party would not be allowed into the UK by the Immigration Service. This was because when they landed at the UK airport, a well-trained immigration officer found that all the children in the party were born on 1 January and hence he suspected that the passports were forgeries of some kind. The actual explanation was that all the children in the party neither knew their actual birth date, nor had any documentation such as birth certificates. Hence when touraid arranged for them to have passports issued, they simply gave 1 January as their date of birth. After this experience, visiting children were allowed to pick or were allocated different 'dates of birth'.

Although the visiting children enjoy enormously the opportunity to travel to the UK and participate in the activities organized for them, the main aim is to establish long-term relationships that have a 'legacy' impact. The range of impacts on the children that tour the UK can be educational, economic, sporting, social, and psychological. Educational impacts have included disadvantaged children securing scholarships to improve their education, mentoring and coaching, and educational equipment being pro-

vided. As a result of the media coverage of the tours, corporate and government funding has been stimulated. touraid involvement has enabled the coaches to receive media coverage which strengthened their effectiveness in their communities. For example, in Trinidad and Tobago the coaches are able to be more proactive in their area which is characterized by gun crime and drug abuse. Social benefits have included a Rwandan touring team which comprised children from Hutu and Tutsi communities and their integration being sustained on their return to their homeland and a team from the Kibera slums of Kenya which highlighted social integration after civil unrest between tribes. In addition there are impacts on the host schools, such as the opportunity for teacher exchanges, opportunities for British teenagers to spend a gap year in the institution from which the disadvantaged children came, and opportunities for ongoing cultural and sporting education.

Source: authors' primary research

Questions

1. Identify the risk at each stage in the project process.

2. How might the success of a touraid project be evaluated?

3. What kind of business continuity planning might touraid have to develop?

Chapter summary

To consolidate your learning, the key points from this chapter are summarized as follows:

- **What is a project?**

  A project is a temporary endeavour. It has a definite beginning and end and the delivery of project outcomes is constrained by a defined scope statement, which needs to be delivered at an agreed quality, in a defined time, at an agreed cost.

- **Define project management**

  Project management has been defined as 'the planning, organizing, directing, and controlling of company resources for a relatively short-term objective that has been established to complete specific goals and objectives' Kerzner (2006).

- **Understand the tools used in project management**

  Project management uses a key set of tools to ensure that planning, control, and monitoring are carried out effectively (for example, those mentioned in *A Guide to the Project Management Body of Knowledge* (PMBOK® Guide)). The use of computer systems to generate planning tools such as the Gantt chart and network diagrams also help project managers to effectively control projects.

- **Understand the principles of risk management**

  Risk management can be deconstructed into five major stages: planning, identification, analysis, response, and monitoring and control.

- **Differentiate between a crisis and disaster**

  A crisis is a 'turning point', the breakdown of order in a process leading to an extreme condition. This may be caused by a natural or man-made disaster, but not necessarily.

- **Understand business continuity planning**

  Business continuity planning is ways in which organizations can ensure that their operations and business activities can continue in the event of some kind of crisis.

Questions

Review questions

1. What are the main differences between a project and an operation?
2. In which industries are projects often used?
3. What are the four stages of a typical project?
4. What is a project scope statement?
5. How is project success measured?
6. Name and explain the two types of uncertainty which often occur in projects.

7. How is risk measured in a project?

8. What is the 'snowball effect'?

9. What are the four phases of crisis behaviour?

10. How and why are business continuity plans developed?

Discussion questions

1. Why do you think most high-profile transport or building projects fail to meet either the cost or time originally budgeted?

2. Why do you think there been so much work done on creating project standards (such as the PMI Body of Knowledge), but very little on how to successfully manage the providers and stakeholders of projects?

3. Draw a Gantt chart and allocate resources for a project to run a successful project management module at University.

4. Think of a recent example of a project mentioned on television or in the national newspapers. Do you think that a risk assessment was carried out? What influence did the different stakeholder groups have on the outcome of the project, in terms of cost or time?

5. Compare and contrast the factors to be taken into consideration when designing a business continuity plan for a local high street shop and a large out of town supermarket.

 # Further learning guide

There are a number of associations that address the issues covered in this chapter and their websites provide some useful insights. These include the Business Continuity Institute and the Institute of Risk Management. In addition, in 2004 the UK government enacted the Civil Contingencies Act 2004, which requires all emergency services and local authorities to actively prepare and plan for emergencies. As a result, local authorities have the legal obligation under this act to actively lead promotion of business continuity practices in their respective geographical areas. So check out your local authority's website to see what they are doing.

 # References

Coutu, D.L. (2003) Sense and reliability, *Harvard Business Review*, 81(4), 84–90

Fink, S.L.B.J. and Taddeo, K. (1971) Organizational crisis and change, *Journal of Applied Behavioural Science*, 7, 15–37

Frosdick, S. (1997) The techniques of risk analysis are insufficient in themselves, *Disaster Prevention and Management*, 6(3), 165–77

Gary, L. (2003) Dealing with a project's fuzzy front end, *Harvard Management Update*, 8(6), 3

Hayes, R.H. and Wheelwright, S.C. (1979) Link manufacturing process and product life cycles, *Harvard Business Review*, January–February, 133–40

Kerzner (2006) *Project Management: a systems approach to planning, scheduling and controlling* (9th ed.), John Wiley & Sons Inc: Hoboken, NJ

Nelson, R. (2007) *IT Management: Infamous, Classic Mistakes, and Best Practices,* MIS Quarterly Executive, 6, 67–78

Project Management Institute (2004) A *Guide to the Project Management Body of Knowledge*, Project Management Institute Inc.: Newtown Square, PA. www.pmi.org/Resources/Pages/Library-of-PMI-Global-Standards.aspx

Part D

Operations strategies

Chapter Fourteen

Operations strategy

Learning outcomes

After reading this chapter you will be able to:

→ Recognize the relationship between corporate, business, and operations strategy

→ Explain the relationship between operations, marketing, human resource, and finance strategies.

→ Compare and contrast the market-driven and resource-based view of operations strategy

→ Outline the concept of 'business models'

→ Differentiate between a range of contemporary operations strategies and how these may be used to deliver order winners.

TMO Renewables—developing an operations strategy

Setting up a business based on a new technology and deciding on the long-term strategy takes time. In the early 1970s, Prof. Tony Atkinson noticed that a certain type of bacterium that grows on the sugars derived from biomass (vegetable matter) will produce ethanol—a fuel additive that makes petroleum more efficient. He went on to identify other bacteria 'in the wild' that had an appetite for different kinds of biomass and then developed techniques to encourage them to make ethanol too. So in 2002 TMO Renewables was founded in order to commercially exploit this research.

As petrol is based on a non-renewable resource that may ultimately be exhausted, it is important to develop alternative renewable sources of energy. Ethanol is such a source since it is made from biomass, but the challenge is to do it in such a way as to make it cheaply and sustainably. The traditional way of doing this was by brewing, that is to say, yeast-based fermentation. But this process uses a lot of energy because the biomass has to be heated to high temperatures to prepare it, then cooled for fermentation, and then reheated for distillation. This makes the process costly, time-consuming and an inefficient way to make a fuel additive. However, TMO's technology uses a 'thermophilic (literally heat-loving) micro organism'. This means that fermentation can take place at temperatures in excess of 60°C. This brings a number of benefits. First, very little cooling or heating is required, so there is a significant saving in energy. Second, the organism works faster than ordinary yeasts. And third it breaks down the sugars in biomass more effectively. As a result, using this technology ethanol can be produced economically, using a process that is more-or-less carbon neutral, and makes more efficient use of agricultural land.

Whilst there is a clear business case for adopting this technology, TMO decided that its expertise lay in research and not in large-scale ethanol production. So TMO does not plan to build and operate its own

TMO Renewables was founded in order to commercially exploit research into the production of ethanol.

plants, but to license these to investors and developers with expertise and interests in the fuel business. They propose two different business models. The first model is to 'bolt on' TMO technology to an existing plant that makes ethanol from corn. TMO claim this will instantly and dramatically increase the producer's margin. A trial in Iowa, in 2008, proved that TMO could deliver lower energy consumption, lower costs, and higher output, thus producing a 70% improvement in margin—and this after the payment of a royalty to TMO. The second business model is based on TMO's TM 242 micro-organism, which can be applied to biomass of many different kinds—most notably, perhaps, domestic waste (paper, food) , waste from industry, and the straw from cereal crops, the burning of which is now largely prohibited in Europe.

Because TMO is essentially a research-based company, the majority of their employees work in their laboratory in Guildford. But to attract investors and demonstrate to potential clients that the process works, TMO have built a Process Demonstration Unit (PDU) in Surrey, UK. This is designed to process a variety of different biomass and confirm that it can be done on an industrial scale. Clients are able to provide their own source material in order to see for themselves how effective the TMO process is in processing this material when compared with existing processing plants. To keep their own costs down, but also to demonstrate the relative simplicity of the technology, the PDU was built largely from components (such as vessels, pipes, and valves) available 'off-the-shelf'. It's not the equipment that makes the difference, but the bacteria.

Source: author's primary research

Questions

1 What does TMO have expertise in and how does it exploit this expertise to create order winners?

2 What is its strategy for delivering these order winners and what are the advantages of this?

Introduction

So far in this text, we have considered each aspect of operations management separately. There have been chapters on process choice, location, supply chain, capacity, and quality. And whilst these chapters have made it clear that organizations have a wide variety of choices as to how they manage each of these areas, we have not yet considered the relationship between them. That is the purpose of this chapter. It discusses the concept of **operations strategy**—the way in which organizations plan and integrate all aspects of their operations in order to achieve **competitive advantage**.

In Chapter 12, when we discussed new product development (NPD), we identified that the development process was 'messy'. A number of factors affected whether the NPD process was formal or informal. Well the same thing applies to strategy and strategic planning—it is 'messy' too. Most organizations are likely to have a strategy—but in small and medium-sized enterprises (SMEs) this may well be implicit (just in the owner's head), whereas in large firms it is likely to be explicit, formal and written down so that all managers know what it is. We also saw earlier in Research insight 1.1 (page 14) that operations within an organization might be at one of four stages, in terms of the strategic role that operations might have—ranging from simple goals relating to generally improving operational performance up to the means by which the firm seeks to gain competitive advantage. In this chapter, we are mainly focusing on organizations that are at this fourth stage.

So we begin by defining competitive advantage and reviewing how firms might achieve this. We then discuss the purpose and nature of strategy, and in particular how it relates to other strategies that an organization might have. Two alternative views of strategy are then discussed—the market-driven view and the resource-based view, before we identify some of the generic operations strategies that have emerged over the last 20 years. Finally we go on to explore how organizations may refine these strategies so that they can successfully compete in their markets, by looking at how they may develop specific 'bundles' of order winners (OWs).

Operations strategy a plan for managing operations over the long term to achieve business goals

Competitive advantage the superiority of an organization relative to other competing organizations demonstrated by its performance in the marketplace

RESEARCH INSIGHT 14.1

Labegalini, L., dos Santos, G.A., Moreno, S.M.M.A., Polidório, G.R.S., Faria, S.C. and Csillag, G.M. (2009) Operations strategy research in the Journal of Operations Management (JOM), *2009 EurOMA Conference*, Goteburg, Sweden

This article is not based on primary research in industry, it is based on secondary research of the literature published in one of the discipline's leading academic journals. It reviews the operations/manufacturing strategy literature in the *Journal of Operations Management* (JOM) from 1995–2008. In doing so, it replicates a similar study by Boyer et al. (2005) in another leading journal—*Production and Operations Management* (POMS). By analysing the literature in the same way, it enables comparison between the two journals, and provides an overview of the main topic areas of concern in this area.

Achieving competitive advantage

In the business world, firms compete to just survive. Even survival can be difficult, as the global recession of 2009 and 2010 demonstrated. In the UK over 21,00 businesses were declared bankrupt in 2010, according to the government's insolvency statistics (The Insolvency Service 2011). However—beyond survival—firms also seek to gain competitive advantage, a term promoted by Michael Porter in 1985 in his groundbreaking book. Competitive advantage is the way in which a firm designs its operation, or other activities, so that it maintains a revenue stream and sustains its position relative to other firms in the same marketplace.

Maintaining a revenue stream is important, as firms can become bankrupt even though they are profitable. This is because of cash flow—the rate at which money is flowing into the firm from customers and flowing out of the firm to debtors, such as suppliers, employees, and landlords. In some industries, there can always be positive cash flow, because customers pay for goods before they are made or services before they are delivered. For instance, in the tour operating business, holidaymakers typically book and pay for their holiday several months before they take it. In other industries, cash flow can be weak, because customers pay on credit and debtors are paid in cash. For instance, a small restaurant may have the majority of its customers pay on credit cards, but have to pay cash to suppliers on a daily basis and staff weekly. For firms that have a high level of debt, weak cash flow often means that the level of debt increases and interest charges cannot be met on time. This leads to lenders declaring the business bankrupt. So all organizations need to be concerned about cash flow, and where possible operations should be designed in order to support positive cash flow.

In addition, commercial firms also need to make a profit. This is especially so in industry sectors that routinely require major capital investment in new plant and machinery, such as transportation and hotels. The role of operations is therefore to ensure that processes are as efficient as possible, thereby maximizing the margin between direct costs and sales price. Of course, even in not-for-profit organizations, operations should be efficient, either to maximize the output for the level of resourcing provided and/or to keep down the cost of providing not-for-profit products and services.

But simply making money is not enough. As we saw in Chapter 2, when we discussed markets, the very basis of free market economics is competition. The rationale for which is that competition ensures the most efficient use of resources and that the consumer gets the lowest possible price (at least under perfect competition—see page xx). According to Porter (1985), there are two basic ways firms compete, either on cost or through differentiation. In our terms, we know that operations compete through order winners, one of which is cost, so that speed, flexibility, quality, and dependability must be ways in which firms differentiate themselves from each other. Therefore to compete, organizations will try to provide their goods or services cheaper than their competitors, or more quickly, or more flexibly, or to a higher quality, or more dependably.

But it is slightly more subtle than that. In trying to out do their competitors, firms have two basic choices. They can either compete on the same order winners, but seek to outperform their rivals in delivering these things. Or they can bundle together a unique set of order winners that no other firm is providing. So, for instance, it could be argued that in the theme park business and mainstream motor manufacturing sector, firms are basically competing on the same basis. However, some firms are pre-eminent or have achieved growing market share, because they are simply better at doing these things than their competitors. For instance, the world's premier theme park operator is judged to be Disney, based on the quality of their rides, standards of service, cleanliness of the park, and general smooth operation. To train their employees, who they call 'cast members', they built a training facility, which they call the Disney University, at their park in Orlando, Florida. Because Disney is such an admired company, they commercially exploit this facility by not only running courses for their own staff, but also managers and employees from many other companies, who want to learn the Disney way of doing things. In motor manufacturing, Toyota has a similar world-leading reputation, which derives from the creation of the Toyota Production System, which became the lean manufacturing standard for all large-scale car makers.

On the other hand, in some sectors firms clearly have potential order winners that none of their competitors have, perhaps because they have invented a product or process that is patent protected. This was the case with TMO Renewables, and is often true in the pharmaceutical industry. Such an approach is consistent with the so-called resource based view of operations, which is further discussed below.

In summary, operations need to:

- Operate sufficiently well to get the basics right—positive cash flow and sufficiently high margin.
- Support competitive advantage through the delivery of order winners—either by delivering these order winners better than competitors; or by delivering a different set of order winners; or a combination of these.

However, the extent to which operations is fundamental to a firm's long-term success will vary depending on two key criteria. The first of these is the nature of the firm's value chain and the relative sophistication of the process technology it employs. The value chain is a model developed by Michael Porter (1985) which proposes nine different elements, each of which can add value to the output of the organization. These elements are made up of a chain of five activities—inbound logistics, operations, outbound logistics, marketing, and service—and four supporting functions—firm infrastructure, human resources, technology, and procurement. This might appear to suggest 'operations' has a potentially small role in adding value, but as you know from reading this book, contemporary thinking about operations does not simply consider this as being just 'inside the factory'. We think of operations as being a combination of logistics, operations, service, procurement, technology, and human resources. So in this sense operations can have a huge impact on how the firm performs and achieves competitive advantage. This is the external driver of the firm's approach to operations. Different elements of the value chain apply to different industry sectors. In the supermarket industry, logistics is hugely important, in civil engineering procurement may be key, whereas in the aerospace sector technology may add significant value.

The second factor is internal, and comprises the values of the firm's senior executives, the organizational culture, and the perceived importance of operations to the success of the firm. Some organizations have chief executive officers (CEOs) or executive teams that have a great deal of operations experience, and this is reflected in how they think about strategy. For example, Robert Dudley the CEO of BP was educated as a chemical engineer and worked in both engineering and commercial operations for the early part of his career.

As a result of this, operations can have four different roles within an organization, as illustrated in Figure 14.1. The weakest role for operations occurs when both external and internal drivers are low (quadrant A). In this context, operations policies and procedures are designed to meet strategic objectives, but are not really seen as a means of delivering competitive advantage. In the second scenario (quadrant B), operations are identified as being significant in the sector in which the firm operates, but not considered so by the firm itself. In this scenario, the firm is likely to be adapting its operations activity in response to competitors, rather than proactively managing and exploiting operations. In the third scenario, internal drivers are strong, but external drivers are low (quadrant C). In this instance, the firm is developing its operations to try to gain competitive advantage, but the impact of this is limited by the industry context. Finally, operations are at the core of the firm's strategy when the external drivers are high, and the internal drivers are strong (quadrant D).

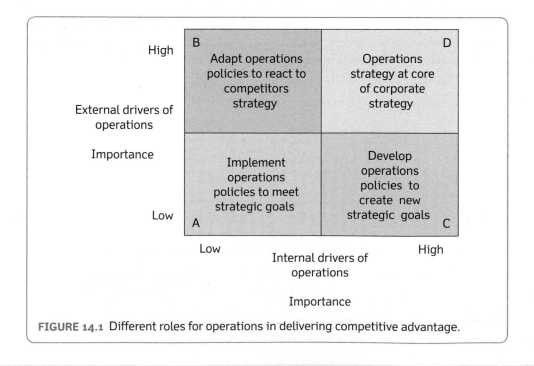

FIGURE 14.1 Different roles for operations in delivering competitive advantage.

The purpose and nature of strategy

The role of strategy is to draw up a long-term plan designed to achieve competitive advantage. It is not simply an action plan designed to improve performance. Therefore an operations strategy has a number of features:

- It sets long-term goals and hence specifies appropriate measures of performance.
- It integrates all aspects of the operation.
- It involves all levels of management within the operations function.
- It is likely to affect and/or involve all the major policy areas we have previously discussed (location, process design, materials management, supply chain, capacity management, human resources, and quality management).
- It will be integrated with other kinds of strategic plan (corporate, business, marketing)—which is what we will discuss next.

Levels of strategic planning and implementation

In many organizations there are potentially three levels of strategic planning and implementation: corporate strategy, business strategy, and operations strategy. Corporate strategy is devised by large organizations in order to provide an overall plan. Within the organizations, there may be a number of different divisions or businesses, for each of which a strategy will be devised. For instance, Whitbread has a corporate growth strategy within which it has three separate businesses—Premier Inn, the budget hotel brand; Costa Coffee; and a restaurants division made up of three or four brands. Each of these operates in a different market and hence as its own business strategy.

Once a business strategy has been set, a strategy for each of the functional areas within the business—marketing, human resources, finance, and operations—is devised and executed. This is illustrated in Figure 14.2.

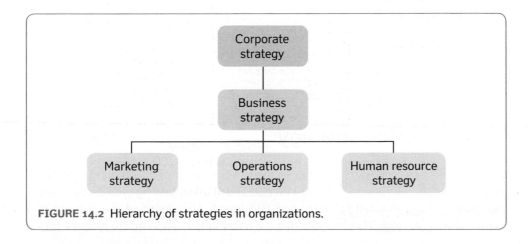

FIGURE 14.2 Hierarchy of strategies in organizations.

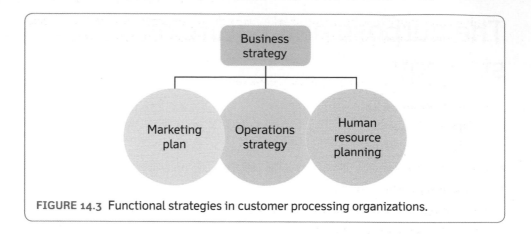

FIGURE 14.3 Functional strategies in customer processing organizations.

Relationship between functional strategies

In manufacturing businesses, these functional strategies have clear demarcation between them, even though they need to be integrated one with the other. This is largely because the production of goods is separate, both in terms of time and place, to the purchase and consumption of those goods. However, in customer processing organizations, production and consumption are simultaneous—as we saw in Chapter 1 when we discussed the concept of 'servuction'. It is therefore more difficult in services to differentiate between functional strategies, as illustrated in Figure 14.3.

This also illustrates the notion that firms can achieve competitive advantage not just through operations but also through their other strategies. Some firms are hugely successful at marketing—creating and maintaining a high level of brand awareness through promotional activities. In other organizations, it may be the management of human resources that leads to success, especially in the so-called knowledge-based sectors of the economy Such sectors include high-tech manufacturing, education, health, telecommunications, finance, and insurance.

Strategy in small and medium-sized enterprises

Having established the notion of a hierarchy of strategies, as illustrated in Figure 14.1, we need to consider if all businesses engage in all three levels of planning. Research (Jones et al. 2004) in SMEs suggests that they do not. SMEs have no need for complex planning processes because they manage relatively small businesses operating in local markets, over which the owner can often have direct, personal control. As firms grow larger they tend to separate out the levels and develop the functional areas identified in Figure 14.2.

Manufacturing strategy

Earlier in this text we have referred to strategy in a number of chapters. In Chapter 6, Research insight 6.2 about Berry and Hill (1992) discussed linking systems to strategy (see page 159). In this article, Berry and Hill specifically identified the concept of a manufacturing strategy. They propose that it is essentially an approach to manufacturing planning and control that integrates market objectives, process choice and the organization's infrastructure. Hence they identify elements of manufacturing strategy as:

- Process choice issues:
  - Choice of job-shop, batch or mass production
  - Process positioning
  - Capacity decisions
  - Role of inventory
- Infrastructure issues:
  - Role of support functions
  - Planning and control systems
  - Quality assurance and control
  - Systems engineering
  - Clerical processes
  - Payment systems
  - Work scheduling
  - Organizational structure.

They then go on to discuss a number of alternative strategies in which the mix of these elements is based around whether or not products are made-to-order (MTO) or made-to-stock (MTS), and hence shop-floor control is based on a 'pull' system or 'push' system.

It must be remembered that Berry and Hill (1992) were writing at a time when new systems and capabilities, facilitated by computers, were being introduced into manufacturing. In the early 1990s, materials requirement planning (MRP), just-in-time (JIT), and optimized production technology (OPT) were all relatively new. These have been discussed in Chapter 6, and will be discussed in more detail in Chapter 15. Firms that introduced these new systems were often disappointed by the impact they had on performance. They were expensive investments that appeared to provide a low return on capital employed. They were not, as Berry and Hill (1992) explain, the 'panaceas' that many people thought they would be. In particular, manufacturers still thought in terms of 'trade-offs'—Hayes and Wheelwright's (1979) basic concept that processes had to lie along the diagonal, as illustrated in Figure 3.3. This trade-off is the notion that a wide range of products can only be produced in low volumes, whilst high-volume production required standardized outputs.

However, it takes time to develop new systems and to implement these successfully. We saw in Chapter 2, in Research insight 2.1 from the same authors (Berry at al. 1999), this time from the late 1990s, the increasing sophistication of manufacturing strategy and how it is linked to marketing strategy. So over the last 20 years the basic manufacturing strategy concept has become more sophisticated and evolved into a number of forms, which have been given specific names. As we shall see, a number of things were required for these strategies to emerge:

- More sophisticated information technologies, both in terms of hardware and software.
- Recognition of the role of the supply chain and the emergence of this as a major discipline, along with specialist logistics companies.
- Breaking away from the concept of 'trade-offs' towards the concept of 'win-wins'.
- Growth in demand from emerging markets.
- Emergence of large-scale manufacturing companies in developing countries based on relatively low labour cost, new infrastructure, and drive to compete globally.

Boots Contract Manufacturing (BCM) was the manufacturing arm of the retail chain Boots, now it is a completely stand alone business within Alliance Boots, making health care products for a range of customers. It employs 1200 people in its Nottingham factory, which produces 26 million units per month. On its website BCM promotes 'innovation, responsiveness to customer needs, and proven track record'.

BCM makes over 5000 different products across health care, skincare, personal

BCM engages in research and development of packaging for health care products. © istock/Dmitry Souharevsky.

hygiene, cosmetics, dental care, baby and toddler, fragrances, and sun cream. Such products are made in manufacturing vessels, in which formulas are mixed in batch sizes between one and nine tonnes (the End of chapter case in Chapter 3 explains this in more detail). The Nottingham plant has 52 vessels and 40 packing lines which can package products in a variety of containers, such as jars, tubes, cartons, bottles, and pumps. Whilst its clients research the product formulas, BCM engages in research and development of packaging.

One of the biggest initiatives BCM implemented was a new information technology (IT) system. This provided complete visibility over its customer's forecasts and levels of inventory, allowing the company to deliver an automated replenishment service, which is known as Vendor Managed Inventory (VMI). VMI allows BCM to improve the accuracy of forecasts and hence to respond to fluctuations in demand, so that they can adopt a level capacity strategy in terms of production and therefore improve efficiency. BCM are able to manage their customers' inventory so that their retail clients can concentrate on their core business. By having a better insight into what its main customers are going to need, BCM can schedule its production better to take advantage of economies of scale—producing for multiple customers' markets from one batch, for instance—and it can then benefit from fewer changeovers, lower inventory levels, and plan its own supply of raw materials more effectively too. This helps to ensure that it competes on cost with other manufacturers. The new IT system has undoubtedly contributed heavily to an improvement in overall equipment effectiveness (OEE) around the plant. Three years ago, OEE was 45%, now it is up to around 65%.

Another aspect of its service level is BCM's speed to market. Most clients provide a brief that specifies precisely the product formula and how it is to be packaged. In these cases, BCM can begin production within four weeks. In addition, BCM has the ability to convert raw materials very quickly and process them through the facility quickly error free. This means BCM does not have cash tied up in work-in-progress. It also helps their customers to react to trends very quickly. BCM's responsiveness also means that customers who have been let down by another supplier can come to BCM and still get their order supplied on time.

BCM has low levels of employee turnover based on good communication and employee empowerment. As a result Alliance Boots in 2010 was one the UK's top big companies to work for according a *The Sunday Times* survey.

Sources: 'Get by with a little Help from your Friends', The Manufacturer *November 2010 and* www.bcm-manufacturing.com/

Questions

1. What is BCM's manufacturing strategy?

2. How does this manufacturing strategy relate to the firm's other functional strategies, i.e. marketing strategy, human resources, and finance?

Alternative perspectives on strategic operations

In Chapter 3, Research insight 3.1 by Lowson (2003) provided an introduction to the concept of operations strategy, explained how it evolved, and reviewed two alternative ways of thinking about it—the resource-based view and the market-driven view. We identified that these two viewpoints (or 'paradigms') occur throughout the operations management literature and influence different researcher's interpretation of nearly every aspect of operations. So we briefly review these two alternatives here.

Market-driven view

In fact, you have already been introduced to the market-driven view, because this is essentially the approach advocated by Michael Porter. His 1980 book *Competitive Strategy* articulated the thinking of that time that strategy was largely driven by the market and external, environmental influences—rivalry between firms, the power of customers and suppliers, the threat of new entrants into the market, and threat of new products. This viewpoint was essentially an economic perspective, or more specifically industrial economics.

Resource-based view

The resource-based view offers a different perspective in that it says strategy is largely determined from within the organization, due to the resources that it has under its control. So firms develop competitive advantage from a set of particular resources—such as assets, processes, or knowledge—that acquire value and become difficult to imitate. An example of a firm that has competed on this basis is Apple Macintosh, who developed and exploited their own operating system in the personal computer market. Prahalad and Hamel (1990) refer to these key resources, skills and technologies as core competencies—the things an organization is good at. Hence strategy should be based on these competencies rather than on reacting to what competitors are doing.

Reconciling the two viewpoints

In the academic literature, researchers typically adopt one viewpoint or the other. But in industry and commerce, most managers happily adopt both viewpoints and develop strategies based on market analysis and their core competencies.

RESEARCH INSIGHT 14.2

Grant, R. (1991) The resource-based theory of competitive advantage: Implications for strategy formulation, *California Management Review*, 33(3), 114–35

This article was one of the first to explain the resource-based view and explain how it was different to the market perspective. It explains how an organization would go about developing a strategy based on this approach.

Business models

An alternative way of thinking about strategy is to think in terms of the organization's **'business model'**. A business model can be defined as all the factors that describe a business, including the market served, how it creates value, and the factors that will sustain it over the long term. Probably the best way to differentiate between a strategy and a business model is to consider how they originate. The way an organization develops its offer and organizes its transactions can be planned or emergent. In simple terms, most business models are planned, whereas many operations strategies are emergent. Examples of business models that have been deliberately planned are firms that have started a business based around low cost or e-commerce. For instance, Southwest Airlines is credited as being the first low-cost airline, Federal Express revolutionized postal services, and Amazon.com created a whole new way of purchasing books (and now other products). On the other hand, examples of emergent strategies include servitization (the way manufacturing firms have moved into offering services) and ubiquitization (how service firms developed their chain operations).

It is often the case that new entrants into markets plan and design a new business model in order to compete against the existing players in that market. Almost by definition, since they have no established reputation, new firms have to come up with offers or ways of doing business that have new features. Spring and Mason (2010) suggest that there are three main elements of a business model, as illustrated in Figure 14.4. These are the 'network architecture', market offering, and technology.

Network architecture

This comprises four subelements—markets, transactions, capabilities, and relationships. Markets refers to the specific customers that are to be served by the new enterprise. As

> **Business model**
> a system designed for competing effectively in a specific marketplace

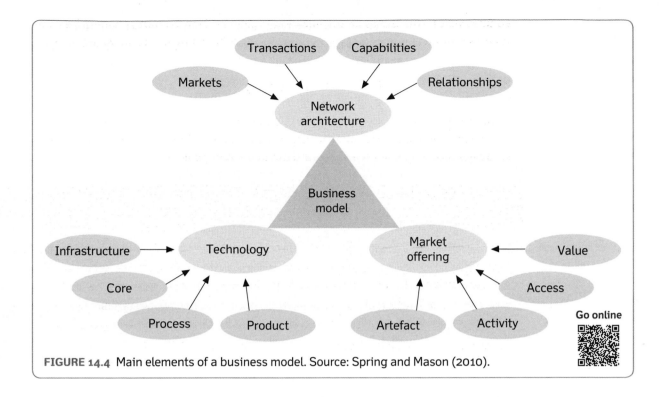

FIGURE 14.4 Main elements of a business model. Source: Spring and Mason (2010).

we saw in Chapter 2, the two main types of market are business-to-business (B2B) and business-to-customer (B2C). Transactions describe the way in which the organization will engage with its customers and enable them to purchase the offer. In recent years, many new business models have been created based around transactions conducted on the Internet—so called 'e-commerce'. Capabilities are those things the organization needs to have in order to conduct its business. Finally, as we have discussed in many preceding chapters, any contact with customers (or suppliers) creates relationships, and how these are designed and maintained is a key element of any new business model.

Market offering

It is suggested that there are four basic types of market offering—artefacts, activity, access, and value. Artefacts are what we generally know as products, i.e. 'things' (such as a tube of sun cream, mobile phone, or motor cycle). Activity refers to services that are performed on or to the customer (medical care) or on behalf of the customer (parcel delivery). Access also tends to refer to services, but in this case services that enable customers to use facilities or things offered by the organization (hotel rooms or car hire). Finally value refers an offer which is none of these, such as websites like Google and Facebook.

Technology

This element of a business model also has four subelements—infrastructure, core, process, and product. Infrastructure relates to the physical environment needed to host the organization, such as buildings, warehouses, or, in the case of an airline, hangers and runways. Core technology refers to the specific plant or machinery an organization might need in order to create a transaction, such as a transportation fleet (for an airline). Process technology is how the infrastructure and core technology is deployed, such as how an airline might schedule its aircraft fleet. Product technology refers to the specific characteristics of the offer, such as in the airline case the cabin interior design and décor, inflight entertainment system and other onboard features.

OPERATIONS INSIGHT 14.2
Yum! restaurants—two operations in one

In the early 2000s, Yum!, the US-based restaurant chain, decided to multibrand its operations made up of five main brands—Pizza Hut, Long John Silvers (seafood concept), KFC, Taco Bell (Mexican style food), and A&W Restaurants (hamburger concept). The basic idea behind multibranding is that a single property can be used to operate two different operations under the same roof. In doing so it faced a number of operations management challenges.

A clear advantage of multibranding is that the right combination of two brands within one setting should lead to a higher overall utilization of the assets. This was because the brands had high traffic at different times of day, both for in-restaurant dining and take-away sales. So combining a KFC with Long John Silvers resulted in the restaurant being busy with mainly KFC customers during the day, whilst LJS customers tend to use the restaurant during the evening. Hence a key decision was with regards the pairing of the brands. Yum! decide to adopt only ten specific pairs that they felt would create high utilization when combined.

With regard to process design the issues included the extent to which kitchen equipment in one restaurant was compatible with the needs of the other brand; how the food was held prior to sale (hot or not); and opportunities for the rationalization the two different production and service systems. There were clearly opportunities to rationalize the materials inventory, i.e. share foodstuffs across the two brands such as frying oil. The supply chain could also be rationalized with regards to equipment supply—so, for instance, the number of seating suppliers was reduced from 30 to 4.

Whilst merging the two systems and technologies was relatively straightforward, developing the in-restaurant human resources to deliver two different brands was more challenging. Yum! found that training costs increased and the workforce was concerned about doing more demanding work for the old rates of pay. Moreover, long-serving staff had an emotional attachment to the brand and were used to wearing that brand's uniform. Since staff turnover in this sector is typically high, Yum! management were concerned that multibranding might push this even higher. They therefore actively developed a Yum! organizational culture aimed at integrating the managers and employees into a single entity.

Sources: authors' primary research and www.yum.com

Questions

1. In making this decision to multibrand, did Yum!'s senior executives have a market driven view or resource-based view?

2. Consider the main elements of a business model, how might these be affected by Yum!'s decision to multibrand?

Contemporary operations strategies

In Chapter 3, we discussed the evolution of process type, and identified the emergence of a number of generic operations strategies. Such strategies emerge and are followed by firms that have strong external and internal drivers of operations performance (as identified in Figure 14.1). Before discussing these it is worth pointing out two issues. First, the terms used to describe these strategies are not precisely defined—different authors use these terms in different ways. In a moment, in Figure 14.1, we are going to identify a wide range of 'different' strategies, but differentiating between these is not always easy. Second, and linked to the first, these strategies have some degree of overlap, so that actions taken in one strategy may also be relevant to another. Hence in discussing these strategies, we shall emphasize the differences between them, when in reality there are also many similarities. It is worth noting that it is not what the strategy is called that is important. What is important is the strategy's effectiveness in delivering competitive advantage in the market in which the organization operates.

Lean production

Essentially 'lean' refers to the stripping out of all kinds of waste from any process to make it as efficient as possible. This was the strategy developed by Toyota in Japan. It is now widespread throughout motor manufacturing, but the principles have been applied to many other sectors of the manufacturing industry. At the heart of lean manufacturing is the idea that three order winners can be delivered simultaneously—cost, quality, and dependability—that is to say, a win-win approach. Whereas historically these were seen as a trade-off, lean enables cost to be reduced as there is less waste, rework, and returns; it ensures products are made right first time every time so that quality is assured; and it increases the dependability of processes and outputs. This is discussed in much more detail in Chapter 15.

Agile manufacturing

Agile manufacture is also based on the notion of a win-win scenario with regard to order winners, but in this case the delivery of cost and speed. Such agility has largely come about through the introduction of IT into the design and production processes. The factory layout and equipment in use is designed to allow switching between one product and another very easily. Hence an agile company is able to respond to a customer order more speedily because its systems allow it to. An outcome of focusing on making processes agile is that most firms adopting this approach have also improved their dependability. This, too, is discussed in Chapter 15.

Mass customization

Whilst there is some overlap between 'lean', 'agile', and mass customization, at the heart of this strategy is the notion of combining cost and flexibility. This is because mass customization seeks to produce low-cost goods based on mass production principles but customized for individual customers. This often involves 'postponement'. This means delaying the assembly of the product until the last possible moment, so that only products that have been ordered are made. This keeps cost down because finished goods inventory is almost non-existent, and flexible because the customer gets exactly what they wanted. What might be sacrificed is speed, because the customer has to wait whilst the product is made for them. This is issue is explored in some detail in the End of chapter case on Dell computers.

The three operations strategies we have discussed so far (lean, agile, and mass customization) have specifically been developed to create win-wins and deliver across a range of different order winners. However, firms and organizations have also developed operation strategies for other reasons, and it is to these different strategies to which we now turn.

Two strategies focus not on creating a new bundle of order winners, but on doing existing ones even better. These are the continuous improvement (CI) strategy and the low-cost strategy.

Innovation and continuous improvement

With regards to the adoption of a CI strategy, firms and organizations do not change their order winners but seek to make a myriad of small improvements in all that they do, so that these order winners are performed to a higher and higher standard. The main difference between innovation and CI is the scale and speed of change. Rapid and significant change is radical innovation, whereas CI is many small changes. All firms and their operations have to change over time as consumer tastes change, new competitors emerge, and new technologies become available. Some firms use innovation to be first into the market with new products or services, and/or use CI to seek to stay ahead of the competition in their market. In the UK, firms like Virgin and Dyson have a reputation for being radically innovative. This strategy is discussed in more detail in Chapter 16.

Low-cost competition

In the low-cost model the firm creates a business model in which the entire focus is on cost and pursues this relentlessly. New business models have also emerged whereby firms are able to compete on costs that are significantly lower than the established players in the market. The airline industry has been revolutionized by so-called low-cost carriers, first in the United States with Southwest Airlines, and then in the UK with easyJet and Ryanair. We saw in Operations insight 2.1 (page 36) easyJet's low-cost model.

Finally there are four other strategies, which are not entirely 'pure' operations strategies because they are linked to marketing too, but which have major operations management issues. These are servitization (sometime referred to as servicization)—how manufacturing firms are developing into service providers; ubiquitization—how service firms develop their service provision and markets; e-business—the use of the Internet and worldwide web to deliver services; and globalization—the making and selling of goods or the delivery of services on a worldwide basis.

Servitization

This refers to manufacturing firms becoming service providers with added value services for customers who buy their products. For instance, IBM was originally the world's largest manufacturer of mainframe computers. But by 2008 over half its revenue was generated from services such as maintenance agreements, project management, and consulting.

Ubiquitization

This is a strategy adopted by service firms in order to physically distribute their products and services 'everywhere'. Examples of this are banks who have installed ATMs in a wide variety of locations, soft drink manufacturers who distribute their products through vending machines, and hotel and food service chains that seek to maximize their geographic coverage in order to create a critical mass of locations to support customer loyalty.

e-business

The advent of the Internet and its adoption by a high proportion of the population has led to new business models being created that exploit this marketing channel. The archetype of this approach is Amazon.com, who revolutionized the sale of books and subsequently other products through their online shopping strategy.

Globalization

It can be argued that globalization is not simply an operations strategy, but a corporate strategy. However, making products or delivering services on a global basis has very significant implications for how operations are managed. This is discussed in more detail in Chapter 17.

Other 'strategies'

In addition to these listed strategies, a number of other operations 'strategies' have been proposed and discussed in the literature. Many of these have been discussed by Lowson (2002) and Table 14.1 identifies and defines these. We would argue that these 'strategies' are not generic strategies, i.e. applied across many industry sectors, and as such are an element of the main strategies we have discussed earlier (as Table 14.1 also explains).

OPERATIONS INSIGHT 14.3
Fine Industries—developing new business opportunities

Fine Organics was a subsidiary of a global chemical company that decided in 2007 to rationalize its portfolio in what was a highly competitive industry. Seeing the opportunity to own and run their own business, the managers of the company negotiated a management buyout (MBO). In 2008 they established Fine Industries, within which Fine Organics is the main operation. On completion of the second year of operation the directors launched four new companies to both complement Fine Organics and add further value to Fine Industries—

other sectors of manufacturing have also done so. This leads to the question—if all firms in a sector have adopted the same basis strategy how do firms then compete?

As we have seen earlier, one way to compete is to do the same thing as competitors, but do these things better. Hence we saw the emergence of low-cost business models and the adoption of continuous improvement. But there is another way. Remember that Neely (2008) has extended each of the five main order winners into a total of 32 elements (see Chapter 3). Hence strategies can be devised and competitive advantage sought based around these more specific elements.

For instance, if all car makers have adopted lean and so are competing on cost, quality, and dependability, then within each of these OWs they may focus on different order winning elements. One example of this might be the quality element 'aesthetics'. Some car makers may work especially hard at designing their cars to be aesthetically pleasing. On the other hand some may focus on the quality element 'features', ensuring that their models have more or better features than their competitors. Yet another manufacturer may seek to make their vehicles more 'serviceable'. This is illustrated in Figure 14.5, which shows the OWs that car makers might compete on, with those that maker A has chosen being highlighted. This manufacturer is therefore known for producing reliable, dependable, and low-cost vehicles.

This idea of competing on different elements of order winners is similar to what Robert Lowson (2002) called 'clusters of value'. He envisaged a time when consumers would be 'the nucleus of activity, dictating and driving all demand preferences for variety' (Lowson 2002: 17). He suggested that all processes—suppliers, the operation itself, and distribution —would be designed flexibly so that they constantly evolved and adapted to meet changing needs in the marketplace. In this future scenario, existing strategies—lean, agile, low cost, CI—would all meld into one. It could be argued that we are already seeing this in the automotive sector.

One way to gain insight into what a firm's OWs might be is to look at its advertising. Since OWs are designed to appeal to customers, it is not surprising that the organization will draw these to people's attention.

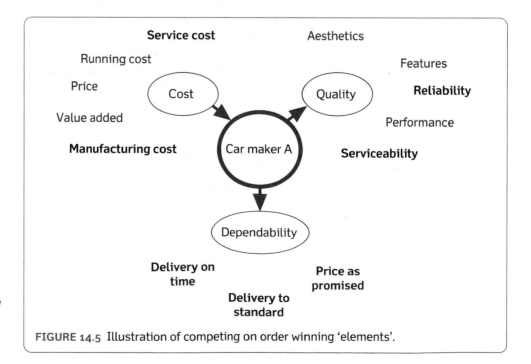

FIGURE 14.5 Illustration of competing on order winning 'elements'.

Go online

RESEARCH INSIGHT 14.3

Frohlich, M.T. and Dixon, J.R. (2001), A taxonomy of manufacturing strategies revisited, *Journal of Operations Management*, 19(5), 541–58.

This article is interesting because it evaluates how manufacturing strategies evolved over the 1990s and how different regions of the world had different strategies. In an earlier study, by Miller and Roth (1994), a sample of manufacturing companies were asked to rate the relative importance of 11 competitive capabilities, most of which are similar to OWs (for instance, price, design flexibility, conformance, performance, delivery speed, and dependability). Three types of strategy emerged, called 'marketers', 'caretakers', and 'innovators'. In their study, Frohlich and Dixon therefore used data from 1994 and 1998 to investigate if these same clusters continued in North America, but also whether they existed in other regions of the world. They found that in North America the caretaker and innovator strategy was still evident, but that the marketer strategy had been replaced by one that they termed 'designers'. This new strategy was focused on product design capabilities, as well as conformance and dependability. They identify this strategy as requiring firms to 'excel on multiple fronts', i.e. compete on a bundle of order winning elements, as we have discussed previously.

Conclusions

In this chapter we have outlined the importance of operations strategy and how it relates to the other strategies within an organization. In doing so, we have highlighted some generic strategies that have been adopted by many firms in a variety of different industry sectors. We have only had space to describe these briefly, but three of these now become the subject of the next three chapters—where the strategy is explained in much more detail. We have also discussed the concept of a 'business model' which is a way of describing in more detail exactly how a firm seeks to achieve its competitive advantage. It is highly likely that the most successful firms will be those with highly developed and well-understood business models, albeit that such firms also need to constantly adapt their model to fit with the environment in which they operate. This was demonstrated in Operations insights 14.2 and 14.3 (pages 374 and 377), and also in the End of chapter case about Dell Computers.

END OF CHAPTER CASE
Dell Computers—customized computers for everyone

Dell was set up in 1984 by Michael Dell, and by 1992 it was listed in the Fortune 500 list of the world's largest companies. By 2001 it was the global market leader in the personal computer industry with 13% market share, and in 2005 it topped *Fortune* magazine's list of America's 'Most Admired Companies'.

This success was based on a very clear business model—direct selling to consumers. This enabled Dell to compete on two main order winners—cost and flexibility.

Cost was kept low for a number of reasons. First, Dell took orders directly from customers, so there

Flexibilty was an order winner for Dell as customers were able to specify the precise features of their computer.

were no margins for distributors such as wholesalers or retailers. Second, inventory was low as products were produced to order. Third, much of Dell's manufacture, assembly, and logistics support was outsourced, considerably reducing their own inventory and overheads. Dell's other order winner—flexibility—also arose out of the direct selling approach. Customers were able to specify the precise features of the computer, and thereby only pay for what they wanted. But this has had other advantages too. It was argued that by selling direct, the sales force became a highly effective technical support team that provided high levels of customer service. Moreover, this direct contact enabled Dell to closely track customer preferences and emerging trends, thereby enhancing their new product development activity and technological innovation.

Dell's business model was enshrined in the 'Five Tenets of Dell'. These were:

- Most efficient path to the customer. 'We believe . . . [in] a direct relationship, with no intermediaries to add confusion and cost'.

- Single point of accountability. This means that the 'resources necessary to meet customer needs can be easily marshalled in support of complex challenges'.

- Build-to-order. 'We provide customers exactly what they want . . . through easy custom configuration and ordering'.

- Low-cost leader. '. . . we consistently provide our customers with superior value'.

- Standards-based technology. Dell specifies standard, interchangeable technologies from amongst the world's best suppliers , thereby benefiting from their research and development.

However, in 2006, Dell began to lose market share to HP, one of its major competitors. In 2007, Dell's worldwide market share was 14.3%, but HP had grown to 18.2%. The relative decline in Dell's fortunes and HP's success was largely attributed to HP's distribution strategy. Firstly, with the growth of e-commerce, most other computer manufacturers had developed their own direct selling model, which also enabled customers to build to order. Hence Dell's model was no longer unique in the marketplace. But unlike Dell, HP had a well-developed wholesale and retail distribution system. This included original equipment manufacturers (OEMs) and independent software vendors (ISVs), who 'bundled' HP's products in with their own; independent distributors and resellers; and major retailers. Moreover, HP had adopted a partnership approach with these stakeholders. It recognized that margins were relatively small, but it strived to offer these distributors the best possible deal. It also ensured that its own sales force was incentivized to work with these partners rather than compete against them. Both of these things made distributors more likely to use or promote HP's products over other brands.

HP's business model, based around diverse channels of distribution, therefore had some specific advantages. First, many customers wanted to 'feel and touch' the product in a store and to see how it performed before buying it. This was especially true in some of the newer and most rapidly expanding markets around the world, where for social and cultural reasons customers preferred to buy directly from retail outlets. Second, buying from a shop eliminated the waiting time that arose from ordering a customized product online. Third, customers felt more secure with regards to technical support if they purchased from a retailer or distributor, as they could return the product to the shop or outlet themselves, as well as speak with 'experts' on a face-to-face basis.

It was also argued that Dell somewhat overhyped the advantages, or benefits, of build-to-order. Although the level of customer choice appeared to be high, in reality the alternatives were fairly limited, and certainly no better than those provided by competitors. This was because, in striving to keep costs down, Dell had a fairly limited range of components and features. Moreover, it was further argued that by focusing on standardization, Dell was unable to exploit new and exciting products and services being developed within the industry.

Another major disadvantage of Dell's build-to-order model relates to its supply chain implications. It is by definition a 'pull system'—the product is not assembled until it is ordered. This was entirely satisfactory when competitors had a push-based system to supply their wider range of distribution channels, which was relatively inefficient. This traditional global distribution system (push-based) relied on members in the supply chain anticipating needs in the next echelon of supply chain. Based on these forecasts, components or computers would be produced and put into inventory until orders were received. As a result inventory was held at many stages along the supply chain—manufacturers, freight forwarding companies, international air carriers, warehouses, and distribution centres. It could take up to four weeks for a product to reach its point of sale. As a result, this relatively inefficient system led to late delivery, stock shortages, and damaged products. It was clearly a poor business model as it resulted in deterioration of stock value, lack of responsiveness to market needs, reduced working capital, and disagreements among channel members.

But during the 2000s, HP and other vendors transformed their supply chain, to partly overcome the problems identified. Hence HP and others began imposing stricter and stricter specifications on defect rate and manufacturing/assembly time. By investing in just-in-time and lean production, OEMs were able to achieve 100% no-defect-rate production and speed up production to just two days. But the other major change was to redesign the supply channel, so that finished products were air-expressed and shipped directly by integrated logistics service companies such as FedEx and UPS. This meant that computers go directly from source to major retail customers, without going through a range of different supply chain stakeholders. The delivery time cycle from factory to retailers was shortened to between two to five days, depending on the location and the type of express service used. Thus by 2005, 90% of computers were being ordered, shipped, and delivered in less than 7 days. This global direct distribution model enabled HP to be much more flexible and responsive to customer needs. It also meant that new innovations could be incorporated into computers and get to market relatively quickly.

To respond to the growing threat from HP, in 2007 Dell developed a new distribution strategy. It launched a channel partner programme and began to distribute is product through retail outlets. In North America it signed a distribution agreement with Wal-Mart, the largest US retailer, in the UK it formed an alliance with Carphone Warehouse, and in France it began selling though Carrefour retail outlets. Late in 2007, Dell launched its PartnerDirect channel partner programme aimed predominately at value added resellers (VARs). VARs offered customized products and solutions largely to small and medium-sized businesses, a B2B model, rather than Dell's B2C direct selling. PartnerDirect was designed to assist VARs with sales and marketing, as well as technical support. Partners would be able to use the Dell logo, order shipments direct online, have a specific partner portal, receive technical support, and be given access online to Dell's knowledge base. However, this programme was not well received by VARs. Compared with other players in the market, Dell did not provide high margins, co-market effectively, have a dedicated channel executive who knew that specific market, nor provide a specialized team to provide technical support dedicated VARs typical customer base.

Despite these changes to its distribution strategy, Dell continued to lose market share. In 2009, HP, Lenovo, and Toshiba all grew by more than 10%. The big improvement came from Acer, which grew by 21% to get to 0.2% short of Dell as the number two worldwide PC vendor. Dell actually achieved a 9.9% drop in shipments for 2009.

Sources: www.dell.com; www.hp.com; Dedrick and Kraemer (2007); Knowledge@Wharton (2007); Wilkens (2010)

Questions

1. What made Dell's original operations strategy so successful?

2. Why did it have to change this strategy?

3. Why does the new strategy appear to be not working?

Chapter summary

To consolidate your learning, the key points from this chapter are summarized as follows:

- **Recognize the relationship between corporate, business, and operations strategy**

  Corporate strategy is the overall plan and goals for the organization. Business strategies are devised for different parts of the organization. And operations strategies are the specific plans that are implemented within the operations function to achieve business goals.

- **Explain the relationship between operations, marketing, human resource, and finance strategies**

  Within a business strategy all the functions—operations, marketing, human resource and finance—have to have strategies that fit with each other so that the goals of the business can be achieved.

- **Compare and contrast the market-driven and resource-based view of operations strategy**

  The market driven view suggests that strategy was largely driven by the market and external, environmental influences—rivalry between firms, the power of customers and suppliers, the threat of new entrants into the market, and threat of new products. On the other hand, the resource-based view says strategy is largely determined from within the organization, due to the resources that it has under its control.

- **Outline the concept of 'business model'**

  A business model is all the factors that describe a business, including the market served, how it creates value, and the factors that will sustain it over the long term. It has been suggested that it comprises three main elements—network architecture (which include the four subelements of markets, transactions, capabilities, and relationships), market offering (comprising artefacts, activity, access, and value), and technology (of four kinds—infrastructure, core, process, and product).

- **Differentiate between a range of contemporary operations strategies and how these may used to deliver order winners.**

  Contemporary operations strategies include lean production, agile manufacturing, mass customization, continuous improvement, low-cost competition, servitization, ubiquitization, e-business and globalization. Each of these may deliver different 'bundles' of OWs depending on industry context. For instance, lean production delivers some of the elements of cost, quality, and dependability, whilst agile delivers elements of cost and speed.

Questions

Review questions

1. What is mean by the term 'competitive advantage'?

2. What criteria influence the choice of strategy?

3. How are the market-driven view and the resource-based view of strategy different to each other?

4. What is the relationship between lean manufacturing and order winners?

5. How is agile manufacturing different to lean production?

6. What is meant by the term 'mass customization?

7. Which two strategies depend on doing the existing strategy better?

8. What are the 12 components of a business model?

9. What kind of firms engage in the servitization strategy, and what kind engage in ubiquitization?

10. How do generic operations strategies get further refined so that firms can achieve competitive advantage?

Discussion questions

1. In what ways are Boots Contract Manufacturing and Avery Weight-Tronix operations strategies similar?

2. What are the implications of TMO Renewables strategy from the point of view of integrating its functional strategies (marketing, operations, human resources, and finance).

3. Select a firm that you are familiar with and explain its business model.

4. To what extent are the different operations strategies that have been identified in this chapter mutually exclusive?

5. Compare and contrast how Ford, Alpha Romeo, and Volvo compete on OWs.

6. What ethical and sustainability issues arise out of creating an operations strategy?

Further learning guide

Most textbooks on operations management discuss the concept of operations strategy, but there are some that focus entirely on this topic. Examples of strategic operations management texts include Lowson (2002) and Brown et al. (2004). There are also some ground-breaking books that explore or explain specific strategies, such as Pine (1993) explaining mass customization and Heskett et al. (1997) who proposed the so-called 'service profit chain'. There is also the broader strategic management literature which place operations strategy in context, such as Porter (1980, 1985).

References

Berry, W.L. and Hill, T. (1992) Linking systems to strategy, *International Journal of Production and Operations Management*, 12(10), 3–15

Berry, W.L., Hill, T., and Klompmaker, J.E. (1999) Aligning marketing and manufacturing strategies with the market, *International Journal of Production Research*, 37(16), 3599–618

Brown, S., Lamming, R., Bessant, J., and Jones, P. (2004) *Strategic Operations Management*, Butterworth Heinemann: Oxford

Boyer, K.K., Swink, M., and Rosenzweig, E.D. (2005), Operations strategy research in the POMS journal, *Production and Operations Management,* 14(4), 442–49.

Dedrick, J., and Kraemer, K.L. (2007) *Market Making in the PC Industry*, Personal Computing Industry Centre: Irvine, CA

Heskett, J., Sasser, W.E., and Schlesinger, L.A. (1997) *The Service Profit Chain*, Harvard Press: Boston, MA

Jones, P., Van-Westering, J., and Bowen, A. (2004) Best practice in operational planning and control, *Hospitality Review*, 6(1), 42–7

Knowledge@Wharton (2007) *Can Dell's Turnaround Strategy Keep HP at Bay?*, September 5 [online]. http://knowledge.wharton.upenn.edu/article.cfm?articleid=1799

Lowson, R.H. (2002) *Strategic Operations Management—The New Competitive Advantage*, Routledge: London

Miller, J.G. and Roth, A. (1994) A taxonomy of manufacturing strategies, *Management Science*, 40(3), 285–304

Pine, B.J. (1993) *Mass Customization: the new frontier in business competition*, Harvard Business School Press: Boston, MA

Porter, M.E. (1980) *Competitive Strategy*, Free Press: Boston, MA

Porter, M.E. (1985) *Competitive Advantage: Creating and Sustaining Superior Performance*, Free Press: Boston, MA

Prahalad, C.K. and Hamel, G. (1990) The core competence of the corporation, *Harvard Business Review*, May/June, 79–91

Spring, M. and Mason, K. (2010) *Business Model Innovation*, ESRC Aim Servitization Workshop, London, 17 March

The Insolvency Service (2011) *Statistics Release: Insolvencies In The Fourth Quarter 2010*, The Insolvency Service: Birmingham. www.insolvency.gov.uk/otherinformation/statistics/201102/index.htm

Wilkens, M. (2010) *Acer Ascends, Dell Dives in 2009 PC Market*, iSuppli Press Release, March 9

Chapter Fifteen

Lean and agile production

Learning outcomes

After reading this chapter you will be able to:

→ Define lean production and its five main principles

→ Identify the eight wastes of lean production

→ Explain the application of the tools and techniques used in lean production

→ Explain total productive maintenance

→ Review the development of lean thinking and its application to customer processing operations.

→ Explain agility and explain the tools to implement it

→ Outline mass customization

Mars Drinks—reducing cost and removing waste

Mars Drinks has two factories on its Basingstoke site. One factory makes the machines that dispense beverages, whilst the other makes the drinks products themselves. The former is an electromechanical assembly operation working a single-shift system, producing in low volume, and facing considerable variation in the size and predictability of demand. However, the drinks factory is a high-speed packaging operation, operating 24/7 to manufacture products under the company's Klix and Flavia brand names.

Since 1998, both operations have developed the lean approach to production. Over a ten-year period, half the space in the machine factory was saved, and inbound warehousing was eliminated. Linked to this, productivity went up around 30%, and manufacturing control costs were down 50%. In particular, raw materials and work-in-progress have been reduced by at least 50%, whilst the contingency stock of finished goods is smaller than it was. Similar advances in the drinks factory have also been accompanied by a dramatic reduction in inventory. Whereas before the lean initiative the plant might hold 25 days' worth of finished stock, afterwards its stock was down to five days' supply, with most orders being met the day after they were ordered.

The company's approach to lean was centred around principles, leadership, and people, rather than so-called lean 'tools', such as kanbans, statistical process control, or Ishikawa analysis. Mars Drinks created a programme called principle-centred leadership, which started with the supply function and was then spread across most areas of activity. The basic object of the exercise is to establish shared principles and values with respect to leadership and line management excellence, and what makes the difference is that these principles and values are self-discovered and co-created by the line managers themselves. As a consequence, Mars report positive employee outcomes in terms of reliability, safe working, absenteeism, staff turnover, and productivity. It has also led to more interdependence across departments.

In 2008, due to the economic downturn caused by the banking crisis, the demand for office drinks in the UK declined, creating pressure on Mars Drinks sales income. The increasing cost of coffee and polystyrene—core manufacturing ingredients for this company—simultaneously created manufacturing cost pressures. To combat the effects of this financial squeeze, the manufacturing team was tasked with driving big improvements in manufacturing unit conversion costs (MCCs). Outcomes of this included working with employees to create more flexible working patterns to better match factory capacity with demand; driving down material waste by chasing down any overspend in this area; maximizing waste stream recovery for every waste classification; and finding creative ways to reduce operational engineering

Increasing cost of coffee and polystyrene contributed towards manufacturing cost pressures.

spend. With these and other initiatives, the team had already reduced MCCs by 15% in less than two years.

The manufacturing team also continuously balances quality, cost, and delivery (QCD) with safety, engagement, and sustainability (SES). The initials QCD and SES are displayed all around the factory as a reminder of their importance. Mars Drinks looked at each step of its manufacturing process to find ways of either reusing or recycling materials—from the refurbishment of the machines to baling its cardboard for resale. Reflecting this commitment to sustainability, Mars Drinks has recently reduced the amount of production waste sent to landfill by its drinks factories in Basingstoke from 600 tons per year to zero. The company also uses the Waste To Energy (WTE) process, generating electricity from incinerating waste and sending it back into the national grid for future use. Through WTE Mars Drinks saves enough electricity every year to power at least 30 homes.

The manufacturing management team also considered downtime. If a problem is encountered, such as raw materials being unavailable or not to specification, a report is raised for that shift to investigate. A Five Whys analysis (explained in Chapter 9) is then conducted—asking questions to identify the root cause in order to remove the problem and ensure that it does not occur again. A dedicated space—the so-called 'PRIMP' room—provides a focus area for these investigations. It is a type of incident room, with magnetic sheets lining the walls, enabling action lists and planning documents to be displayed.

Sources: adapted from: www.klix.co.uk; 'Principles and People', The Manufacturer, September 2007; 'Excellence in Execution', The Manufacturer, December 2010; www.marsdrinks.co.uk

Questions

1. Why has the machine factory been able to reduce raw materials and work-in-progress inventory by 50%, whereas the drinks factory has mainly been able to reduce finished goods stock?

2. Mars Drinks' approach to inventory management seems to be based around people rather than materials processing systems. Why might this be?

Introduction

As we have discussed earlier in Chapter 3, mass production was the dominant approach to planning, controlling, and operating production during the early and mid 20th century as demonstrated by Ford's Highland Park plant for the Model T car. Making as many cars as possible did result in high levels of production output but also a high level of stock of unordered product. This was acceptable for Ford in the early days as all cars were the same. However, with increasing customer choice and technology advances over the ensuing years it is now inconceivable that a car manufacturer would manufacture large batches of identical cars and then put them into store awaiting orders. In the late 1970s pioneering work was undertaken by Shigeo Shingo and Taiichi Ohno on waste reduction and the development of groundbreaking **lean** production methods at Toyota in Japan. The outcome of their innovative work was the establishment of the Toyota Production System (TPS). Womack and Jones (1996) in their seminal book *Lean Thinking – Banish Waste and Create Wealth in Your Corporation* explained the revolutionary production methods that they observed in Toyota. The book provided a vision of a world transformed from Ford's early mass production model to a Toyota-derived lean enterprise. It followed their earlier book *The Machine that Changed the World*

Lean the elimination of all types of waste from any process

(1990), which gave a vision of a world without waste and with a total quality culture. These techniques have now received universal acceptance as a methodology for improving operations and delivering quality products and services at an acceptable cost in the shortest time possible. But it must be remembered that the terms 'lean thinking', 'lean production', and 'lean manufacturing' can mean different things to different people. Pettersen (2009) concludes that 'there is no consensus on a definition of lean production . . . [and there are] different opinions on which characteristics should be associated with the concept'.

In this chapter we consider five main topics. First we look at the five key principles of lean production and in particular how they can be extended beyond automotive production, where they originated, to any organization. We then go on to examine how these principles are applied to remove waste from the process. This leads on to a discussion about the tools and techniques that can be applied to identify and remove waste in production, including a discussion on total productive maintenance. Fourth, we look at significant trends in lean and its applicability to customer processing operations. Finally we consider agility and examine ways in which firms can be more responsive to consumer needs, without abandoning lean principles.

Lean production

Lean production is often misunderstood to mean a collection of tools (such as the five 'S's', just-in-time (JIT), or kaizen, discussed in Chapter 16) or a way of removing waste. Lean production does indeed use these tools to remove waste; however, at the core of the lean philosophy is the notion of putting the customer and what they value first. Understanding customer value allows firms to understand what waste is and how to remove it using the lean tools and techniques. Before we explore and define the elements of waste, and explain how to use tools and techniques to remove it, we will examine the five principles of lean production.

The first principle is to specify what value means from the standpoint of the customer. The key question to ask is 'If I were the customer what would I be willing to pay for?'. Often levels of sophistication in a product or service are not required by customers so they would expect to pay less without them and a bit more for them. Customers buying a mobile telephone are offered wide variety of packages that vary in price according to the features offered. Companies need to understand the market requirements when designing products and services to ensure that they have the right balance.

Second, identify the steps in the process that are required to deliver value to the customer. This is called the value stream. The value stream in Figure 15.1 shows a typical manufacturing operation. It is different to the 'value chain', discussed in the last chapter in that the chain is a generic model applied to any kind of business, whereas a value stream is a specific model applied to a specific operation. There are a number of steps in the process which add value before the operation is complete. However, we can also see that there are areas that contain non-value adding activities that generate waste, such as a huge amount of waiting as work-in-progress (WIP). The total throughput time for the completion of the operation is 336 hours (nearly two full weeks) whilst the value added time (when work is actually being carried out on the product (WIP)) is only 5.6 hours, or 1.67% of the total operation time. This is a hugely wasteful and inefficient process and from the customer's perspective they have to wait for their products for two weeks and also pay for the inefficiency. (This is not an uncommon situation and many industrial

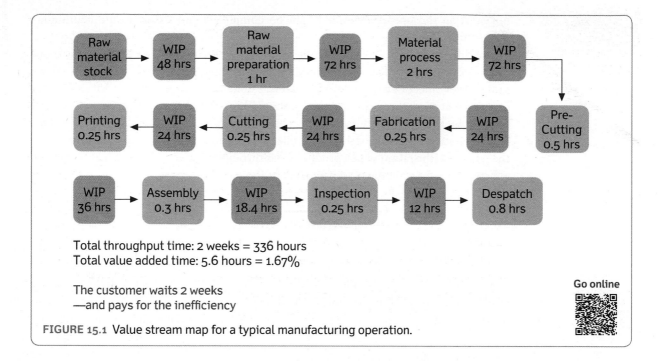

Total throughput time: 2 weeks = 336 hours
Total value added time: 5.6 hours = 1.67%

The customer waits 2 weeks
—and pays for the inefficiency

FIGURE 15.1 Value stream map for a typical manufacturing operation.

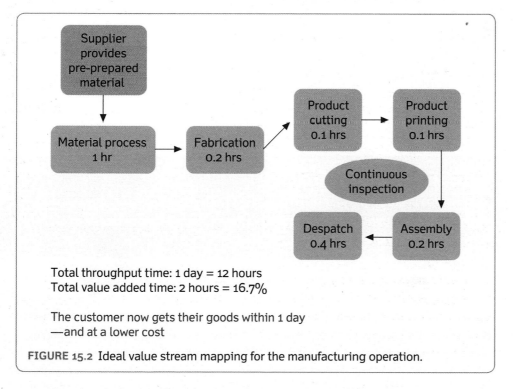

Total throughput time: 1 day = 12 hours
Total value added time: 2 hours = 16.7%

The customer now gets their goods within 1 day
—and at a lower cost

FIGURE 15.2 Ideal value stream mapping for the manufacturing operation.

operations when measured like this show a value added percentage of less than 5%, according to the Institute of Operations Management research.)

If the majority of waste is removed from the operation by reorganization and restructuring of the process, then a much faster throughput can be achieved without the unnecessary waiting time. Figure 15.2 shows an ideal value stream map which highlights the improvement. This time the product is completed within 12 hours using material that is pre-prepared by the supplier, and lean production principles of pull planning, by not starting the operation until it can be completed and using in-line continuous inspection.

The third principle relates to getting value to flow through the value stream without interruption, rework, double handling (i.e. moving materials or product to and from the same place unnecessarily) and waiting. This is done by load levelling so that there is an even pace or work through each work station. This is what the Japanese term heijunka. Measurement of the time for products to pass through each work station and the complete operation need to be tightly controlled. This is done by measuring and monitoring the takt time (the rate at which products pass through an operation). The takt time is the effective 'heartbeat' of the manufacturing facility.

$$\text{Takt time} = \frac{\text{Effective working time per shift}}{\text{Customer requirement per shift}}$$

Therefore if a facility operates for eight hours (480 minutes) per shift and the customer requirement is 960 per shift, then the takt time = 0.5, i.e. 30 seconds. Thus the company needs to ensure that two units pass through the operation every minute, in order to ensure output meets the customer's actual, or forecast, demand.

Fourth, once the obstacles to flow have been identified and eliminated goods are then manufactured at the pull rate of the customer's demand. If the customer only wishes to buy one product at a time why produce a large batch? Pull planning techniques are a vital part of lean production as they ensure that no part enters the operation unless an order is attached to it.

The fifth principle is the requirement to strive for perfection. Customer value is not static so manufacturing organizations continually seek to deliver increased levels of value, whether this is in terms of cost, quality, and/or delivery. Continuous improvement, or kaizen, as we will discuss further in Chapter 16, is another essential element of lean production.

RESEARCH INSIGHT 15.1

Hines, P., Holweg, M., and Rich, N. (2004) Learning to evolve—A review of contemporary lean thinking. *International Journal of Operations and Production Management*, 24(10), 994–1011

This article begins by giving a brief history of lean production. It then identifies that this approach has been criticized in a number of ways and discusses these issues. The authors then suggest that the development of the lean strategy has evolved through four stages, which they term cells and assembly lines, shop floor, value stream, and value systems. The article, along with its extensive list of references, provides a good overview of this topic.

Waste elimination (MUDA)

Waste reduction and removal is essential to delivering customer value through production processes. Waste is the opposite of value. The original seven production wastes were identified and categorized by Shigeo Shingo as part of the Toyota Production

System. An eighth waste has been added to the list and reflects that waste related to underutilizing the talents and skills of the people employed in the process. Each of these wastes is explained as follows.

1. Transportation—excessive movement of products, information, and people resulting in wasted time and resource.

2. Inventory—unnecessary raw material, WIP, or finished goods inventory leads to delays in process and storage handling. In Figure 15.2, inventory in the form of WIP was held at every stage in production.

3. Motion—inefficient movement created by poor workplace and equipment design. This can be in relation to how far apart different areas of activity are, or on a much smaller, 'ergonomic' scale in terms of how an individual's work area is laid out. **Ergonomics** applies scientific principles to workplace design to assure human well-being. A good example of this is how office chairs are designed to be adjustable, keyboards made user-friendly, and computer screens positioned correctly on desks.

4. Waiting—periods of inactivity for the process, information, and people.

5. Overproduction—producing too many products discourages the efficient flow of goods through activities, for example, large-batch production leading to excess inventory and delays in the process, brought about by the unavailability of storage space or work areas being blocked.

6. Overprocessing—producing goods or services with inappropriate tools and procedures leading to inefficient use of resources—'using a hammer to crack a nut' (Bicheno 2004), or providing products to too high a specification compared to what the customer really needs. It could be argued that word processing software and smart phones have become like this—with most users not using many of the features of these products.

7. Defects—errors in administration or production leading to rework and additional costs. This is the area where the drive for efficiency overlaps with the drive for quality.

8. Skills—the waste of untapped human potential through the poor use and application of the talents and skills of the people employed in the process. As we have seen when discussing quality management, employees are no longer engaged in simple tasks, but expected to identify, analyse and resolve production issues on the shop floor, without the intervention of management.

Ergonomics
the application of scientific principles to workplace design to assure human well-being

Lean tools and techniques

There are a number of tools and techniques commonly used by companies employing a lean production strategy. Each of these is designed to address one or more of the eight wastes. By becoming 'lean', companies are exposing themselves to the inefficiencies and constraints that get in the way of fast throughput operations. A common analogy used to explain lean is of a ship crossing a piece of rough water in a storm. So long as there is a high tide the ship is most likely to navigate itself through the storm unharmed. However, if it is low tide then there is a greater chance that the ship may hit some rocks. In the same way companies have a buffer against rough going by keeping inventory.

Without this level of inventory (as demanded by lean production) they are exposing themselves to the 'rocks' of inefficiency and poor organization. These need to be addressed within the company before embarking on a lean production strategy. Generally lean production is only suitable for repetitive processes which are tightly controlled.

Single minute exchange of dies

Taiichi Ohno of Toyota believed that the waste associated with overproduction due to large batch sizes was at the root of many quality and cost issues in production. Large batch sizes lead to high inventories and long lead times. Phrases such as minimum order quantity (MOQ) and economic order quantity (EOQ) reflect the cost of changing equipment from one product type to another. The downtime costs associated with machine changeovers led many manufacturers to stipulate minimum batch quantities to reduce the number and frequency of these changeovers.

Reducing the cycle time of machinery through minimizing machine downtime resulted in the concept of Single minute exchange of dies (SMED). The idea came through the challenge of reducing the changeover time of dies in injection moulding machines from several hours to less than ten minutes; hence the 'single minute' phrase. Reduction in cycle time is achieved by doing as much as is possible with regards to the changeover while the machine is running, and so minimize the activities—and time these take—when the machine is stopped. Examples of this technique includes quick-release clamps for when the machine has stopped and pre-heated dies that allow for quick return to production. The use of more labour to execute the changeover helps to achieve the desired timescale. We can see the same technique being used by Formula 1 racing drivers every time they go into the pits to change tyres. A group of highly trained mechanics can change four tyres, add more fuel, and get the car back on track in less than ten seconds. SMED was adopted by Apex Linvar, as discussed in Operations insight 10.1 (see page 259)

Workplace organization—5S

The concept of workplace organization is one of the cornerstones of lean production and underpins a company's ability to perform SMED and total productive maintenance (TPM). The idea is very subtle and profound in its impact on the performance and ability of an organization to execute lean. The tool consists of five steps and requires discipline and a drive for continuous improvement. The five steps are explained below and the original Japanese words are included for completeness.

Step 1 (seiri)—sort: this first stage focuses upon the removal of all parts, materials, and equipment that are not required in the immediate future. Any unnecessary items are relocated to ensure that they do not affect the prime working area and its productivity. Time and effort can be wasted in terms of motion as people walking around the unwanted items as well as time spent looking for inventory that is obscured by the unnecessary parts or equipment.

Step 2 (seiton)—set: the catch phrase 'a place for everything and everything in its place' is usually mentioned when firms begin step 2. The purpose of this step is to arrange materials and tools in the optimum place for both the operator and the production area. Optimum locations reduce motion that is associated with picking up and

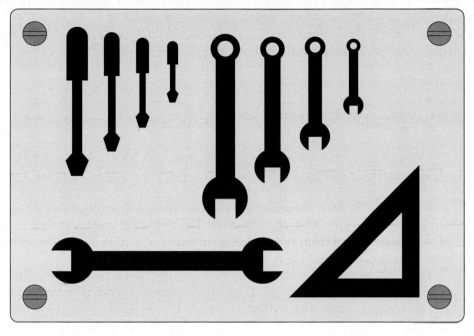

FIGURE 15.3 Shadow board. © Robert Gebbie Photography.

putting down items and the time required to locate them. Typically a factory would establish shadow boards which make it easy to identify where a tool is located and where it should be returned to (see Figure 15.3).

Step 3 (seiso)—shine: the cleaner the workplace the easier it is to see if something is out of place and identify if there is a problem with the process. For example, in a tool shop that operates lathes, drilling, and milling machines it is easier to detect an oil leak if the floor is clean and free from dirt and grime.

Step 4 (seiketsu)—standardize: once the first 3S's are executed the next challenge facing the organization is to maintain the standard that has been achieved. Discipline through standardization and establishing routines in working practices that maintain the new standards are essential otherwise the danger of returning to the 'old' ways exists.

Step 5 (shitsuke)—stick though continuous improvement: driving forward ongoing improvement is the fifth and most challenging step of 5S. This step moves the organization from a reactive to proactive stance. Instead of reacting to the oil leak the firm asks why the oil has leaked and what they can do to prevent the spillage happening again.

Total productive maintenance

One of the other principal concepts that is deployed in manufacturing environments relates to maintenance of equipment. Historically firms would repair equipment once it had broken down or during the planned annual factory closure. This mainly reactive approach led to disruption in production as machinery failed or had to run slowly.

Japanese manufacturers developed the concept of TPM. This is often carried out in conjunction with total quality management (TQM), which we explained and discussed in Chapter 9. TPM focuses on equipment, and in particular its condition and maintenance. A typical TPM programme has seven steps, as follows:

- Step 1—initial deep cleaning, in order to identify equipment defects or problems, such as contamination or the accumulation of dirt, that have not previously been identified.
- Step 2—development of procedures and tools aimed at preventing these defects from occurring, such as moving or modifying the equipment to make it easier to clean.
- Step 3—establish standards for cleaning, lubricating, and maintaining each type of equipment and train staff up to these standards.
- Step 4—establish general inspection procedures and schedules.
- Step 5—develop employee autonomy to conduct an inspection.
- Step 6—orderliness and tidiness become the norm.
- Step 7—full autonomous maintenance.

To implement such a programme and achieve these steps a number of organizational changes are typically made. The maintenance team is integrated within the production department rather than being a separately managed unit. Employees become both operators and maintenance staff, and training is undertaken to encourage operators to feel like they 'own' the equipment. Finally, good habits are developed so that cleaning is seen as a part of the quality process rather than a chore. TPM shifts maintenance away from the historical view that machine performance is someone else's concern to a situation where it is everyone's duty of care.

Kanban

Kanban materials requirement planning technique

'Kan' means visual and 'ban' means card. A **kanban** is a classic signalling method that has been in existence for many years in various businesses. It is the basis for the 'pull planning' process where demand is pulled by customer orders, as opposed to the more traditional 'push' process used for many years by Western companies. In some operations the kanban can be a bin (which has a related card with it) or a marked area on the factory floor. When the bin or space is empty it signals to everyone that it needs to be replenished. This type of visual manufacturing is very important in lean production environments. Kanban supports the operation of a 'single-piece flow' where products are completed one at a time without interruption.

Within manufacturing dual kanban cards (as shown in Figure 15.4) are used to signal the need to deliver more parts and a similar card signals the need to produce more parts. When the consuming production cell takes stock there is a gap on the shelf which is the signal for the supplying cell to produce more stock to replace the item(s) taken. For instance, in a flight kitchen (see Operations insight 4.2, page 97) that operates with work stations, each type of equipment needed to lay up a meal tray is in a bin of a standard inventory amount, say 200 items. When the work station is set up, bins are removed from the stores, which signals they need to be replaced (i.e. 'produced') with new, fresh bins being made up in the flight wash-up area, where equipment is washed to make it ready for use. Typically each work station has two bins of each item of equipment, so that when the first is empty, the operative can continue lay up by moving onto the second bin. The empty first bin serves a signal that it needs replacing (a

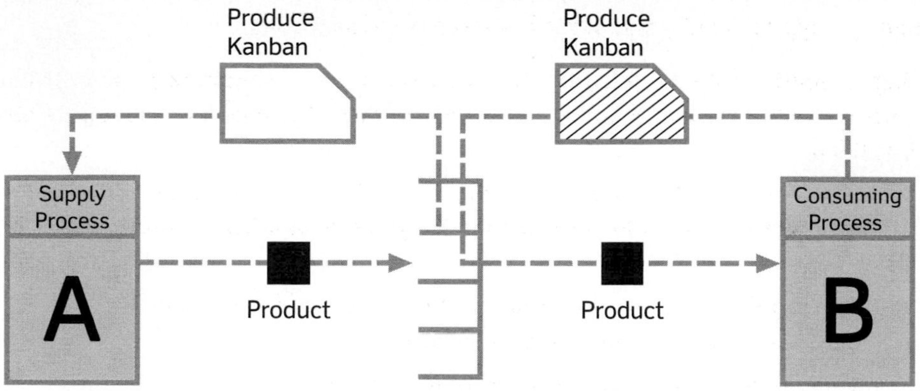

FIGURE 15.4 Dual kanban system. Rother, M. and Shook, J. (1998) *Learning To See: Value Stream Mapping to Add Value and Eliminate Muda*, © Copyright 1998 Lean Enterprise Institute, Inc. Cambridge, MA. All rights reserved.

'deliver' signal), which another operative does from the stores. Thus one operative can serve several workstations in terms of ensuring they always have the equipment that they need.

RESEARCH INSIGHT 15.2

Singh, B., Garg, S.K., Sharma, S.K., and Grewal, C. (2010) Lean implementation and its benefits to production industry, *International Journal of Lean Six Sigma*, 1(2), 157–68

This article provides an in-depth case study of how lean was applied to a specific production facility. Comparing the current and future state of production it was found that reduction in lead time was 83.14%, reduction in processing time was 12.62%, reduction in work-in-process inventory was 89.47%, and reduction in manpower requirement was 30%. The rise in productivity per operator was 42.86%. The article provides insight into how lean thinking is implemented and the process of value stream mapping.

Just-in-time production

JIT is a system for producing and delivering what is required just when it is needed. In order to achieve and operate a JIT system it is critical that 5S, SMED, TQM, poka-yoke, and TPM are in operation to minimize interruptions to flow. All of these techniques have already been discussed here or in previous chapters. JIT can refer to internal as well as external production and delivery. Internally JIT is represented by kanban cards.

Externally the concept is normally demonstrated as small and frequent deliveries of parts. This approach in the 1980s led to a negative image of JIT as being a way for manufacturers to push inventory back to suppliers at their expense. Car parts suppliers today support JIT by suppliers establishing premises close to or adjacent to their customer to reduce transit times and costs.

Lighting Design International is a UK based business that was facing increasing demands from customers for shorter lead times and reductions in prices. The company are a leading edge technology firm making lights with innovative design features. These features result in architects and interior designers specifying this company's products when they engage in projects for clients. This highly creative firm had led to a very broad portfolio of products supported by a very wide range of suppliers and parts. The operations director's challenge was to develop a manufacturing strategy that could deliver the demands of its architectural and designer customer base.

The business decided that the way forward was to implement a lean strategy. The strategy would be deployed in multiple stages. Firstly the product range would be segregated into high-volume regular demand products (lean) and low-volume irregular product types (materials requirement planning (MRP)). Secondly the lean categorized products would be manufactured in a focused factory. The other items would remain in the traditional factory and be planned and coordinated through the MRP system. The product split is shown in Table 15.1.

The impact of the implementation of lean and the focusing of management time and resources on the two different factories had a significant impact on the service offered to the customer base. Lead times were reduced from eight to 12 weeks for all products to two to four weeks for MRP items and zero to two weeks for lean. Costs were also significantly reduced for both production areas.

Achievement of these changes (shown in Table 15.2) were as a result of implementing 5S, SMED, kanban, value engineering, reduction of number of suppliers and their lead times, plus the simplification of administration processes.

The firm still faced the challenge that the customer wanted both lean and MRP items at the same time not two to four weeks later. This customer challenge led to the development of

TABLE 15.1 Comparison of lean versus traditional factory

	Low volume	High volume
Number of products	>5000	<800
Material flow	Push	Pull
Material control	MRP	Kanban
Demand predictability	Low	High
Minimum order quantity	1 unit	Pallet
Service offer	Made to order	Made to stock
Ethos	Traditional	Lean

TABLE 15.2 Performance of traditional versus lean factory

	Before	After	
		MRP	Lean
Product codes	6000+	>5000	850
Product development	24 months	6 months	6 months
Lead times	8–12 weeks	2–4 weeks	0–2 weeks
Costs	100	85	73

an agile factory to drive down the response time for MRP products which is discussed later in this chapter in Operations insight 15.3.

Source: authors' primary research

Questions

1. Why did Lighting Design International decide to have two separate factories?

2. What is likely to have led to costs falling by 27% for products manufactured in the lean factory?

Lean thinking and customer processing operations

Waste and general inefficiency is just as prevalent in an office or customer-facing environment as it is in a manufacturing operation. Consequently the philosophy and ideas associated with lean have transferred across to customer processing operations and terms such as lean thinking or lean enterprise have begun to be used to reflect this.

However, there is one important way in which manufacturing and services differ, and this is in terms of how value is measured. For products, value is often best expressed in terms of the functionality of the product. Thus it is reasonably straightforward for manufacturers to decide if value is being added to a product or not. But in the service setting, customers often identify a significant proportion of their satisfaction with the service as being derived from their interaction with service staff. Hence rapport between employees and customers adds value. But since the nature of this can vary from one service encounter to another, it may be difficult to apply lean thinking to this setting. For instance, some consumers dislike self-service (which is a 'lean' approach) and prefer to shop or bank in a traditional way.

Despite this, lean thinking has been applied to a wide variety of different customer processing operations—theme parks, financial services, hotels, and restaurants. For instance, in the 1990s, Horst Schulz, chief executive officer of Ritz-Carlton Hotels initiated a programme to improve quality and reduce costs in his chain of 20 five-star hotels. Although not labelled a lean initiative, much of what Ritz-Carlton did was consistent with this strategy. Schulz's team identified 18 key processes and engaged in a detailed analysis of these in order to redesign them to be more efficient. More recently Julien and Tjahjono (2009) report on the application of lean thinking to a well-known UK safari park. Through value stream mapping, the introduction of redesigned processes and the elimination of waste, they estimated an annual saving of £91,000 without negatively affecting the customer experience.

Another service sector that has especially adopted lean thinking is the health care sector. Powell et al. (2009) review this and conclude that it works best in support departments, rather than clinical or medical areas that deal with patients. This is partly because value stream mapping is a challenge in this setting, but so are the values of the people working within the health community, especially clinicians. Medical and clinical staff are used to the idea of developing new processes and improving existing ones. They do this routinely in terms of surgical procedures and medical treatments, through 'clinical trials'. Such trials are based on a rigorous research design, detailed analysis of outcomes, and very clearly established samples and time lines. However, this approach is very different to the typical way in which lean initiatives are introduced. Lean is usually endorsed by a champion, or several champions, within the organization, often based on their enthusiasm rather than their rigour as researchers. To embed lean thinking these champions share good news stories about the effect of the lean initiative, rather than rigorously analyse data. Hence medical staff may well treat lean initiatives as simplistic and unsupported by evidence, thereby negating their effect in hospitals and other health care settings. Despite this, there are lean initiatives in the National Health Service (NHS). For instance, Hereford Hospitals NHS Trust has undertaken three different programmes looking at the 'patient journey', waste in the pathology department, and turnaround time in pathology.

Agility and agile manufacturing

Agile the design of processes, tools, and training to enable quick response to customer needs

The principle of lean and mass production is based on being very good at the things you can control. **Agile** manufacturing deals with the things we cannot control. Agility is the ability to thrive and prosper in an environment of ever increasing and constantly changing customer demands. Agility means using market knowledge and a flexible organization to exploit opportunities in a dynamic and volatile market (Naylor et al. 1999). Agility is a business-wide capability that embraces organizational structures, information technology (IT), logistics processes, and mind sets (Aitken et al. 2005). Maskell (2001) explains agile in terms of four common axioms:

- The market requires low-volume, high-quality, and customer-specific products.
- Agile products have a very short life cycle and development time.
- Product lead times are very short.
- Everything is changing and is unpredictable.

Agility in essence is about the speed of response to develop, produce, and deliver product in a very quick turnaround.

We will consider four main areas of agility. First we look at the characteristics of agile manufacturing and how these principles relate to order winners. This leads on to a discussion about the differences and synergies between lean, mass customization, and agile approaches. Thirdly, we look at the tools and techniques that are used to deploy agility in manufacturing, supply chains, and retail management. Finally, we conclude with a consideration of ethical and sustainability issues of agile manufacturing practices.

Agile characteristics

Agile manufacturers need to design or develop their products specifically to customer's specifications. For instance, Pipex (see End of chapter case) are agile enough to respond to critical incidents that require them to do a rush job, such as when several metal manhole covers were stolen and new, plastic replacement covers were needed urgently. Product design and manufacturing have to be closely linked to deliver fast customer response. The idea of routing and developing products through a traditional linear and sequential process does not support the needs of an agile operation. Product design, engineering, and the production process have to operate collaboratively if the business is to be successful (Figure 15.5).

The consequence of operating alongside one another is that new product development takes less time and the firm's technical capacity and capability increases. In traditional manufacturing, operators would be expected to execute repetitive tasks within predefined parameters in terms of build time, assembly costs, and product routing. Standard operating procedures will exist to inform the operator step by step which activity to perform next and when. Within an agile environment the operations are non-routine as each product will be designed and assembled according to its unique customer requirements. Since operators will not perform repetitive standardized tasks the firm and its staff have to have the ability to optimize the product build as they

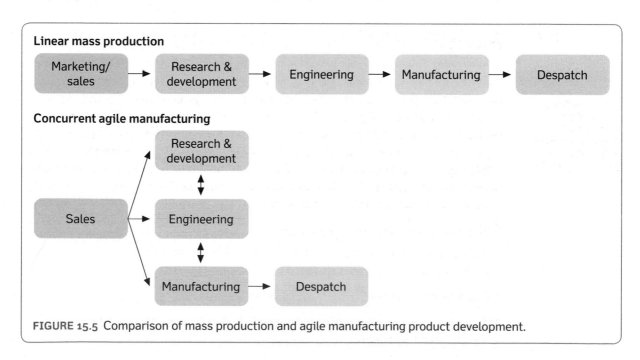

FIGURE 15.5 Comparison of mass production and agile manufacturing product development.

assemble the item. This may mean cutting, drilling, and punching parts from a computer or a hand-drawn diagram and executing the electrical tasks based on a wiring diagram of a similar product. Due to the nature of the agile operation people have to be able to analyse, diagnose, and resolve problems as they occur as opposed to standard manufacturing where specialists are called upon to resolve issues.

Short product life cycles are common for agile operations as the manufactured items are usually bespoke and may only ever be produced once. Product batch sizes tend to be small and the variety of items to be made extremely large. Operations insight 15.2 demonstrates the characteristics of agile manufacturing.

OPERATIONS INSIGHT 15.2
Engineering in art—going agile

In London, a traditional engineering firm produced metal fasteners for sale to other local and UK-based customers for use in the their equipment. With the demise of their customer base due to relocation of clients to the Far East and the entry into the market of low-cost overseas competitors the firm had to rethink its strategy.

The directors of the company analysed their company strengths in terms of knowledge and ability of their engineers to cut, shape, and polish metal to a high quality. They also recognized that the market for architectural engineering

Directors recognized the ability of their engineers to polish metal to a high quality as one of the companies strengths. © James Blacklock: Fotolia.com.

was increasing. This market required the production of small batch, bespoke items that could be tailored to client's specific and changing demands. The original drawings produced by architects and their clients were never finalized until the product was finished. Clients also wanted the ability to drop in and see their 'creations' as they evolved. This meant that the engineering firm had to have the ability to alter production at the last moment, as the client might wish to develop each design further.

The firm managed to turn its business from mass production to agile manufacturing through the skills and knowledge of its engineers. The firm has become renowned for its agility based on the principles of meeting customer needs through a fast, responsive workforce

Source: authors' primary research

Questions

1. What are the process type implications of changing this company's strategy?
2. What become this company's new order qualifiers and order winners?

Efficient customer response and enabling information technology

Engaging with market knowledge requires firms to develop close links both down- and upstream. Agility depends on the quick flow of information from customers and suppliers enabled by information technology. One of the approaches used by retailers and manufacturers is efficient consumer response (ECR). ECR supports the shrinking of time windows to meet customer demand by integrating and rationalizing replenishment and product development across the supply chain. ECR is achieved through effective collaboration and alignment of demand management with supply chain management. Through reducing the time it takes to transfer demand information from the retailer to the manufacturer the replenishment cycle time can be complete in hours instead of days and weeks. Through the use of enabling technologies such as electronic data exchange (EDI) and electronic point-of-sale (EPOS) information can be transmitted directly to manufacturers to start production. Technology continues to advance and businesses are now using radio frequency identification devices (RFID) which can be used to create intelligent shelves to inform the retailer and manufacturer about the location of the item in the supply chain. RFID assists with tracking of product throughout the factory and the extended supply chain. Firms can see when a component is going to arrive and then track its movement along the manufacturing process and finally on to the customer. When the product is used or sold a signal can be transmitted to the manufacturer to produce a replacement. The same technology is used by overnight parcel delivery services such as UPS and Federal Express—RFID tags track the packages that are being transported to help ensure they meet their 24-hour delivery promise.

OPERATIONS INSIGHT 15.3
Lighting Design International B—adding agile to lean

As seen in Operations insight 15.1, Lighting Design International traditionally produced high volumes of inventory in its UK plant and shipped the product 300 kilometres to a central warehouse to ensure product availability to retailers within 48 hours. The cycle time for process from product assembly to finally being delivered to the customer's shelf took on average six weeks due to the level of inventory in the pipeline. Even with such a high level of inventory service was inadequate due to product promotions and unreliable demand forecasts.

The firm decided to re-engineer its processes by creating modular products in terms of subassemblies (unbranded light bulbs). Through postponing the final branding and packing and implementing EDI/EPOS data capture the firm was able to reduce the cycle time to 12 hours. When the consumer product was scanned at the till (EPOS) a message was sent to the supplier (EDI) via the retailer's inventory replenishment to the manufacturer's production machine. Each product was branded and packed for a specific store and delivered within 12 hours.

Source: authors' primary research

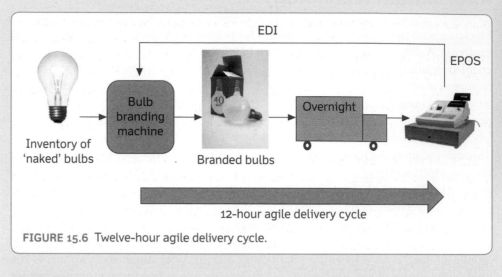

FIGURE 15.6 Twelve-hour agile delivery cycle.

Questions

1. How does adopting an agile approach change or enhance Lighting Design International's order winners?

2. What are the advantages of moving to modular components?

Amazon.com book supplies similarly rely on the power of enabling IT to drive their business and satisfy consumers. Orders are placed by consumers via the Internet and then Amazon use their own supplier network of independent retailers and manufacturers to satisfy the demand. Amazon has become an example of an agile distribution and Internet retail business.

Agile product development

Practitioners of and researchers into agile manufacturing emphasize the application of **'soft' technology**. Such 'technology' can be similar to soft systems (discussed in Chapter 10), that is to say, the human, social, and organizational aspects of the operation, or it is can also be in reference to policies and practices that are adaptable, such as Six Sigma, statistical process control, and other quality tools. Soft technology performs an important role in agile manufacturing since it is essential to maintain quality and efficiency, whilst being agile.

'Soft' tools are also used in some agile contexts. This refers to equipment, such as moulds or dies, which are used in pressing or stamping machines, which are made from lighter materials and hence can only produce a limited number of products/components before they have to be replaced. The benefits of 'soft' tools are twofold. Firstly the time to manufacture soft tools is shorter and secondly the cost is a fraction of normal 'hard' tools. 'Hard' tools are expensive as they are manufactured from steels and take several weeks or months to prepare, run, and de-bug. These 'hard' tools would be used by lean and mass production firms as they can be used repeatedly before they have to be

Soft technology policies and techniques for assuring the efficient and effective organization of work

Soft tools temporary dies and moulds used for the manufacture of one-off products or small batches

repaired. Time is critical for an agile business hence the use of 'soft' tools in prototyping and customer production.

For agile firms to be successful they rely upon suppliers, however, the relationships with these key resources can be short lived. Lean manufacturers operate with few long-term suppliers who link in with their kanban and JIT systems. Agile firms, such as in textiles and clothing manufacturers, develop fluid clusters of suppliers who come together face-to-face or electronically for a specific project. The work is distributed by the manufacturer against very short lead times with all parties focused on delivering customer value. Individual companies in an agile supply chain need to align their operations by redesigning the flow of information, goods, and business control practices.

Students occasionally operate with agile networks when executing assignments. Tasks are split between group members based on expertise and ability. The completed tasks are then re-integrated before the assignment deadline. The focus of the network is to deliver the product (assignment) on time with the highest quality at least cost (to the students resources). The operation works well when all network suppliers execute their task on time to the quality required. This allows the integrator (student) to easily and quickly complete the product on time for the customer (lecturer).

Comparison of agile and lean manufacturing strategies

Both of these strategies have common attributes but they vary in the significance of the affect of volume, variety, variability, life cycle, and delivery lead time. The main purpose of lean is to manufacture high-quality products at a dependable rate with lowest cost. Agile is focused upon delivering high-quality products in the shortest possible delivery time at a cost the market will accept. In essence lean is about quality at lowest cost and agile is about quality and speed of delivery. Table 15.3 compares the attributes of the two approaches.

TABLE 15.3 Comparison of agile and lean attributes

Attribute	Agile	Lean
Typical products	Bespoke (e.g. clothing)	Commodities (e.g. transistors)
Product variety	High	Low
Product life cycle	Short (weeks)	Long (years)
Product volume	Low	High
Demand variability	High	Low
Set-up costs	Low	High
Product development	Short	Long
Product standardization	Low	High

Mass customization

Another strategy which has similarities to both lean and agile manufacturing is mass customization. A key feature of this strategy is 'modularity'—designing the parts or components of a product so that they can be used in many different ways. The example that is always given because it is so familiar to everyone is Lego, which can be used in thousands of different ways to assemble many different things. By using standardized components or subassemblies, the operations can stay 'lean'—as these are mass produced. But by making them interchangeable, they are also 'agile'—as they can produce many different products from a relatively small set of components. This requires postponing assembly until the last moment, or even waiting until the customer orders the product. So long as the operation is sufficiently agile, it is still able to maintain a relatively high speed of delivery. For instance, this is how BMW manufacture the Mini, Swatch make watches, and Benetton make their clothes. Swatch has literally thousands of different watches that are designed to be worn as a fashion accessory. They are able to be priced competitively because although the straps, faces, and colours may vary widely, many key components, such as the watch mechanism itself, is mass produced. In Benetton's case they changed the way that woollen garments were produced. Traditionally these are knitted from dyed wool, but Benetton designed and made garments from undyed wool, and then dyed the whole garment according to any season's colours. In this way, they could track retail sales and dye garments according to the strength of demand for any given colour.

Comparing the three strategies in Figures 15.7, 15.8, and 15.9 against certain attributes highlights the differences in the three approaches in terms of competitive advantages and disadvantages.

These three manufacturing strategies should not be considered to be mutually exclusive. Firms during the life cycle of their products can move between the strategies to suit the market conditions and drivers. Operations insights 15.1 and 15.3 highlight the example of a lighting company that deployed all three strategies during the life cycle of the product. Initially the product concept was produced in the agile factory to keep cost low and test the market for the product. Once the market response was positive the product was standardized and hard tools were produced for the components. During the growth stage the product was moved to the lean factory to drive down costs and increase volumes. As the market and product matured, mass customization was introduced to increase response times, availability, and product variety. Finally as the product declined it was produced in the agile factory again.

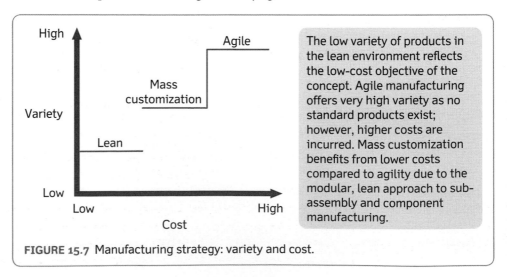

FIGURE 15.7 Manufacturing strategy: variety and cost.

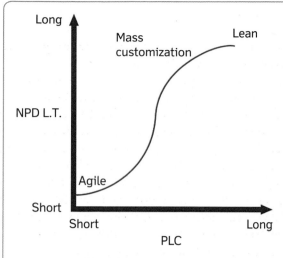

Agile manufacturing derives its competitive advantage through very short product development and delivery time. Products are normally only produced once, meaning that the cost advantage gained by standardization of components and assembly processes is not possible. Longer new product development times and costs are found in lean and mass customization as effort and time is spent developing standardized work

FIGURE 15.8 Manufacturing strategy: NPD lead time and product life cycle.

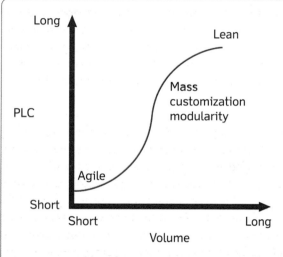

Higher volumes offer manufacturers the opportunity to deploy lean and the modularity which supports mass customization. The cost of establishing the standards for the products and processes are recovered over the longer life cycle. Agile products are very often bespoke small-volume items (e.g. furniture) that may only be manufactured once.

FIGURE 15.9 Manufacturing strategy: product life cycle and volume.

RESEARCH INSIGHT 15.3

Aitken, J., Childerhouse, P., Christopher, M., and Towill, D. (2005) Designing and managing multiple pipelines, *Journal of Business Logistics*, 26(2), 73–96

This paper highlights the fact that there is now a growing recognition that supply chains should be designed from 'the customer backwards' rather than from 'the company outwards'. If such a view is accepted then the implication is that since the organization will likely be serving multiple markets or segments, there will be the need to design and manage multiple 'pipelines' to service those different customers. To assist decision-makers in their choice of appropriate supply chain design a framework is proposed based upon multiple criteria. It also refers to the paper by Naylor et al. (1999) where the term 'leagile' is introduced as the particular value stream configuration in which upstream processes are lean and are then followed by downstream agile processes.

Conclusions

Lean production has taken a number of guises over the years. Starting off deeply embedded in manufacturing as part of the Toyota Production System and using JIT techniques to remove the wastes from processes it has now broadened its use into all types of enterprise and companies who adopt lean principles are now doing so from a customer value standpoint. As this chapter has demonstrated, by using the five principles of lean production companies can identify those steps in the process which add value and which the customer is prepared to pay for and to eliminate those which he is not.

Lean production can deliver quality improvements through the elimination of defects, dependability improvements through reducing inventory and working towards a single piece flow to ensure goods are delivered on time, and cost improvements by eliminating the eight wastes in the value process chain. It is also associated with kaizen, or continuous improvement (discussed in Chapter 16).

Increasing customer prosperity is challenging manufacturers to provide bespoke products for individual needs. The advent of the Internet has given rise to consumer demand based on quick and tailored responses. Agile manufacturing offers firms and their supply chain a competitive edge through speed of response in terms of product development and delivery lead times. With the support of IT, cooperation between firms in the supply chain and a mindset that accepts and expects change agility offers a solution and competitive advantage. Agility is the ability to thrive and prosper in an environment of ever increasing and constantly changing customer demands. Demands continue to rise and agility offers firms an approach to meet these growing challenges.

END OF CHAPTER CASE
Pipex px®—agility becoming lean

Pipex px® in 2011 was recognized by the Institute of Mechanical Engineers as the best small to medium-sized enterprise (SME) in the UK for the products it manufactures. With two sites, one in Plymouth and another in Scotland, the company use three types of plastic-based materials to make a variety of different outputs. Thermoplastics are used to make tanks, chambers, vessels, drainage pipes, and manhole covers; advanced composites are used to make lightweight, robust piping that can be used safely under high pressures; and fibre-reinforced plastic (FRP) composites can be made into structures such as gratings, parapets, and even footbridges and platforms for use on the railways and many other applications. Pipex px® serves a wide range of clients in many industry sectors—such as power, water, chemical, industrial, transport, oil and gas, marine, offshore, subsea, architectural, and civil construction.

Nearly everything Pipex px® manufactures is made to suit client specifications. Thus Pipex px® has project managers who oversee the different contracts they have negotiated. Such a contract will typically begin with a site survey in order to carefully measure the features of the site where the product is to be located. This may be challenging. The infrastructure to which Pipex px® products may be connected, such as water and drainage pipes, varies greatly in terms of the dimensions (which may be imperial or metric) and materials from which they are made (such as clay, metal, or plastic). Hence measurement has to be extremely precise in order to ensure a failsafe fit between the new and existing infrastructure. To assist in this, Pipex px® has an extensive Technical Standards library on site so that it can refer to relevant specifications and drawings. Once the site survey is complete, the product is designed using computer-aided design

(CAD) software, which also enables a virtual three-dimensional model of the product to be produced. Before it goes into production the client can see this model in order to confirm it meets their specification.

The CAD software also produces fabrication drawings which are reviewed by the operations manager in order to schedule production and estimate the time it will take to fabricate. Once scheduled, these drawings are passed on to the relevant operative who will begin the process of fabrication. Pipex px® do not extrude plastics themselves but purchase it from suppliers, either in pipe or sheet form. Operatives therefore have two main tasks—to cut the pipe or sheets to the right length and shape, and then thermally weld them together to make the final product. A feature of what Pipex px® does is that for some products that will be finally assembled on site, it pre-assembles these in its factory to ensure that all the components fit together and any snags are removed. They then disassemble the product for transportation to the site. This allows them to offer a 'rapid installation' service, since they have already practised and checked assembly.

As a typical job shop operation, Pipex px® is inherently agile. The very wide customer base it serves, and the range of products it fabricates, demonstrate this. The challenge for an operation of this kind is how to be lean. To address this issue the opera-

tions team have adopted a number of initiatives. The factory moved from an old site to its current site in Plymouth only four years ago, and in doing so the opportunity was taken to review and reorganize the operation so that equipment was located effectively and efficiently in four separate 'factories'—one specializing in gratings and handrails, another in large chambers and vessels, one for pipe fabrication, and one devoted to skills and innovation. Moreover some of the equipment in use is unique to Pipex px®, having been designed by the firm's works director. Such equipment includes a flat sheet bonding press, a large diameter pipe shaver, tank welder, and butting equipment. This gives the firm a technical capability that its competitors do not have, as well as the ability to undertake some processes at a lower cost.

Another lean initiative is the firm's total quality management approach, with everyone taking responsibility for the quality of products. There are three levels of quality inspection:

- No inspection required: where a work order is for the supply of non-fabricated standard products then no inspection is required.

- Inspection level 2: the factory manager or a nominated deputy will carry out all level 2 inspections; they will inspect critical elements of the build to check for quality and compliance against the order. When satisfied they will sign the bottom section of the red production box on the drawing to signify that the completed items have been inspected by the signatory and are ready for shipment.

- Inspection level 1—in addition to a Level 2 inspection: project managers are responsible for the control of all level 1 inspections, where the client specifically specifies testing/inspection requirements in the order and/or orders which are to be fabricated to a specific standard (e.g. BS 4994, PED, etc.). This level of inspection is applied to complex products designed for challenging environments.

Mandatory level 1 test requirements are stipulated on the inspection form and additional inspection criteria are to be planned and detailed by the project

Pipex uses three types of plastic-based materials to make a variety of different outputs such as lightweight, robust piping.

manager on the test certificate form; project managers arrange the necessary checks to fulfil the customer/design requirements. The customer can also choose to inspect products before release from Pipex px®; in these instances the customer (or appointed third party) signed the inspection sheet to confirm acceptance.

All operatives receive extensive training, especially in thermal welding, which is technically challenging, and have a qualification approved by the Thermal Welding Institute. Pipex px® is also a recognized NVQ (National Vocational Qualification) centre and has a number of NVQ assessors working for it who conduct training, not only in technical skills but also in quality inspection techniques. The company has a number of accreditations that reflect its reputation for quality. These include ISO 9001 and ISO 14001, as well as recognition relating to health and safety, LRQA certification OHSAS18001, and being an approved supplier to public sector bodies and utility firms. Many products used in civil engineering projects are required by law to have a record of the manufacture retained for 12 years in the event of a potential failure.

In 2009, the workforce was reorganized so that it worked ten-hour shifts over four days, rather than eight-hour shifts over five days. This enabled the more efficient scheduling of work activities within the longer shift period. Moreover flexible working was introduced so that all employees are now trained to work on any of the four factory floors as work demands. But it also had the benefit that overtime is now worked on Fridays, and productivity levels on this day are much higher than they were when overtime was scheduled for a Saturday or Sunday.

In 2011, the operations team also began a review of inventory and stock holding. In order to reduce this Pipex px® have rationalized their yard from three stores to one, storing all materials according to their properties (sheet/pipe) rather than the ownership of Pipex px® factory division. Pipex px® have reduced the holding levels by moving stock back to the supplier, 'calling off' when required. The form has also improved its supplier relationships by introducing a preferred supplier list, reducing the number from 600 to under 100 preferred suppliers.

Linked to these lean initiatives are environmental, sustainability, and business improvement strategies that also cut costs by up to 15%. Water used for testing is recycled and is collected in a large thermoplastic tank, constructed by Pipex px® themselves, this water is then reused for testing and cleaning of products. Likewise, there has been a major focus on reducing energy costs, especially electricity. Staff have been trained to switch off machines when not in use, and poka-yokes installed to help ensure that this happens. Finally, cutting sheeting to size and shape results in off-cuts and waste. This waste has been minimized in the first instance by re-nesting the CNC (computer numerical control) machine to ensure minimal waste is produced. The small amount that is produced is collected and recycled.

Source: author's primary research

Questions

1. What are Pipex px®'s order winners?
2. How does agility contribute to delivering these OWs?
3. What are the challenges facing a job shop operation in trying to be lean? How has Pipex px® addressed these challenges?

Flexible working was introduced so that all employees are trained to work on any of the four factory floors.

Chapter summary

To consolidate your learning, the key points from this chapter are summarized as follows:

- **Define lean production and its five main principles**

  Lean production is a philosophy which aims to put the customer first in the process and to remove any excess waste so that costs are reduced to a minimum. It is often associated with just-in-time (JIT) operations using a pull planning system which uses signals, or kanbans, to generate orders to start production.

- **Identify the eight wastes of lean production**

  The eight wastes are: transportation, inventory, motion, waiting, overproduction, overprocessing, defects, and employees skills

- **Explain the application of the tools and techniques used in lean production**

  Tools used in lean include single minute exchange of die (SMED), 5S, total productive maintenance (TPM), and kanban. The five S's are derived from five Japanese terms (seiri, seiton, seiso, seiketsu, and shitsuke) and have been 'Westernized' to sort, set, shine, standardize, and stick.

- **Explain total productive maintenance (TPM)**

  TPM focuses on the condition and maintenance of equipment. It is an equipment-focused programme, often linked with total quality management.

- **Review the development of lean thinking and its application to customer processing operations.**

  Lean has been applied in a number of service sectors, such as hotels and hospitals. It has tended to be applied to back-of-house operations. However, it can be argued that the adoption of self-service technologies front of house reflects the lean philosophy.

- **Define agility and explain how it is implemented**

  Agility is the ability to thrive and prosper in an environment of ever increasing and constantly changing customer demands. The tools to implement agility are enabling technologies (EDI, EPOS, RFID), collaboration between suppliers and customers through ECR and supplier clusters, product postponement, and agile new product development through concepts such as soft tools.

- **Outline mass customization**

  Mass customization enables a wide variety of products to be manufactured applying mass production principles. It therefore combines aspects of both lean and agile manufacturing. A key element of mass customization is component modularity, i.e. components that can be mass produced but used in a wide variety of ways when fitted together with other modular components.

Questions

Review questions

1. What are the main components of a lean production operation?

2. How does lean production differ from batch or mass production?

3. How can lean operations be implemented in a service environment?

4. How does total productive maintenance contribute to lean production?

5. What are the main attributes of an agile production operation?

6. How does agile production differ from lean production?

7. What are 'soft technology' and 'soft tools'?

8. How can agile operations be implemented in a service environment?

9. What is mass customization?

10. How is the product life cycle related to these three different manufacturing strategies (lean, agile, and mass customization)?

Discussion questions

1. How can lean supply systems be implemented as part of the global supply chain? Is there a conflict?

2. If more companies are going to adopt lean thinking and JIT approaches to their operations, what will be the implication for SME's?

3. How can firms or organizations increase their flexibility to be able to cope with changes in demand?

4. Discuss the development of lean thinking and its application to customer processing operations.

5. What are the ethical implications of adopting lean and agile production?

6. How can lean and agile production contribute to sustainability?

Further learning guide

Lean thinking and agile production are among the most talked about and researched topics in the field of operations management. As a result there is a huge amount of information available from a wide range of sources. But perhaps the best way to understand this topic is to see it action. YouTube has many hundred of short videos showing lean and agile tools and techniques being applied in factories all over the world. We recommend that you pick two or three industry sectors, such as auto manufacture (Toyota, Ford, Audi, Volkswagen), telecommunications (Sony-Ericsson, HTC, Nokia), and electronic goods (Hitachi, Phillips, Sony), and view a sample of videos about how specific firms are using lean and agile manufacturing to make their products.

For further reading on this subject see Naylor et al. (1999).

References

Aitken, J., Childerhouse, P., Christopher, M., and Towill, D. (2005) Designing and managing multiple pipelines, *Journal of Business Logistics*, 26, 2, 73–96

Bicheno, J. (2004) *The New Lean Toolbox: Towards Fast, Flexible Flow*, (3rd ed.), PICSIE Books: Buckingham

Julien, D.M. and Tjahjono, B. (2009) Lean thinking implementation at a safari park, *Business Process Management Journal*, 15(3), 321–35

Maskell, B. (2001) The age of agile manufacturing, *Supply Chain Management: An International Journal*, 6(1), 5–11

Naylor, J., Naim, M., and Berry, D. (1999) Leagility: Interfacing the lean and agile manufacturing paradigm in the total supply chain, *International Journal of Production Economics*, 62(1/2), 107–18

NHS *Lean thinking* [online] www.institute.nhs.uk/quality_and_value/lean_thinking/lean_thinking.html

Pettersen, J. (2009) Defining lean production: some conceptual and practical issues, *The TQM Journal*, 21(2), 127–42

Powell, A.E., Rushmer, R.K., and Davies, H.T.O. (2009) *A systematic narrative review of quality improvement models in health care*, NHS Scotland: Edinburgh

Rother, M. and Shook, J. (1998) *Learning To See: Value Stream Mapping to Add Value and Eliminate Muda*, The Lean Enterprise Institute: Brookline, MA

Womack, J., Jones, D., and Roos, D. (1990) *The Machine That Changed the World*, Rawson Associates: New York

Womack, J. and Jones, D. (1996) *Lean Thinking*, Simon & Schuster Inc.: New York

rig for every part. For instance, the Dyson website identifies that a tumble test shakes and rattles components in a steel box for days, another rig slams cleaner heads into a steel table leg at 30 kilometres/hour, and at another a robot arm pushes machines back and forth for the equivalent of 21 years. During development a Dyson vacuum will be dropped onto a hard floor 5318 times and run 1357 kilometres on a turntable rig. Performance is tested in temperatures as low as −20°C in an environmental chamber. Even the noise of the vacuum cleaner is tested in the laboratory's semi-anechoic chamber. The chamber can also measure sounds as quiet as a whisper up to 130 decibels, the equivalent of a jet engine.

Also in Wiltshire is the Dyson microbiology lab, set up in 2001. It has the sort of equipment usually associated with hospital laboratories. Scientists and microbiologists use the lab to research ways of eliminating allergens to make the home cleaner and safer for allergy sufferers. They also research the dust mite,

which Dyson regards as 'enemy number one'. Dyson is the only vacuum cleaner manufacturer with its own microbiology laboratory. And if all this lab-based testing is not enough, employees routinely take products under development home with them, so that they and their families can test them under 'real-life' conditions.

The R&D facility is organized so that engineers are grouped together in one space. Access is only possible if you have the right pass and your thumb print is recognized. Even then, certain areas are out of bounds. Only Dyson himself has totally unrestricted access. Within the facility there are eight concept areas and 20 specialist labs close by.

Sources: developed from www.dyson.co.uk

Questions

1. What makes Dyson an innovative company?
2. Why does Dyson employ an eclectic range of people in its R&D facility?

Introduction

Firms, and indeed whole industry sectors, need to innovate and improve just to survive. History is very clear on this point—those enterprises which do survive, do so because they are capable of regular and focused change. Innovation is also strongly associated with growth. This is because it leads to competitive advantage in two ways. First, a continuously improving organization gets better at what it does all the time. And secondly, an innovative organization finds new and better ways of doing things. Hence this chapter is concerned with how innovation and continuous improvement can be used as a strategy for beating the competition.

In this chapter we explore the difference between so-called radical innovation and **continuous improvement** (CI) and see how these can be used strategically to achieve competitive advantage. We saw in Chapter 12, which dealt with new product development, that innovation was anything new that a firm did. This means that innovation might be relatively minor, such as a line extension (for instance, developing a new flavour of crisps), or a major, new invention (such as Dyson's bagless vacuum cleaner). This was illustrated in Figure 12.2 (see page 311). Another way of thinking about this is to think in terms of innovation being incremental or radical. Incremental innovation takes place on a day-to-day basis and involves many tiny changes to processes and slight adaptations to products or services over an extended period of time. Generally the CI strategy works on this basis. Radical innovation, on the other, is a major change, typically based

Continuous improvement the systematic improvement of processes and outputs through incremental innovation

on invention, which significantly changes what the firm produces, and may well change the way a whole sector of industry operates, as discussed on page 309.

An alternative way of thinking about the difference between these two types of innovation is to think in terms of order winners (OWs). Incremental innovation tends to be focused on improving the performance of the firm in delivering existing OWs—improving delivery speed, adding a new feature to a product, shaving a few pence off the unit production cost, or whatever. Radical innovation, however, tends to be concerned with creating an entirely new or significantly improved 'bundle' of order winners that differentiates the product or service from anyone else. For instance, the low-cost airline business model is very different to that of traditional carriers, thus creating significantly different prices to these airlines.

We have looked at the radical innovation process in Chapter 12. In this chapter, we take a more strategic view, by focusing on incremental innovation, or CI. We consider the underlying philosophy and principles of CI, before considering the tools organizations use to support this strategy. We also consider performance measurement because in order to improve, an organization needs to measure this improvement carefully. We conclude by looking at what is termed the 'learning organization' and consider the implications of a new strategy based around so-called open innovation.

Continuous improvement

The specific concept of CI originated in the USA with a government initiative called 'Training Within Industry', established during World War II. Shortly afterwards, the CI concept was introduced to Japan by several experts, notably Deming, Juran, and Gilbreth. As a result, CI was refined and further developed by Japanese companies, and came to be known as 'kaizen'. Kaizen means CI involving everyone—managers and workers alike (Imai 1986). Then when Japanese firms, especially Toyota and Toshiba, began to impact on the global economy, European and American manufacturers started to look again at this whole concept.

Kaizen the Japanese philosophy of achieving process improvement through incremental change

There is some confusion as to whether CI is a strategy in its own right or part of another strategy. Kaizen has been linked with the adoption of total productive maintenance, total quality control (TQC), total quality management (TQM), Six Sigma, and lean production (which are discussed in Chapters 9 and 15). This is because kaizen is an improvement concept which is very much concerned with quality, and especially standards of performance. In this chapter, we shall consider CI as a distinct strategy, by focusing on principles and practices not discussed elsewhere in this text.

Principles of continuous improvement

Lowson (2002: 85) has suggested 'ten guiding principles' of CI. These are:

1. Process-driven across all organizational functions
2. Total employee involvement
3. Good labour–management relations
4. Effective leadership and cross communication
5. Adaptability to changing environment

6. Visibility and control of all processes

7. Reducing waste (discussed in Chapter 15)

8. Customer orientation

9. Standardization

10. Quality awareness and quality control (discussed in Chapter 9).

Many of these features are discussed in more detail later in this chapter.

Rationale for and impact of continuous improvement

A number of different reasons have been put forward for adopting this strategy. External drivers may include significant growth in level of competitor performance, either in terms of their quality level or their cost performance, or both. Whereas internal drivers may be that the rate of employee turnover has increased or customer satisfaction with a service or product is declining.

Bessant (2003) has shown that CI in UK firms leads to improvement in various areas of their operations, such as increasing flexibility, increasing plant availability, and cost reduction. A survey conducted by Hyland et al. (2007) asking 89 Australian organizations in which CI activities contributed to the different areas of business performance, showed that CI was important to help improve organization cooperation and communication, increase employees' skills and competencies, and improve customer relations. Another study in Jordanian manufacturing conducted by Al-Khawaldeh and Sloan (2007) confirmed that CI had positive impacts for the organization such as cost reduction, higher customer satisfaction, better customer relations, and increased productivity along with improved safety and working conditions. Furthermore, there may be indirect benefits of CI implementation such as improved image, enhanced customer loyalty, and the ability to attract new customers. In summary, CI has positive impacts on the organization, both directly and indirectly, as well as internally and externally.

OPERATIONS INSIGHT 16.1
Naval Command Headquarters— developing continuous improvement

Naval Command Headquarters had gone through three major change programmes between 2002 and 2008. These were driven by government policy and the need to save money by reducing manpower, as well as rationalizing operations. Much of this change had involved the use of external consultants, which had not always proved satisfactory, as work in the armed services has some unique characteristics not found in other organizations, as well as a well-defined military organizational culture. In order to get buy-in from naval personnel, it was therefore decided to develop change management expertise within the organization. A special team (the CI team) was established to implement the new approach with an initial remit for three years. Due to the success of the initiative, this has subsequently been fully integrated into the organization as a full-time, permanent team.

Naval Command Headquarters had seven clearly identifiable divisions (value streams), many of which are similar to functions in non-military organizations, such as operations, logistics, human resources, and finance. These were used as the building blocks for implementing the new system and value stream leaders were nominated at a senior level for each division. Each division had a number of business units (typically between ten and 20 people) and the organization had nearly 80 business units in total.

To get the CI process started, a regular business review was conducted by a fully trained facilitator from the CI team. This was based around each business unit scoring itself against ten set questions across levels one to five. This 'score' would act as a benchmark for future reviews and interventions. The ten questions were formed around three core principles of 'purpose, process, and people'. It was felt that any business unit must have clarity of purpose first before deciding what processes to put in place and then a suitable manpower and organizational structure to run the processes. Gaining clarity of purpose proved more difficult than at first envisaged and it sometimes took considerable time and effort. Each event produced a simple action grid with a number of items for the team to work on to improve their performance. Initially this activity was planned every six months but experience showed that one a year was more realistic. Occasionally larger issues would emerge and further events, facilitated by the CI team, would be needed to tackle these. Likewise, the notion of 'scoring' performance was replaced because this led to simply trying to improve scores, rather than actual performance.

These events were renamed continuous improvement reviews (CIRs) and was emphasis placed on the actions required to improve rather than scores.

Over two years' experience of this system has seen an improvement in the team's awareness of their purpose and much greater levels of engagement in the CI process. The success of the programme is demonstrated by team leaders regularly asking the CI experts for help. The CI team is fully occupied without the need to promote itself within the organization.

Source: www.royalnavy.mod.uk and author's own research

Questions

1. What are the key features of the Naval Command Headquarters approach to CI?
2. What are the issues that arise with regard to implementing a CI programme?

Continuous improvement implementation and tools

The first stage of implementing CI is to establish a standard operating procedure (SOP). SOPs are policies, rules, directives, and procedures for all major operations. This often requires flowcharting of each process in order to identify each step in the process (as discussed in Chapter 10). Once the process and the expected level of output is clear, it is then necessary to ensure employees have the appropriate training to achieve the desired standard.

Another issue is communication. Imai (1986) found that one of the problems for managers attempting to engage employees with an improvement programme was communication, partly because managers were not effective communicators, but also because they use a different terminology to the shop floor workers. He suggested also that leadership needs to be based on personal experience and conviction, not just on authority, rank, or age.

As well as leadership, human resource practices (also discussed in Chapter 11) can be used to reinforce the CI strategy. For instance, Nissan Cars has used the annual appraisal system to gain cooperation from employees. The company gives its employees opportunities to share and discuss their improvement objectives for the coming year.

The next stage in implementing CI is to work on improving processes and performance. This requires employees not just to be trained in the work they are doing, but in the skills and expertise need to improve processes and outcomes. Kaizen is synonymous with problem-solving in the workplace, using techniques such as Pareto analysis, Ishikawa analysis, and failure mode and effect analysis (FMEA) (also discussed in Chapter 10). As well as problem-solving skills, Kaizen also includes the concept of checklists. The 3M checklist is made up of muda (waste), muri (strain), and mura (discrepancy); whilst the 4M checklist is man (operator), machine (facilities), material, and method (to which measurement is sometimes added as a fifth 'M').

In most organizations, processes and the problems that arise from them are not the sole responsibility of a single person, it involves a team of workers. So teamwork is another key factor for kaizen. Many attempts have been made to identify the characteristics of an effective team. The consensus of opinion identifies the following:

- Members depend on one another to achieve the organization's formal goals.
- Members trust each other.
- Members have common objectives.
- Members make decisions by consensus.
- Members are strongly committed to the group.
- Members solve conflict by working through the problem.
- Communication is a key factor by which group feelings can be expressed freely.
- Members will be open with one another and will listen to one another.

It is also possible to identify the signals which indicate poor team work:

- Low productivity.
- A decrease in customer satisfaction levels.
- Hostility and conflict among team members.
- An increase in the number of requests for transfers.
- Poor cooperation between management and staff.
- High levels of absenteeism, poor timekeeping or labour turnover.
- Blaming others for poor performance.

Involving employees in problem-solving and process improvement pushes responsibility down through the organization. This is consistent with the concept of empowerment (defined and discussed in Chapter 11). This gives employees the freedom to make decision and to take action without management's approval. It can be defined as the process of enabling or authorizing an individual to think, behave, take action, and control work and decision-making in autonomous ways. But it is only really effective if employees genuinely feel empowered—so-called 'psychological empowerment'. This is the state of feeling able to take control of one's own destiny. Research into this concept (Spreizer 1995) has identified four key elements of this. The first is 'meaning', that is to say how the work role fits with the employee's own values and belief. The second is 'competence', how well the employee believes they can do the work. The third is 'self determination', the extent to which employees believe they have control over their own work. And finally 'impact', which is the degree to which employees believe they can influence work outcomes.

Another form of employee involvement is the 'the employee suggestion system' (ESS). Imai (1986: 15) has given a definition of suggestion systems as 'an integral part of the established management system, and number of workers' suggestions is regarded as an important criterion in reviewing the performance of these workers' supervisor'. The concept of a suggestion scheme predates CI and was first implemented in the USA by Eastman Kodak Co. in 1898. It can now take a number of forms. An American-style suggestion system will focus on economic benefits from ideas by providing financial incentives as the rewards for employees. Meanwhile, the Japanese style is more likely to focus on the morale-boosting benefits of positive employee participation. In some organizations teamwork, empowerment, and the ESS are linked. Employees put the ideas or suggestions into a box and then review these themselves every month. If necessary they can vote for the ideas or suggestions which should be implemented first. The remaining suggestions can be kept for the next team meeting. It is argued that this approach encourages employees to participate more fully in the scheme.

However, employee suggestions schemes are not always successfully implemented. Fairbank and Williams (2001) identified examples of failure and identified the reasons for this. They were the lack of motivation to participate in the systems, slow processing time or delayed response to suggestions, unattractive or unattainable rewards and recognitions, and a misunderstanding of the scheme's purpose. Another study by Arthur and Smith (2001) found an increase and decline of employees' participation in ESS over time. This indicates that keeping a high level of employee involvement in a suggestion scheme may be challenging. Therefore organizations may have to implement a scheme for a specific amount of time, such as once or twice a year, to gain some creative ideas from employees. Or the scheme might be set as a traditional campaign that happens every year to gain attention from employees.

RESEARCH INSIGHT 16.1

Rapp, C. and Eklund, J. (2002) Sustainable development of improvement activities – the long-term operation of a suggestion scheme in a Swedish company, *Total Quality Management & Business Excellence*, 13(7), 945–69

Many organizations are faced with problems associated with both the implementation and long-term maintenance of their CI programmes. The purpose of this article by Rapp and Eklund is to identify factors important for the sustained use of suggestion schemes. They use a case study of a Swedish firm that has had a suggestion scheme for nine years to explore how it has developed and changed over this period of time. They found there were three periods in the development of the suggestion scheme, which they call Initiation, Decline, and New Interest. They go on to identify key factors which seem to influence the sustainability of the suggestion scheme, which include someone championing the scheme, its simplicity and flexibility, the resources and commitment needed from managers and shop-floor workers, and the speed of feedback to employees submitting suggestions.

Linpac Packaging, which is based in St Helens, Lancashire, produces plastic packaging for a variety of different sectors, including retail, fruit and produce growers, bakeries, and sandwich makers. It has a product range of more than 10,000 items, including manufacturing trays, films, and disposable tableware. Its customers include supermarket chains such as Aldi, Carrefour, and Morrisons, as well as a range of food manufacturers.

In November 2009, Linpac's performance was recognized by winning *The Manufacturer*'s Operations & Maintenance Award 2009. This gave recognition to a key aspect of the business which had greatly added to the success of the firm, namely CI. Linpac based this on the shop floor, where workers were empowered to identify areas for improvement, run their own action teams, and put right any snags that they identify. The role of management was to create a 'can do' environment throughout the organization. As a result, employee morale and motivation had increased which in turn had led to a drop in absence rates.

The culture of Linpac is based around the philosophy 'Don't work harder; work smarter'. One aspect of this is to ensure that the right materials are used every time—so that in 2009 the plant made a reduction of 50% in their non-right first time processes. This improvement was helped by a shift towards automating processes. Not only has this improved productivity, it has also meant upskilling the workforce. With more sophisticated manufacturing processes, they spend less time engaged in repetitive tasks and much more time on CI activities such as problem identification and problem resolution. In 2009, the company implemented a real-time data collection system. This means that performance data is input at the end of each production line, so that action teams can analyse those aspects of operation which are driving improvements across the business. Large monitors are placed throughout the shop floor, enabling staff to keep up to date with production successes,

In addition the company has adopted total productive maintenance (TPM), which they term their Asset Care programme. On each shift there is an Asset Care Champion—a machine operative who has undergone workshops and related training to become highly skilled in their understanding of asset care. By maintaining the plant and equipment, unplanned downtime was reduced and output volume increased, so that in 2008 OEE improved by 16%. It was believed that through increasing availability, reducing unplanned downtime, and reducing manufacturing waste, a target of 15% further improvement was possible.

Another feature of CI is the effect it has had on health and safety at work. There was a 60% reduction in accidents in the company and it is planning to achieve zero injuries in the future. However minor the injury, every incident is put through a seven-step problem-solving exercise, in order to find a solution which will ensure that the accident will not reoccur.

Sources: www.linpac.com and 'Packing a Punch', The Manufacturer, *March 2010*

Questions

1. In what ways has the work of employees changed over the last few years?
2. How does TPM contribute to CI? (See also Chapter 15.)

Often the CI will also include employee incentives designed to encourage participation in CI and to encourage an exceptional performance. Some firms have incentive schemes to reward employees who have achieved an effective performance, especially when they discover the best solutions of problem-solving. An alternative to financially rewarding employees is some sort of recognition scheme. These may reward employees by highlighting their contribution through the employee notice board, organizations' internal media (magazine and newsletter), competitions, and awards. This can be implemented at different levels such as individual rewards, team level, and work units.

Barriers to implementing continuous improvement

A number of reasons have been identified preventing the successful adoption of CI. These included:

- Resistance to change.
- The lack of trust by the employees to the management motives.
- The lack of clear purpose and anticipation.
- The lack of participative skills due to limited experiences and understandings.
- The lack of ongoing commitment from the top management.

It has also been claimed that it is rather difficult to motivate employees to have a sense of involvement and be willing to work by using their competence to implement innovation within the organization, as each of them has different reasons for working. Another problem is that those people who want to engage with innovation may lack the formal skills and experience needed or are afraid to propose the ideas as it may look silly or too simple.

RESEARCH INSIGHT 16.2

Bessant, J. and Caffyn, S. (1997) High-involvement innovation through continuous improvement, *International Journal of Technology Management*, 14(1), 7–28

This article discusses continuous improvement through mobilizing a high level of involvement of the workforce in sustained incremental problem-solving. As explained in the Abstract, it identifies that:

although the potential benefits of such high involvement are considerable, implementing programmes of this kind is not easy. This paper reports on a five year research programme exploring implementation issues in CI and presents a framework model for the development of CI which draws upon extensive case study work. In particular, it identifies a series of levels of CI performance and the blocks and enablers associated with them.

Performance measurement

In the 1990s, many organizations started to redesign performance measurement to align it with the organization's strategy and it became an important factor in the achievement of corporate goals. There are various factors that can be used to measure success or failure of CI implementation, such as an increase in customers, higher levels of customer satisfaction, reduction in waste, and an increase in annual turnover. But two main tools are used—the balanced score card and benchmarking.

The balanced scorecard was developed by Robert Kaplan and David Norton (1992). It is a methodology that translates the objectives of the organization into measures, goals, and initiatives in four different areas, namely financial, customer, internal business process, and learning and growth. For instance, Whitbread used this approach and measured six items across all its brands—revenue, profit, customer satisfaction, health and safety, and employee satisfaction—and had one other item specific to each of its brands, such as occupancy in its hotel chains and seat turnover in its restaurants. Kaplan and Norton (1992) argue that this approach to performance measurement can be used to clarify and update the business strategy, link the objectives of the organization to annual budgets, facilitate and support organizational change, and increase the understanding of the company vision and mission statements across the organization.

Benchmarking can be defined as a systematic way of judging the way your business performs against a reference point, exploring where and why your operation does not work as well as it could and implementing ways of closing the gap. It was discussed earlier in Chapter 9 (see page 238). However, particularly in the UK manufacturing sector, there has been an emphasis on benchmarking as external comparison, either within the same industry or indeed outside the industry, wherever CI best practice can be found. This has partly been prompted by the UK government who has encouraged the idea of 'world-class manufacturing' and financially-supported programmes designed to transform different sectors of industry through best practice initiatives.

OPERATIONS INSIGHT 16.3
The NatWest Customer Charter—setting improvement benchmarks

In 2010, NatWest launched a marketing initiative based a round a Customer Charter. What makes it unusual is that this makes publicly available performance improvement targets that are underpinned by a CI strategy. It clearly shows that this company believes that its success and competitive advantage lie in its operations capability to deliver good products and service to its customers. The bank not only made the commitments in the Charter, but also promised to report on its delivery of these targets every six months. The first such report appeared in February 2011. The results of its strategy are summarized in Table 16.1.

Questions

1. Which of the goals listed in Table 16.1 have been achieved? Why do you think this is?
2. Which of the goals listed in Table 16.1 would most benefit from a CI strategy? Why?

TABLE 16.1 NatWest progress report on selected operational goals

Goal	Performance
We will keep over 800 of our branches open on Saturdays	We have opened at least 846 of our busiest branches every Saturday
This year we will open for early mornings and late evenings in an initial 200 branches	We have extended the opening hours in 206 of our busiest branches, used regularly by 2.8 million of our customers. On average these branches are open 46 hours per week
A queue measurement tool will be rolled out to our 300 busiest branches	In November we measured queue times in our 300 busiest branches. 75% of customers were served within 5 minutes and the average waiting time was 4 minutes. [But] . . . there are times and places where customers have waited longer and we have much more to work on. We are testing a new tool to measure queues. We will monitor the results of this and assess how effective it is at both measuring queues and more importantly helping us to minimize them. We will then decide whether to use this system in our busiest branches or find a different solution
9 out of 10 customers will rate us friendly and helpful	8 out of 10 customers rated us friendly and helpful during 2010 . . . we know we have more work to do
All of our branch literature will be simplified and rewritten in line with your feedback	Using customer feedback and in association with the Plain English Campaign, we have re-written the literature in our banking halls. Some of this updated literature was available in branches from December, but the remaining revised banking hall literature will not be available until the end of February 2011
We will roll out a new Customer Review Programme to make it easier for you to choose the right product	We have rolled out our new Customer Review Programmes across our branch network to enable our staff to help customers choose the right products for them. 6300 of our staff have been trained to use these programmes
We will send Personal Annual Statements to over 1 million current account customers	We issued more than 1 million Personal Annual Statements in 2010. These statements give customers an overview of their account activity for the previous year on banking products they hold with us such as Current Accounts, Savings Accounts and Loans
We will ensure our telephone banking centre is available to help you 100% of the time, always giving you the option to speak to a real person based in the UK	All our telephone banking centres remain in the UK with staff on hand to help 24 hours a day, 7 days a week
We will answer 90% of calls in less than a minute	We answered 91.4% of your calls in less than a minute
We'll despatch all lost and stolen replacement debit cards the next working day	We sent all replacement debit cards within 24 hours to customers who had lost or had their debit cards stolen, unless they had also requested a new PIN
We will have a dedicated support team in place to look for signs that customers are falling into financial difficulty	We have a dedicated team of 85 full-time staff who actively monitor and help customers who are heading into financial difficulty. Since we established this team, we have spoken to 122,485 customers
All of our employees will be offered a day off for local volunteering with an aim of providing more than 22,000 days each year to community volunteering	We offered all of our UK Retail employees the opportunity to take a day of paid leave to volunteer in their local communities when we launched the Charter. During 2010, one-third of our employees took up the offer and gave 7547 days of volunteering to their local communities. This excludes the work we did with Sport Relief which was the equivalent of 1674 additional days
We will aim for 75% of our customers to be satisfied with the way their complaint has been handled	57% of our customers were satisfied with the way their complaint was handled. We have conducted an internal review of our complaint handling process and identified a number of issues which we are committed to putting right
We will launch a new Customer Listening Programme to ensure our customers can share their needs and frustrations at first hand with our staff, including executives	We have launched a new Customer Listening Programme where invited customers share their experience of banking with head office staff and executives. This has provided excellent insight about improvements to our products and processes, several of which are underway

Source: www.natwest.com (a second set of results were published in August 2011 and can be found on the Natwest website)

The learning organization

The term 'learning organization' is one that consultants and organizations have used a great deal over the last 20 years. It is characterized by the idea that both individual and collective learning are key to the long-term survival of the modern organization. But exactly what it means is difficult to establish. Some authors argue that it actually does not exist, but is an ideal towards which organizations should seek to move. Moreover academics have tended to research 'organizational learning'—the processes of learning within an organization, whilst consultants have promoted the concept of the 'learning organization'—a template of what an organization should be like in terms of policies and procedures for making learning happen.

The emergence of the idea of the 'learning organization' is closely linked to the work of Donald Schön (1973). He developed a framework that linked living in a context of increasing change with the need for learning. He suggested that society and all of its institutions are in continuous processes of transformation, so we must all learn to understand, guide, influence, and manage these transformations. To do this, individuals and organizations need to become adept at learning. Another important contributor to this debate was made by Peter Senge (1990) who explored 'the art and practice of the learning organization' in his book *The Fifth Discipline*. He suggested five disciplines, namely personal mastery, mental models, shared vision, team learning, and systems thinking.

Since then there has been an ongoing debate as to the nature of such an organization. There is no agreement about whether it is initiated and developed by senior management, or if it is a more 'bottom-up' or democratic development. There is also a difference between those who focus on the technical aspect of the learning organization, as opposed to the social aspects. The technical approach seeks to measure specific aspects of performance such as the 'learning curve', which can be thought of as the rate at which production cost falls as the volume of production increases. In other words, the more you make the cheaper it becomes, because you have learned how to do it better. On the other hand, the social view of the learning organization investigates interactions and processes. Kerka (1995) suggests that the following characteristics appear in some form in the more popular definitions of the learning organization:

- Provide continuous learning opportunities.
- Use learning to reach their goals.
- Link individual performance with organizational performance.
- Foster inquiry and dialogue, making it safe for people to share openly and take risks.
- Embrace creative tension as a source of energy and renewal.
- Are continuously aware of and interact with their environment.

However, there are some issues with the learning organization concept. Most of these relate to whether or not learning is truly embedded in the organization itself, or whether it is only a few individuals, mainly in managerial positions, that lead and control change or improvement. Finger and Brand (1999) found that simply focusing on the learning organization concept did not achieve performance improvement or organizational transformation. This was because it does not adequately take into account other aspects of an organization, such as hierarchical structures and the organization of work. Second, whilst individual and some collective learning might take place, this is not automatically linked to the organization's strategic goals. And finally, the concept is somewhat vague. Because of this it may help facilitate change, but will of itself not create change.

In this article, Garvin begins by clarifying the meaning, management, and measurement of a learning organization. He then goes on to discuss the five 'building blocks' of this concept. These are:

- Systematic problem solving.

- Experimentation with new approaches.

- Learning from the organization's experience and past history.

- Learning from the experiences and best practices of others.

- Transferring knowledge quickly and efficiently throughout the organization.

The article then explores in some detail the approaches and tools an organization might use to implement these.

Open innovation

A relatively recent development has been the emergence of so-called '**open innovation**'. This is the idea that innovation should not be confined to an R&D department, or even the whole organization, but be implemented across organizations. In Chapter 12, we identified the different potential stages in the new product or new service development process. Two of these stages were 'ideation', the creation of new ideas, and 'realization', the actual design and testing of the product or service. It is argued that both ideation and realization depend on information, and that getting the right kind of information is challenging within one single organization. So open innovation has been developed in order to involve unknown others in the innovation process through formal and informal relationships.

One particular example of open innovation is so-called '**crowdsourcing**'. This is when an organization takes a function that it used to do itself and outsources it to an undefined network of external stakeholders through an open call to participate in this activity. This basic concept has also been given other names, such as wikinomics, and interactive value creation.

As a result of this, new organizations have been created to enable open innovation to occur. These are often based on the Internet. For instance, Innocentive.com is a web-based community of scientists who are invited to respond to R&D challenges posted on the website by companies seeking solutions to production or development problems. Other similar websites include NineSigma and Yet2.

Another mechanism for open innovation is to set up 'idea contests'. For instance, Volkswagen set up a contest called 'App my Ride', designed to solicit ideas as to what kind of apps could be developed to be used in conjunction with their motor cars. This leads into the concept of 'co-creation' whereby consumers not only provide ideas but are also provided with the means to develop their own product. In one example of this, the

Open innovation
the use of markets to obtain and exploit new ways of doing things within an organization

Crowdsourcing
outsourcing tasks to a large group of undefined people, usually through an open invitation online

Turkish bank GrantiBank made it possible for customers to select alternatives from ten different features of a credit card. As a consequence of this it was possible to design 10,000 variants of how this credit card would operate, in terms of fees, interest rates, bonuses, and discounts. Clearly there is a link here with the operations strategy of 'mass customization'.

Conclusions

In this chapter we have looked at ways that organizations can change for the better, by focusing their attention on continually improving their processes. Best practice adopters of CI have adopted a CI philosophy, called 'kaizen' in Japan, have top management commitment, and a workforce empowered and trained in CI tools and techniques. Such firms include Honda, Toshiba, and Sony. This has led to organizations also adopting approaches to performance measurement, often referred to as the balanced scorecard, which are more sophisticated than simple financial targets or sales figures. One outcome of CI is that companies may truly become what is known as 'learning organizations'. As well as developing themselves internally, organizations are also beginning to exploit the opportunity the worldwide web provides for open sourcing innovation. Through placing open calls for ideas or for tasks to be done, firms access the capabilities of people outside the organization that support them to be innovative.

END OF CHAPTER CASE
Brompton Bicycle—radical and incremental innovation

Andrew Ritchie set up Brompton Bicycle from his bedroom overlooking the Brompton Oratory in South Kensington in 1976. He had decided that with his background in engineering he could design a better folding bike than ones currently on the market. His first model, Prototype 1, had 18-inch (46-centimetre) wheels and the handlebars folded down on either side, but the rear wheel folded under the bike just like every Brompton produced since. With the development of Prototype 3, which featured 16-inch (41-centimetre) wheels and a simpler, lighter folding mechanism, the Brompton folded neatly and conveniently into a suitcase-size package. This was safe and clean to handle, as the chain and sprockets were on the inside of the package, shielded between the wheels. This design also brought several incidental advantages. With the rear of the frame free to pivot, adding a rubber block to work against the main frame provided suspension at the rear. This is an advantage on a small-wheeled bike, as it reduces shock loads into the frame and

gives the feel of a 'real bike'. Another advantage of the rear pivot was the 1.02-metre wheelbase, which compared favourably with much larger machines and ensured a decent ride and good handling. The only (minor) disadvantage of the design was the need for a chain tensioner to keep the chain taut when both folded and unfolded.

The P6R model. Each Brompton consists of some 1200 parts.

However, these prototypes were fairly crude. The brazed steel frames and other components were quite heavy (the first machines weighed almost 15 kilograms), and specialized plastic components were, of necessity, made by hand. Ritchie's original plan was to license production of his deign to an existing manufacturer. But no one was interested in doing this. The alternative was to start manufacturing the bikes himself, but again he was unable to interest any venture capitalist. So five years after starting, Brompton Bicycle only began production when 30 of Ritchie's friends agreed to buy a bicycle in advance. Although the budget was ridiculously low, some rudimentary tooling was eventually in place and the bikes duly appeared in 1981 from rented premises in the offices of an engineering design company near Kew Gardens. Word-of-mouth marketing allowed Ritchie to continue production until February 1983. By this time 500 bicycles had been hand-made and sold for £200 each, but further investment was needed.

Julian Vereker, an entrepreneur, was an enthusiastic customer and when he heard that production could cease forever, he joined the company in 1985 and provided it with the necessary investment. Before manufacture of the new Brompton (unofficially called the Mark 2) began, it was completely re-engineered, a process that absorbed a considerable amount of time and money. Weight reduction was a priority in these early days. A bike of 14.1 kilograms was too heavy for some people. So lighter components were introduced and the Brompton gradually became leaner. A key element in the weight-reduction strategy was the material used in the wheels: switching from steel to aluminium rims brought considerable savings, and also improved wet-weather braking. Weight was cut to about 11.3 kilograms.

In April 1987, at the Cyclex exhibition, the Brompton won the Best Product award against an international field. This was a turning point. Dealers had been wary of stocking and selling folding bikes because they had a reputation for being unreliable and unsafe. But Brompton seemed to have produced a much more reliable product, so some dealers placed orders. To meet these, in November 1987 the company moved to premises in Brentford, West London and began production, gradually increasing output to 60 bikes a month. At this stage, further design improvements were made. Customers were given the choice of three or five-speed gears, and the rear rack was replaced by a lighter bolt-on design, making it optional. A quick-release carrier block was also developed for the front of the bike, as well as a folding left-hand pedal. Although this added to the cost, this brought the total width of the machine down to just 10 inches (25 centimetres). For taller owners, an extended seat pillar was introduced.

By late 1988, production had increased to 90 per month, and bikes were being retailed through a network of 40 UK dealers with prices starting at a reasonable £235. Overseas sales were making an impact too, with small numbers of machines finding their way to Germany, Holland, Austria, France, and Belgium. This led to a backlog of orders that proved impossible to satisfy and inevitably prices rose, the basic model retailing for no less than £336 by early 1990, against competitors as cheap as £200. Most road testers adored the Brompton and the accolades continued to convince more than enough potential customers that it was worth paying extra for a superior product.

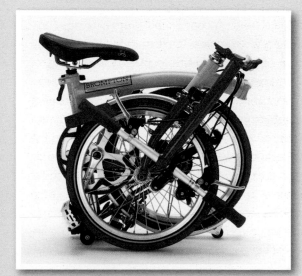

The SL2 model folded. The chain and sprockets on the inside thereby shielded between the wheels.

The early 1990s were years of steady expansion for Brompton, as production picked up and the bikes were steadily improved. Having first expanded into a neighbouring railway arch, the company moved into significantly larger premises in Chiswick Park in late 1993. With room to expand and several new staff, production gradually increased, reaching 100 machines a week within a year. Soon the waiting list had been absorbed, and the factory was in a position to actively generate new business, which was not long in coming.

In April 1995 the company won the Queen's Award for Export in recognition of increased sales in Germany, Holland, Scandinavia, and elsewhere. In late 1996, the Brompton was declared Bike of the Year by the German ADFC (German Cyclists' Federation) and sales exploded. In March 2000, the Brompton 'Mark 3' was launched. It featured improvements in areas criticized on the Mark 2, notably the brakes, now upgraded to dual-pivot callipers. Brompton was also finally in a position to make its own tyres, and Ritchie decided to put tread and a dynamo contact strip on the fastest tyre then available to the 16-inch (41-centimetre) wheel market: the Primo, which was effectively a racing tyre. Together with numerous lighter (yet stronger) components, the new tyres and brakes transformed the bike.

Some re-engineering and re-tooling in 2003 allowed the company to extend the wheel-base by a few centimetres, further increasing the stability of the ride without compromising the size of the folded package, but this otherwise significant improvement was overshadowed by the raft of developments unveiled in early 2005, when Brompton announced the biggest upgrade in its eventful history, described by Ritchie as 'a technical and marketing advance far greater than anything we've done since the Brompton was first introduced 17 years ago'. The new options created new terminology across the range. The classic handlebar design was given a name (the M Type) to distinguish it from two new handlebar options—a low, straight bar (S Type) and a square design offering high and low riding positions (P Type). The old 'L'

(lightweight) and 'T' (touring) labels would henceforth appear at the end of the model name, and the 'T' was replaced by the letter 'R' (rear rack). Hence, old models like the T6 became an M6R and the L3 became an M3L. With the range of gear options extended to include a single speed and a two-speed (using a new gear-free Brompton rear hub, with or without the derailleur), the model range was extensive.

The introduction of new lightweight materials, principally titanium frame parts, added to the complexity but was perhaps the most significant development of all. Having tried the UK and Europe, cost considerations ultimately ensured that the titanium frame parts would be sourced from China and Russia, with rigorous controls ensuring that Brompton's trademark quality was maintained. The lightweight options (denoted by the suffix X) inevitably added to the cost but ensured that bikes like the S2L-X (weighing 9.65 kilograms) were among the lightest folding bikes on the market; the single-speed, mudguardless S1E-X weighed in at just under 9 kilograms.

The last five years have seen further changes to the Brompton range, but much of the process of improving the Brompton takes place in a never-ending process of small incremental steps. All kinds of minor changes occur in relation to the manufacturing process itself. For instance, the tubes and hinge parts that make up the frame of the bike need to be smooth to allow for brazing (i.e. fixing together) and subsequently for painting. Brompton have been experimenting for years with the use of a 'rumbler', which is a machine like a washing machine, in order to automate this process (which is otherwise done by hand—using files). They have recently found that they can achieve the level of finish that is required by adding the right concentrate of citric acid. Likewise, bicycles used to be hand-built by a single worker each with their own work station. They are now assembled by a production team that moves the bike from one station to another to fit the wheels, brakes, and other features of the bike.

The Brompton consists of some 1200 parts, over three-quarters of which are unique to their bicycles (exceptions include the chain and various screws, washers, and other sundry fixtures). As most parts have had to be designed in-house to meet their particular needs, they have also had to design and build the machines, tools, and fixtures needed to manufacture them, including over 500 purpose-made press tools, moulds, braze jigs, and assembly fixtures. They are continually refining their manufacturing methods, raising productivity, and every year sees a large investment in new machinery and equipment. In addition, 50% of management resource is dedicated to design and development. In 2011 they planned to manufacture 30,400 bicycles, an output of around 110 per working day. Potentially, each one of these bicycles could be unique. As well as all the optional features, it is now possible to order a bike in one of 16 different colours. This choice of colour and options now means that there are theoretically over two million variants of the bicycle.

Sources: author's primary research and www. brompton.co.uk

Questions

1. Identify examples of radical innovation undertaken by Brompton Bicycle.

2. Identify examples of incremental innovation.

3. How does continuous improvement relate to Brompton Bicycle order winners?

Chapter summary

To consolidate your learning, the key points from this chapter are summarized as follows:

- **Define innovation and continuous improvement**

  Innovation may be of two types. If it is infrequent, rapid, and significant, then it is 'radical innovation'. If it is frequent and small scale, then it is 'incremental innovation'. An operations strategy designed to result in incremental innovation is termed 'continuous improvement' (CI).

- **Identify and explain the principles and practice of continuous improvement**

  The principle of CI is based on the continuous review of process performance and the systematic adjustment of processes to improve performance. To achieve this, CI tools are given to, and CI skills are developed in, the workforce, who are empowered to engage in improvement activities.

- **Discuss the balanced scorecard and benchmarking**

  These are two possible ways in which the impact of CI can be measured. The balanced scorecard extends performance measurement into non-financial, and potentially non-conventional, areas—such as employee satisfaction or retention, or reject and wastage rates. Benchmarking, on the other hand, is concerned with enabling an operation or organization to compare performance against itself over time, or against others.

- **Discuss the learning organization and open innovation**

  The learning organization can be defined as a template of what an organization should be like in terms of policies and procedures for making learning happen. But this can be contentious, as measuring learning is difficult to do in this kind of context. Open innovation is defined as the formal discipline and practice of leveraging the discoveries of others as input for the innovation process through formal and informal relationships. It is often achieved through an open call for ideas online.

 # Questions

Review questions

1. What are the similarities between the principles of CI and TQM?

2. What is the concept of kaizen?

3. How can the impact of CI be measured?

4. Why is flowcharting an essential tool for CI?

5. How can the barriers to implementing CI be overcome?

6. What is benchmarking and how does it contribute to CI?

7. How does the balanced scorecard contribute to CI?

8. What is a learning organization?

9. What is open innovation?

10. What are the advantages of open innovation?

Discussion questions

1. Is an employee suggestion scheme necessary if employees are empowered?

2. How might a bicycle manufacturer engage in benchmarking?

3. What six or seven measures might a private hospital have for its balanced scorecard?

4. What are the benefits of crowdsourcing? What might be the downside?

5. What are the ethical implications of continuous improvement and or radical innovation?

 # Further learning guide

A good place to start is the Kaizen Institute (**www.uk.kaizen.com**). Although a consulting company, their website has a great deal of information and case studies on CI tools and their implementation. One of the values of the Association for Manufacturing Excellence is continuous improvement (**www.ame.org**). It is based in the USA, but publishes online a great newsletter, with articles not just on CI but a range of other operations topics. You should also look at the crowdsourcing websites and compare the business models of Innocentive, NineSigma, and Yet2, each of which is slightly different. Finally the Brompton Bicycle company has a great website that explains how its folding bikes are design and manufactured (**http://www.brompton. co.uk**), whilst there are a large number of videos online about Dyson and Dyson products.

References

Al-Khawaldeh, K. and Sloan, T. (2007) Continuous improvement in manufacturing companies in Jordan, *International Journal of Technology Management*, 37(3/4), 323–31

Arthur, J.B. and Smith, L.A. (2001) Gainsharing and organizational learning: an analysis of employee suggestions over time, *Academy of Management Journal*, 44(4), 737–54

Bessant, J. (2003) *High-Involvement Innovation: Building and sustaining competitive advantage through continuous change*, Wiley: Chichester

Fairbank, J.F. and Williams, S.D. (2001) Motivating creativity and enhancing innovation through employee suggestion systems technology, *Creativity and Innovation Management*, 10(2), 68–74

Finger, M. and Brand, S.B. (1999) The concept of the learning organisation applied to the transformation of the public sector, in Easterby-Smith, M., Burgoyne, J., and Araujo, L. (eds.) *Organizational learning and the Learning Organization*, Sage Publications: London, 130–56

Garvin, D.A. (1993) Building a learning organization, *Harvard Business Review*, July/August, 78–91

Hyland, P.W., Mellor, R., and Sloan, T. (2007) Performance measurement and continuous improvement: are they linked to manufacturing strategy? *International Journal Technology Management*, 37(3/4), 237–46

Imai, M. (1986) *Kaizen: The Key to Japan's Competitive Success*, McGraw-Hill: New York

Kaplan, R.S. and Norton, D.P. (1992) The balanced scorecard: Measures that drive performance, *Harvard Business Review*, January/February, 72–9

Kerka, S. (1995) *The Learning Organization: Myths and Realities*, ERIC Publications: Columbus, OH

Lowson, R.H. (2002) *Strategic Operations Management*, Routledge: London

Schön, D.A. (1973) *Beyond the Stable State. Public and private learning in a changing society*, Penguin: Harmondsworth

Senge, P.M. (1990) *The Fifth Discipline. The art and practice of the learning organization*, Random House: London

Smith, M.K. (2001) The learning organization, in *the encyclopaedia of informal education* [online] www.infed.org/biblio/learning-organization.htm.

Spreizer, G.M. (1995) Psychological empowerment in the workplace: Dimensions, measurement and validation, *The Academy of Management Journal*, 38(5), 1442–65

Chapter Seventeen

Internationalization, globalization, and corporate social responsibility

Learning outcomes

After reading this chapter you will be able to:

→ Define terms related to internationalization and globalization

→ Identify the key challenges of internationalization

→ Identify and explain alternative approaches to managing international operations

→ Discuss the implications of corporate social responsibility for operations managers

Gripple originated as the manufacturer of a new device, called the 'gripple', for joining fencing wire together. Since then it has become the manufacturer of a wide range of products such as wire joiners and tensioners, pipe clamps, and anchoring and suspension systems used in agricultural, manufacturing, and construction industry settings. For instance, the iconic 'Gherkin' building in London had 27,000 Gripple components used in its construction. It invests up to 5% of revenue into research and development and hence its products tend to provide low-cost, but highly effective solutions for its customer base.

It began manufacturing in Sheffield, and now has highly automated factories covering 50,000 square feet, from which 90% of its output is exported to countries all over the world. In 2000, it established a sales and marketing office in France in order to promote its products to Europe, and one year later it opened a sales office in Chicago, in order to exploit the North American market. Reflecting this growth in international markets, Gripple has also expanded its operations internationally by setting up a production facility in the USA and another in India, and a manufacturing joint venture in Australia. In 2011, 80% of output was manufactured in the UK, with the USA and India contributing 15% and 5% respectively. In 2011 it also opened a new facility in Brazil.

The decision to manufacture internationally was based primarily on the company recognizing that it needs to be close to the customer in order to offer an industry leading level of service and responsiveness, and to maintain control over the manufacture of its products, many of which are patent protected. The company emphasizes that it has not 'offshored' manufacturing to reduce unit costs. Proximity to markets means that Gripple is able to minimize logistics cost, ensure swift delivery to customers, and offer its full product range, at the same time as minimizing and stock holdings.

The No2 Gripple Hanger; one of the companys most popular products.

In undertaking this international expansion, the company was anxious to ensure that the same business ethos and culture developed in the UK was adopted overseas. Hence UK employees were used to help set up international operations, and locally sourced employees were taken to Sheffield to be inducted into the Gripple culture. Key aspects of this culture have been replicated everywhere. For instance, since its early days the company adopted open-plan working so that managers do not have separate offices. Likewise, all Gripple employees must become shareholders in the company, and this applies equally to international employees as well as those based in the UK. Overseas production facilities are managed by teams comprising expatriate British managers and local managers, who work to company-wide systems and standard operating procedures (SOPs).

Source: author's primary research

Questions

1. What are Gripple's order winners (OWs) and how does internationalization fit into this?

2. What aspects of their operations did Gripple focus on when expanding overseas?

Introduction

In 2000 $78 trillion worth of goods and services were traded internationally, of which about 20% is in services. From 1950–2000, the world economy grew sixfold, but the volume of world trade grew 22 times greater over this same period. Cross border trade was 8% of world gross domestic product (GDP) in 1950, by 2000 it was 25%. Foreign direct investment (FDI) has also grown. In 1985 companies invested $50 billion in overseas factories, equipment, and offices. In 2000, FDI was £1.3 trillion. So a feature of today's business world is that many organizations operate in more than one country. Indeed some companies now have a global presence—banks like HSBC, international hotel and restaurant chains like Hilton and McDonalds, and manufacturing firms in motor manufacturing, electronic goods, and soft drinks. Multinational corporations account for nearly 80% of US trade.

To illustrate this, a study in 1997 (quoted by Legrain 2002: 110) looked at the different countries that contributed to the production value of an apparently 'American' car. Only 37% of its value was actually created in the USA. Assembly in South Korea accounted for 30%; components made in Japan contributed 17.5%; Germany added 7.5% for design services; minor parts valued at 4% came from Taiwan and Singapore; the UK contributed 2.5% in terms of marketing; and 1.5% came from data processing undertaken in Ireland and Barbados.

The interconnectedness of the world was also brought into sharp focus by the tragic events in Japan in 2011, when that country was struck by a tsunami which resulted in a major nuclear incident. Within a few days of these events, companies all over the world were affected by the disruption to Japan's manufacturing capability and transportation network. Apple were unable to source parts for its new iPad 2, such as its flash memory—used for audio and video storage—and the battery, which is made only by Apple Japan. Other affected iPad components included the DRAM memory, built-in compass, and the touchscreen glass. Sony Ericsson faced similar problems with its mobile phones. General Motors suspended production at a Louisiana truck plant in the US, and BMW, Volkswagen, Fiat, and Daimler Peugeot were all affected. Boeing's Dreamliner was also threatened by delays, as Jamco manufactured the plane's galleys in northwest Japan and shipped them through Yokohama. Whilst the production facility was unaffected, deliveries and shipments were disrupted by fuel shortages.

Before discussing the implications of this for operations management, it is necessary to understand the different terminology that may be used in this area, such as **globalization**, internationalization, multinational, international trade, and international business. The chapter then goes on to identify the challenges facing a firm that is moving operations from a domestic base to an international one. This leads into discussing various features of internationalization—offshoring, franchising, and managed services —and the risks associated with becoming international. Finally the chapter concludes by considering corporate social responsibility, the ethics of globalization, and its implications for sustainability.

Globalization the development of an organization's operation on all five continents

From internationalization to globalization

When organizations are relatively small it is inevitable that they tend to serve only local markets, in their home country. It also means that they recruit their managers and staff from local labour markets, source their raw materials and capital goods locally, and operate in the context of one country's laws and regulatory regime. Indeed, with increased concern about sustainability, some firms make a virtue out of this by promoting how local their operations are. For instance, restaurants promote on their menus locally sourced meat and fish products, and woollen manufacturers promote locally sourced wool. However, with the advent of the Internet, even small companies can start to trade internationally relatively easily. The worldwide web does not recognize national boundaries so that customers may place orders from anywhere in the world.

Firms begin to internationalize when they begin to engage in international trade. International trade refers to firms that either buy raw materials or goods from outside their home country, and/or sell these in international markets. These days, due to the nature of the world economy, many organizations would be engaged in international trade in some way or another.

A firm really only becomes truly international when it moves some part of its operations out of its home country into another host country. This operation could be identical to that in the home country, or it could be designed to produce completely different outputs. For instance, the first Hilton hotel outside the USA was built in Puerto Rico and operated to the same standards and specifications as all the other Hilton hotels. Whereas GKN, has different factories, in different countries, producing different products.

There have been numerous studies (Harzing 2000) of this process of **internationalization** and a variety of terms used to describe different forms of international company. Most typologies are based around two key characteristics, sometimes referred to as Bartlett and Ghoshal's integration-responsiveness grid, as illustrated in Figure 17.1. This refers to key aspects of international business. First how closely integrated and coordinated the operations are from one country to another. Second, how responsive these operations are to local markets. The characteristics of each of these types are as follows.

> **Internationalization** the movement of some part of a firm's operations to outside its home country

- **Multinational**—these firms have country-centred strategies, and may be made up of autonomous country subsidiaries. There is limited central control. Research and development (R&D) is likely to be carried out locally. Hence the culture and human resources are very international in scope, i.e. polycentric.

> **Multinational** an organization with operations in several different countries, on more than one continent

- Global—firms of this type are often organized into product divisions, and they have a global strategy, along with a centralized R&D function. Products and services will conform to brand standards across the world. Their culture often reflects that of their home country, i.e. ethnocentric.

- Transnational—these firms have complex global strategies and may have complex organizational forms, such as a matrix structure. Their approach tends to be geocentric.

- International—although found on the matrix in Figure 17.1, very few studies have actually identified firms that operate with these characteristics, i.e. both low integration and low responsiveness.

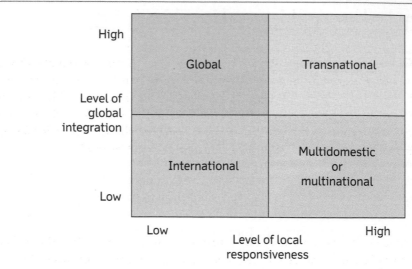

Go online

FIGURE 17.1 Types of international companies. Based on Bartlett and Ghoshal (1989).

Whilst it is useful to have terms that can be used to distinguish between different types of company, Birnik and Moat (2009) suggest that it is too simplistic to think of firms behaving in this way across all functions of their business. They take what they call an 'activity-based view'. That is to say it depends on the specific operational activity as to what extent it should be integrated or responsive. Hence they suggest that 'transnational approach' be adopted for activities such as the development and operation of web-based systems, corporate marketing, and corporate development (such as mergers, acquisitions, and divestments). A 'global approach'—a central strategy with local execution—ensures standardization. It is most appropriate for activities such as quality management, accounting, budgeting, and some elements of the marketing mix. Thirdly, a 'multinational approach' can be adopted towards activities which need to be country-based, such as local procurement, customer services, and human resource recruitment and development. Finally, some activities may be both low integration and low responsiveness, such as facilities management. Hence it is unlikely that any specific firm is purely multinational, transnational, or global, even though firms are often described (perhaps wrongly) as one or the other.

What makes this even more challenging is that there is no universal agreement as to what differentiates between an 'international' organization and a 'global' one. One suggested criterion for being global is that the firm must operate on every continent. But a firm could be quite small, only operating in a limited number of countries, and meet this criterion. For instance, some consulting firms and advertising agencies have an office on every continent, but would probably be regarded as international companies, rather than global. Likewise a manufacturer might have assembly plants on only two or three continents, but be regarded as global because its products were distributed all over the world. It should also be noted that globalization has come to refer not only to organizations and corporations, but also to the cultural, economic, social, and political integration of nation states and peoples. And as we shall discuss towards the end of this chapter, it is a concept that is highly controversial.

Key challenges

There are three main issues an organization must address when it moves out of its home country and begins to operate internationally. The first issue is how to enter the new market and control its activities there. This is the issue of integration, identified in Figure 17.1. The second is how to organize human resources internationally. And the third is the extent to which the product or service may need to be adapted to local market conditions—the issue of local responsiveness identified in Figure 17.1.

Entry mode choice

One of the first decisions to be made by a firm considering international development is the so-called entry mode choice. This relates to the degree of ownership the firm will retain over the assets it has outside its own country. There are two alternative theoretical frameworks for explaining this—transaction cost economics and the resource-based view. Both identify a range of factors that influence a firm towards developing, owning, and operating its own facilities overseas, or being happy to engage in asset light alternatives, such as joint ventures, franchises, and outsourcing. The main factors are:

- Ease with which a contract can be established with an overseas partner.
- Cost of finding, negotiating, and monitoring overseas contracts.
- Extent to which the firm has assets and expertise exclusive to itself.
- Laws and regulations of the host country and their similarity with the home country.
- Degree of cultural similarity between the home and host country.
- Degree of economic, social, and political stability in the host country.
- Level of investment and related risk.
- Level of market opportunity and growth potential.
- Safety and security risks.

The impact of these is summarized in Table 17.1. Research (such as Jones et al. 2004) also suggests that firm-specific factors may also influence how firms go about entering new countries. These are firm size, the sector in which the firm operates, and their level of international experience. For instance, in the hotel industry, most of the six truly global hotel chains (IHG, Starwood, Hilton, Accor, Marriott, Wyndham) do not own the hotels they operate, partly in order to reduce risk. One of the most rapidly expanding markets in the world is China. In this country it is extremely difficult to set up operations unless in some form of partnership with a local organization. GKN, for instance, has set up joint ventures in China, which is the most common way foreign firms enter this market.

Very few countries will score positively on all factors, as the End of chapter case on Shell illustrates. Shell has extensive operations in Nigeria because of the oil and gas reserves found there. The market opportunity and growth potential are high, but social and political stability is fragile. So it is an extremely challenging and risky environment in which to manage operations. In 2010, Shell estimated that criminal gangs were

TABLE 17.1 Influence of factors on entry mode choice

Factors in host country	Full ownership of international assets	Joint ventures or some other partial mode
Availability of overseas partner	Limited	Broad
Cost of establishing & monitoring contract	High	Low
Proprietary expertise	Yes	No
Similarity of laws and regulation	Yes	No
Similarity of culture	Yes	No
Economic, social, political stability	Yes	No
Investment risk	Low	High

stealing oil at a rate of 100,000 barrels a day, whilst 26 employees and contractors were kidnapped and one contractor killed. Eighty per cent of the oil spills in Nigeria could be directly attributed to sabotage and theft.

Organizational approach

A second key issue is the extent to which the organization will behave ethnocentric-ally, polycentrically, or geocentrically. These three alternatives are briefly explained in Table 17.2 which shows the main focus for each, as well as how these may relate to organizational functions, different types of product, and different locations geographically.

Ethnocentrism is based on the tendency of people to act according to past experi-ences, learned behaviours, and norms—how they do things in their home country. This often results in home nationals believing they are more advanced and responsible than foreign colleagues, so the managerial policies and processes developed at home are

TABLE 17.2 Alternative approaches to international organization

	Ethnocentrism	Polycentrism	Geocentrism
Definition	Based on ethnicity	Based on political orientation	Based on geography
Strategic orientation/focus	Home country oriented	Host country oriented	Global oriented
Function	Finance	Marketing	R&D
Product	Industrial products	Consumer goods	–
Geography	Developing countries	N/a	US and Europe

N/a, not applicable
Source: Bartlett et al. (2008)

applied overseas. This is most evident in relations with subsidiary organizations or product divisions in developing countries. As result, the organization's headquarters tends to make all the decisions. Policies and standards of performance are the same throughout the organization. Ethnocentric organizations are usually identified with the nationality of the owner. For example, BP is seen as a British company because its headquarters are in the UK, as became very evident during the Gulf of Mexico oil spill crisis (see Operations insight 13.2, page 350). The ethnocentric attitude is a centralized approach. For instance, all training and development in the organization is centrally conducted. This also means managers are recruited in the home country and then sent out to work in international operations. Hence there may be higher financial costs in order to pay for the transfer costs of managers coming from the home country to work and live overseas. It may also create problems and incur cost if the expatriate worker does not fit into the work practices and cultural attitudes of the country they have been sent to. Another disadvantage might be that the organization does not exploit or develop the expertise of the local labour market, which may make it less responsive and flexible in terms of doing business in that country.

On the other hand, polycentrism is defined as a host country orientation. Under this approach, an organization's managers believe that local conditions and techniques are the best way to deal with local market conditions. This is especially with regards to the marketing function, and activities such as market research, pricing, customer service, and distribution. Local managers are deemed to have better understanding of local conditions. But this polycentric approach can lead to problems related to coordination and control. First it may mean that economies of scale cannot be achieved, as resources are divided up across many locations. Second, because subsidiary businesses or divisions work independently of one another, the concept of the learning organizations (as discussed in Chapter 16) cannot be developed. Third, facilities will be replicated in more than one location, potentially creating diseconomies of scale—in other words each local facility is too small to be truly efficient. Finally, by focusing on local policies and techniques the subsidiary could appear to be a local, rather than international, company and have less appeal to local consumers who are seeking international brands.

The geocentric approach focuses on a more transnational approach to management. A geocentric firm has no bias towards either a home or host country approach. It adopts a contingent philosophy and adopts whatever appears to be the best policies and procedures for the context. For instance, in the marketing field products may conform to a global brand, but be priced and distributed in different ways according to local conditions. For instance, Costa Coffee have stores in eastern Europe, the middle East, and Asia and each of their country websites is slightly different reflecting the image and products they wish to promote in each market. Likewise, in managing human resources in company policies and procedures regarding training and development may be standard across the organization, but other aspects may be local to reflect the different employment laws from one country to another. Geocentric organizations tend to adopt global standards which are used as guidelines rather than rigid policies. These guidelines enable new operations to be set up and managed, as well as provide ideas about how to market to new customers, and adapt products or services to meet local conditions. Geocentric organizations tend to have a reward system and incentives based on global or organizational goals, which therefore encourage head office and local managers to work together as a team. This helps reinforce a shared organizational culture amongst all employees, wherever they may be located in the world.

JDR Cable Systems produces specialist cables, some which are called 'umbilicals' because they connect remote sites to essential resources—the way that a deep sea diver may be connected to a ship in order to get air to breathe and to communicate. Its Rotterdam-based business—JDR Smart Solutions—develops and produces cables with seismic, defence, and other specialist applications. Whilst the UK business—JDR Umbilical Systems—serves the offshore oil and gas industry by making products that connect drilling rigs to installations on the sea bed. Expertise in design, project management, and manufacturing is also based in the UK. A third location is in Houston, Texas, which supports JDR products being used for oil and gas exploration in the Gulf of Mexico.

In 2006, JDR built and opened a plant in Thailand. It did so for two main reasons. First, its UK plant was not in a suitable location for manufacturing modern umbilicals. This was due to oil exploration and other offshore operations having moved into deeper waters, so that cables and umbilicals needed to be up to 3 kilometres long, as well as more sophisticated. Because its UK plant was not on the coast, all JDR's output has to be transported by road, and 100 tonnes is the maximum load that can be carried in this way. So it needed a port location from which they could ship long cables of more than 100 tonnes. Second, they identified that their competitors had operations in Europe, the Gulf of Mexico and Brazil, but had none in south-east Asia, which was a developing market. The demand for oil and gas is rapidly rising there because the economies of China, Indonesia and other countries in the region are developing and significant subsea resources have been identified in the seas around these countries.

The company emphasized that it had not set up the factory in Thailand to take advantage of the cheaper labour market there. JDR had highly automated their manufacturing processes in their UK factory, and this same technology was installed overseas. So their labour cost percentage was relatively low anyway. It was partly for this reason that they decided not to outsource production to another company. They regarded their expertise in umbilical production too important to risk sharing it with anyone else. Moreover, JDR wanted to maintain tight control over quality, and judged that in order to achieve this they had to own, manage, and operate their own plant overseas.

Hence the Thai plant, at the Royal Naval Base in Sattahip, was constructed so that it could assemble products of up to 300 tonnes. It is also located on the quayside, with a 12-metre deep berth, so that ships can be directly loaded with the reels of cable. The development was swift, as the plant was equipped and opened within 12 months, due to effective collaboration between experienced UK staff, local machinery and installation companies, and the newly-recruited Thai workforce. The Sattahip operation does not do exactly the same as is done in the UK. The UK factory continues to manufacture all the components for umbilicals, such as electrical cables and high-pressure hoses. These are then exported by container to Thailand, where they are laid up in lengths up to 10 kilometres. These are then made into the finished product by covering them in armoured wire, before being wound on to nine-metre reels ready for shipping. As a result, JDR has a price advantage over its competitors in the region. Its armoured wire costs less because it is locally supplied, and its transportation is less costly because the final heavy reels of umbilicals are moved much shorter distances.

By making Sattahip purely engage in assembly and final testing, the operation is lean. This is monitored remotely from the UK, as the automated machinery and equipment in use in Thailand can be tracked via the Internet. Statistical process control (SPC) analysis is conducted on this data and follow-up action taken if necessary. Likewise, advanced web-cams have been installed so that managers can see what is happening on the shop floor in Thailand. This automation also means that that the Thai workforce is comprised of only 12 operators, each of whom was trained in England.

Source: JDR Cable systems video; www.jdrcables.com; 'Cable Capability', The Manufacturer, *December 2006*

Questions

1. What was JDR's entry mode in Thailand and what were the reasons for adopting this approach?

2. What are JDR's OWs and how do they ensure these are achieved by the Thai operation?

3. Is JDR geocentric, polycentric, or ethnocentric?

Concept adaptation

The third issue is the extent to which products or services may need to be modified in order to meet local needs. In some product categories, the firm is able to market its brand globally, without any modification to the product. Examples of this would be soft drinks, such as Seven Up, or footwear, such as Adidas. However, in other categories there clearly has to be adaptation. For instance, keyboards for PCs need to be made with different alphabetic scripts, such as Latin, Greek, Arabic, and Chinese.

Firms would prefer to make the same product or deliver the same service wherever they are in the world. The rationale for this is based on economies of scale, since adding complexity adds cost. Hence any adaptation a firm makes is due to constraints of some kind. These may either be supply side constraints or market constraints or both. So the first question a firm has to resolve is whether or not the supply side, or upstream, infrastructure can support an unmodified concept. This means considering all the inputs the operation may need and evaluating their availability and cost. If some of these inputs are not available, the firm has the choice of overcoming this by investing itself in the necessary infrastructure, or adapt its concept to fit with local conditions. For instance, resort hotels in North America and Europe are able to source their utilities, such as water, electricity, and sewage disposal from established suppliers. But when such hotels are being built and developed in locations such as the Maldives, these utilities are not available. So the hotel developer has to build not only the resort property but also a power plant and water treatment plant.

It may also be the case that the market drives firms to adapt in order to reflect local customs and taste. In India beef is not eaten by Hindus, so the McDonalds' menu there does not feature beefburgers or Big Macs. Instead it offers Chicken Maharaja Mac,

McVeggie, and McSpicy Paneer. Similarly, when Disney first opened in Paris, they adopted their American policy of not selling alcohol in the theme park. Within a few months, they had to change this policy as the French clientele, who made up the majority of visitors, were so used to drinking wine with their meal. Other market conditions may also affect operations. For instance, a combination of very strong demand and relatively low investment costs mean that four- and five-star hotels in the Far East tend to be larger than hotels in Europe.

Such adaptations have implications for operations and how they are organized and managed. For instance, any organization that had to invest in its own utilities infrastructure will have a much bigger engineering team in-house, the chief engineer is likely to be more qualified, and the executive management team will need to have a better understanding of engineering and technology than would be the case in more developed countries—or outsource this. Likewise, in countries where product modifications are significant, the firm is likely to establish local new product development teams to ensure they meet that country's needs.

Alternative approaches to internationalization

As we have seen, internationalization creates a number of challenges for the firm in terms of how it delivers its products and services, and how it manages its operations. So far we have tended to focus on organizations who either directly manage their own overseas operations, or do so in partnership, such as a joint venture, with others. However, there are ways in which international expansion is conducted by developing supplier relationships. There are a number of different approaches that firms may adopt, often reflecting the characteristics of different industry sectors. These approaches include offshoring, franchising, and managed services.

Offshoring

Offshoring to movement of an operation from a high-cost economy to a low-cost economy

Offshoring relates to an organization having some of its activities operating outside its home country. Although outsourcing and offshoring are often used interchangeably, they are not the same thing. Offshored activities may be directly managed by the organization, or they may be outsourced to a supplier. The kinds of activities that are offshored have the following characteristics:

- Significant wage differences between the home and offshore countries.
- Activity is based around information so that it can be teleworked either through telephones (such as call centres) or the Internet (such as computer-aided design and customer support).
- The work is relatively standardized and hence easy to set up.

The reasons for offshoring are very similar to those for outsourcing, but in particular some governments have introduced policies that encourage this practice. For instance, India has become a significant player in offshoring, particularly dominant in the software industry. This is due to the Indian government in the 1970s putting in place restriction on foreign ownership of companies. This led to many international companies, especially in the information technology (IT) industry, leaving India. Consequently the government developed schools to train students in technology so that they could support their own infrastructure, thereby creating a highly skilled indigenous workforce. In the 1990s the Internet developed making it easy to undertake computer-based work anywhere in the world. As a result when IT companies were faced with the Y2K problem (many experts believed that IT systems would crash at midnight on 31 December 1999 when the year changed to 2000) they turned to Indian expertise to help deal with reprogramming computers. Having done so, these firms recognized that Indian software engineers were English speaking and highly skilled but had pay rates considerably lower than in Europe or the USA. Major Indian companies providing offshore services include Infosys, Tata Consultancy Services (TCS), and Wipro. More recently companies in other industries have started to offshore their production activities, notably to China.

RESEARCH INSIGHT 17.1

Aron, R. and Singh, J.V. (2005) Getting offshoring right, *Harvard Business Review*, December, 135–42

In this article, Aron and Singh discuss a financial services firm that offshored and ran into difficulty. They analyse the reasons for this and then propose a systematic way for deciding what to offshore and how to do it. They identify two kinds of risk—structural and operational—and then use these to identify what activities should be located (offshore or not) and what organizational form should be used to control these (basically retain in-house or outsource). Thus low-risk (both structural and operational) activities, such as data entry, can be offshored and outsourced. Whereas high-risk activities, such as pricing decisions, need to be conducted in-house in the organization's base country.

Franchising

In service sectors, firms often expand internationally by franchising their brand. A franchise agreement allows the franchisee to operate the business operation according to specific procedures laid down by the franchisor. The franchisee invests in the franchise by setting up the operation in the territory assigned to the franchise and then makes two kinds of annual payment. A royalty, most often in the form of a percentage of revenue, and management fees relating to any training and advisory services given by the franchisor. A franchise is usually agreed for a fixed time period, such as 5–30 years, which may be broken down into shorter periods when the agreement is reviewed. The agreement will specifiy a 'territory', i.e. the area in which the franchisee can operate. Within this territory a franchisee may have more than one operation, and some larger franchisees may have more than one territory. One franchisee may manage several such locations. The advantage of franchising internationally is that it gives access to investment capital in a host country, making international growth potentially much faster. The franchisor also reduces the risk of developing internationally and taps into the local expertise of its franchisees.

Managed services

Managed services providers (MSP) originated in the IT sector, when large-scale IT firms began to provide a range of IT services to clients. Such services include back-up, security, data storage, monitoring, and network management. MSPs manage and take responsibility for the provision of services to clients proactively, since it is they (not the client) who determine what type and level of service is needed. Most MSPs charge a flat fee or near-fixed monthly fee, which benefits their clients by providing them with predictable IT support costs. More recently MSP has extended beyond IT into areas such as supply chain management, media, utilities, and facilities management.

Managed services can play a part in the international development of operations because they enable firms to reduce the risk of operating in foreign countries. MSPs provide local expertise, security, and low-cost approaches to key aspects of the operation, as illustrated in Operations insight 17.2 about innocent.

OPERATIONS INSIGHT 17.2
innocent—developing smooth operations to serve Europe

innocent is the UK's number one smoothie maker. Founded in 2000, innocent has become one of the most recognizable retail brands in the UK. innocent began life as a company of just three people selling fruit smoothies at a minor music festival in London. Individual consumers have always been encouraged to contact the firm through email addresses stamped on their bottles, but very quickly this led to a huge volume of emails and so significant data storage requirements. Hence innocent took a MSP approach by contracting with a hosted exchange service provider to manage its email messaging and communications traffic.

Innocent encourage customers to contact them through email addresses stamped on their products

After starting with local retail customers, innocent expanded its geographic coverage and customer base by taking orders via fax, phone, and email. Large retailers began to stock their products, which meant their supply chain needed to be reliable and effective. Contracts with such retailers demanded a more complex system for managing the information flows along the supply chain. In 2002, an electronic data interchange (EDI) system was adopted, which connected head office to innocent's UK warehouse and automated most ordering and invoicing. Shortly afterwards the company started to distribute to Belgium, Holland, France, Ireland, Germany, Austria, and Scandinavia, so the EDI system had to be upgraded. In particular the system had to operate in different languages, as well process information according to internationally recognized data standards and protocols.

As an organization, innocent was already very lean. It did not have 24/7 head office support and it outsourced much of its operations, as mentioned earlier. Hence it was natural for it to look for an outsourced EDI solution. It therefore decided to work with a supplier of 'software as a service' (SaaS) based around cloud computing (a network of remote servers hosted on the Internet). The supplier had the expertise of hosting such systems internationally and could assure a smooth transition to the new system. By automating processing, innocent saved 20 hours a week compared with its old system. And because their new EDI system was well established, they were able to win a new contract with a retailer who used the same system.

Using managed service providers in this way brings innocent many advantages. First, they have a very small in-house IT team. But second, they are able to keep up with the latest technology and comply with legislative requirements concerning data exchange, due to the expertise in these areas of their suppliers. Third, they are able to take on new customers easily, as systems based on the Internet are increasingly compatible with each other. And finally, they can do this across many different countries.

Sources: www.cobweb.com; www.innocentdrinks.co.uk; 'An innocent EDI journey', The Manufacturer, *August 2009*

Questions

1. What are innocent's OWs and how does EDI enable these to be delivered?
2. What are the dangers of adopting the managed service solution to international expansion?

Risks associated with internationalization

As we saw when discussing entry mode choice, there are some risk associated with operating outside an organization's home country. The most obvious of these are:

- Exchange rate and financial risks. The cost advantage of offshoring may depend on the rate of exchange between the country where the costs are incurred and the country where the revenue is derived. For instance, if the value of sterling declines relative to the value of the Indian rupee, moving production to India will become significantly less attractive.

- Regulatory risk (e.g. a change in laws and regulations that affect business activities). Many governments in the developing world have restrictions on who can set up a business in their country. For instance, China requires European and American companies to set up joint ventures in that country.

- Intervention (governmental action to prevent a transaction being completed). In some cases, governments impose sanctions against trading with other countries for a variety of reasons.
- Political risk (change in leadership and policy that may affect operations). In 2011, oil production was affected by political unrest in countries in North Africa and the Middle East.
- Natural disaster, war, and other uncontrollable events. For instance, the 2011 tsunami in Japan led to auto component manufacturers being unable to maintain production. This led to major manufacturers such as GM and Volkswagen being unable to make cars because they relied on just-in-time inventory.
- Lack of control. For instance, Brompton Bicycles licensed production of the folding bike to a Taiwanese manufacturer, but withdrew this when they were dissatisfied with the quality of the bicycles being produced.
- Security. The level of threat from criminals, social unrest, and terrorism varies from country to another and one location to another. This means that facilities and employees may be subject to relatively low levels of security to very high levels. For instance, in Europe very few retail stores have uniformed security personnel at their entrances, whereas in the Philippines and South Africa armed guards are common.

Corporate social responsibility

Globalization as a concept has been portrayed as many different things by a range of pressure groups, from both the left and right of the political spectrum. These accusations include ideas that suggest globalization:

- Erodes national sovereignty.
- Imposes Western, specifically American, cultural values on countries around the world.
- Removes power from democratically elected governments and puts it in the hands of corporate big business.
- Shifts production to the Third World where labour is cheaper.
- Exploits labour in the Third World.
- Results in governments in the developed world creating tax regimes and labour laws to attract production to the detriment of its own citizens.
- Creates brands that are all-powerful.

And events such as the Enron scandal in 2001, when a major energy company collapsed after trading fraudulently and the collapse of the global financial sector in 2009 give some credence to some of these perspectives. Moreover at the start of the new millennium, of the 100 largest 'economies' of the world, 49 of these were nation states, but 51 were multinational corporations.

At the heart of this argument is the extent to which free trade is, or is not, desirable. However, there is strong evidence (see Legrain 2002) to suggest that free trade is not the cause of many of the manifestations of globalization discussed in this chapter. It is true that the share of manufacturing in countries within the Organization for Economic Cooperation and development (OECD) has fallen from 30% to less than 20% between 1970–2002, especially in textiles and metal products. Linked to this, manufacturing employment has fallen, but largely due to unskilled workers engaged in repetitive task being replaced by automation and technology. This has led to the gap between skilled and unskilled workers wages increasing and higher rates of unemployment amongst the unskilled. But it is not trade that has created this situation, it is technology. In a typical steel plant, it is now possible for 3500 workers to make as much steel as 30,000 once did. In agriculture, we now produce more food than ever before, but the number of agricultural workers is at its lowest ever number. So whilst manufacturing's share of GDP in Europe fell around 5% in the 1990s, the manufacturing trade deficit only widened by 0.5% of GDP. In other words, manufacturing's contribution to European economies fell, but this was due to efficiency gains rather than importing goods from outside Europe.

However, such productivity gains have not resulted in massive unemployment in the USA and Europe. As the economy has grown, the population has had more disposable income and there has been a rise in service jobs. In the service sector, productivity growth is much slower, as personal services (such as nursing, hotel keeping, hairdressing) cannot be easily automated. And as a result, work is generally more pleasant for most employees. Service employment compared with manufacturing has more pleasant working conditions, more interesting work, more work-time flexibility, job security, and fewer health-related problems. There are only two potential disadvantages of service work—wages may be lower in this sector and employees are expected to work antisocial hours.

Whilst globalization has been shown not to harm the developed world, it has also been demonstrated to be a positive force in the developing world. A number of studies, such as that by Hartungi (2006) have compared globalizing countries (such as China, India, Brazil, and Mexico) with non-globalizing ones (most of Africa and many Muslim countries, such as Indonesia and Pakistan). In the 1990s, GDP in globalizing countries rose on average 5% per annum, but only by 1.4% in non-globalizing ones. Put another way, living standards would double every 14 years in a globalizing country, but take 50 years to do so in a non-globalizing one.

Legrain (2002) also provides evidence that suggests multinationals are not 'the demons they are made out to be'. Foreign firms tend to outperform domestic ones in a variety of ways, such as:

- They pay their employees more than the domestic firms (6% more in the USA in 1996).
- They create jobs faster (growing at 1.7% a year in the UK in the 1990s, whilst domestic employment fell by 2.7%).
- They invest more in R&D (40% of the UK's total R&D spend in 1996).
- They export more (in Ireland 89% of their output in 1996, compared with 34% by domestic Irish firms).

However, if globalization is driving greater growth might not this be unsustainable? There is little doubt that the world potentially faces an environmental disaster in the relatively near future. The world now uses 70% more energy than 30 years ago and greenhouse gases are increasing by 50%. The global nitrogen cycle is being overwhelmed due to the use of fertilizers, human sewage, and burning fossil fuels. In the Amazon, 20,000 square kilometres of tropical rain forest are cleared every year, creating smog and reducing biodiversity. One-third of all the world's fish species are under threat from overfishing and pollution. Global water use is increasing so rapidly that two out of three people in the world will experience water shortages within the next 30 years.

Globalization can affect the environment in both positive and negative ways. Its negative impacts derive from how it drives economic growth and increases emissions, from the transportation used to ship goods around the world. In terms of positive impacts, it results in shifts of some 'dirty' industry sectors (steel mills, chemical production) from one country to another; but also shifts in so called 'clean' sectors (call centres, computer programming). Second, globalization spreads greener technologies, as firms setting up factories in the developing world often have technologies that are much less environmentally harmful than indigenous manufacturers.

In fact, the key driver of environmental degradation is population growth. The world population was only 2.5 billion people in 1950, and is set to be three times this in less than a decade. There is also a link between growth, wealth, and the environment. As countries develop economically, there is a degradation in the environment due to the growth of industry and manufacturing. However, as the population becomes more wealthy as a result, there comes a point where the citizens start to demand a cleaner environment. Researchers at Princetown University suggest this is at an annual income of $5000 per person, and by the time the average annual income is $8000, almost all measurable pollutants (air, nitrogen, sewage, heavy metals) are falling, as for instance in South Korea (Legrain, 2002: 245). Operations managers in developing countries, however, do not have to follow this historical pattern, because they could 'leapfrog' the environmental impact of manufacturing by adopting modern, 'clean' technologies, so long as the political, social, and economic environment supports this.

RESEARCH INSIGHT 17.2

Chryssolouris, G., Papakostas, N., and Mavrikios, D. (2008) A perspective on manufacturing strategy: Produce more with less, *CIRP Journal of Manufacturing Science and Technology*, 1(1), 45–52

In this article, the authors recognize the impact of globalization and propose that new ways of producing more with less ought to be found. The article focuses on the technologies, relating to novel processes, materials, and information/communication technologies, which could deal with the issues of increased demand for manufacturing goods, finite resources, and the need for sustainable production.

In recognition of these issues, large international organizations have developed **corporate social responsibility** policies designed to address many of the ethical and sustainability issues discussed previously. Operations insight 17.3 illustrates this.

Corporate social responsibility
the adoption by organizations of policies and practices designed to meet the needs of society as a whole

OPERATIONS INSIGHT 17.3
HP—global citizenship

HP is the world's largest IT company and employs around 325,000 people. Its international nature is reflected in where it has sited its R&D facilities—California, England, Russia, Israel, India, Singapore, and China. In an open letter, HP's CEO Leo Apotheker outlines his company's 'Global Citizenship' policy. He writes, 'Social and environmental responsibility are essential to our business strategy and our value proposition for customers. They are also at the heart of an obligation we all share to help create a sustainable global society'. To drive this policy forward, HP has a Global Citizenship Council which has developed and is responsible for delivering the Global Citizenship strategy. This is based around 'commitment to understand the needs of and improve society; respect universal human rights and the environment;

act with integrity and accountability; and operate responsibly and sustainably' with regards its operations, product development, supply chain, and all its stakeholders.

The Global Citizenship Council is made up of senior executives with responsibility for a range of relevant business areas (such as Investor Relations, Labour Relations, or Corporate Communication), as well as functions specific to this area (such as Social innovation or Environmental Sustainability). Reporting to the Council are five committees, in the areas of ethics and compliance, human rights and labour policy, environmental sustainability, privacy, and social innovation.

Although HP has adopted this approach because morally it is the right thing to do, it also appreciates that will help drive the business, and potentially maintain competitive advantage in nine specific ways. One way is that it will address the needs of their customers and provide insight as to their needs. Their main markets are business-to-business (B2B), business-to-customer (B2C), and government agencies. In the B2B market, their customers are concerned about sustainability and are partly driving this by ensuring their suppliers supply sustainable products that are environmentally friendly. Everyday consumers are also concerned about this issue, but may not reflect this in their buying habits. So HP has a programme to show consumers how 'green' initiatives may help them save money. Finally government agencies now have procurement policies that require IT vendors to demonstrate sustainability, as well as provide privacy and data security.

A second business benefit of the Global Citizenship strategy is that it may bring cost savings. For instance, one initiative to reduce energy usage has cut costs by 3%. In 2010, the company collected data from 269 sites, which included all HP manufacturing sites, as well as the largest owned and leased offices, warehouses, data centres, and distribution sites. The total floor space was approximately 7.3 million square metres. It is using this data to monitor energy usage and to benchmark similar operations against each other.

HP believes that innovation, market access, and competitiveness are also outcomes of the strategy. By demonstrating corporate social responsibility, HP is better able to engage in public policy debates and with legislators over issues of concern to the company, such as intellectual property rights, corporate tax regimes, and trade policies.

The strategy also improves employee engagement and external engagement. All new employees have an environmental sustainability module as a part of their training. The company also supports employee interest in this area, and in 2010 supported 29 chapters (groups) with more than 10,000 employees in HP's Sustainability Network. It also hosts an internal website 'environment@hp' which provides information and support to employees. This fits with HP's engagement with external agencies as illustrated in 2010 when 27 offices in 14 countries organized local events in relation to Earth Day, United Nations World Environment Day, and Green Week. Finally the Global Citizenship strategy should result in risk reduction and provide a platform for reputation management.

Source: www.hp.com

Questions

1. What aspects of HP's Global Partnership strategy are unique to them operating in the IT sector?

2. Using HP's extensive web resources on their Global Citizenship strategy, identify which policies and practices are driven solely by ethical criteria.

Conclusions

Globalization is a significant phenomenon in the twenty-first century, not just in terms of business, but politically, socially, and economically. Firms have a choice as to how they go about this process and how they organize themselves once they are international. Hence, there is wide variation between global companies in terms of how their operations are organized, how they are managed, and how they function. For some companies offshoring and outsourcing has been highly successful, but for others it has not. And whilst some might think of themselves as being ethnocentric, geocentric, or polycentric, in reality this may vary from one part or function of the organization to another. Such large firms are also recognizing the impact they have on society and the environment. So many of them have developed policies on corporate social responsibility that are designed to ensure they address issues of concern from major stakeholder groups, other than their shareholders—politicians and law-makers, environmental groups and agencies, and society as a whole.

END OF CHAPTER CASE
Shell—a truly global organization

The petroleum company Royal Dutch Shell in 2011 was the world's second largest company, according to Fortune 500. In 2010 it had outlined to shareholders a three-year strategic plan which was designed to improve competitive performance in the short term, and deliver 'a new wave of production growth'. Leading up to 2020 Shell is planning to transform itself into an integrated energy company that will offer a very wide range of energy 'products' from increasingly sustainable resources. In the five years leading up to 2011, it had invested $2.1 billion on researching alternative energy sources, CO_2 emissions, and carbon capture and storage. In their 'upstream' operations the firm explores for and extracts natural gas and crude oil, whilst 'downstream' Shell refines, supplies, trades, and ships crude oil worldwide, produces petrochemicals for industrial customers, and manufactures and sells a wide range of products.

In 2010, Shell operated in more than 90 countries and employed 93,000 people. The scale of operations was large and varied—it sold 16.8 million tonnes of liquefied natural gas (LNG), produced 3.3 million barrels of gas and oil, operated 43,000 Shell service

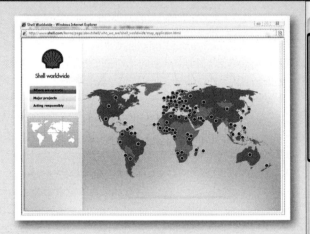

The extent of Shell's international operations can be seen on their website. With kind permission of Shell International Ltd.

stations worldwide selling 145 billion litres of fuel, and operated more than 30 refineries and chemical plants. As a result its turnover was $368.1 billion, and trading profit $20.5 billion. It invested $30.6 billion in capital equipment and $1 billion in research and development.

The company is truly global. It has downstream operations in every country in Europe, largely through its chain of service stations. But it also has upstream operations in 14 European countries. In Africa, oil and gas exploration and extraction is mainly conducted in North Africa (Algeria, Morocco, Tunisia, Libya, and Egypt) and West Africa (Nigeria, Ghana, Gabon), with downstream operations in eighteen other countries. A significant proportion of its upstream business is in Canada, the USA, and Mexico, where it also has downstream businesses. In the Middle East and Asia it is exploring for or extracting oil and gas in 20 countries, as well as refining, supplying, shipping, or selling petroleum products in more than 20 states. And in South America it has upstream and downstream operations in six countries, most notably in Brazil, Argentina, Venezuela, and Columbia. As well as a corporate website, Shell also has specific websites for 73 different countries. For most of these countries the website is in the local language.

In 2009, following the appointment of a new CEO, Shell was reorganized, with a change of responsibilities for the senior management team and a new organizational structure. The purpose of this was partly to reduce costs, but also to speed up decision-making, which in a very large organization like Shell is always a challenge. Four separate business divisions were created.

The Projects & Technology division is responsible all of Shell's major projects, most of which are related to innovation and based around research into technology that will improve the use of energy sources. In addition, the division provides technical services and technology know-how to the other divisions. It is also responsible for safety and environment, and contracting and procurement across the whole of the company. In 2010, it had started up five new major projects, with another eight ongoing and due to start by the end of 2011. These projects are on a massive scale, such as BC10 deepwater in Brazil, Perdido deepwater in the Gulf of Mexico, and Athabasca oil sands project. The Perdido wells are the deepest yet exploited by Shell in the Gulf, at 2600 metres below sea level.

The Upstream Americas division manages operations in North and South America. The division has four main business units—exploration, onshore gas, deepwater oil, and heavy oil—as well as support departments. Due exploiting new oil and gas fields, output was expected to grow by 40% between 2010 and 2014.

The Upstream International division manages the upstream businesses outside the Americas. Within the division activities are organized as geographical units, some business-wide units and supporting units. It engages in a similar range of activities as the other upstream division.

The Downstream division is responsible for all of Shell's manufacturing, distribution and marketing activities for oil products and chemicals. This division's strategy in 2011 had three strands. First, it was planning to maintain its presence in its 'heartland' countries—Europe and USA—whilst expand significantly in high-growth countries such as Brazil, India, and China. Second, it was engaged in continuous improvement in order to drive down cost. Third, the division was rationalizing the number of refineries it operates, focusing production in the most efficient of these. It is organized into some globally managed businesses, such as chemicals, many geographically managed operations, and divisional support departments. For instance, in the UK, Shell has a number of business units such as Shell Gas Direct, which supplies natural gas to industry; Retail, with over 900 service stations; and Shell Gas (LPG), manufacturing and marketing propane and butane. On the other hand, Shell Chemicals is a global business unit, with regional offices in London, Rotterdam, Houston, and Singapore; research centres in Amsterdam, Houston, and Bangalore; and 29 manufacturing sites across the world.

On its corporate website, Shell provides some profiles of its employees in order to illustrate the nature of a career in such an international company. One example is of a graduate who joined Shell in London in 1994, and then worked in Oman, Venezuela, Houston, and the Netherlands. Another instance describes how a finance manager joined the company in Aberdeen in 1980 and has since worked in Gabon, Malaysia, and Singapore. However, it is largely managers and technical specialists that have this kind of experience. In 2010, 90% of Shell's workforce were nationals of the country in which they were working.

As an energy company, Shell has a highly developed corporate social responsibility (CSR) strategy and it produces a Sustainability Report every year. In 2010, this identified the company's main environmental concerns and strategies for tackling these. These were greenhouse gas (GHG) emissions, 'flaring' (the burning off of gas associated with oil extraction), energy efficiency, spills, and water. With regards GHG emissions, Shell set a target in 1998 to reduce these to 5% below their 1990 level. It has met this target every year since 2005, and in 2010 was producing 75 million tonnes from its refineries and chemical plants, 25% lower than the 1990 comparable level. In terms of flaring, this had increased in 2010 over 209, due mainly to starting up new fields, where this is a necessary safety precaution, or taking over operations which did not have the infrastructure in place to capture the emissions. This is particularly challenging in Nigeria due to a lack of funding support from the government and a poor security situation. Sabotage and theft in this country led to 3000 tonnes of lost oil production. Energy efficiency is ongoing as all upstream activities have energy management plans in place. Spills performance in 2010 had improved over 2009 in one respect, in that the number of events was down from 275 to 193. However, it was worse due to an increase in the size of spillages from 1400 up to 2900 tonnes, due mainly to a major spill in at the Montreal refinery in Canada, which

accounted for 35% of the total. Since 2007, Shell has also been monitoring its use of fresh water, which in some regions of the world is increasingly in short supply. In 2010, it consumed 202 million cubic metres, 75% of which was in its downstream operations.

With regards social responsibility, Shell reports in a number of areas. Of major concern is the company's safety record, recorded as the number of cases per million working hours, lost working hours, and number of fatalities. In 2010 each of these showed significant improvement in performance over 2009— 15% fewer injuries, 25% less time off work, and 12 fatalities compared with 20 the previous year. Despite some of their workforce working in extreme conditions, the majority of these deaths resulted from road traffic accidents. In 2010 Shell reported spending $121 million on 'social investments' of which half was spent in the least developed countries of the world. Other issues of concern are equal opportunity, social inclusion, training, and local procurement. Shell conduct reviews of their suppliers routinely to ensure that they comply with labour practices, human rights, and business integrity standards. In 2010 they conducted 34 such reviews in countries such as Taiwan, India, and China.

Sources: www.shell.com and http://sustainability report.shell.com

Questions

1. Identify which activities in Shell are organized internationally, multinationally, globally, and transnationally.

2. Is Shell a geocentric, ethnocentric, or polycentric organization?

3. Why has Shell adopted this approach?

Chapter summary

To consolidate your learning, the key points from this chapter are summarized as follows:

- **Define terms related to internationalization and globalization**

  Internationalization occurs when a firm moves some part of its operations out of its home country into another host country. Globalization refers to when it has operations on all five continents.

- **Identify the key challenges of internationalization**

  The key challenges are entry mode choice, organizational form (geocentric, ethnocentric, polycentric), and concept adaptation.

- **Identify and explain alternative approaches to managing international operations**

  Offshoring relates to an organization having some of its activities operating outside its home country. Offshored activities may be directly managed by the organization, or they may be outsourced to a supplier. Another approach is to franchise or licence overseas operations. This can apply to both manufacturing and so-called managed services.

- **Explain the major ethical and sustainable issues in internationalization and globalization**

  It is argued that economic, social, and political globalization erodes national sovereignty by imposing Western, specifically American, cultural values on countries around the world.

  It may also shift power from democratically elected governments and put it in the hands of corporate big business. Often production is shifted to the Third World where labour is cheaper, and potentially more easily exploited. This can result in governments in the developed world creating tax regimes and labour laws to attract production to the detriment of its own citizens. And finally it creates corporations and brands that have a great deal of power, but which are not subject to national boundaries, nor democratic accountability. Such power may result in the unregulated use of the world's natural resources.

Questions

Review questions

1. How are international companies usually organized?
2. How are multinational companies usually organized?
3. How are global companies usually organized?
4. In what ways are geocentricity, ethnocentricity, and polycentricity different to each other?
5. What is the case for and against globalization?
6. What is corporate social responsibility (CSR)?
7. Why do firms adopt CSR?
8. What are the implications of CSR for operations managers?

Discussion questions

1. What are the similarities and differences between how Gripple, JDR, and innocent have gone about internationalization?

2. How important is it for a firm to retain control of its own assets when developing operations internationally?

3. What are the positive and negative aspects of the globalization phenomenon?

4. What action might a global financial services company take to demonstrate its corporate social responsibilities?

 # Further learning guide

Two of the companies featured in this chapter—Shell and HP—have extensive websites that provide a great deal more information about their operations worldwide, and HP's website provides many pages of information about its 'global citizenship' programme. International management and international business are subjects in their own right, so there are extensive resources, including textbooks and journal articles on this topic. Moreover globalization is also widely discussed in newspapers, on television, and on the Internet. Indeed, typing this search term into a video search engine reveals videos on this topic by Theodore Levitt the marketing guru, Ted Kennedy the US senator, Thomas Freidman the economist, and many others. Finally, corporate social responsibility is also extensively explained in a wide range of different textbooks, as well as on websites including the UK government's Business Link website (**http://www.businesslink.gov.uk**).

 # References

Bartlett, C.A. and Ghoshal, S. (1989) *Managing Across Borders: The Transnational Solution*, Harvard Business School Press: Boston, MA

Bartlett, C.A., Ghoshal, S., and Beamish, P. (2008) *Transnational Management: Text, Cases and Readings in Cross-Border Management*, (5th ed.), New York: McGraw-Hill

Birnik, A. and Moat, R. (2009) Mapping multinational operations, *Business Strategy Review*, Spring, 30–4

Harzing, A-W. (2000) An empirical analysis and extension of the Bartlett and Ghoshal typology of multinational companies, *Journal of International Business Studies*, 31(1), 101–20

Hartungi, R. (2006) Could developing countries take the benefit of globalization?, *International Journal of Social Economics*, 33(11), 728–43

Jones, P., Song, H., and Hong, J.H. (2004) The relationship between generic theory and hospitality applied research: The case of international hotel development, *Journal of Hospitality and Tourism Management*, 11(2), 128–38

Legrain, P. (2002) *Open World: the truth about globalization*, Abacus: London

Glossary

ABC classification a method of identifying and categorizing SKUs according to their demand value

Agile the design of processes, tools, and training to enable quick response to customer needs

Anticipation inventory inventory held in order to absorb large increases in supply or demand

Batch production a production system in which an operation is broken down into distinct processes that are completed on a small number or 'batch' of products at a time

Benchmarking the process of measuring and comparing processes and performance across more than one operation

Bill of material (BOM) a list of all materials, components, and subassemblies which will be needed in order to make the required quantity of a product.

Buffer inventory (also called safety stock) extra material or products made available in case of uncertainty in the supply chain

Bullwhip effect a disproportionately large fluctuation in demand at the supply end following a minor change at the customer demand end of the supply chain.

Business model a system designed for competing effectively in a specific marketplace

Capacity lagging capacity is only added in response to an actual increase in demand

Capacity leading capacity is increased based on a forecast increase in demand

Capacity the maximum possible output in a given time

Category management the strategic management of product groups through trade partnerships which aim to maximize sales and profit by satisfying consumer and shopper needs (Institute of Grocery Distribution)

Cell layout configuration of related equipment and components so that output is produced by a single worker

Chase demand strategy adjusting inputs so that outputs match demand

Competitive advantage the superiority of an organization relative to other competing organizations demonstrated by its performance in the marketplace

Continuous improvement the systematic improvement of processes and outputs through incremental innovation

Corporate social responsibility the adoption by organizations of policies and practices designed to meet the needs of society as a whole

Cost (as an order winner) the ability to provide products or services at a price the customer is willing to pay whilst still retaining a profit for the organization

Crisis the breakdown of order in a process leading to an extreme condition

Crowdsourcing outsourcing tasks to a large group of undefined people, usually through an open invitation online

Demand management strategy adjusting inputs and influencing demand so that inputs and outputs are closely matched

Dependability (as an order winner) the ability of an organization to consistently meet its promises to the customer

Dependent demand demand orders for specific inventory items are directly linked to other items

Disintermediation dealing directly between supplier and customers rather than through intermediaries

Economic order quantity the most cost-efficient quantity of a material to purchase

Economies of scale as the scale of output increases, the average unit cost of production falls

Efficiency the proportion of effective capacity that is achieved

Electronic data interchange (EDI) the transfer of information using the Internet or secure network

Empowerment authorizing employees to make critical decisions about how their work should be done

Enterprise resource planning (ERP) an extension of business systems integration across different companies in the supply network

Ergonomics the application of scientific principles to workplace design to assure human well-being

Failure mode and effect analysis (FMEA) technique for analysing potential failure modes with a system

Finished goods inventory goods which have had all necessary work done on them and are awaiting dispatch to the customer

First-tier supplier those suppliers directly serving the operation

Fixed order period materials are ordered after the same fixed time period

Fixed order quantity materials are ordered in the same quantity each time

Fixed position layout the layout of equipment and processes determined by the context rather than operational efficiency

Flexibility (as an order winner) the ability to change a product or service offering to suit customers' needs

Flow chart a diagram of stages in a process

Flow process production a series of processes through which a product moves or flows continuously

Franchising a licence and related support mechanisms enabling a franchisee to trade under the trade mark/trade name of the franchisor to agreed brand standards

Gantt chart a graphic representation of a project enabling time, cost, and resources allocated to be depicted on a series of bar lines to enable effective planning and monitoring of a project

Globalization the development of an organization's operation on all five continents

Heterogeneity the variety of responses consumers may have to a service experience

Incremental innovation changes made to existing products or technologies to improve performance

Independent demand demand for a particular inventory item is not related to any other item

Innovation putting into practice anything new that an organization has not done before

Intangibility the lack of tangible characteristics of a service operation

Internationalization the movement of some part of a firm's operations to outside its home country

Invention the development of a novel idea

Inventory management the planning and controlling of inventory in order to meet the competitive priorities of the operation

Inventory any quantifiable item that is stored and used in an operation to satisfy a customer demand

Job enlargement increasing the scale of a job by adding more tasks of the same type

Job enrichment increasing the scope of a job by assigning more responsibility for the work done

Job shop the production of very small batches of different products, most of which require a different set or sequence of processing steps

Just-in-time a method for optimizing operations processes by eliminating all forms of extraneous waste

Kaizen the Japanese philosophy of achieving process improvement through incremental change

Kanban materials requirement planning technique

Lean the elimination of all types of waste from any process

Learning organization an organization that develops itself through facilitating the learning of its members

Level capacity strategy keeping inputs constant during periods of low demand to create inventory to meet periods of high demand

Logistics the physical activities involved in the procurement, movement, storage, and accounting for raw materials, partially processed, and finished goods

Lot for lot exactly the same number of items is ordered as used or issued from stock

Make or buy the decision as to whether manufacturing fabrication should be in-house or done by a supplier

Manufacturing resource planning (MRP II) an extension of materials requirements planning to include finance, sales and marketing, and human resources planning on one database

Manuscape the physical and psychological setting in which manufacturing is organized and delivered

Mass production the manufacture of standardized products in large quantities, based on standardized components and assembly-line processes

Mass service the delivery of services based on standardized customer processing steps and assembly-line principles

Master production schedule (MPS) a plan for producing the necessary products in the correct sequence

Materials requirements planning (MRP) a system which aggregates demand from customers taking into account any existing stock

Multinational an organization with operations in several different countries, on more than one continent

Multiple sourcing obtaining the same type of product or service from more than one supplier to ensure continuity of supply

Multiskilling training employees to do a variety of tasks

Network diagram a diagram which shows activities and their dependencies in the correct sequence for a project

Offshoring moving an operational activity to another country

Offshoring to movement of an operation from a high-cost economy to a low-cost economy

Open innovation the use of markets to obtain and exploit new ways of doing things within an organization

Operations management the management of processes that convert inputs (such as materials, labour, and energy) into outputs (in the form of goods and services)

Operations strategy a plan for managing operations over the long term to achieve business goals

Order qualifiers characteristics of a product or service that are required for them to be considered by a customer

Order winners characteristics of a product or service which directly contribute to winning business from customers

Organizational culture the shared attitudes, values, and beliefs of employees within an organization

Outsourcing the shift of production from in-house to a supplier

Overall equipment effectiveness (OEE) a measure of a machine's utilization, speed, and reliability

Pareto analysis a statistical technique designed to identify a limited number of causes with the greatest effect

Perishability the inability of service providers to inventory their services

PERT Programme Evaluation Review Technique. A method to determine the expected completion of a project using probability theory

Pipeline inventory any inventory that is in transit and cannot be used on any other orders

Poka-yoke Japanese term for a fail safe device

Process layout the layout of equipment and processes in clusters of similar type to allow for flexible operation

Process a systematic arrangement of actions design to achieve specific outcomes

Procurement the process involved with selecting suppliers, negotiating contracts, purchasing items, and evaluating suppliers

Product layout the layout of equipment and processes in a specific sequence in order to manufacture standard outputs

Product life cycle the sequence of stages which products or brands follow after being developed, namely introduction, growth, maturity, and sales decline

Professional services these are generally services that are provided uniquely to each customer or client

Project management the planning, organizing, directing, and controlling of resources to complete the specific goals and objectives of a project

Project a planned set of interrelated processes executed over a pre-determined time

Project a temporary endeavour with a definite beginning and end in which the delivery of outcomes is constrained by a clearly defined scope statement

Prosumption is a model of consumer purchase and usage of a product or service that involves the consumer in its production or delivery

Quality (as an order winner) the ability to provide products and services that meet customers' expectations

Quality assurance the design of production or operations in order to maintain quality

Quality control processes designed to monitor production or operations in order to maintain quality

Quality all the features or characteristics of a product or service that allow it to satisfy stated or implied needs

Queuing system the organization of customers for processing through a service experience

Radical innovation the commercialization of products or services that have a big impact on both the market and the company

Radio frequency identification (RFID) a system whereby tracking devices using global position satellite technology are used to identify and locate inventory items

Raw material the essential ingredients, components, and subassemblies needed to make a product

Reorder point the level of inventory which triggers more material to be ordered

Revenue management a system for managing advanced reservations through pricing and other mechanisms to maximize profitability

Reverse logistics the complete supply chain dedicated to the reverse flow of goods for return, repair, or recycling

Risk management the process whereby organizations methodically address the risks attached to their activities with the goal of achieving sustained benefit within each activity and across the portfolio of all activities

Scope statement a definition of the purpose of a project, usually including project objectives, deliverables, milestones, specifications, limitations, and exclusions

Service encounter the interaction between the customer and service provider

Service failure a deviation by the service delivered from the specified service

Service firm life cycle the sequence of stages which service firms follow after being set up namely entrepreneurship, multi-site rationalization, growth, maturity, and decline

Service recovery the actions taken in response to a service failure with the aim of restoring customer confidence and satisfaction

Service shop the delivery of services which require a different set or sequence of customer processing steps

Servicescape the physical and psychological setting in which a service experience is organized and delivered

Servuction system a model of an operation that identifies the relationship between equipment and employees, and back of house and front of house

Simultaneity the co-production and delivery of a service in the consumer's presence

Simultaneous multiple containment describes how a process may have subprocesses and how these subprocesses may also be part of a different process too

Single sourcing obtaining all of one type of product or service from one supplier

Six Sigma a disciplined methodology that uses data and statistical analysis to measure and improve a company's operational performance by identifying and eliminating 'defects' in manufacturing and service-related processes

Soft systems the social, political, or organizational aspects of any operational process

Soft technology policies and techniques for assuring the efficient and effective organization of work

Soft tools temporary dies and moulds used for the manufacture of one-off products or small batches

Speed (as an order winner) the ability to provide products or services with as short a time delay between customer order and delivery

Stakeholders those people or organizations affected in any way by the project

Stock keeping unit (SKU) an individual item or product held in stock

Stock turn a method of measuring inventory and supply chain management efficiency

Supply chain management the planning, design, organization, and control of the flow of information and materials along the supply chain in order to meet customer requirements in an efficient manner

Supply chain operations reference (SCOR®) model a framework that sets clear guidelines on the management of the key processes in the supply chain (plan, source, make, deliver, and return)

Supply chain a sequence of business and information processes that link suppliers of products or services to operations and that link operations through distribution channels to end users

System clearly identifiable, regularly interacting or interrelating groups of activities

Technology the use of technical means to achieve process outcomes

Theory of constraints (TOC) an operations control system based on the identification of bottlenecks or constraints in the production flow process

Tiers of supply and demand the levels in the chain or network, determined by how near they are to the operation

Total quality management the adoption of quality assurance at all levels of the organization

Utilization the proportion of design capacity that is actually achieved

Variability the extent to which each product or service may be customized or not

Variation how the level of demand changes over time and thereby affects the volume of outputs. This may be short term (hourly or daily), as well as seasonal

Variety the size of product range or number of services offered

Vertical integration the extent to which a company owns the upstream supply side organizations, the downstream distribution organizations, or both, in its supply network

Volume the size or scale of the output, i.e. how many items are manufactured or customers served in a specified time period

Work breakdown structure (WBS) this breaks down the work involved into individual work packages which can then be allocated certain resources, namely labour, time and cost. WBSs are often represented diagrammatically and resemble an organization chart in a series of levels

Work in process (WIP) inventory partially completed products consisting of a combination of raw materials, but which are not yet completed

Index